THE TRAGEDY OF

HAMLET

Prince of Denmark

THE TRAGEDY OF

HAMLET

Prince of Denmark

William Shakespeare

J. J. M. Tobin, Editor and General Editor of the Series
University of Massachusetts–Boston

WADSWORTH
CENGAGE Learning™

Australia • Brazil • Japan • Korea • Mexico • Singapore • Spain • United Kingdom • United States

WADSWORTH
CENGAGE Learning˙

Evans Shakespeare Editions:
Hamlet, J.J.M. Tobin, Editor
and General Editor of the Series

Senior Publisher: Lyn Uhl

Publisher: Michael Rosenberg

Development Editor:
Michell Phifer

Assistant Editor: Erin Bosco

Editorial Assistant: Rebecca
Donahue

Media Editor: Janine Tangney

Senior Marketing Manager:
Melissa Holt

Marketing Communications
Manager: Glenn McGibbon

Content Project Manager:
Aimee Chevrette Bear

Art Director: Marissa Falco

Print Buyer: Betsy Donaghey

Rights Acquisition Specialist,
Text: Katie Huha

Rights Acquisition Specialist,
Images: Jennifer Meyer Dare

Production Service: MPS Limited,
a Macmillan Company

Cover Designer: Walter Kopec

Text Designer: Maxine Ressler

Cover Image: Brian Vaughn
(left) as Hamlet and Dan
Kremer as Clown in the Utah
Shakespeare Festival's 2006
production of Hamlet. (Photo
by Karl Hugh. Copyright Utah
Shakespeare Festival 2006.)

Compositor: MPS Limited,
a Macmillan Company

For product information and
technology assistance, contact us at **Cengage Learning
Customer & Sales Support, 1-800-354-9706**

For permission to use material from this text
or product, submit all requests online at
www.cengage.com/permissions
Further permissions questions can be emailed to
permissionrequest@cengage.com

Library of Congress Control Number: 2010942818

ISBN-13: 978-0-495-91118-0

ISBN-10: 0-495-91118-6

Wadsworth
20 Channel Center Street
Boston, MA 02210
USA

Cengage Learning is a leading provider of customized
learning solutions with office locations around the globe,
including Singapore, the United Kingdom, Australia,
Mexico, Brazil, and Japan. Locate your local office at:
international.cengage.com/region

Cengage Learning products are represented in Canada by
Nelson Education, Ltd.

For your course and learning solutions, visit
www.cengage.com

Purchase any of our products at your local college store
or at our preferred online store **www.cengagebrain.com**

Printed in the United States of America
1 2 3 4 5 6 7 14 13 12 11

Other titles in the *Evans Shakespeare Editions*
from Cengage Learning

TABLE OF CONTENTS

Critical Essays

Classic Essays

Modern Essays

ACKNOWLEDGMENTS

A S GENERAL Editor of this Series, I want to thank my eight Co-Editors: Douglas Bruster, Heather Dubrow, John Klause, Nina Levine, Vincent F. Petronella, Lawrence Rhu, Katherine Rowe and Grace Tiffany for their wisdom, cheerfulness and patience through this long process. The old Latin tag "forsan et haec olim meminisse iuvabit" has rarely been truer than here. I am grateful for support from my colleagues in the English Department at the University of Massachusetts-Boston and from the chairpersons, Robert Crossley and Judith Goleman, as well as Dean Donna Kuizenga of the College of Liberal Arts and Provost Winston Langley. Valuable additional help has come from Michael Melford and my friend and former colleague Robert A. Greene. I wish also to thank Cengage for its commitment to this project, especially on the part of Publisher Michael Rosenberg, Development Editor Michell Phifer and Copy Editor Susan McClung. I trust that the spirit of our friend and mentor Gwynne Blakemore Evans will be pleased by our efforts to do him honor. My wife, Rosemary Barton Tobin, has supported this project with her loving wisdom and with her keen eye for textual subtleties in particular.

As Editor of *Hamlet*, I wish to repeat my thanks to those mentioned above and add particular acknowledgement of my students in English 382 and 383, the shrewd advice of my longtime friend, Vincent F. Petronella, and the still-felt influence of the late P. Albert Duhamel. Lastly, I wish to dedicate this book with the deepest gratitude and a keen sense of the limits of language, to Susannah Barton Tobin, without whose love of Shakespeare and of Gwynne Evans, this Series would not be what we hope it is and this volume would not exist.

LIST OF ILLUSTRATIONS

Color Plates

Pl. 1. *Ophelia* by Sir John Everett Millais 1852.
Pl. 2. Swordfight Scene from Kenneth Branagh's 1996 film of *Hamlet*.
Pl. 3. Bill Murray as Polonius and Kyle MacLachlan as Claudius in the 2000 film of *Hamlet* directed by Michael Almereyda.

Illustrations in the Text

Fig. 1. Joseph Fiennes as Shakespeare in *Shakespeare in Love*.
Fig. 2. Shakespeare's First Folio, title page.
Fig. 3. Visscher, engraving of the Thames.
Fig. 4. Jude Law as the Prince in the 2009 Donmar Warehouse production.
Fig. 5. Ethan Hawke as the Prince in the 2000 Almereyda film.
Fig. 6. Sir Laurence Olivier as the Prince and Eileen Herlie as Gertrude in the 1948 film.
Fig. 7. Marianne Faithfull as Ophelia and Nicol Williamson as the Prince in Tony Richardson's 1969 production.
Fig. 8. Sarah Bernhardt as the Prince in an 1887 production.
Fig. 9. Mark Rylance as the Prince in the 1988 Royal Shakespeare Company production.
Fig. 10. David Tennant as the Prince and Patrick Stewart as the Ghost in the 2008 Royal Shakespeare Company production of *Hamlet*.
Fig. 11. Sir Laurence Olivier in the 1948 film.
Fig. 12 Sam West as the Prince in the 2001 Royal Shakespeare Company production.

THE TRAGEDY OF

HAMLET

Prince of Denmark

ABOUT THIS SERIES

J. J. M. Tobin

THE EVANS Shakespeare Editions are individual editions of essential plays by William Shakespeare, edited by leading scholars to provide college and university students, advanced high school students, and interested independent readers with a comprehensive guide to the plays and their historical and modern contexts. The volume editor of each play has written an introduction to the play and a history of the play in performance on both stage and screen. Central sources and contexts for the play are included, and each editor also has surveyed the critical commentary on the play and selected representative influential essays to illuminate the text further. A guide to additional reading, viewing, and listening concludes the volume and will continue the reader's relationship with the play.

Each volume includes an overview of Shakespeare's life and the world of London theater that he inhabited. Our goal for these editions is that they provide the reader a window into Shakespeare and his work that reminds us all of his enduring global influence.

The text for these plays comes from *The Riverside Shakespeare*, edited with notes and textual commentary by the late Gywnne Blakemore Evans. Evans was known for his unrivaled scholarly precision, and his *Riverside* text is an essential and much-admired modern edition of Shakespeare. The Evans Shakespeare Editions preserve the *Riverside* line numbering, which is the numbering used in the invaluable *Harvard Concordance to Shakespeare* by Marvin Spevack.

Beyond his scholarly work, Evans was a generous mentor to many of the editors in this series and a tremendous influence on all of us. His kind-hearted nature made it impossible for him truly to dislike anyone. However, despite an identification with the most traditional and canonical of cultural texts, he reserved a raised eyebrow and stern words for those whose politics lacked empathy and understanding for the full diversity of human experience. In this attitude too, as in all his writing and teaching, it was evident that he was a scholar who understood Shakespeare. This series is dedicated to his memory.

SHAKESPEARE'S LIFE

J. J. M. Tobin

HAKESPEARE WAS a genius, but he was no unreachable ivory-tower poet. Instead, Shakespeare was a young man from the provinces who made good in the big city of London. Just when and how he came from the provinces remains a mystery. He was born in 1564, the eldest son of an initially quite successful father whose position as alderman and then bailiff (mayor) of the town of Stratford allowed his son to attend the local Latin Grammar School. There, Shakespeare received an education that, contrary to some critics' belief, provided him with the historical perspective and verbal flexibility that helped define his writing.

The schoolboy grew into a young man who married an older woman, Anne Hathaway, and became the father of a daughter and a set of twins, a boy and a girl, by the age of twenty-one. The boy, Hamnet, would die before his twelfth birthday. When the playwright's father, John Shakespeare, only recently recovered from two decades of legal and financial difficulties, died in 1601, having earlier secured the coat of arms of a gentleman (Duncan-Jones 90–102), Shakespeare was left in Stratford with a family of four women: his wife, his two daughters, and his mother, Mary, *née* Arden. Shakespeare's own familial experiences, from the fluctuations of his father's fortunes, to the strong influence of several female relatives, to the tragic loss of a beloved son, doubtless added heart and depth to the incisive portrayals of characters that he created in his plays and poems.

Accordingly, given the fact that all description is necessarily selective, Shakespeare often had in mind his own experiences when he chose narrative and dramatic sources for the foundation of his comedies, histories, and tragedies. The few facts of his life that survive are open to all sorts of interpretations, some of which reveal more about the interpreter than about the facts themselves, while others carry with them a greater degree of likelihood. A few critics have noted that Shakespeare was the eldest boy in a patriarchal world, the first surviving child born in a time of plague after the infant deaths of two siblings. As a child, he doubtless saw and remembered his father dressed in the furred scarlet gown of a bailiff in 1568, going about his appointed supervisory tasks, a figure both familiar as a person and strangely exalted as an official, and as Stephen Greenblatt has noted, all by means of a costume (Greenblatt 30–31). He was likely to have been the indisputable favorite of his mother, acquiring a self-confidence that often leads young men with even a modicum of talent on to success.

Richard Wheeler has pointed out that Shakespeare's choice of source material in which a female is disguised as a boy, best illustrated in *Twelfth Night,* has psychological roots in the playwright's wish to have repaired the loss of his son, Hamnet, whose twin sister, Judith, remained a constant reminder of the absent boy (Wheeler 147–53). Finally, although his marriage and fatherhood indicate some clear grounds for heterosexuality, Shakespeare also wrote beautiful poems about a young man, and his plays often feature male bonding and pathetic male isolation when the bond is broken by marriage, as in the instances of Antonio and Bassanio in *The Merchant of Venice* and a second Antonio and Sebastian in *Twelfth Night.* These scenarios offer putative evidence of at least homosociability.

Of course, over-reliance on causal links between the playwright and the experiences of his creations would logically have Shakespeare a conscience-stricken killer like Claudius or Macbeth, a disoriented octogenarian like Lear, and a suicidal queen like Cleopatra—interpretative leaps that even the most imaginative critic is unwilling to make.

Between the birth of the twins in February 1585 and the writer Robert Greene's allusion to Shakespeare as an actor-turned-playwright in September 1592, there is no hard evidence of his whereabouts, although many theories abound. Perhaps he was a schoolmaster in the country; perhaps he was attached to the household of a Catholic landowner in Lancashire. Certainly one of the most plausible theories is that Shakespeare joined the traveling theatrical troupe called the Queen's Men in 1587 as it passed through Stratford and then came to London as a member of their company. If so, he joined an exciting theatrical world with competition for the entertainment dollar among several companies with plays written by both authors who were university graduates and a minority who were not. It was a world that on its stages carefully reflected the political issues and events of the moment, but did so indirectly because of restrictions created by governmental censorship and by the potential dangers posed by a personal response to criticism by the powerful men of the time.

These dramas were composed for a public audience of mixed class and gender, from work-cutting apprentices to lords of the realm and every possible class gradation in between. They were also performed occasionally for a private audience of higher status in smaller indoor venues.

The London of these plays was a fast-growing city, even in a time of plague, full of energy, color, commerce, varieties of goods, animals, and people of all social degrees. The population numbered perhaps 200,000 by the end of the sixteenth century. It was governed by a Lord Mayor and a municipal council quite concerned about issues of crowd control, the spread of disease, crime, and the fallout of all three in neighborhoods either just at the edge of their partial jurisdiction, Shoreditch in the north and Southwark, Bankside, in the south, or fully within it, like the Blackfriars. Playhouses, three-tiered amphitheaters, and the earlier open-plan inn-yards with galleries above, brought together all three of these problems and more, and they were threatened constantly with restriction by the authorities, who also had the subtle financial desire of taxing players whose performances were not protected by aristocratic patronage.

By the time he joined the newly formed Lord Chamberlain's Men in 1594, Shakespeare had already written his first four history plays (*1, 2, & 3 Henry VI* and *Richard III*), the farcical comedies *The Taming of the Shrew* and *The Comedy of Errors*, and the grotesquely interesting tragedy *Titus Andronicus*. Many, but certainly not all, of his 154 sonnets were also written in the mid-1590s. When the Lord Chamberlain's Men moved into the newly constructed Globe Theater in late 1599, having had five good years at the Theater and the nearby Curtain in Shoreditch, Shakespeare had scripted four more history plays, *King John, Richard II,* and *1 & 2 Henry IV* (and part of a fifth play, *Edward III*), six comedies, including *The Two Gentlemen of Verona, Love's Labour's Lost,* three of the five so-called "golden comedies" (*A Midsummer Night's Dream, The Merchant of Venice,* and *Much Ado About Nothing*), and *Romeo and Juliet,* the tragic companion to *A Midsummer Night's Dream.*

The opening season at the Globe doubtless included the last of the English history plays written solely by Shakespeare, *Henry V*, the pastoral comedy both debunking and idealistic, *As You Like It,* and the most frequently taught of the plays focused on Roman history, *Julius Caesar.* Before the death of Queen Elizabeth in late March of 1603, Shakespeare had certainly written his most famous play, *Hamlet,* his most intensely claustrophobic tragedy, *Othello,* the bourgeois domestic comedy *The Merry Wives of Windsor,* the last of the "golden comedies," which we find alloyed with both satire and melancholy, *Twelfth Night,* and the uniquely powerful satirical comedy *Troilus and Cressida,* as well as the enigmatic poem about martyrdom, *The Phoenix and Turtle.*

Outbreaks of the plague affected Shakespeare both as a dramatist and as a poet, for the virulence of the disease, when deaths reached more than fifty a week in London, forced the authorities to close the theaters in order to restrict contagion. Shakespeare was thus left with added time free from the incessant pressure to produce dramatic scripts, and he then composed his two Ovidian narrative poems, *Venus and Adonis* (1593) and *The Rape of Lucrece* (1594). The most extended theater closings were from June 1592 to May 1594 and from March 1603 to April 1604, but there were other, briefer closings. The plague was an abiding and overpowering presence in the lives and imaginations of the poet and his audiences.

After the accession in 1603 of James VI of Scotland as James I of England, when the Lord Chamberlain's Men became the King's Men and before the company activated for themselves the lease in 1608 of the Blackfriars, a smaller, indoor theater that was to draw a higher and more homogeneous class of spectator, Shakespeare created his other great tragedies, *King Lear, Macbeth, Antony and Cleopatra*, and *Coriolanus*, as well as the bitter *Timon of Athens* (although there is no record of its ever having been performed), and the two "bed-trick" plays, *All's Well That Ends Well* and *Measure for Measure*, comedies in which a lecherous man is fooled by the substitution of one woman for another in the darkness of the night. For that indoor spectacle-friendly Blackfriars theater, Shakespeare wrote the romances *Pericles, Cymbeline, The Winter's Tale*, and *The Tempest*, with their wondrous atmospheres and radiant daughters. By 1611, Shakespeare was moving into partial retirement, co-authoring with John Fletcher, his younger colleague and successor as principal playwright of the King's Men, *Henry VIII, The Two Noble Kinsmen*, and, probably, the lost *Cardenio*.

The division of his plays into these categories—comedies, histories, tragedies, and romances—reminds us that the first step taken by the playwright (indeed any playwright) was to determine the basic genre or kind of play that he wished to write, however much he might expand its boundaries. Genre creates expectations in the mind of the audience, expectations that no dramatist of the time was willing to frustrate. Regarding kind, Polonius tells us with unconscious humor of the versatility of the players who come to Elsinore: "The best actors in the world, either for tragedy, comedy, history, pastoral, pastoral-comical, historical-pastoral, tragical-historical, tragical-comical-historical-pastoral" (2.2.396–399). In that boundary-blurring, increasingly capacious definition of genre, he also informs us of Shakespeare's own gift in all kinds of writing and the fact of his often combining many of these genres in a single work. When, at the end of Plato's *Symposium*, Socrates argues that logically, the greatest tragic writer should also be the greatest comic writer, he was prophetic of Shakespeare, even if he doesn't go on to argue that these principles of tragedy and comedy could and should be connected in the same play. And Shakespeare indirectly repays Socrates for his prophecy by alluding to the philosopher's death in Mistress Quickly's description of the dying Falstaff in *Henry V*, 2.3.

Shakespeare is Shakespeare because of a combination of philosophical tolerance, psychological profundity, and metaphoric genius; that is, he is generous-minded, aware of what makes people tick, and is able to express himself more vividly and memorably than anyone else in the language. And it is his language that truly sets him apart, while simultaneously creating some occasional static in the mind of the modern reader.

There are six areas of this problematic language worth special attention: word choice, false friends, allusions, puns, iambic rhythm, and personification. Shakespeare's vocabulary has words that are no longer part of today's language, chiefly because they refer to things and concepts no longer in use, such as "three-farthings," coins of small value, in the Bastard's metaphoric "Look where three-farthings goes" (*King John*, 1.1.143). Such terms are easily understood by looking at the footnotes, or by checking *The Oxford English Dictionary* or a Shakespearean lexicon, like that of Schmidt; C. T. Onions's *A Shakespeare Glossary;* or *Shakespeare's Words,* by David and Ben Crystal. More difficult are false friends, words spelled the same as words we use today but that have different meanings. One example of this issue is "brave," which as an adjective in the sixteenth and early seventeenth centuries meant primarily "splendid" or "glorious," as in Miranda's expression of awe and excitement in *The Tempest*: "O *brave* new world/That has such people in't" (5.1.183–84), or "virtue," which in Shakespeare's language usually means "strength or power," as in Iago's argument for personal responsibility to Roderigo and the latter's lament that "it is not in my *virtue* to amend it [being in love with Desdemona]": "*Virtue*? A fig! 'tis in ourselves that we are thus or thus" (*Othello*, 1.3.318–20).

Equally problematic, but just as easily understood by reference to footnotes, are instances of classical and biblical allusion, where Shakespeare assumes a recognition by all or some of the audience of glancing references to Greek and Roman deities, frequently to elements in that most abiding narrative in Western literature, the Trojan War, as well as historical and legendary figures, as in Hamlet's "My father's brother, but no more like my father/Than I to *Hercules*" (1.2.152–53) or his subconscious reminder in the graveyard of the fact that his father was the victim of fratricide, "How the knave jowls it to the ground, as if 'twere *Cain's* jaw-bone" (5.1.76–77).

More difficult at times are Shakespeare's puns—plays on words, sometimes comedic and sometimes intentionally non-comedic, but in each case designed to bring more than one meaning in a single word to the attention of the audience and the reader. Shakespeare's puns are almost always thematically significant, revelatory of character, or both, and attention to the possibilities of the presence of punning can only increase our understanding and pleasure in the lines. There are such simple etymological puns as "lieutenant," the military title of Cassio in *Othello*, where the word is defined as one who holds the place of the captain in the latter's absence—exactly the fear Othello has about the relationship that he imagines exists between his wife, Desdemona, and Lieutenant Cassio. There are also puns that fuse the physical and the moral, as in Falstaff's comment that his highway robbery is condoned by the goddess of the moon, "under whose *countenance* we steal" (*1 Henry IV*, 1.2.29) where the word "countenance" means both "face" and "approval." Falstaff's pun is in prose, a good example of how Shakespeare, commonly regarded as the greatest of English poets and dramatists, wrote often in prose, which itself is full of the linguistic devices of poetry.

When Shakespeare was writing in verse, he used iambic pentameter lines, ten syllable lines with five feet, or units, of two syllables each, in the sequence of short–long or unstressed–stressed. Consider, for example, Romeo's "But soft,/what light/through yond/er win/

Everett Collection, Inc.

Fig. 1. Joseph Fiennes as William Shakespeare fighting through writer's block in the film *Shakespeare in Love*: a handsome dramatist without the receding hairline of contemporary portraits and busts.

dow breaks" (*Romeo and Juliet*, 2.2.1), or Antony's "If you/have tears/ prepare/to shed/them now" (*Julius Caesar*, 3.2.169).

Scanning the rhythm of these lines is made easier by our knowledge that Shakespeare and the English language are both naturally iambic and that proof of the correct rhythm begins with marking the stress on the final syllable of the line and moving right to left. The rhythm with the emphasized syllables will lead the actor delivering the lines to stress certain words more than others, as we imagine Shakespeare to have intended, even as we know that stage delivery of lines with an unexpected stress can create fruitful tension in the ear of the audience. For example, Barnardo's "It was about to speak when the cock crew" (*Hamlet*, 1.1.147) is a pentameter line, but the expected iambic rhythm is broken in the last two feet, especially in the sequentially stressed final two syllables, which by their alliteration and double stress combine in form to underscore the moment of interruption in the play's narrative. Such playing off the expected is part of Shakespeare's arsenal of verse techniques.

In addition to these issues of unknown terms, false friends, allusions chiefly classical and biblical, meaningful puns, and verse rhythm itself, there is the metaphoric language that is the glory of Shakespeare, but each instance of this feature demands careful unpacking. Consider the early example of Romeo's personifying Death as an erotic figure keeping Juliet as his mistress, linking the commonly joined notions of love and death: "Shall I believe/That unsubstantial Death is amorous,/ And that the lean abhorred monster keeps/Thee here in dark to be his paramour?" (5.3.102–05). This link already had been anticipated by the Chorus in the prologue to the play, which speaks of "The fearful passage of their death-marked love" (1.6).

More compactly, later in his career, Shakespeare will have Hamlet, in prose, combine Renaissance and medieval views in similes and metaphors, comparisons with and without "like" or "as," in order to describe the multifaceted nature of man: "…how like an angel in apprehension, how like a god! The beauty of the world; the paragon of animals; and yet to me what is this quintessence of dust?" (*Hamlet*, 2.2.306–08). Macbeth in his play will argue against his wife's view that a little water will cleanse his guilty hands, "No; this my hand will rather/The multitudinous seas incarnadine,/Making the green one red" (2.2.58–60). Here Shakespeare has been careful to combine the mouth-filling hyperbole and its Latinate terms "multitudinous" and "incarnadine" (an illustration of the technique that he had learned from Christopher Marlowe) with a crystal-clear synonymous expression, "Making the green one red" for the benefit of all in the theater, even as everyone hears the hypnotically mellifluous line that came before it.

Sometimes Shakespeare scorned the opportunity to use high-flown language, even when one might expect it most, as in the Roman play *Antony and Cleopatra*, when the queen uses a noun as a verb in her bitter image of herself live on the Roman stage played by a child actor, "And I shall see/Some squeaking Cleopatra *boy* my greatness/I'th' posture of a whore" (*Antony and Cleopatra*, 5.2.219–221). Shakespeare gives to Cleopatra's handmaiden Charmian the least hyperbolic expression in a context linking the erotic and funereal (analogous to that situation described by Romeo), "Now boast thee, death, in thy possession lies/A *lass* unparallel'd" (5.2.315–16), where the simple pastoral monosyllable charms the audience, which all along had sensed the antithesis of the playful girl within the cunningly imperious and imperial queen.

While nothing can fully explain the development of this language, its raw material comes largely from Shakespeare's reading, as do the basic elements of plot and character. The same man who was to save and increase his money and property in London and Stratford was, as a craftsman, equally economical, preferring to alter and expand upon material given to him in the literary sources that lie behind all his compositions rather than to create from experience alone. He is the chief counter-example to Polonius's admonition "Neither a borrower nor a lender be" (*Hamlet* 1.3.75)—Shakespeare is a world-class borrower, but one who reshapes and transforms the borrowed materials.

Certainly he had a most retentive memory and could and did recall, at times subconsciously, both single expressions and rather lengthy passages from his reading. "It is often as if, at some deep level of his mind, Shakespeare thought and felt in quotation," as Emrys Jones has noted (Jones 21). Dryden's comment that Shakespeare "needed not the spectacles of books to read Nature; he looked inwards and found her there" ignores Shakespeare's conscious manipulations of his reading as a chief source for his achievement. Nevertheless, Dryden gives us the basic image useful for picturing Shakespeare's genius. The playwright's metaphorical spectacles had two lenses, one of which was focused on life as he knew it and one on the writings of his predecessors and contemporaries: historians both classical and English, proto-novelists, poets, pamphleteers, and essayists, and playwrights who had in their own ways dealt with themes that interested him.

It is by looking at what Shakespeare himself perused that we see his manipulative genius at work, omitting, adding, preserving, and qualifying those plots, motifs, and images viewed through one lens of his binoculars. An important question is just how much of the original theme and significance is brought over in the creative borrowing, a question made more difficult to answer by the fact that in the composition of his plays, Shakespeare often modified and sometimes even inverted the gender and number of the persons in the original mate-rial. See, for example, the model in the story of Cupid and Psyche from Apuleius' *The Golden Asse* (1566), where Psyche almost murders Cupid, for the description of the deaths of the little princes in *Richard III*, as well as for the presentation of the murder of Desdemona in *Othello*. The closer one looks at this source and the affected passage, the more one sees that the young man from Stratford, despite being accused by his London-educated colleague and rival Ben Jonson of having "small Latin and less Greek," was a sufficiently good Latinist to check the translation of Apuleius that he was using against the original, even as he would later check Golding's translation of the *Metamorphoses* against Ovid's Latin for use in *The Tempest*.

We don't know the workplace of Shakespeare, the desk or table where he kept his books, nor do we know for certain who provided him with these volumes, some of which were quite expensive, such as *Holinshed's Chronicles*, North's *Plutarch*, and bibles, both Bishops' and Geneva. But, if we imagine a bookshelf above his desk and envision the titles that he might have ordered there chronologically, we would first see the classics, most importantly Ovid and Virgil; then the Bible, espe-cially Genesis, the Gospel of St. Matthew, and the Book of Revelation; medieval and Renaissance writers, including Chaucer and Erasmus; and then his own immediate predecessors and colleagues, especially Thomas Kyd, Christopher Marlowe, Robert Greene, and Thomas Nashe. Sometimes the most unlikely source can provide a motif or a character, but for more important ideas, we may note what he would have learned from four exemplary volumes on this imagined shelf.

From Seneca, the Roman philosopher, tutor to the emperor Nero and playwright of closet tragedies (that is, of plays meant to be read in the study rather than performed on stage), Shakespeare learned to balance a sensational theme—fratricide and incest—with a plot structured with care and characters subtly developed with an attitude quite fatalistic. From Plutarch, the Greek historian who wrote paral-lel lives of Greek and Roman leaders, he learned the importance of the nature of the private man when serving in public office and how that nature is revealed in small gestures with large significance—what James Joyce, the "spiritual son" of Shakespeare, would later refer to as "epiphanies." From Machiavelli, the notorious early-sixteenth-century political theorist, or from the image of Machiavelli, he saw what he had already known about the role of deception and amorality in political life. From Michel de Montaigne, the sixteenth-century father of the essay, he added to his already operative skepticism, a ca-pacity to question received notions about the consistency of the "self" and the hierarchical place of human beings in creation.

Fig. 2. Later, on other writers' bookshelves, would be Shakespeare's own First Folio (1623), containing thirty-six plays, half of them appearing in print for the first time. It does not, however, include any of the longer poems or sonnets.

To enjoy Shakespeare, it is not at all necessary to understand the sources that he mined, but to study Shakespeare, the better to appreciate the depth and complexity of the work, it is extremely useful to examine the foundations upon which he has built his characters and plots. We can trace, for example, the many constituent elements that have gone into the creation of Falstaff, who, together with Hamlet, is the most discussed of Shakespeare's creations. The elements include, among still others, the Vice of the morality plays; the rogue from Nashe's *The Unfortunate Traveller;* the *miles gloriosus* or cowardly braggart warrior from the Roman comic playwright (and school text) Plautus; the cheerful toper from the Bacchus of Nashe's *Summer's Last Will and Testament;* parodically, the Protestant martyr Sir John Oldcastle from Foxe's *Book of Martyrs;* and even the dying Socrates of Plato's *Phaedo.* Not that Falstaff is at all times all these figures, but in the course of his career in four plays, alive in *1 & 2 Henry IV,* dying offstage in *Henry V,* and radically transformed in *The Merry Wives of Windsor,* he is each of them by turn and counterturn, and still so much more than the mere sum of all these literary, dramatic, and historical parts.

In terms of giving voice to multiple perspectives, to characters of different ages, genders, colors, ethnicities, religions, and social ranks, Shakespeare is unrivaled. No other playwright, then or since, makes other selves live while simultaneously concealing his own self or selves, a talent described by Keats as "negative capability." Shakespeare was also an actor; that is, a person interested in imitating imaginary persons. He was thus doubly a quite creative mimic. Some of the selves mimicked are versions of the "Other," those foreigners or aliens from around the world, including Africans (Aaron, Morocco, Othello), Jews (Shylock, Tubal, Jessica), Frenchmen and Frenchwomen (the Dauphin, Joan of Arc, Margaret of Anjou), non-English Britons (Irish: Macmorris; Scots: Jamy; Welsh: Fluellen), as well as such other continental Europeans as Spaniards (Don Armado) and Italians (including several Antonios), to say nothing of the indefinable Caliban.

Some of his topics, his subjects for dramatic treatment, came often from already set pieces at school, as Emrys Jones, among others, has shown. For example, a set question to be answered, pro and con, was, should Brutus have joined the conspiracy to assassinate Caesar, the answer to which helps create the tensions in *Julius Caesar* (Jones 16). Such an on-the-one-hand and on-the-other school exercise became part of Shakespeare's dramatic strategy, where plays provide the tension created by opposites and the consequent rich ground for multiple interpretations by readers and audiences. There were also sources in earlier stage productions, including plays about Romeo and Juliet, King John, King Lear, and Hamlet. Marlowe especially provided structures to imitate and diverge from in his plays of a weak king (*Edward II*) and of several extraordinary ambitious characters, among whom are a villainous Jew (*The Jew of Malta*), and a rhetorical conqueror (*Tamburlaine*), brilliant efforts which become in Shakespeare's hands the still more dramatic *Richard II, The Merchant of Venice*, and *Henry V*.

Shakespeare's borrowing was frequent and pervasive, but his creative adaptations of those raw materials have made him ultimately not just a borrower but in fact the world's greatest lender, giving us four hundred years of pleasure and providing countless artists, whether painters, novelists, film directors, or even comic book writers, with allusive material. Of course, we would happily surrender our knowledge of a number of these borrowings if only we could have some sense of the quality of the voice of the leading man Richard Burbage, of the facial expressions of the comic actor Will Kemp, the sounds of the groundlings' responses to both the jokes and the set soliloquies, and the reactions of both Queen Elizabeth, who allegedly after watching *1 & 2 Henry IV* wanted to see Falstaff in love, and King James, who doubtless loved the image of his ancestor Banquo in *Macbeth*.

Shakespeare's last years before his death in April 1616 were spent back in Stratford. Although little is known of that time, we are left with the enigmatic coda to his life: his will, in which he famously left to his wife, Anne Hathaway Shakespeare, "the second-best bed"—it is unclear whether it was a cruel slight or a fondly personal bequest. Care of his estate went to his elder daughter, Susannah, while a lesser inheritance went to his wayward younger daughter, Judith, and any children she might have. He died a landowner, a family man, and a once well-known playwright. His will did not cite what has become his greatest legacy—the plays and poems that we read today—but the clues that these works leave about his life, and certainly the testament to his talent that they represent, are more valuable than even the most detailed autobiography. To be sure, however, the local boy who made good, worked hard, had flaws, and lived a complicated family life has more in common with many of his readers, then and now, than does the iconic Shakespeare, who has been mistakenly portrayed as a distant genius paring his fingernails while creating many of the greatest works in world literature.

ELIZABETHAN THEATER

J. J. M. Tobin

MASS ENTERTAINMENT today has become ever more frac-
tured as technology provides myriad ways to take in a film
(and myriad ways for Hollywood to try to make money).
Movie theaters now have to compete with home theaters and couches
in a way they never had to before in order to put people in the seats.
The attractions of high-definition screens and stereo surround-sound
are not the draw they once were now that individuals can access such
technology in their own homes, and stadium seating and chair-side
concessions don't make up the difference. The appeal of first-run films
is fading too, now that movies go to DVD in a matter of weeks and are
also available for immediate streaming through a Netflix subscription.
All of these technologies, however, whether enjoyed in the cinema or
at home, contribute to the moviegoer's sensation of being transported
to another time and place (a journey, moreover, that lasts not much
longer than an hour and a half). Hard to imagine, then, that a little
over four hundred years ago, when the battle for the entertainment
dollar took place on the stage rather than the screen, most members
of the Elizabethan audience gladly stood for more than two hours
without benefit of a padded seat, buttered popcorn, or Junior Mints
(although they did have dried fruit and nuts), or the pause button
in order to watch the plays of Shakespeare and his fellow dramatists
performed. The legendary plays we read today on these pages were
once the sixteenth- and early-seventeenth-century equivalents of the
Harry Potter series or *Avatar*—artistic creations to be sure, but first and
foremost moneymakers for their producers.

Theatrical performances in Elizabethan England took place all over
the country in a wide variety of venues. As we know from the work of
A. Gurr and others, if we put aside the sites used by touring companies
like the Queen's Men of the 1580s (to which Shakespeare himself may
have been attached), the guildhalls and marketplaces in cities and towns
like Norwich, Bristol, and Stratford, or the halls of the universities of
Oxford and Cambridge, and instead concentrate on London itself, we
see that there were five basic performance locales (Gurr, esp. 115 ff.).
There were, of course, the inns and inn-yards, in large part roofed
against the weather and useful especially during the winter months.

The most celebrated of these inns in the history of London theater were the Bel Savage, the Bull, and the Cross Keys, these latter two on the same London street. These were the locations most frequently of concern to the mayor and other municipal authorities anxious about unruly crowds and increased chances of plague contagion, until 1594, when it was declared by the Lord Chamberlain of the Queen's court that there would be only two adult companies—his own, the Lord Chamberlain's Men (Shakespeare's group) and his father-in-law's, the Lord Admiral's Men, troupes that would upon the succession of King James be called the King's Men and Prince Henry's Men—and they would not perform anymore in city inns.

Second, there were two indoor halls, one in a building abutting St. Paul's Cathedral, not too far from the Bel Savage Inn, and the other in the refectory of the old Blackfriars monastery, each used by the children's companies of boys who put on plays with adult political and moral themes. Shakespeare and his company in 1596 had hoped to use the Blackfriars because Blackfriars was a liberty—that is, a district that, for reasons of its religious history, was independent of the secular control of the sheriff—but were refused by a powerful NIMBY (not in my backyard) movement of influential residents. They then leased the building to a second generation of a children's company and had to wait until 1608 to take possession of what would turn out to be both a "tonier" and quite lucrative theatrical space.

Third were the dining halls of the Inns of Court, the London law schools or, perhaps, more accurately, legal societies, where noteworthy performances of *The Comedy of Errors* (Gray's Inn) and *Twelfth Night* (the Middle Temple) took place. There, special audiences with their appetite for contemporary satire allowed for the lampooning of particular individuals whose traits and foibles would be represented by grimace, gesture, voice imitation, and even clothing, as in the case of Dr. Pinch in *The Comedy of Errors*, Malvolio in *Twelfth Night*, and Ajax in *Troilus and Cressida*. When these plays were moved to the larger public stage, the personalized elements could be withdrawn and the characters could continue as general, non-specifically humorous figures.

Fourth was the Queen's court itself (after the death of Elizabeth in 1603, it became the King's court), where at Christmastide, the major companies would be invited to perform for the pleasure of the monarch. Indeed, throughout the long period of tension between the city authorities and the court, the justification for allowing the players to perform their craft in public was that they needed to practice in order to be ready at year's end to entertain the monarch. This argument assumed a quite disproportionate ratio of practice to performance, but it was a convenient semi-fiction that seemed to satisfy all concerned. These court performances were rewarded financially by the Master of the Revels and were less expensive than other kinds of royal entertainment, including masques with elaborate scenery and complicated production devices, the high costs of which later contributed to the downfall of Charles I, James's son and successor. Legend has it that Queen Elizabeth so enjoyed some of the performances featuring the character of Falstaff that she wished to see him in love, a comment which was allegedly the stimulus for *The Merry Wives of Windsor*, which was said to have been written in two weeks, the better to satisfy the queen's request. A close look at the multiple sources used in the creation of this middle-class comedy suggests that the legend may be well founded.

Last, there are the purpose-built amphitheaters, beginning with James Burbage's the Theater (1576) in Shoreditch, just to the north of the city limits; and the Curtain (1578) nearby. To the south, across the Thames, were the Rose (1587), the site of the Lord Admiral's company and most notably the performances of Christopher Marlowe's plays; the Swan (1596); the Globe (1599), built with the very timbers of the Theater transported across the river in the winter of 1598 after the twenty-one-year lease on the old property had expired and several subsequent months of renting; and, back to Shoreditch in the north, the Fortune (1600), explicitly built in imitation of the triple-tiered Globe.

There was competition for the same audience in the form of bull-baiting, bear-baiting and cockfighting, and also simple competition for attention from such activities as royal processions, municipal pageants, outdoor sermons, and public executions with hangings, eviscerations, castrations, and quarterings, not to mention the nearby temptation of the houses ("nunneries") of prostitution. Nonetheless, these theatrical structures proved that, if you build it, they will come.

And come they did, with hundreds of performances each year of thirty or more plays in repertory for each company, plays of chronicle history, romance, tragedy (especially revenge tragedy), satire, and comedy (slapstick, farcical, situational, verbal, and, from 1597, "humorous"; that is, comedy dependent upon characters moved by one dominant personality trait into behavior mechanical and predictable, almost monomaniacally focused). The two major companies could and did perform familiar plays for a week or more before adding a new play to the repertory. A successful new play would be performed at least eight times, according to Knutson, within four months to half a year (Knutson 33–34). New plays were house-fillers, and entrance fees could be doubled for openings. When sequels created a two-part play, performances were only sometimes staged in proper sequence, even as moviegoers will still watch on cable *Godfather II* or *The Empire Strikes Back* without worrying that they had not just seen *The Godfather* or *Star Wars*.

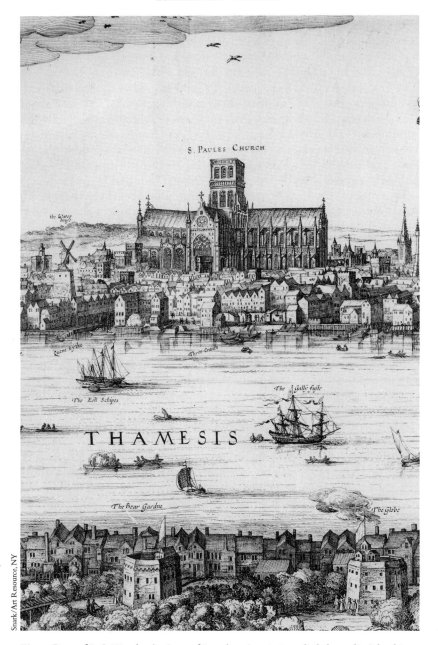

Fig. 3. Part of J. C. Visscher's view of London (c. 1616 or slightly earlier) looking north from the Bankside and showing the Bear Garden Theater and, to the right, the Globe Theater (or possibly the Swan).

The players seemed willing to play throughout the week and throughout the year, but municipal officials repeatedly insisted that there be no performances on Sundays and holy days and holidays, nor during Lent. These demands had some effect, although their repetition by the authorities clearly suggests that there were violations, with performances on occasional Sundays, even at court, on some holidays, and on some days in Lent.

Of course, even though almost half of Shakespeare's plays had already been performed at the Theater and elsewhere, we think of the Globe, open for business probably in the late summer of 1599, as the principal venue for Shakespeare's work, perhaps with *As You Like It* the first production. The current New Globe on the Bankside in Southwark, erected in careful imitation of what we know to have been the methods and materials of the sixteenth century, allows for a twenty-first-century experience analogous to that of the Elizabethan theatergoer. It may be that the diameter of the current theater, of one hundred feet, is a bit too wide, and that seventy-two feet is rather closer to the exact diameter of not only the Globe but several of these late-sixteenth-century London theaters. If so, the judgment that such Elizabethan theaters could hold between 2,000 and 3,000 people suggests that spectators, particularly the groundlings—those who had paid a penny to stand throughout the two-to-three hour performance—were packed in cheek by jowl.

The geometry of the Globe itself is that of a polygon, but it appears circular. From a distance, one would know that a play was to be performed that day by the presence of a flag flying high above the tiring house, the dressing area for the actors. Once inside the building, the theatergoer would note the covered stage projecting from an arc of the circle almost to the center of the uncovered audience space, such that the groundlings would be on three sides of the stage, with those in the front almost able to rest their chins on the platform which was raised about five feet from the floor. This stage was not raked—that is, inclined or tilted towards the audience—as it often is in modern theaters today. Raking both creates better sightlines and potentially affects stage business, as in the case of a fallen Shylock in productions of *The Merchant of Venice*, who at one point struggles in vain to stand on a pile of slippery ducats (gold coins). This move is made even more difficult by the slight incline. However, instead of raking the stage, the Rose, and perhaps the Globe and the Fortune, had the ground on which the audience stood slightly raked (Thomson 78–79), to the great advantage of those in the back of the theater.

Behind the stage, protected by a backdrop on the first level, was the tiring house where the actors dressed and from which they came and went through two openings to the left and right. There were few surprise entrances in the Elizabethan theater, as the audience could always see before them the places of entry. Covering the upper stage and a large part of the outer stage would be the "heavens," supported by two columns or pillars behind which characters could hide in order to eavesdrop and which could serve metaphorically as trees or bushes. The underside of the "heavens" was adorned with signs of the zodiac, the better to remind the audience that all the world is a stage. At the back of the stage in the center, between the two openings of exit and entrance, was a discovery space within which, when a curtain was drawn, an additional mini-set of a study, a bed, or a cave could be revealed.

From below the stage, figures, especially ghosts, could ascend through a trapdoor, and mythological deities could be lowered from above. From the second tier of the galleries, still part of the tiring house, characters could appear as on battlements or a balcony. Music was a very great part of Elizabethan theater, and musicians would be positioned sometimes on that second level of the tiring house. Less musical but still necessary sound effects, say one indicating a storm and thunder, were achieved by such actions as the offstage rolling of a cannonball down a metal trestle or repeated drumming.

Although the groundlings were the closest to the talented actors, for those members of the audience who wished to sit in the galleries (Stern, esp. 212–13) and were willing to pay more money for the privilege, there would have been the comfort of the familiar, as V. F. Petronella has pointed out, inasmuch as these galleries included rooms not unlike those in the domestic buildings near the Globe. However, the familiar was balanced with the rare via the figures on the stage who represented kings, nymphs, fairies, and ghosts, personages not usually found in the Southwark area (Petronella, esp. 111–25). These audiences themselves came from a great range of Elizabethan society, male and female, from aristocrats to lowly apprentices, with all gradations of the social spectrum in between. The late Elizabethan and early Jacobean period is so special in theatrical history in part because of the work of a number of gifted playwrights, Shakespeare preeminent among them, but also in part because of the inclusive nature of the audiences, which were representative of the society as a whole.

When the King's Men in 1609 began to perform in the smaller, indoor Blackfriars Theater while still continuing at the Globe in the summer months, they were able to charge at Blackfriars five or six times the entry fee at the Globe for productions that pleased a grander and wealthier group, but at the cost of having a more socially homogeneous audience. Although the Blackfriars was a more lucrative venue,

Shakespeare's company still profited from productions at the Globe, to the degree that when the Globe burned down during a performance of *Henry VIII* on June 29 1613, the company immediately set about rebuilding the structure so that it could reopen the very next year. One wonders whether Shakespeare came down from semi-retirement in Stratford for the new opening or was already in London working yet again in collaboration with John Fletcher, his successor as principal playwright of the King's Men.

In the more heterogeneous atmosphere at the Globe, whether the first or second version, audiences watched action taking place on a platform of about twelve hundred square feet, a stage which could be the Roman forum at one moment, the senate house at another, and a battlefield at still another. Yet the audience was never at a loss in recognizing what was what, for the dramatist provided place references in the dialogue between and among characters (and some plays may also have featured signs indicating place). The action was sometimes interrupted by informative soliloquies, speeches directed to the audience as if the character speaking on the stage were totally alone, whether or not he or she actually was. By convention, what was said in a soliloquy was understood to be the truthful indication of the character's thoughts and feelings. These soliloquies must have been in their day somewhat analogous to operatic arias—plot-useful devices, but also stand-alone bravura exercises in rhetorical display. Othello's "flaming minister" speech (5.2.1–22) is a good example of the show-stopping effect of the soliloquy, and Edmund's defense of bastardy in *King Lear* (1605; 1.2.1–22), in a passage of identical length seldom fails to elicit applause at the last line even from today's audiences, who otherwise are accustomed not to interrupt the flow of a performance.

The actors and the audience were proximate and visible to each other during these daylight performances, putting them on more intimate terms than is the case in theaters today. Performers were dressed onstage in contemporary Elizabethan clothing, with the kings and dukes wearing specially purchased, costly garments whose fate as they grew worn and tattered was to outfit the clowns with social pretensions. There were also attempts to provide historical atmosphere when needed with helmets, shields, greaves and togas appropriate to the ancient world. Perhaps as few as ten men and four boys, who would play the women's roles in this all-male theatrical world, could perform all sixteenth-century plays. The boys would remain with the company until their voices cracked, and some then became adult members of the company when places became available. They were apprentices in a profession where the turnover was not great—a bonus to the dramatist who could visualize the actor who would be playing the character he was creating but not so advantageous for a young actor looking for a permanent place within a stable group. Because plays were very seldom performed in an uninterrupted run, actors needed powerful memories. It was a time when the aural rather than the visual understanding was much greater than in our own time, but even so, the capacity of actors to hold in their heads a large number of roles from many different plays was extraordinary, and new plays were constantly being added to the repertory.

Even as one man in his time plays many parts, so did Shakespeare's company of actors. The skills and particular strengths of these actors must have given Shakespeare a great deal of confidence about the complexity of the roles that he could ask them to create. Such an element of the familiar increased the pleasure of the audience when it could recognize the same actor behind two different characters whose similarity might now be perceived. Celebrated instances of doubling include, in *A Midsummer Night's Dream*, Theseus/Oberon and Hippolyta/Titania; and, in *Hamlet*, Polonius/First Gravedigger and, most strikingly, the Ghost/Claudius. The audience would likewise be affected by their experience with an actor in a current play having performed in a previous play that they had also seen. One example of this link between roles that allows the audience to anticipate the plot comes in *Hamlet,* when Polonius tells us of his having played Caesar. Caesar, of course, was killed by Brutus in Shakespeare's *Julius Caesar.* The actor now playing Polonius had played Caesar previously in *Julius Caesar,* and in that production, he was killed by Brutus, played by Richard Burbage (son of James). In this performance of *Hamlet,* Burbage was playing Hamlet, and he would shortly kill Polonius, in a repeat of history.

The theater is the most collaborative of enterprises. We should think of Shakespeare as a script-writer under considerable pressure to provide material for his colleagues, all of whom viewed the play to come as a fundamentally money-making project. Shakespeare had multiple advantages beyond his inherent verbal and intuitive gifts. Not only did he write for a group of actors whose individual talents he could anticipate in the composition of his characters, but the script that he was creating was often a response to recent successes by rival companies with their own revengers, weak and strong English kings, and disguised lovers.

The performances themselves relied greatly on the power of the audience's imagination to fill in what was missing because of the limitations of the Elizabethan stage, as the self-conscious Prologue in *Henry V* (1599) makes clear by appealing to the audience to imagine whole armies being transported across the sea. Other Elizabethan dramatists did attempt to be "realistic" in ways that are laughable even beyond the well-intended efforts of Quince, Bottom, and the other Mechanicals in *A Midsummer Night's Dream* (1596). Consider, as noted by G. B. Evans, Yarrington's *Two Tragedies in One* (1594–c. 1598), 2.1: "When the boy goeth in to the shop, Merry striketh six blows on his head and, with the seventh, leaves the hammer sticking in his head; the boy groaning must be heard by a maid, who must cry to her master." Three scenes later, a character "Brings him forth in a chair with a hammer sticking in his head" (Evans 71). Such grossly imperfect efforts increasingly gave way to conventional signals expressive of the limitations of the stage. Four or five men with spears and a flag could represent an army, and a single coffin could represent a whole graveyard. While the Globe stage lacked scenery as we know it, it was not lacking in props. Not only were there a trapdoor grave and a bank of flowers, but also a good number of handheld props like swords, torches, chalices, crowns, and skulls, each a real object and potentially a symbol.

Sometimes convention and symbolism gave way to nature in the case of live animals. Men in animal skins are safer, of course, but some animals, like dogs and bears, are trainable. It is certain that Crab, the dog in the *Two Gentlemen of Verona* (1595–96), was "played" by a true canine, and it is quite likely that the bear that pursues Antigonus in *The Winter's Tale* was only sometimes a disguised human being; but at other times, it was a bear, managed but real, possibly even a polar bear reared from the time of its capture as a cub. Further reflection on the known dangers associated with working with bears and our knowledge of the props listed in *Henslowe's Diary* of 'j beares skyne' (Henslowe 319) suggest that Elizabethan actors were more comfortable with artificial bears, thereby avoiding any sudden ursine aggression, revenge for all the suffering their colleagues had endured at the bear-baiting stake.

The authorities whose powers of censorship were real and forceful did not worry much about whether animals were live onstage or not, but they did care about theological issues being discussed explicitly and about urban insurrection, as we know from the strictures applied to *The Book of Sir Thomas More*, a manuscript play in which Shakespeare most probably had a hand. For all their apparent sensitivity to political issues, the government seems not to have interfered with plays that show the removal—or even the murder—of kings, although the scene of the deposing of Richard in *Richard II* (1596) was thought too delicate to be printed during the lifetime of Queen Elizabeth, who recognized Richard as a parallel figure and pointedly said: "Know ye not I am Richard the Second." Scholars debate whether some of these potent themes regarding right versus might, illegitimate succession, and successful usurpation were recognized imperfectly by the government and so escaped into performance if not always into print. Another theory is that the authorities allowed the audiences to be excited and then pacified by these entertaining productions, a release of energies that returned the audience at the play's end to an unchanged social and political reality.

While it is now customary to refer to this reality as part of the Early Modern Period, it is still important to remember that the two main cultural forces of the time, the Renaissance and the Reformation, came together in a perfect storm of new ideas about values. The Renaissance brought us the rebirth of classical culture and an emphasis on the dignity of human beings, and the Reformation stripped levels of interpretative authority in favor of the individual's more direct reliance on Scripture. These new ideas, sometimes in concert and sometimes in tension, have led increasingly over four hundred years to our current distant but clearly related theories of skepticism and pragmatism.

It is just as important to remember that when James Burbage built his theater in 1576, he was not so much interested in the idea of the dignity of human beings or in the proper interpretation of Scripture as in the making of money. When his son, Richard, and his son's friend and partner, William Shakespeare, and their fellow shareholders were creating and performing their scripts, they were counting the house above all else. Theater was an essential part of the entertainment industry, and for some, it was especially lucrative. If a man was an actor, he made a little bit of money; if a playwright, a little more; if a shareholder in the company that put on the play, a very great deal more; and if a householder in the building in which the plays were performed, even more still. Shakespeare was all four, and as we read his scripts, we should remember that the artist was also a businessman, interested in the box office as much as or more than any hard-to-imagine immortality. The Elizabethan theater was the forerunner of the multiplex, a collaborative, secular church in which the congregation/audience focused on the service before them, and Shakespeare and his fellows focused on both the service and the collection plate.

And yet with all the primary focus on material gain, Shakespeare and his competitors and collaborators were aware of the cultural importance and historical traditions of drama itself. Their own work continued myths and rituals that had begun in Athens and elsewhere more than two thousand years ago. It may well be true, as Dr. Samuel Johnson famously said, that no man but a blockhead ever wrote for anything but money, and Mozart might have been partially correct when he said that good health and money were the two most important elements in life. Yet we also know that just because a work has been commissioned doesn't rule out the presence of beauty and truth, as indeed Mozart's own works reveal. Michelangelo was paid by Pope Julius II to paint the Sistine Chapel, but nobody thinks of the fee the artist earned when she or he looks at the creation of Adam or the expulsion of Adam and Eve from the Garden of Eden. Shakespeare's career in the Elizabethan theatrical world turned out to be quite lucrative, but given the many profound reasons for which we read and study *A Midsummer Night's Dream, King Lear,* and *The Tempest* today (among so many other plays and poems), we see that the dramatist who created these works and gained so much material success was nevertheless grossly underpaid.

WORKS CITED

Crystal, David and Ben Crystal. *Shakespeare's Words.* London: Penguin, 2002. Print.

Duncan-Jones, Katherine. *Ungentle Shakespeare: Scenes from His Life.* London: Arden Shakespeare-Thomson, 2001. Print.

Evans, G. Blakemore. *Elizabethan-Jacobean Drama.* London: A&C Black, 1988. Print.

Foakes, R. A., ed. *Henslowe's Diary.* 2nd ed. Cambridge: Cambridge UP, 2002. Print.

Greenblatt, Stephen. *Will in the World: How Shakespeare Became Shakespeare.* New York: Norton, 2004. Print.

Gurr, Andrew. *The Shakespearean Stage 1574–1642.* 3rd ed. Cambridge and New York: Cambridge UP, 1992. Print.

Jones, Emrys. *The Origins of Shakespeare.* Oxford: Clarendon, 1977. Print.

Knutson, Rosalyn. *The Repertory of Shakespeare's Company, 1594–1603.* Fayetteville: U of Arkansas P, 1991. Print.

Onions, C. T. *A Shakespeare Glossary.* Oxford: Clarendon, 1911. Print.

Petronella, Vincent F. "Shakespeare's Dramatic Chambers." *In the Company of Shakespeare: Essays on English Renaissance Literature in Honor of G. Blakemore Evans.* Eds. Thomas Moisan and Douglas Bruster. Madison and London: Fairleigh Dickinson and Associated UPs, 2002. 111–38. Print.

Schmidt, Alexander. *Shakespeare Lexicon.* Berlin: Georg Reimer, 1902. Print.

Stern, Tiffany. "'You that walk i' in the Galleries': Standing and Walking in the Galleries of the Globe Theater." *Shakespeare Quarterly* 51 (2000): 211–16. Print.

Thomson, Peter. *Shakespeare's Professional Career.* Cambridge: Cambridge UP, 1992. Print.

Wheeler, Richard P. "Deaths in the Family: The Loss of a Son and the Rise of Shakespearean Comedy." *Shakespeare Quarterly* 51 (2000): 127–54. Print.

INTRODUCTION

H<small>*AMLET*</small> HAS been and is a large part of not only Western but also world culture. The play lives today in theater, television, and film—and even in graphic novels. Its hero is a young man who, unlike his tragic peers Othello, Lear, Macbeth, Antony, and even Coriolanus, has two, perhaps even three, parents. One could argue that the play is a powerful example of Philip Larkin's notorious line about the harmful effects that parents have on children. Of course, Prince Hamlet is much more than the son in a dysfunctional family. He's a student with a best friend. He has a girlfriend. He has problems, and these problems, although ratcheted to the level of the horrific and the preternatural, are nevertheless, at their base, familiar to us. The pleasure that we find in the play is partly in our watching his struggles to resolve the tangled plot in which he is enmeshed and partly in our appreciation of the truth and beauty of his observations about life and its pressures. We understand him because he is involved in a community, even as he is detached as a commentator. None of Shakespeare's heroes combines involvement and detachment so well. By the end of the play, we are grateful that he is our representative in these struggles.

Shakespeare wrote *Hamlet* probably in 1600, approximately halfway through his career. He had devoted most of the first half of his career to writing history plays and comedies. Of course, Shakespeare had written tragedies before *Hamlet*, including history plays with tragic elements. In *Titus Andronicus* (1594), he expressed the extreme level to which bloody revenge can rise; in *Romeo and Juliet* (1596), he pushed the envelope of chance as an influence in life about as far as it could go; and in *Julius Caesar* (1599), a play almost as full of blood as *Titus Andronicus* and focused on the already fascinating political issue of what to do with a difficult incumbent leader, he discovered the rich topic of the gap between thought and deed. As Brutus expresses it:

> Between the acting of a dreadful thing
> And the first motion, all the interim is
> Like a phantasma or a hideous dream.
> The Genius and the mortal instruments
> Are then in council; and the state of a man,
> Like to a little kingdom, suffers then

The nature of an insurrection.

(2.1.63–69)

Tragedy itself is a term defined in many different ways. Certainly Shakespeare saw it as something more than merely the main character's fall from eminence into defeat, more than the death of that character, certainly more than a kind of condign punishment for that character's errors and weaknesses. Increasingly, he saw it as involving forces larger than one human being and the moral decisions made by that character, who always has imperfect information.

There is a view that we enjoy plays like *Hamlet* because, subconsciously, we are relieved that all this suffering that we are watching is happening to others and, by an economy of cosmic energy, therefore is less likely to happen to us. However, a nobler and more likely reason is that these characters show, at the very least, qualities of courage and imagination which make us proud to share the same humanity. Some critics, following the lead of Kenneth Burke, see in the best of these plays a tragic rhythm in which the protagonist acquires a purpose, undergoes suffering, and finally, in the midst of that suffering, is granted a perception about the nature of the world and his life in it. Not all Shakespeare's plays satisfy this rhythm, but as an initial critical matrix, and as applied to *Hamlet*, it is a useful device. We see its protagonist given a task, we see him stagger under the weight of its burden, and we wonder at the means and nature of his perception of a Providential understanding of life.

In terms of background to the play, a good deal was happening in the life of England and in the life of Shakespeare himself in 1600. The kingdom was being ruled still by Queen Elizabeth, now in her forty-second year on the throne. She had begun to fail physically, and while everyone knew it, not very many were willing to talk about it in public. Her former favorite, the Earl of Essex, had failed militarily in Ireland in spite of many heralded promises (to which Shakespeare had referred in *Henry V*) and was about to lead an abortive rebellion in February 1601, one that would result in his arrest and execution and the imprisonment in the Tower of London of his chief lieutenant, Shakespeare's sometime patron, the Earl of Southampton. There were also rumors and speculations as to the legitimate successor of the childless Elizabeth, most of which surrounded James VI of Scotland. He eventually did succeed her, and his own mother, Mary, Queen of Scots, had a violent and tangled set of relationships with a murdered husband and lover— elements thought to be obliquely echoed in *Hamlet*. England had triumphed in its defeat of the Spanish Armada a dozen years before but was still a small nation in the midst of foreign threats. Less sensational were the economic tensions with Denmark over fishing rights and the War of the Theaters between adult and children's companies, ripe with personal lampoonings as well as the latent issues of the proper function of drama. (See Bednarz, *Shakespeare and the Poets' War,* for a full description of this latter conflict.)

We believe that our first critical move involves the recognition that all description is necessarily selective—neither you nor I nor Shakespeare can or could say everything about anything. We ask, why this kind of a play as opposed to that? Why this kind of a character and not some other? We can only speculate about Shakespeare's motive. He himself had just four years earlier suffered the death of his only son, Hamnet, back in Stratford; and in the same town, his father, John Shakespeare, was entering the last year of his life. These familial issues may have affected Shakespeare's choice of tragedy as the genre for this play of 1600, but it is also certain that the genre of tragedy was a popular one, that the Elizabethans in general enjoyed blood and gore, not only in public executions and bear-baiting arenas but also on the dramatic stage. Indeed, some of the Elizabethan and even Shakespearean protagonists, like Gloucester in *King Lear* and Macbeth himself, look very much like tortured animals and sometimes describe themselves as bears chained to a stake, set upon by dogs.

The particular subcategory of tragedy at issue in *Hamlet,* revenge tragedy, was a popular genre with considerable variety available to the scriptwriter in the creation of the conduct of the revenger. The audience, thrilled by the tension between the force of the biblical statement, "Vengeance is mine, saith the Lord," and the instinctual drive to reach what Francis Bacon called "a kind of wild justice," knew that the hero could act quickly or with delay, move with prudent reflection or with no moral qualms at all. Spectators who came to the theater to see a revenge play doubtless held the expectation that the villain would get his comeuppance; in addition, they came with considerable curiosity as to the kind of action and reaction this particular revenger would display. In the case of *Hamlet,* where many members of the audience had seen an earlier version of the story, the *Ur-Hamlet,* there would have been the special pleasure derived from the anticipation of seeing the working-out of a familiar plot together with the delight in the likelihood of seeing something in the conduct of the revenger that was, if not completely different, at least significantly so.

Shakespeare and his company doubtless saw *Hamlet* as being the kind of play that would guarantee a full house. But if only bloody action were required to fill the seats and the standing room around the stage, he need not have provided all the soliloquies and all the philosophical reflections on the nature of life and choice he did. One might dismiss as biographically simplistic the suggestion that a man who had recently lost his only son and was about to lose his father, never mind one who was wondering about the future of his own country, might have wanted to express himself at length on these issues of belief, obligation, and futurity. Whatever the exact proportion of box office pressure and personal concerns, however, the result is the greatest moneymaking play in the English theatrical tradition, as well as the most psychologically and philosophically rich drama in the English language.

Shakespeare's play exists in three versions, themselves part of a lengthy tradition of the Hamlet story, which goes back to a Norse saga of the ninth century. The saga is preserved in a Danish history written in Latin in the twelfth century, the *Historiae Danicae,* by Saxo Grammaticus. It is continued, with additional misogynistic elements, in a sixteenth-century French collection of tragic stories by François de Belleforest. Finally, the Hamlet story appeared on the Elizabethan stage in a play (possibly by Thomas Kyd, the author of the seminally influential *The Spanish Tragedy*) known as the *Ur-Hamlet.* All these versions of the *Hamlet* story are about adrenaline-producing vengeance and its entanglement with notions of personal and familial honor— topics that in differing ways were already part of Shakespeare's earlier efforts in tragedy, *Titus Andronicus, Romeo and Juliet,* and *Julius Caesar,* and that later would be an essential part of many of his other tragedies, from *Othello* to *Antony and Cleopatra* and *Coriolanus.*

The three versions of *Hamlet* available to the postmodern reader and, with luck, the viewer are the *Quarto 1* (the "bad" quarto) of 1603, short and sometimes garbled in transmission, perhaps through the memory of the actor who played Marcellus (although more scholars are now skeptical of this theory), but reflecting in part genuine Shakespearean material from a staged version. That material is not present in the same way or, in the case of the conversation between Gertrude and Horatio, present at all in *Quarto 2* of 1604, the fullest version, which includes all seven soliloquies and is thought by some scholars and critics to reflect best the play as Shakespeare composed it in and for the theater of his own imagination, as well as for the stage. Nor is it included or arranged in the same way in the Folio version of 1623, which is based on a theatrical production revealing a few additions and a number of cuts, the latter perhaps made by or at least approved by Shakespeare himself. The excisions included the moving seventh soliloquy of 4.4. Students will decide which of the latter two versions better suits their own image of Shakespeare, either the artist at his desk or table or the man of the theater collaboratively adjusting to the needs of the stage in general or for specific performances—or they will see that one can have both in eclectic texts which should indicate by brackets those passages introduced from one version into another.

The play is about an individual, the prince, but it is also about the royal family, and to a lesser extent about the family of Polonius, Laertes, and Ophelia. Accordingly, the tragedy is like the plays of the ancient Greek dramatists Aeschylus, Sophocles, and Euripides (some of which Shakespeare could have known through Latin translation or through the Latin remakes of Seneca, which we know were several times translated into English in the sixteenth century). In these plays, the protagonist is a member of a politically prominent and variously dysfunctional family whose difficulties affect the state and gain the attention of the gods. Often, their scripts involve the particular destruction of women, whether as vulnerable victims or as "willfully" independent queens like Clytemnestra and Medea.

Critics have noted in *Hamlet*, as in ancient drama, the large number of broken ceremonies or maimed rites, including the violation of decorum regarding a proper period of mourning for King Hamlet and the imperfect burial of the apparent victim of suicide, Ophelia, and beginning with the odd changing of the guard with which the play opens, as Barnardo (rather than the man on duty, Francisco) asks the Danish equivalent of a sentry's question, "Who goes there?" Ceremonies, rites, and rituals are the formal devices that human beings have constructed as protective barriers against the chaotic and appetitive force of fundamental nature. The ease with which these devices can be spoiled or overturned only adds to the audience's concern and certainly to the poignancy of the prince in his loneliness and vulnerability.

The figure from ancient drama most frequently compared with Hamlet is Oedipus, the character whose peculiar (or, Freudianly, hardly all that peculiar) relationships with his father and his mother are thought to be shadowed in Hamlet's feelings toward Claudius and Gertrude. Yet there is an even more intriguingly influential figure from ancient drama: Orestes, obliged in spite of the taboo against matricide to avenge the honor of his father, Agamemnon, murdered by his wife and Orestes' mother, Clytemnestra, and her lover, Aegisthus. These literary and dramatic ghosts hover over the play in ways that remind us that despite the Christian world in which he was writing, Shakespeare was very much a part of a dramatic tradition that winds back to the days of Oedipus, Orestes, and, moving to the epic, even the Aeneas of Virgil, who meets his ghostly father in the underworld.

Sixteenth-century familial issues resonate in the play, from the historical fact that Henry VIII, the father of Elizabeth I, in whose reign Shakespeare was writing and at whose court he and his fellows often performed, had married his late brother Arthur's widow, Katherine of Aragon, to the conflicting views on interclass marriage held by Polonius and Gertrude. Polonius's argument that Hamlet is socially beyond

Ophelia—after all, however important Polonius has been to the Danish government, he is at best a civil servant and his daughter a ranking member of the middle class, not the ruling royal class—clashes with Gertrude's happy acceptance of the idea of marriage between Ophelia and her royal son: "I hop'd thou shouldst have been my Hamlet's wife" (5.1.244). Polonius is right in terms of the statistical probability of such a marriage in England, but Gertrude is correctly responding to the increasing ease of intermarriage between moneyed merchant families and the nobility. Elizabethan instances of middle class and aristocratic, if not royal, intermarriage were frequent enough. Such unions were usually based on the coincidence of the financially successful middle-class side's desire for social advancement and the land-poor aristocrat's need for ready money.

A DETECTIVE STORY AND THE MISSING EVIDENCE

The play as we have come to know it is a detective story, a mystery, analogous to Sophocles' *Oedipus Rex*. This mystery takes place in a dark, ambiguous world filled with intriguing persons, some of whom are intriguers bent upon entrapping the detective himself. These persons range from a most politically able antagonist and criminal (Claudius), a minimally supportive yet conflicted mother (Queen Gertrude), and the duplicitous, high-ranking bureaucrat (Polonius) through the all-too-vulnerable love interest (Ophelia), the unwitting tools (Rosencrantz and Guildenstern), the rival sons of slain fathers (Fortinbras, Laertes, and the doubly fictional Pyrrhus), and finally, to the faithful friend and moral exemplar, Horatio. Things become a little less mysterious when we come to understand the thoughts, feelings, and plans of the revenger, through both his direct address to us (in soliloquy) and his dialogue with his confidant, Horatio.

What is very clear is that the play begins with the appearance of someone or something back from the dead and ends with the protagonist and several other key members of his world slain. In between these two moments, the prince has many opportunities to reflect on life and its end, and while he is never really afraid of death itself, he does worry about what might happen after death. In terms of the theological concern with eschatology (the four final human experiences: death, judgment, heaven, and hell), this prince doesn't fear death but does worry about a divine judgment that would punish him for what he wants to do—that is, until he returns from his near-fatal voyage to England, when he is confident that Providence will guide him.

In his search for the truth, the princely detective judges his situation and the persons surrounding him on the bases of testimony and eyewitness behavior, while we try to understand the protagonist himself and his suspects by considering a quartet of ways of interpretation: examining what others do, what others say, what the protagonist does in analogous circumstances, and what others say about the protagonist (in the last instance always taking into consideration the vested interests of the speaker). Shakespeare's fascination in all his plays with epistemology, that branch of logic that concerns the issue of how we know what we know, is revealed especially vividly with such fragile items of evidence as the testimony of a ghost, the ambiguous audience response to and by an indignant yet guilty antagonist, and the words of liars bent on entrapping the hero.

There are some missing pieces of information and some figures whose absence creates an important part of the atmosphere of the play and whose presence would have perhaps demystified it to our regret: What was Hamlet Senior really like, and his opponent, Fortinbras Senior? What was Wittenberg like as a university, especially with its odd combination of Lutheran associations and its pedagogical interest in human anatomy? What was Paris like as a playground for Laertes? These issues pale in significance when compared with the greater uncertainties whose solutions are just out of our reach: the precise physical and metaphysical nature of the Ghost, the depth of the relationship between Hamlet and Ophelia, the exact nature of Gertrude's involvement with Claudius before the death of Hamlet Senior, even the true nature of Claudius himself, who behaves soberly and quite competently but is described by his hostile nephew as politically incompetent, physically ugly, and morally alcoholic and lecherous.

Some of the ambiguity in the play is psychological: Does Claudius respond to the murder of Gonzago, the mousetrap designed to catch his conscience, with guilt or with indignation? Some of the ambiguity is syntactical or grammatical: Is the "he" who is dead and gone in Ophelia's mad song her late father, Polonius, or her former love or lover, Hamlet (in keeping with the question of the degree of intimacy in their relationship?) or both? Some is even textual: Did Hamlet Senior smite on the ice the "sledded Polacks" or a "leaded pole-axe"? Is the flesh referred to in Hamlet's first soliloquy "solid" or "sullied" or "sallied? Are Hamlet's promises to Ophelia pious "bonds" or "bawds?, among many other questions.

And there is even the semantic ambiguity in words and phrases about which there is no question as to their textual clarity. Consider, for example, Hamlet's lament at the end of the first act that "The time is out of joint—O cursed spite/That ever I was born to set it right!" presents an image illustrating Hamlet's dismay at being assigned this particular task. Yet what is the illustration? Is Hamlet a clock-repairer, objectively and detachedly setting time in order? Or is he an orthopedic physician, or at least a bone-setter (in Philip Brockbank's phrase), reducing a dislocated humerus into its shoulder socket, an act involving considerable painful involvement in the restoration of the body politic? Which is he—or rather, which does he think he is? The original audience certainly knew mechanical clocks, and in those early days of medical science, they clearly knew of the importance of bone-setters.

Is Claudius to be judged by the words of Hamlet, or should the audience listen to Claudius's own expression and watch his own acts? The same kind of problem, easily resolved by a confident director, occurs in *King Lear*, where Goneril complains of the riotous behavior of Lear's entourage of one hundred knights, but there is no evidence in the text that they behaved badly and, indeed, we have Lear's explicit denial that they are riotous. A director might include these riotous knights in the background or, more likely, as a conspicuously silent and decorous group. Similarly, a director must decide what to do with Claudius: Is he frighted by false fire, or is it that he reacts with indignation, such that Hamlet's interpretation of the mousetrap's success is mistaken?

And what of Hamlet's age? He is a student at the University of Wittenberg, presumably a relatively young man, but later we infer from the gravedigger's remarks that the prince is actually thirty years of age. Has Shakespeare been recalling the odd practice of aristocrats sending their sons to school at a late age, so that while we can imagine that Hamlet's grammar school experience might have had chronological embarrassments, his being a university student at thirty would not be a contradiction? Are we confident that the gravedigger's statement is correct? If so, has Hamlet always been thirty in the play? Has Shakespeare perhaps been careless in now making him thirty? Or is thirty not such a bad age for someone who has traveled emotionally and experientially a very great distance between Act 1, scene 2, and Act 5, scene 1?

Our difficulties in understanding these mysteries mirror those of our protagonist, who wrestles with so many of his own doubts and surrounding ambiguities. These mysteries only add to the depth of our intellectual and emotional involvement.

TRIPPINGLY ON THE TONGUE: PUNS AND ALLUSIONS

More than anything else, Hamlet is a master of words, some of which correspond to the "real" world. He is a rhetorician in the best sense of that often-maligned term, able to convince us of the depth of his feelings and the complexity of his life. His words, while occasionally deliberately "wild and whirling" (1.5.133), often carry added meaning through puns and allusions, those glancing references to classical mythology, the Bible, and ancient and modern history. Hamlet is the best evidence against Dr. Samuel Johnson's opinion that a pun (or "quibble," as he called it back in 1765) was the fatal Cleopatra for which Shakespeare lost the world and was content to lose it. Hamlet's puns are often comical yet sometimes noncomedic, but they almost always reveal themes and character in a shorthand way, as even a brief perusal of his first instances of word-play in Act 1, scene 2 suggest: *son/sun, kin/kind, sallied/solid, cannon/canon*, etc. This habitual punning is sometimes said to be an aspect of Hamlet's "feminine" nature, which makes him reluctant to kill and reluctant to state exactly what he means, rather than expressing himself in a more "manly" fashion, allowing the audience to choose an either/or resolution to his delaying word games. Such punning, of course, is one of the absolute glories of Shakespeare's art, an art that teaches us to welcome multiplicities. His allusions today sometimes require footnotes, but the references are so placed in the text that the contexts themselves would often have made and do make the essential meaning clear to the sixteenth-century groundling and the twenty-first-century sophomore pulling an all-nighter.

The recognition of puns and allusions is often a source of self-congratulatory pleasure. Shakespeare credited his original audience with sufficient knowledge and alertness to contribute to the meaning of the play. They "got it" without having to be hit over the head, and in "getting it," they joined Shakespeare himself as creators of meaning. Today, with the help of glosses in footnotes and secondary reading, lectures, and conversation, we too are in a position to "get it." This shared making of meaning is operative in all Shakespeare's plays but reaches its greatest height in *Hamlet*, which has the greatest number of occasions for supportive, contributing involvement.

In terms of creating meaning by recognizing allusion, when Hamlet, prompted by such a comparison in Belleforest, refers frequently to Hercules, he means the half-divine archetype of heroic strength with his celebrated labors, but when he links Hercules with Laertes (5.1.291), he is thinking of the comic Hercules of early Renaissance drama, who was portrayed as a ranter. Most of the other classical allusions are associated with Olympus (Jove, Mercury, Mars, Vulcan) or above that mountain, as in Hyperion; or with the Trojan War, the central narrative of European literature, with Priam and Hecuba and Pyrrhus, Aeneas, and Dido. In addition, there are references to the historical figures of ancient Rome, Caesar, Nero and Roscius. Midway between the gods and men, there is the world conqueror who carried the Homeric story of the Trojan War with him on his adventures, Alexander the Great. These allusions in their immediate contexts cast light on the persons with whom they are linked, and they largely expand the universe of the play, temporally as well as geographically.

Another striking feature of the play's language beyond punning and allusion is the by now oft-noted use of the rhetorical figure of verbal doubling, of creating one entity out of two, known as "hendiadys" (see especially the work of George T. Wright and Frank Kermode). Example will tell more than abstract definition: Consider Horatio's "The *sensible* and *true* avouch" (1.1.57), "the *gross* and *scope* of mine opinion" (1.1.68), "the dead *waste* and *middle* of the night" (1.2.198) and Hamlet's "*Angels* and *ministers of grace*" (1.4.39), "Hath op'd his *ponderous* and *marble* jaws" (1.4.50), and "within the *book* and *volume* of my brain" (1.5.103).

These instances of two nouns or two adjectives, where we normally would expect a noun modified by an adjective, create moments in which the reader or the particularly acute listener has to transfer the noun into the adjective or the adjective into the noun—a process that slows down the momentum of an already-delaying revenger. It is in our sorting out of the doublings that we become again, as in allusion, more involved in the drama and more contributive to its meanings. Like the prince, we are moving forward, if not with the greatest speed.

There are some single common nouns with added energy derived from their punning nature, like "nunnery," "fishmonger," and "privates," and suggestive proper names from classical myth and history such as the aforementioned Hercules, the archetypal hero of strength and demigod; Nero, the emperor, and matricide; and Roscius, the actor who both is and is not the person he plays. The infinitive of the simplest of copulative verbs, "to be," opens the door to theological and philosophical questions about the meaning of life, as the prince demonstrates the truth of the statement that it all depends on what the meaning of "is" is. Even the smallest indefinite article, "a," becomes significant when placed before the noun "divinity" in Hamlet's remark to Horatio, "There's a divinity that shapes our ends" (5.2.10), by suggesting a pagan force perhaps equivalent to Fortune, the subject of the penultimate chapter of Machiavelli's *The Prince* (see Roe's *Shakespeare and Machiavelli*), rather than a term for the Christian god who clearly appears in Hamlet's subsequent explanation to Horatio that the readiness is all, with its allusion to the gospel of St. Matthew (5.2.219ff.). And how much added force comes in the most famous line of all when the article is definite rather than indefinite: ". . . that is *the* question" (3.1.55).

NAMES: PROPER AND IMPROPER

Names and direct statements involve us still more deeply in the play. It is true that a rose by any other name would smell as sweet, and equally true that Shakespeare can be absolutely indifferent to the names he gives to some of his characters (Gadshill is both a person and a place in

1 Henry IV). In *Hamlet*, however, he seems to have given his audience (and particularly his reading audience) a good deal of help understanding exactly what is going on by using thematically significant names. The names of the characters in *Hamlet* resonate at different velocities, with some having greater thematically connotative significance than others. For sixteenth-century theatergoers, the names "Hamlet" and "Horatio" would have immediately brought to mind two revenge plays which they had already seen: the *Ur-Hamlet,* as already discussed; and *The Spanish Tragedy,* with a father pursuing revenge for a murdered son named Horatio. When Shakespeare substitutes "Hamlet" as a name for Hamlet's father for the "Horwendil" in Belleforest, he creates yet another instance of the pervasive doubling in the play (Welsh, 24). Here, he provides opportunities for immediate comparisons and contrasts between the prince and his paternal namesake, differences and similarities that both we in the audience and the prince in the action of the play can and do draw. "Gertrude" is a natural expansion of "Gerutha" in Saxo and of "Geruthe" in Belleforest, the latter a text Shakespeare certainly knew. But it is richly suggestive, in the opinion of Welsh, that Shakespeare either deliberately or subconsciously fused in an instance of "Shakespeare outdoing Freud" (Welsh, 24)—putting together the first syllable of the name of Amleth's mother, "Ger," with the last syllable of the name of Amleth's quite sensual second wife, "Herme*trude,*" thereby underscoring the theme of maternal sexuality with which the prince is obsessively concerned in the closet scene (Act 3, scene 4; see again Welsh).

For the educated members of the audience, the Roman names "Claudius" and "Marcellus" would have suggested, in the case of Claudius, interconnections between and among tyranny, poisoning, unfaithful wives, and ultimately, in the person of a stepson Nero, matricide. In the name Marcellus, best known from Virgil's *Aeneid* Book 6, a text that Shakespeare would have had to study and translate at the Stratford grammar school, we have a host of interconnected elements, beginning with the very situation of the ghost of a father explaining the nature of the moral and political responsibilities that he was placing on the son and an armored hero who defeats his rival in single combat. We even have an allusion to a hero who succeeds by delaying, along with images of purple flowers and a request to look at a particular ghost, one named Marcellus, as Marcellus himself does in the play (1.1.40). In addition, current theatergoers who had heard the first shot fired in the War of the Theaters by Ben Jonson in *Cynthia's Revels* would have noted that the name "Ophelia" plays off against the purely virginal nymph "Aphelia" in Jonson's play. The first letter in Ophelia's name was frequently evoked in the Elizabethan era as a symbol of the "nothing," the word men used to refer to female genitalia. See in this very play, 3.2.112 ff., for an example of such wordplay. This instance of sexually allusive nomenclature perhaps makes more complex our reading of the character of Ophelia and her relationship with Hamlet.

These richly significant and suggestive names are better appreciated in the reading rather than in the theatrical viewing, where the action unfolds rapidly and the opportunity for retrospective reflection is absent, but this play was read (see Erne) and appreciated for its richness from the very beginnings of its critical history. A contemporary, the rhetorician Gabriel Harvey, expressed it thus: "The younger sort takes much delight in Shakespeare's *Venus and Adonis*: but his *Lucrece*, and his tragedy of *Hamlet, Prince of Denmark* have it in them to please the wiser sort."

Of course, Hamlet is not only a hero in the making, but he is also at times a clever manipulator of the action of his world, commenting as a chorus on the success of his efforts. He does so sometimes with intemperate self-congratulatory glee, as if he were the Vice of the morality plays or that earlier Shakespearean master of the soliloquy, Richard of Gloucester, or even the professional jester Will Summers, the personal clown of Henry VIII and a character in the pageant play about natural political succession by Shakespeare's extremely useful associate, Thomas Nashe, *Summer's Last Will and Testament*. The prince is also a lover, with Ophelia (see Color Plate 1) the immediate object of his love and Polonius, her father, as the obstacle that stands between them in the proper fulfillment of that love, a more articulate Egeus from *A Midsummer Night's Dream*. This triangle derives not only from the typical situation of comedies where the father is defeated (or of tragedies, where he is not, as in *Romeo and Juliet*), but, particularly in its description in Act 1, scene 3, from Apuleius' *Metamorphoses*, a second-century "novel" of a man transformed into a donkey whose many adventures include his overhearing of the story of Cupid and Psyche. That tale, like his own, tells a story of sin/transgression, punishment, and salvation in which a socially superior male (Cupid) loves and impregnates a girl (Psyche) to the dismay of a parent (Venus) whose concern is with the social embarrassment resulting from the child of these lovers and their irregular union. This Latin text had been translated into English as *The Golden Asse* (1566) and was used by many other Renaissance playwrights and nondramatic writers (among them Edmund Spenser and later John Milton) for plots and elements of language, and throughout his career by Shakespeare himself, including material later in *The Golden Asse* that influenced the accidental poisoning of Gertrude.

As a student whose academic career has been interrupted but who is hardly a dropout, Hamlet also has read and reflected on Erasmus' *The Praise of Folly*, where he has learned more of the wisdom inherent in some kinds of fools, and Montaigne's *Essais*, probably in John Florio's translation, which was not published until 1603 but clearly circulated in some areas of England before then. It was available to Shakespeare, who courted and received the favor of the Earl of Southampton when Florio was a member of Southampton's household as a tutor. From Montaigne, Hamlet would have had enhanced his skeptical questions of fundamental views of the universe, stopping just shy of cynicism.

While Greece and Rome, continental Europe, and contemporary England make up the major currents of allusion that flow into the world of the Renaissance university-educated prince, one other essential source is his Bible, most importantly Genesis and the Gospel of St. Matthew. In Genesis, the book in the Jewish testament most alluded to by Shakespeare, there is the story of Cain and Abel, of the fratricide that is the first recorded murder, one to which Shakespeare has Claudius subconsciously and revealingly refer in his counsel to Hamlet, "From the first corse till he that died to-day" (1.2.105).

From the Gospel of St. Matthew, Shakespeare's favorite book of the New Testament, there is at 5.2.219-20 a reference to the Providential care that God takes of every individual: "Are not two sparrows solde for a farthing, and one of them shal not fall on the ground without your father" (Geneva version). Between these two biblical references of fraternal violence and divine solicitude hangs much of the action and meaning of the play.

"MORE THINGS IN HEAVEN AND EARTH": OBJECTS IN THE PLAY

The action, shaped from such sources, is set on a physical, temporal and spatial grid that gives both fixity and expansiveness. While the prince tells Polonius and us that he is reading "Words, words, words" (2.2.192) (see Fig. 4), we remember that this most articulate verbal hero and his most voluble play are also about *things*. Many such things are handheld objects, like the foils that, while of the same length, are not of the same degree of sharpness or "envenomness" (see Color Plate 2); the union, the pearl that masks the fatal poison; the skull of Yorick emptied of all the seats of memory; Ophelia's duplicitous prayer book; Hamlet's letter to Ophelia, whenever composed, read by Polonius to Gertrude and Claudius; the referred-to sealed letters from Claudius to the King of England, unsealed, changed, and resealed by the prince and, perhaps, also the pole-axe that King Hamlet once smote upon the ice during an angry parle. These objects, sometimes actually seen onstage and other times told of with such vividness that we believe that we have seen them, if only in our mind's eye, remind us just how physical, how full of significant materials having shape and size, this celebratedly verbal work really is.

In *Hamlet*, the role of time past is obviously critical, with its dominant fact of a murdered king and father weighing heavily upon the present moment. Correspondingly, time's most essential faculty, memory, which occupies a seat in the prince's mental theater, keeps alive the dead king as well as the idea of the necessity of doing justice by him, at least in terms of his spirit. The working-out of this problem of doing justice takes place in a great many venues—places that help give the play both an expansive spatial range and a series of particular locales. Geographically, several European nations and cities are visualized on stage or alluded to in dialogue, including, beyond Denmark, Norway, Poland, England, France, Rome, Vienna, and Wittenberg. In addition, within the castle of Elsinore itself are spaces, both confined and open, that reflect forces political and private, public and personal, as well as those influences of the supernatural, or at least preternatural. These

Fig. 4. Jude Law as the prince in the 2009 Donmar Warehouse production. We do not know the title of the book that Hamlet carries as he enters at 2.2.168, but its text allows the prince to relate its contents to Polonius.

elemental powers are either chance or Providence, imagined in the play, respectively, as a fickle woman, Fortune, or as a kind and supportive father who watches over even the fall of a sparrow.

The play begins on the battlements high above the castle walls, open to the night sky, and moves inside to the splendidly lit and cel-ebrationally colorful throne room, where Claudius shows executive skill in matters foreign and domestic. The action then moves to rooms like Gertrude's closet, not properly a bedroom but a decorous sitting room or study that is also the site of Hamlet's indecorous indictment of his mother's behavior. And in that indictment, there is the vivid image of the stained royal bed. Connecting these venues are the castle corridors through which espionage agents and one princely coun-terspy move purposefully past and behind convenient and dangerous arrases.

What does speak forcefully down the corridor from the early modern world to the present is this theme of espionage. Rosen-crantz and Guildenstern, Reynaldo, the servant of Polonius, and even Ophelia are agents of Claudius and Polonius, who "by indirections [hope to] find directions out" (2.1.63). Meanwhile, the prince proves expert at opening secret letters disclosing the target of a royal English hit man and at replacing his own name with those of the ignorant agents Rosencrantz and Guildenstern. While there are spaces of privacy—personal rooms of retreat and meditation for Ophelia and Gertrude—these venues are not safe from intrusion and spying. All the world knows "seems" and tries, for varying reasons of self-interest, to get to "is" (1.2.76)—that is, people practice deception while wishing to unmask the deceptions of others.

However, no corridor runs directly to the heart of the prince, and no space or set of spaces opens directly onto Hamlet's inner nature. For understanding this last subject, the best we can do is to attend carefully to the action, dialogue, and, especially, the soliloquies with which Hamlet speaks most clearly to us.

Although these puns, allusions, and significant names of which we have spoken contribute to the truth that Hamlet is the most articulate and multifaceted of Shakespeare's creations, he is to be understood as we understand any other character in this play. When we look at what he does, from grieving bitterly over the remarriage of his mother to his finally slaying Claudius, not premeditatedly but on the spur of the moment, and in reaction to both the death of his mother and the as-sault upon himself, we can agree with him about the impropriety of her marrying so soon after her husband's death, quite apart from the vexed question of "incest" as a consequence of a widow marrying her brother-in-law. Considering only the revenge plot itself, by the time we have seen Claudius and Laertes plot against Hamlet, we again have no hesitation—even if he has had some between these two events—in involving ourselves with him as our representative. Only upon reflection do we reconsider his cruelty to Ophelia and the Machiavellian coldness with which he murderously has substituted the names of Rosencrantz and Guildenstern for his own as the assassination target.

When we listen to what he tells us directly, we can believe that he is telling the truth as he understands it. Such is the convention of the Elizabethan soliloquy—no one in such a speech misleads the audience. And in these soliloquies, we can follow the irregular arc of Hamlet's commitment to his assigned task and understanding of his role. Our emotional involvement is manipulated by the dramatist as the play unfolds by his providing fluctuations in the attitude of the protagonist, that one character with whom we are most concerned. Whatever the interest created by the differing antagonistic and supportive characters, the play is primarily the prince's story.

For all Shakespeare's philosophical tolerance and psychological insight, two special virtues that we treasure in him, we can never stress enough that his language sets him above and apart from all other English poets and dramatists, and it is in *Hamlet* that Shakespeare has created the most memorable lines, in both verse and prose.

A good many passages in *Hamlet* are in prose, and that prose provides some of the loveliest and most famous lines. As an example, look at the lines following the prince's statement to Rosencranz and Guildenstern, "I have of late—but wherefore I know not—lost all my mirth, foregone all custom of exercises . . ." (2.2.295 ff.). Here, Shakespeare has fused ideas and rhythms from Psalms, Montaigne, and the pamphlets of Gabriel Harvey and Thomas Nashe, as well as other sources, the better to create an intellectual collision between a Medieval view of man as the "quintessence of dust" (2.2.308) and the Renaissance argument for the dignity, the value, of man, "the paragon of animals" (2.2.307). Although rhetorically heightened, this prose is naturally forceful. Indeed, it and other heightened passages are made to appear "real" by having, as has often been noted, the passage recited by the Player about Hecuba after Hamlet's own fifteen-line version (2.2.450ff.) and the lines in "The Mousetrap" (3.2.154ff.) expressed in an especially archaic manner, such that the rhetoric elsewhere in the play seems natural.

SPEAK THE SPEECH: SOLILOQUIES

Some of those lines, whether prose or poetry, and their thoughts are interconnected by resonating terms or reflecting images that help to tie together the many parts of this, the longest of Shakespeare's plays.

By focusing on the poetry of the seven soliloquies, even at the risk of appearing as merely Hamletists (that is, critics who focus solely on the prince at the expense of the whole play), we can chart the thoughts and feelings of the protagonist and hold more easily in our heads the structure of much of the first four acts of the play.

The first soliloquy is especially full of revealing ideas and emotions. It raises the issue of the divine prohibition against suicide; it introduces the notion of the world as a corrupt garden; it contrasts Hamlet's late father and his uncle, with the latter likened to a satyr, a creature both ugly and lecherous; and it considers that women are both fickle and wrongheaded in their selection of a mate, both indecorous in the timing of the match and mistaken in the object of the choice. Two allusions to classical mythology remind us how far the Danish characters are from their legendary counterparts: Gertrude, although as copious in the shedding of her tears as Niobe, is quick to dry those tears in time for a remarriage; and Hamlet himself is no more like Hercules, a heroic figure of the highest order, than Claudius is like Hamlet Senior. Yet we should note that not being so heroic as Hercules still leaves Hamlet a good deal of room to be humanly heroic. He must bear all these painful thoughts silently—and it is essential to recall that at this point in the action, he and we are ignorant of the fact that Claudius has actually murdered Hamlet Senior.

In the second soliloquy, Hamlet promises to *remember* the Ghost and its commandment to revenge. We recall that tragedies are rituals that require the death of the sacrificial hero, a truth underscored by Christ's words at the institution of the Lord's Supper, itself a eucharistic, symbolic reenactment of sacrifice, words which resonate here: "Do this in the *remembrance* of me" (Luke 22:19 [Geneva version]). Shakespeare, whatever his own beliefs, was in the habit of adding moral and religious weight to his secular tragedies by using allusions to biblical episodes, particularly from the gospels and their narratives of the life of Christ. We see this usage in, for example, the explicitly Christlike sufferings of the tormented York in *3 Henry VI* and the similarly Christlike calm of Othello when we first meet him, confronted with drawn swords, episodes analogous to those described by Matthew and Luke (see Jones, *The Origins of Shakespeare*).

There are no classical allusions, but two images of significance: one of the memory being a seat in the theater of the brain and the other, from a different perspective, that the brain itself is a book into which messages are written. Hamlet has given himself a supportive backup, a book version of what he has witnessed in the theater, anticipating our own experience of seeing the Ghost and then reading its words in our volume of Shakespeare.

The third soliloquy, the longest of the seven, which together contain more than two hundred lines of poetry, has a three-part structure with a coda. In the first section, Hamlet berates himself for not doing what he appears to have every reason to do: kill Claudius, prompted by the tearful grief expressed by the actor playing a distraught and only fictional Hecuba. In the second, beginning at line 582, Hamlet catches himself in the midst of his merely verbal display—"Why, what an ass am I." Third, he shifts into action with the plan of watching the king at a play, the better to observe his probable guilty reaction. He concludes with the understandable concern that the Ghost may be an agent of the devil, bent on leading him into damnation, and therefore evidence more powerful than ectoplasmic testimony is required. Claudius's response to *The Murder of Gonzago* does seem to indicate guilt, but the judgments of the prince and Horatio are not identical. For other, subsequent, reasons, we know that Claudius is guilty, but the device of the play-within-the-play as catcher of the king's conscience opens the door to an issue that fascinated the epistemologist in Shakespeare: How do we know for certain what we know, especially when ocular and auricular "proofs" aren't always reliable?

The fourth and most famous soliloquy (3.1.55–87), "To be or not to be," has at least three issues which continue to stimulate critical response: (1) Is the basic topic of the speech suicide? (2) Are the many "ills" that Hamlet lists difficulties that he himself is facing? (3) What does "conscience" mean at line 82?

Without intending in any way to curtail debate, we may note that in the instance of (1), the argument against the idea that the passage is essentially about suicide is best articulated by Harold Jenkins in the Arden *Hamlet* (1984): "the 'question' of 'to be or not to be' concerns the advantages and disadvantages of human existence, the discussion of which includes the recognition of man's ability to end his existence by suicide" (Jenkins 485). As for (2), the majority of critics have argued that the particularized "whips and scorns of time" (l. 69) belong to humankind in general rather than to the prince himself. While some of the elements of injustice can be made to apply to him, the entire series of abuses and injustices seems to be the product of Hamlet's educated capacity to generalize about life and its difficulties beyond even the heaviest metaphoric "fardels" (l. 75) that he may be said to bear. As for (3), "conscience" is a term that appears eight times in the play, and usually means the moral faculty concerned with issues of right and wrong; however, it can also mean "consciousness," "awareness," and perhaps also in some instances, "inner thought," unspecified as to moral or intellectual quality. Debate over the meaning of the term at 3.1.82 is especially vigorous, with the true interpretation lying perhaps in an eliding of both "awareness" and "moral faculty" into each other, an instance of not "either/or" but "both/and."

The fifth soliloquy (3.2.388–99) is that of a man almost filled with heedless passion—"Now could I drink hot blood" (3.2.390), but the "could" still suggests something short of his taking actual revenge. The prince's thoughts are refocused upon his mother and, in keeping with the Ghost's distinction between the punishment that Claudius deserves and the punishment that Gertrude merits, "Leave her to heaven" (1.5.86), Hamlet resolves to berate her but not harm her physically. Here, the key allusion comes in the name "Nero" (3.2.394), the Roman emperor who had his own mother killed. With all that is unnatural in the play, especially fratricide and incest, Hamlet is resolved not to add to the number of unnatural elements. The groundlings who had never heard the name "Nero" nor perhaps known any Roman history beyond the name "Julius Caesar" would nevertheless have appreciated the significance of this reference by means of the helpfully explanatory following line, "Let me be cruel, not unnatural" (3.2.395). The entire audience, armed with the evidence of Hamlet's response to the king's reaction to the Mousetrap, would have seen that Hamlet is apparently ready to kill Claudius.

The sixth soliloquy shows us a still extraordinarily yet-to-be vengeful prince, one who in misinterpreting Claudius's spiritual condition—the usurper king, in his imperfect effort at prayer, failing to earn forgiveness by not relinquishing the fruits of his crime, the crown and the queen—resolves to wait for a better circumstance in which he can kill both the soul and the body of the king. There are no allusions to historical or mythological personages, but there are glancing references to at least three of the seven deadly sins guaranteed to help damn Claudius's soul: gluttony, in the form of intemperate drinking; wrath; and lust. There is also an elegant balance of metaphors drawn from food preparation, which are understandable if we are to imagine Claudius as an offering to heaven: "*season*'d for his passage" (3.3.86) and "no *relish* of salvation in't" (3.3.92). What strikes the audience most is the irony of the situation—the absolute best moment for killing Claudius combined with Hamlet's misunderstanding. When critics praise the prince for his Christian humanism or his morally valuable reflection and consequent hesitation, they sometimes fail to note that this particular moment of hesitation has a barbaric ethic behind it, one that would have stunned even some in that original Globe audience.

The seventh soliloquy, which is excised from the early-seventeenth-century production of the play reflected in the Folio version of 1623 and shortened by nine lines even in the BBC 1980 TV version, returns the prince to square one on the revenge board, but it offers a still-more-serious reflection on will and appetite, purpose and honor, as well as serving as a thematic parallel to the third soliloquy, "O, what a rogue and peasant slave am I!" (2.2.550 ff.). As in each set speech, there is a comparison and contrast between the prince and his lack of emotion and action, with Hamlet's response to the emotional suffering of Hecuba and to the Norwegian army's actively risking death in a matter of honor—although, significantly for our appreciation of his fitfully skeptical nature, the prince called that honor "a fantasy and trick of fame" (4.4.61), a phrase that the cynical Falstaff might have used.

HONOR: SOMETIMES MORE THAN A FANTASY AND TRICK

Both explicit and latent in these soliloquies and in dialogue is a concern with honor and dignity. For all his singularity, Hamlet is, like most of the male characters in the play (with the significant exception of his antagonist, Claudius), deeply concerned with the idea of honor. Polonius is anxious over the possibility that he will be embarrassed by being the grandfather of an illegitimate child of Ophelia. His son, Laertes, in addition to being concerned about the insufficient dignity given to his sister in her funeral rites, is hesitant to forgive Hamlet for his slaying of Polonius until such a gesture on his part is approved by experts in such nice matters of conduct, "elder masters of known honor" (5.2.248). Fortinbras Senior and Hamlet Senior had fought in single combat prompted by the former's "most emulate pride" (1.1.83). Hamlet himself has been, in his own desire, a rival to Claudius, a rival to his revenge-brother, Laertes, for primacy as the love of Ophelia ("forty thousand brothers/Could not with all their quantity of love/ Make up my sum" 5.1.269–71), a rival to young Fortinbras and his Norwegian army, and even a rival to the Player, who does a better job of expressing grief than the prince himself.

Most memorably, he refers to his posthumous reputation, his "wounded name" (5.2.344) as his central concern when Horatio loyally tries to join him as "more an antique Roman than a Dane" (5.2.341) in death. Unlike some earlier Shakespearean figures, like Hotspur of *1 Henry IV*, Hamlet does not so much seek honor as *the* goal in life so much as he tries to avoid dishonor, whether as a Dane carrying the burden of national weakness (1.4.13 ff.) or as a son with a father slain and a mother stained (5.2.63 ff.). He is at times closer to Falstaff in his awareness of the limitations of honor in the sense of external recognition, especially in the graveyard (5.1.202 ff.), when the prince discusses the ultimately humble fates of Alexander and Julius Caesar; and when the clay stopper of a bung-hole in a barrel of beer creates by its link to alcohol an association to Claudius and his drinking behavior, which besmirches the honor of Denmark.

In his analysis of honor as so easily destroyed (1.4.13ff.), as sometimes trivially mistaken as a goal, that "fantasy and trick of fame" (4.4.61), as no protection against material recycling to "base uses" (5.1.202ff.), as yet important enough to be his first thought as he dies, "Report me and my cause aright" lest he suffer that "wounded name" (5.2.339ff.), the prince shows himself ever so much more self-aware and philosophically analytical than his tragic peers varyingly and nonreflectively concerned with reputation, from Othello through Lear and Macbeth and on to Antony and Coriolanus. In spite of the clear Christian references in the final act and the prince's presumed heavenly reward, his intense concern, as he is dying, with honor in this world looks very much as though now he believes that honor, as the external respect paid to an individual by others, is the only principle of force that can preserve the self or selves from annihilation (see Watson, *The Rest is Silence*). Falstaff, earlier in the canon, had described to us just how limited that principle is.

We might have heard yet further articulations of the prince's moral and psychological struggles were it not for the fact that descriptions of events replace soliloquy. We look in vain in his soliloquies for an evolution in Hamlet's responses, a development or progress towards a purposeful end. Instead, we see a variety of moods and promises that oscillate between confidence and doubt, simple aggression and skeptical hesitation, until a divine force understood by the prince to be operative in his world takes the largest problem from him of what to do and when to do it. That force manifests itself through events that happen offstage, the discovery on board ship of the deadly letter of Claudius and the subsequent fight with and capture by the pirates. Those shipboard events, described but not shown, produce a literal and figurative sea change in the prince, as he now believes that Providence is actively concerned with him and his problem. For some, he has become less interesting inasmuch as whatever subsequent activity is shown, it is against the backdrop of a larger passivity. He who was the agent has become the patient, the "bonesetter" of Act 1, scene 5 has been himself cured by a greater physician.

Of course, religion and religious issues have been important throughout this text. We begin with the ghost in the opening scene and its arrival from Purgatory and move through the punning allusion, in the description of the fate of Polonius's body, to the nature of the transformation of the body of Christ in the Eucharist and to the pivotal council, the Diet of Worms, where Luther allowed that he could do no other. We are then confronted with the nature of Ophelia's death and consequent rights and wrongs of her burial in sanctified earth, as well as with the metaphoric role of Claudius as parodic priest transforming sacramental wine into the blood-corroding poison in the cup of Act 5, scene 2. Finally, we see Hamlet as the sacrifice of the entire play, headed for his heavenly reward accompanied, according to the loyal Horatio, from this earth by flights of angels. Our ostensibly nonsectarian and skeptical humanist dramatist has filled his tragedy with Christian themes, allusions, and ironies.

CONCLUSION

But beyond religious issues, at the heart of the play, a play full of interrogation (cf. Levin, *The Question of Hamlet*), is the question of what it is to be, to exist as an individual, a person, a self. A large part of the problem in the world of Hamlet, just as in life, is the nature of role-playing, where we each find or are given roles that help determine who we are. The prince himself is denied meaningful, self-creating, and self-sustaining roles from the very beginning of the play. He is no longer the expected heir of a beloved father, no matter what the soon-to-be-proven duplicitous Claudius will ambiguously say about Hamlet's being "most immediate to our throne" (1.2.109). He is suddenly no longer a university student when Claudius denies his request to return to Wittenberg. And he is no longer a lover, now separated from Ophelia by her father's command to her that she "be something scanter of [her] maiden presence," (1.3.121), by his recognition that she is deceiving him when they meet and that Claudius and Polonius are hiding nearby in order to eavesdrop (3.1.43ff.), and/or even by his linking Ophelia with Gertrude such that he doubts the fidelity of any woman. In this last response, with his fusing of Ophelia and Gertrude, he is providing evidence of the truth observed by Ernest Schanzer, that the most common aspect of Shakespeare's tragedies is the protagonist's "disillusion with the person dearest to him" (Schanzer, 24).

There is role-playing and *role-playing*, the difference between the honest functioning in a given place in society—the activity that makes us who and what we are—and the calculated pretense of being something and someone we are truly not. There may well be a self that lies behind the actions and roles that create the outer self that we can observe in others and even our "selves," but there is, in certain characters' calculated duplicities, clearly something other than what their actions seem to suggest. They are faking it (see Miller, *Faking It*). Hamlet is at pains throughout the play to distinguish between these differing kinds of role-playing.

By the end of the play, Hamlet is both restored to his community and yet, oddly, still alone. He has seen in his mother's last words her concern for him; in his killing of Claudius, he has satisfied the demand of his ghostly father (however much he is silent regarding whether he himself finds the actual killing of Claudius satisfying); he has, with the nomination of Fortinbras as king, perhaps helped free the Danish throne from criminality and also evoked the profoundest loyalty from his friend Horatio. With parents, friend, country—and even a heavenly escort, the flights of angels—he is no longer alone. And yet, there will be no Hamlet III, no son of our Hamlet. The prince may be said to have cleansed his world of the corruption of his elders, but in that effort, he himself has been stained, a corruption that is washed away only by his death. We value him for his having fought, if not *the* good fight, at least several good fights, as he has challenged duplicity and power. Horatio may hear the song that the angels sing as they escort Hamlet the prince to heaven, but for most of the audience, the angels are but a faint chorus for a brave but solo player.

PERFORMANCE HISTORY

ERFORMANCE HISTORY, the accumulated record of the play in
production across the centuries, can provide useful material
for actors, directors, and critics, as well as for students who
often in their time play all these roles in class or at their desks. It is
useful to remember that what has come down to us over the centuries in the form of eyewitness testimony of theatergoers—sometimes
famous theatergoers—or professional reviewers, scholarly or journal-
istic, is the personal, subjective response of one man or woman. That
reviewer is reacting on a given afternoon or evening to a particular performance of a given company that might have been altered
by something as simple as the use of an understudy or by the wet
feet of an audience on a rainy day. What we have are unique reports
that only apparently have hardened into concrete truths, but they
are still the best evidence we have of what a play has been or can be.
With the arrival of the twentieth century, we also have recordings
and films, often adaptations of stage performances, versions of the text
that, however cut and rearranged in different modes, are part of the
"*Hamlet* experience."

For the student preparing to take her place in the chain of *Hamlet*
performances in the theater of her own imagination, this essay considers celebrated performances that reveal the most essential and at
times controversial of the infinite choices that directors and actors
must make in deciding how to perform this play. Each of us contributes to the texture of the play's history and depth with the choices we
contribute to any production of the play, whether in a scene in front
of the blackboard with a folded book in our hands or on the grandest
stage with the Royal Shakespeare Company.

Any production of *Hamlet* necessarily begins with the script—How
much of this lengthy play should be included? How much abridged?
After the script is set come the casting and directing of the actors—
What image do they present? How do they enunciate the lines? And,
to bring the production together, the director makes decisions about
how the entire play looks—What are the costumes? The props? What
is the setting? Each new actor and director will be treading well-worn
territory but adding a new dimension.

THE SCRIPT

An unabridged performance of *Hamlet*—that is, one in which every line of the play is spoken in the order presented in the longest script from Shakespeare's time—typically takes more than four hours. The attention span of a modern audience is somewhat shorter, but the tradition of cutting the text, of adding material and of rearranging the order of lines and scenes, began in the time of Shakespeare himself.

As you already know in part from the Introduction, the different versions of the play are represented by Quarto 1 (Q1), Quarto 2 (Q2) and the Folio of 1623. The probable order of these scripts is first Q2, the longest version, perhaps designed for an ideal theater in the mind of Shakespeare, without the limitations of the Globe or any other Elizabethan venue. The Folio reflects a performance of the play with significant cuts of some two hundred lines and the addition of nearly ninety lines, some devoted to allusions to the War of the Theaters. Q1, though printed first, appears to be chronologically last, as it reflects a very seriously abbreviated version of the already-cut script of the Folio, perhaps for a performance on a tour outside London. The most notable change in Q1 from the earlier two texts is the placing of the "To be or not to be" soliloquy in Act 2, scene 2, rather than in Act 3, scene 1, where we have it now. In addition, the seventh soliloquy, "How all occasions do inform against me," of Act 4, scene 4, is absent from both Q1 and the Folio.

Lest we bemoan the damage done by others to Shakespeare's text, we should remember that Shakespeare himself is known to have made changes to his script as a result of second thoughts and changed venues. After his death, his company made still more changes, with the result that we should hardly be surprised that subsequent actors and directors have made even more cuts and alterations, albeit now without the authority of the original scriptwriter or of his colleagues. Of course, if it is a script— and it is—rather than a sacred text, it is open to perpetual change. By the end of the twentieth century and the beginning of the twenty-first, directors and actors themselves, those who create new interpretations and new productions in the current moment, are considered by some to be as important as, or even more important than, Shakespeare himself. After all, they are doing with Shakespeare as their source only what he had done with Thomas Kyd and François de Belleforest.

Perhaps following the example of Shakespeare's own day, at the time of the Restoration (1660), huge cuts were made by actors and managers who thought they were improving the text. The actor-play-wright-theater-manager William Davenant (1606–68) "cut Voltemand, Cornelius and Reynaldo, Polonius' advice to Laertes, most of Laertes' advice to Ophelia, all of Hamlet's advice to the players, and Fortinbras's first appearance; while, of the famous longer speeches, only 'To be or not to be' survives in its entirety" (Arden, 98–99). By the middle of the eighteenth century, perhaps the most striking cut and elaborately recreated version was that of David Garrick (1717–79), who took care to create space to enhance his own role as the prince by omitting the gravediggers and the funeral of Ophelia, partly in response to the neoclassical criticism of the alleged crudeness of the gravediggers' discussion and the unseemliness of the fighting in the grave.

These practices of earlier centuries continue today, and the sophisticated technology of today's films show what the results of such familiar rearranging, following the tradition set by Q1 and developed by Davenant, can be. Among the most celebrated (or maybe "notorious" would be a better word) of the rearrangings of Shakespeare's text is that of Laurence Olivier in his 1948 film, where the "dram of eale" speech of 1.4.23-38 was moved to the beginning of the film so as to suggest the key to unlocking the mystery of Hamlet. Olivier meant by this shift to suggest that a single weakness in an otherwise splendid nature is sufficient to cause its downfall. As if such rearranging were not sufficient, there is a voiceover (Olivier's) telling the audience that this is the story of "a man who could not make up his mind."

Another significant rearrangement appears in Franco Zeffirelli's 1990 *Hamlet* (which preserves less than half of Shakespeare's text) with Mel Gibson as the prince, where Fortinbras is eliminated (as he so often has been in performances throughout history), and the international theme is consequently reduced, making the play necessarily less a political drama and more a personal and familial story.

The reverse approach to such cutting involves highlighting the political drama by *adding* lines, as was done in Bucharest, Romania, in the late 1980s, when the play had a consecutive run of more than six months. Claudius was portrayed as the Romanian dictator Nicolae Ceausescu, and when Claudius is succeeded by Fortinbras, the young Norwegian, Fortinbras proves himself to be yet another dictator who, using newly added language not in Shakespeare's original, orders his guards, the still-living Rosencrantz and Guildenstern, to execute Horatio, the sole truth teller in the tragedy (Kennedy; quoted in Liston, 1944).

Such productions in Eastern Europe during the time of Soviet domination and state power were what they were because in the eye of the audience, Denmark is, as the prince says, "a prison" (2.2.251). In one 1989 production in East Berlin, capital of the German Democratic Republic, when Laertes is granted permission to return to Paris from Denmark in Act 1, scene 2, he is handed a green visa (the color of West German passports). He uses that visa to pass through the barbed-wire fence surrounding the Danish kingdom, separating it in the theater from the audience, which "howled with delight" at the symbolically colored document (Kennedy, quoted in Liston, 1944). At that time, and in that place, Fortinbras and the political theme were at the forefront of the play, never cut as in so many contemporary Western productions.

A most extreme version of editorial creative independence is seen in the reordering of the entire play in Charles Marowitz's deliberate dismembering of the text in his Royal Shakespeare Company 1964 production of *Hamlet*, a collage of scenes that the director believed opens up the mythic essence of the tragedy.

But Marowitz is only one of a number of creative rearrangers who are following the logic of Davenant, Garrick, and other early stage interpreters of Shakespeare. The film director Michael Almereyda describes his 2000 *Hamlet* with the same vocabulary as Marowitz, "not so much a sketch but a collage, a patch-work of intuition, images, and ideas" (quoted in Anderegg, 180).

In keeping with Marowitz and not unrelated to Almereyda is Peter Brook, who in 2001 in London, Paris, Vienna, and New York produced *The Tragedy of Hamlet*. "Brook's production sought in *Hamlet* for a set of pan-religious spiritual truths supposedly accessible to all cultures at once, attempting to set the play timelessly and everywhere." (Dobson, 302).

© Miramax/Courtesy Everett Collection

Fig. 5. Ethan Hawke as the prince in the 2000 film version, in which a thoroughly wired and self-referential, postmodern Hamlet wields his camcorder, one of his many advanced technological tools.

"As with Brook's earlier Francophone *Hamlet* piece *Qui est là?*, all began as ever with 'Who's there?', but here it was spoken by Hamlet as the way into his dialogue with the Ghost; then came 'O that this too too sullied flesh would melt', then a little of the court scene that usually precedes it; later 'To be or not to be' came only after Hamlet's despatch towards England." (Dobson, 301). Like Marowitz, Brook is shuffling and cutting the cards in the belief that the resulting hand is not aleatory but profoundly purposeful and significant, almost as if a divinity had shaped the result by preserving the essential in the midst of so much cuttable material.

THE ACTORS

The play is full of many complex characters, but Hamlet is the central figure. All decisions as to how the play should be performed depend, therefore, upon the director's understanding of Hamlet's nature. There are three basic interpretations of what he is essentially like: He is purposefully strong; he is gently reflective; he is wily. Of course, in the richness of his character, in different proportions, he is one, two, or all three. Hamlet is the protagonist, and while "protagonist" is not always synonymous with "hero," for most directors and most readers and viewers, Hamlet is indeed a hero. Heroes themselves are heroes of strength, of wisdom, or of cunning, and sometimes a bit of two or all three.

Without oversimplifying too much, directors, while realizing the multiplicity of elements in Hamlet's character, stress in any particular production one of these three qualities more than the others. Is he primarily a courageous son working his way towards revenge in spite of obstacles both external and internal? Is he in fact too much the sweet student and philosopher, somewhat along the lines of Samuel Coleridge's view? Or is he the crafty trickster of northern sagas and folk tradition? The history of performance of the play demonstrates this range of choices.

Part of the balance of courage, sweetness and cunning is struck in the initial casting of the actor playing the prince—how old and fit is he, and thus, how does his very face reflect the three relevant characteristics in varying degrees? The gravedigger tells us that the prince is now thirty years old (5.1.143–7 and 5.1.162), an age understandable given all that Hamlet has been through, but a bit old for the Wittenberg student that we met earlier in the play. The very first Hamlet, Richard Burbage, was about thirty-two when he played the part, and subsequent Hamlets have been young, old, and middle-aged. The balancing of a too-mature prince and a too-youthful Gertrude can accentuate the idea of sexual tension between the two, e.g., the

Fig. 6. The forty-year-old Laurence Olivier as the prince and the twenty-seven-year-old Eileen Herlie as Gertrude in the 1948 film, which rearranged parts of the text and provided a heavily Freudian interpretation of the play.

forty-year-old Olivier of the 1948 film and his queen, the twenty-seven-year-old Eileen Hurlie.

Conversely, having an actor who possesses a middle-aged paunch hardly seems a romantic figure for a young Ophelia to love, as in the case of Nicol Williamson and Marianne Faithfull in Tony Richardson's 1969 film. In the theater, Simon Russell Beale, a critically successful Hamlet of 2000, played to his lack of physical fitness by patting his ample stomach when he came to the line that told of his having "forgone all custom of exercises" (2.2.296-7). This was an actor and a prince intelligent and confident enough to laugh slyly at himself. Beale, whose success gave comfort to actors of an ample girth and a certain age, might himself been comforted by the 1987 production of *Hamlet: The Tragedy of a Fat Man*, with the almost 240-pound Steve Western as the prince.

Nothing is so altered from the original productions and so affects the way Hamlet may be portrayed as is the gender of the prince himself. Hamlet has often been seen as having a delicate, feminine quality (sweetness, perhaps, or, uncharitably, weakness), one that made it tempting to have a woman play the role. Four of the most famously successful actresses playing Hamlet onstage or in film were

Courtesy Everett Collection

Fig. 7. Marianne Faithfull as Ophelia and Nicol Williamson as the prince in Tony Richardson's 1969 production. The casting of a famous singer and then-girlfriend of Mick Jagger as the virginal Ophelia lent some complexity to the role.

the following: Sarah Siddons (1755–1831) was commonly judged the greatest tragic actress of her time. Charlotte Cushman (1816–76) was a large-boned American with a powerful voice whose square jaw presented a "positively mannish" image (Shattuck, 1914). The French actress Sarah Bernhardt (1834–1923) played the prince in 1887 and then in 1899, when she was in her fifties; and the next year, she was filmed performing a single scene. Finally, the Danish actress Asta Nielsen (1881–1972) played the prince in a 1920 silent film not as a man with feminine qualities but as a princess, a woman disguised as a prince. As critics have noted, Nielsen thus created a tragic version of Shakespeare's comic heroines disguised as boys, like Rosalind in *As You Like It* and Viola in *Twelfth Night*.

Bernhardt in her French translation cut less of the play than did many English actors and directors of her day. Her performances were stylized rather than naturalistic, in spite of her roughhousing with Rosencrantz and Guildenstern, whose heads she knocked, and with Polonius, whose shins she kicked. Overall, her performance "relates strongly to the operatic tradition" (Wells, "Travesti Hamlet," 2). One

Fig. 8. The French actress
Sarah Bernhardt (1844–1923)
played the prince as an
ardent revenger in an 1887
production. Later, in her
fifties, she reprised the role
of a character she viewed as
in his early twenties.

Courtesy Everett Collection

Lafayette – Photo – London.
SARAH-BERNHARDT (HAMLET.)

critic described Bernhardt's superb performance with some details that
reveal her genius for appropriate stage business: "But what exquisite
ideas she had! The crossing of herself before she follows the Ghost; the
speaking of the speech to the players on the miniature stage, making
Hamlet for the moment an actor addressing the audience; the feeling
of his father's picture on the walls when the Ghost has gone and
materialism has come again; the effect of the poison in Hamlet's veins
when his hand is scratched in the duel with Laertes; the kissing of
his dead mother's hair,—all these are exquisite points never imagined
before" (Scott, quoted in Salgādo, 257).

According to many reviewers of female princes, a woman is not
an unlikely Hamlet—in fact, she may be the ideal Hamlet. Indeed,
Bernhardt argued that women are better able to play young men
because they "can combine the light carriage of youth with the
mature thought of a man" (see Wells, "Travesti").

The history of female Hamlets (and there have been more than
fifty), as well as the general issue of physicality in casting the prince,
reminds us also of the profound effect upon audiences of an actor's
voice. We have had a variety of such voices, from the mellifluously
elegant diction of John Gielgud to the late-nineteenth-century Henry

Irving (1838–1905), a brilliantly intense actor with "a queer and unmelodious voice" (Shattuck, 1916), who, when hearing his own recorded voice, responded as each of us might when hearing for the first time just what we sound like, "My God!" Certainly some slack must be given Irving and other Hamlets whose voices are preserved from the early, imperfect days of sound recording.

Visually, some film actors come trailing clouds of previous performances, so that the heroism of the prince is underscored by the achievements of the lethal weapon–brandishing actor in his earlier films, as in the case of Mel Gibson in Zefferelli's 1990 film. When choosing an actor to play the prince, the director certainly looks for both voice and, especially in film, attractiveness. By the standards of his day, Richard Burton, with his deeply musical Welsh voice and handsome face, combined the two ideally in the 1964 New York production directed by Gielgud.

These actors, of whatever size, shape, gender, voice, or attractiveness, recite the lines that survive any cutting and in the order of any directorial rearranging; but in every performance, they must make decisions as to what words of the "words, words, words" (2.2.192) spoken by the prince and the other characters are to be featured—that is, particularly stressed over others. Olivier thought that in an iambic line, there is but one word that can be stressed effectively. Olivier, who had seen John Barrymore's 1925 London production, must have noted that Barrymore had a tendency "to choose a single word (e.g., 'fit and seasoned for his *passage*' for an 'explosion'" (*Sunday Times*, 22 Feb. 1925) (Dawson, 70). Many actors have intuitively accepted this practice and have wrestled with the choice of word. Sometimes that choice is to channel one or more of the great Hamlets of the past for whom we have audio and video recordings; other times, it propels the actor upon a new path and a new interpretation. In the celebrated fourth soliloquy, would one choose to stress the second word, "be," the conjunction "or," the adverb "not," the second "be," the demonstrative "that," the copulative "is," the definite article "the," or the final noun, "question," or even one of the prepositions, "to"? Upon such apparently small decisions rest great effects. A good test is to compare the delivery of that soliloquy in the recordings of Gielgud and Burton and the films of Olivier (1948), Derek Jacobi (1980), Gibson (1990), and Kenneth Branagh (1996).

In a global Shakespearean world, with every nation believing, rightly, that Shakespeare is their Shakespeare, England preserves its position as first among equals. As such, it is sometimes the testing ground for American Hamlets, three of whom have been especially admired by the British critics since the success of Edwin Booth in 1880. Booth was praised particularly for his straight-faced delivery of the comic lines with Rosencrantz and Guildenstern in Act 2, scene 2 (thought to be a uniquely American style). Subsequent acclaimed performances were by John Barrymore in his 1925 production, the television actor Richard Chamberlain in a 1970 version, and the former director of the London New Globe, Mark Rylance, in his pajama-clad version of 1988.

Although the focus of the play is Hamlet, important choices must be made about the supporting characters, including (and to some, especially) Ophelia and Polonius. We do not pass over other crucial members of the cast, having already discussed the significance of the age of the actress playing Gertrude. And in the case of Claudius, his age and appearance are less important than the preservation of his lines. If Claudius loses too many words, he has not the weight to be a fit opponent of the prince. When he does have those words, he can be as formidable as was Patrick Stewart (in a BBC TV production in 1980 and at Stratford in 2008). Ophelia and Polonius, daughter and father, pose a particularly rich array of decisions for actors and directors to make.

Ophelia is for most judges close to the figure that Ellen Terry, herself a celebrated Ophelia in the nineteenth century, described in her notebook: "Her brain, her soul, and her body are pathetically weak." Modern productions, however, whether onstage or on film, tend to

Fig. 9. In a 1988 Royal Shakespeare Company production, the American actor and theater director Mark Rylance depicts the prince in his mental and physical disarray, sopping the blood of the slain Polonius at 3.4.211ff.

accentuate the erotic energy that derives from Ophelia's source figures in Saxo Grammaticus and Apuleius' *The Golden Asse* by having her play scantily clad during the mad scene of Act 4, scene 5, as in the 2008 Stratford version with David Tennant as an intelligent Hamlet and Mariah Gale as the distraught and abandoned Ophelia.

Other directors have tried to strengthen Ophelia, even in a limited way, both by having her indicate by tone and facial expression that she will only apparently obey her father and later by allowing her to warn Hamlet by gesture that her father and Claudius are overhearing their conversation. But the text does not give directors much to support this interpretation.

The desire to flesh out this character has extended to such collateral productions as Stephen Berkoff's 2006 *The Secret Love Life of Ophelia*, directed by Bruce Downie, an epistolary dialogue of the love between Hamlet and Ophelia. In Shakespeare's play, we have an example of Hamlet's side of the correspondence, when Polonius reads an extract that he doesn't much like, in which his daughter is described as "beautified" (2.2.1109), "proof" of his argument that Hamlet's "madness" is the result of frustrated love. Frances Barber, the Ophelia in the Royal Shakespeare Company's 1984 *Hamlet*, played Ophelia "as an adjunct to Hamlet, supplying that which he lacks, but [Barber] is aware that this reading does not have to make her weak, only powerless.... Barber's full conception of Ophelia is that she is 'strong, spirited, forthright, but powerless, only an observer'" (Holmes 128).

As to the portrayal of other supporting characters, in recent stage productions and films, just as in Elizabethan times, the choice of actor provides a signal as to which interpretation a director has chosen. The character of Polonius, for example, provides much creative opportunity for directors and actors alike—Is he an insufferable bore? A comic fool? A "bureaucratic bully," as was Donald Sinden in 1994 (Crowl, 1995, quoted in Liston, 1938)? Some of each? In the 2000 film of *Hamlet* starring Ethan Hawke as the prince, comedian Bill Murray played Polonius (see Color Plate 3). That choice seemingly hinted at the comedy to follow, but Murray's Polonius is also both authoritarian and sensitive—in fact, after ordering Ophelia to end her relationship with Hamlet, he bends to tie the loose lacing on her sneaker, with the lacing itself symbolic of freedom and restraint.

Kenneth Branagh went the comedic route in his 1996 production, casting comedian Billy Crystal as the gravedigger, a humorous choice both for the comic's delivery and for his American accent, standing out among the British straight players. By contrast, the casting of the noted Shakespearean stage actor Ian Holm as Polonius in Zeffirelli's production signaled a more "straight man" version of the character— so much a straight man, indeed, that his delivery of the aphoristic lines, including "To thine own self be true," might mistakenly be remembered as having been spoken by Hamlet. In the 1995 film *Clueless* (itself an adaptation of Jane Austen's *Emma*), the heroine corrects a rival who had attributed the line to Hamlet: "I think I remember Mel Gibson accurately, and he didn't say that. That Polonius guy did."

APPEARANCE: STAGE, COSTUME, AND PROPS

In addition to the text and the casting of the characters, much of the meaning of the play is conveyed by staging, including the size of the stage, the proximity of the audience, the dominance of the set, and the proportion of human figures to their environment. Actors who speak the words also create meaning by inhabiting a space full of semantic significances. Some of the essential choices in this realm come in the selection of costume color, particular props, and elements of scenery.

We know that there is a tradition that only Hamlet wears black; the celebrated Ellen Terry as Ophelia wanted to wear the same color, only to be told by the director's advisor, "There is only one character in this play who wears black, Madam" (Holmes, 127). Gielgud, profoundly interested in the effect of costume, "agrees that Ophelia and Laertes should both wear black after the death of Polonius, at which Hamlet should change to a different color" (Holmes, 127). Tyrone Guthrie's Old Vic production in 1938 used modern dress, but it was the modern dress of court society, with off-the-shoulder evening gowns for the women and "dress suits with colorful sashes, orders, and court swords" for the men. Hamlet himself was dressed more "casually, in black and purple," while the gravediggers were dressed in the coveralls of twentieth-century workmen (Shattuck, 1922).

Moving from the formal to the casual, there is also the idea that rehearsal clothing is best, as Gielgud argued for his own 1964 production in a program note for the Lunt-Fontanne Theater: "This is Hamlet acted in rehearsal clothes, stripped of all extraneous trappings, so the beauty of the language and imagery may shine through unencumbered by an elaborate reconstruction of any particular period" (quoted in Holmes, 119). Pushing surprise costuming to the extreme, in Joseph Papp's 1968 New York production, *"Naked" Hamlet*, "Hamlet appears sometimes in his underwear, sometimes in a white suit and black beret, sometimes in baggy pants and leather jacket. . ." (Shattuck, 1924).

In this play, there are many thematically important costumes and properties, but three particularly stand out: the dress of the Ghost, who in Shakespeare's time wore in the closet scene a "night gowne" (garb that perhaps humanizes the old warrior); the sword with its cruciform handle, the better to be sworn upon; and, of course, the skull of Yorick. "The key to every *Hamlet* is its ghost. A solid ghost demands an active, believing hero, thwarted by events; an insubstantial one, all light-effects and echoes, a brainsick prince, nerveless and Oedipal" (Ronald Bryden, quoted in Wells, 274). Some ghosts are fully armored and helmeted, with a bit of white gauze over the figure, some are only heard and indicated by a light (a green light, in the case of the famous 1925 Barrymore production), and some are heard in the closet scene (Act 3, scene 4) but unseen by the audience, who respond to the differing reactions on the faces of Hamlet and Gertrude, as in the Zeffirelli film of 1990. In the 2010-11 National Theatre Nicholas Hytner production with Rory Kinnear as the young prince, a striking effect came from Gertrude's seeing the ghost in the closet scene. Perhaps one of the most startling ghosts was the ten-foot-tall figure who towered over David Warner's prince in the 1965 Peter Hall production. His height was the external sign of a father's irresistibly powerful influence over a son staggering under the burden of paternal expectations. And there have been in other productions an equally effective illustration of this powerful paternal force by providing no external ghost at all, but rather making the prince

Fig. 10. The use of actors known from television or cinema (here the stars of the British show *Dr. Who* and of *Star Trek: The Next Generation*) bring to some in the audience associations beyond Shakespeare. In this 2008 Royal Shakespeare Company production, David Tennant was a successfully intelligent and moving prince, and Patrick Stewart remained the definitive Claudius of his time, seen here doubling as the Ghost.

himself speak the lines that belong to his ghostly father—Hamlet's internalizing of that father's expectations.

Directors focus not just on the Ghost's appearance but also on the sword that he asks Hamlet to swear upon (Act 1, scene 5) and the foils that the prince and Laertes use in the often spectacular and spectacularly dangerous duel of Act 5, scene 2. While the sword is often used as a symbolic cross, the foils in the action of the dueling scene terrifically increase the audience's tension. John Barrymore, who combined an athleticism that Olivier would later channel with a subdued soliloquizing as he was seated or recumbent, was notoriously aggressive in the duel, to the dismay and near disfigurement of his Laertes (Dawson, 82).

No scene in the play is more iconically familiar than that of Hamlet in the graveyard studying the skull. The skull is personal for the prince because it is that of Yorick, the court jester who playfully carried the young Hamlet on his back many years ago (and the juxtaposition of Yorick's skull and Hamlet suggests that Hamlet is the successor jester to his childhood playmate), but it is also a *memento mori,* the reminder of death that comes to all: Alexander, Caesar, Hamlet Senior, Polonius, Rosencrantz and Guildenstern, and now Ophelia, and eventually to

Fig. 11. The athletic Laurence Olivier (Hamlet, left) dueling with Laertes, played by Terence Morgan, in the final scene of his 1948 film.

© ArenaPal/Topham/The Image Works

Fig. 12. Sam West as Hamlet in the 2001 Royal Shakespeare Company production, contemplating a skull, just before this flippant yet profoundly insightful prince makes an unreasonable demand upon Yorick by using his skull as a football.

all onstage and in the audience. It is the knowledge of the inevitability of death that leads to philosophizing, to asking questions about the nature of the self and the obligation for justice. In some productions, Hamlet will fondle the skull; in others, he will pick it up not with his hand but with the point of his sword, a gesture that wonderfully anticipates his own involvement in the deaths of Laertes, Claudius, and himself. Every production has a skull among its props, where it can even function as a football (see Fig. 12, the 2001 Royal Shakespeare Company production with British actor Sam West as the kicker).

Out of these decisions involving the text, the actors, and the appearance of stage, costume, and props, comes *Hamlet*, the play. And we haven't mentioned the parodic *Hamlets*, such as Tom Stoppard's *Fifteen-Minute Hamlet*, the even-faster Reduced Shakespeare Company's rapid-fire version (going both backward and forward), and Arnold Schwarzenegger's campy prince in *The Last Action Hero*, with his pronunciation of "father" as "fadder" and his comment to Claudius just before killing him, regarding the murder of that "fadder," "Big mistake!" and so many more YouTube amateur versions.

Performances of *Hamlet* and performances of adaptations of *Hamlet* have become part of our shifting sense of the play. Performances that were once thought of as a violation of the text have become an aspect of the play's expanding and mutating script, Shakespeare's and yet more than Shakespeare's. Some scholars, and a few critics, will object to the "liberties" taken with the order of the words that Shakespeare has left us (multifaceted though that gift is). Most audiences have come to delight in the variety of modern and postmodern approaches. Yet it is possible that in that happy majority, there are some who think along the lines of young Stephen Daedalus in James Joyce's *A Portrait of the Artist as a Young Man*, that while God has many names, in different languages, God's real name is God. In the midst of all these splendidly creative versions of the play, *Hamlet* has a real nature, one that is known to each of us as *Hamlet*, that play with Shakespeare's "words, words, words."

WORKS CITED FOR INTRODUCTION AND PERFORMANCE HISTORY

Anderegg, Michael. *Cinematic Shakespeare*. Lanham: Rowan & Littlefield, 2004.

Bednarz, James P. *Shakespeare and the Poets' War*. New York: Columbia UP, 2001.

Brockbank, Philip. "Hamlet the Bonesetter." *Shakespeare Survey* 30. Ed. Kenneth Muir. Cambridge, UK: Cambridge UP 1977.

Crowl, Samuel. *Shakespeare Observed: Studies in Performance on Stage and Screen*. Athens: Ohio UP, 1992.

Dawson, Anthony B. *Shakespeare in Performance, Hamlet*. Manchester and New York: Manchester UP, 1995.

Dobson, Michael. "Shakespeare Performances in England." *Shakespeare Survey* 55. Ed. Peter Holland. Cambridge, UK: Cambridge UP, 2002.

Erne, Lukas. *Shakespeare as Literary Dramatist*. Cambridge, UK: Cambridge UP, 2003.

Holmes, Jonathan. *Merely Players? Actors' Accounts of Playing Shakespeare*. New York: Routledge, 2004.

Jenkins, Harold, ed. *Hamlet,* by William Shakespeare. Arden Shakespeare, Second Series. London: Methuen, 1982.

Jones, Emrys. *The Origins of Shakespeare*. Oxford, UK: Clarendon Press, 1977.

Kennedy, Dennis, ed. *Foreign Shakespeare: Contemporary Performance*. Cambridge, UK: Cambridge UP, 1993.

Kermode, Frank. *Shakespeare's Language*. New York: Ferrar, Straus, and Giroux, 2000.

Levin, Harry. *The Question of* Hamlet. London: Oxford University Press, 1959.

Liston, William T. "Shakespeare's Plays in Performance from 1970." Appendix B. *The Riverside Shakespeare*, ed. G. Blakemore Evans with J. J.M. Tobin. Boston: Houghton Mifflin, 1997: 1932–50.

Miller, William I. *Faking It*. Cambridge, UK: Cambridge UP, 2005.

Roe, John. *Shakespeare and Machiavelli*. Cambridge, UK: D.S. Brewer, 2002.

Salgado, Gamini. *Eye Witnesses of Shakespeare: First Hand Accounts of Performances 1590–1890*. London: University of Sussex Press, 1975.

Schanzer, Ernest. *The Winter's Tale*. London: Penguin, 1986.

Scott, Clement. *Some Notable Hamlets of the Present Time: Sarah Bernhardt, Henry Irving, Wilson Barrett, Beerbohm Tree, and Forbes Robertson*. London: Greening & Co., 1900.

Shattuck, Charles H. "Shakespeare's Plays in Performance: From 1660–1971." Appendix A. *The Riverside Shakespeare*, ed. G. Blakemore Evans with J. J.M. Tobin. Boston: Houghton Mifflin, 1997: 1905–31.

Thompson, Ann and Neil Taylor, eds. *Hamlet* by William Shakespeare. Arden Shakespeare Third Series. London: A&C Black 2006.

Watson, Robert. *The Rest Is Silence: Death as Annihilation in the English Renaissance*. Berkeley: University of California Press, 1994.

Wells, Stanley, ed. *Shakespeare in the Theater: An Anthology of Criticism*. Oxford: Oxford UP, 1997.

——. "Travesti Hamlet," 24 Dec. 1997, *Times Literary Supplement*, 18.

Welsh, Alexander. *Hamlet in His Modern Guises*. Princeton: Princeton University Press, 2001.

Wright, George T. "Hendiadys and *Hamlet*." *PMLA* 96 (1981): 168–93.

ABBREVIATIONS

F1, F2, etc. First Folio, Second Folio, etc.
O1, O2, etc. First Octavo, Second Octavo, etc.
Q1, Q2, etc. First Quarto, Second Quarto, etc.
(c) corrected state
(u) uncorrected state
conj. conjecture
ed. editor; edition
l(l). line(s)
n.s. new series
om. omit(s), omitted
o.s.d. opening stage direction
s.d(d). stage direction(s)
ser. series
sig(s). signature(s)
s.p(p). speech-prefix(es)
subs. substantially
(T) additional notes by current editor

KEY TO WORKS CITED IN EXPLANATORY AND TEXTUAL NOTES

Reference in explanatory and textual notes is in general by last name of editor or author. Not included in the following list of works so cited are editions of the play or special studies referred to in the selected bibliographies appended to the "Note on the Text" following the play.

AEB, *Analytical and Enumerative Bibliography*
ALEXANDER, Peter, ed., *Works*, 1951
BOSWELL, James, ed., *Works*, 1821 (21 vols.)
BULLEN, Arthur H., ed., *Works*, 1904–7 (10 vols.)
BULLOCH, John, *Studies on the Text of Shakespeare*, 1878
BULLOUGH, Geoffrey, *Narrative and Dramatic Sources of Shakespeare*, 1957–75 (8 vols.)
CAMBRIDGE, *Works*, ed. W. G. Clark and W. A. Wright, 1863–66 (9 vols.); ed. W. A. Wright, 1891–93 (9 vols.)
CAPELL, Edward, ed., *Works*, [1768] (10 vols.)
COLLIER, John P., ed., *Works*, 1842–44 (8 vols.); 1853; 1858 (6 vols.)
COLLIER MS, Perkins' Second Folio, 1632 (Huntington Library)
COWDEN CLARKE, Charles and Mary, eds., *Works*, 1864–68 (3 vols.)
CRAIG, William J., ed., *Works*, 1891
CRAIK, George L., *The English of Shakespeare*, 1857
DANIEL, P. A., *Notes and Conjectural Emendations*, 1870
DELIUS, Nicolaus, ed., *Works*, 1854–60 (7 vols.); 1872 (2 vols.)
DYCE, Alexander, ed., *Works*, 1857 (6 vols.); 1864–67 (9 vols.); 1875–76 (9 vols.) *Works of Beaumont and Fletcher*, 1843–46 (11 vols.)
ELN, *English Language Notes*
ELR, *English Literary Renaissance*
FARMER, Richard, in *Works* (Johnson-Steevens), 1773
FURNESS, H. H., ed., *New Variorum Edition*, 1871–1928 (vols. 1–15; vols. 16–21 by H. H. Furness, Jr.)
GLOBE, ed. William G. Clark and W. A. Wright, *Works*, 1864
HALLIWELL, James O., ed., *Works*, 1853–65 (16 vols.)
HANMER, Thomas, ed., *Works*, 1743–44 (6 vols.); 1745; 1770–71 (6 vols.)
HARNESS, William, ed., *Works*, 1825 (8 vols.)
HARRISON, G. B., ed., *Works* (Penguin), 1937–56 (37 vols.)
HEATH, Benjamin, *Revisal of Shakespeare's Text*, 1765
HERFORD, Charles H., ed., *Works*, 1899 (10 vols.)
HINMAN, Charlton, *The Printing and Proof-Reading of the First Folio of Shakespeare*, 1963 (2 vols.)
HLQ, *Huntington Library Quarterly*
HUDSON, Henry N., ed., *Works*, 1851–56 (11 vols.); 1880–81 (20 vols.)

JEGP, *Journal of English and Germanic Philology*
JENNENS, Charles, ed., *Hamlet* (1773)
JOHNSON, Samuel, ed., *Works,* 1765 (2 eds., 8 vols.); 1768 (8 vols.)
KEIGHTLEY, Thomas, ed., *Works,* 1864 (6 vols.)
KELLNER, Leon, *Restoring Shakespeare,* 1925
KITTREDGE, George L., ed., *Works,* 1936
KNIGHT, Charles, ed., *Works,* 1838–43 (8 vols.); 1842–44 (12 vols.)
KÖKERITZ, Helge, *Shakespeare's Pronunciation* (1953)
LIBRARY, THE, *Transactions of the Bibliographical Society*
MALONE, Edmond, ed., *Works,* 1790 (10 vols.)
MASON, John Monck, *Comments on . . . Shakespeare's Plays,* 1785
MLR, *Modern Language Review*
MUNRO, John, ed., *Works* (The London Shakespeare), 1958 (6 vols.)
NEILSON, William A., ed., *Works,* 1906
NEILSON-HILL, *Works,* ed. W. A. Neilson and C. J. Hill, 1942
N & Q, *Notes and Queries*
O.E.D., *Oxford English Dictionary*
ONIONS, C. T., *A Shakespeare Glossary* (2nd ed. revised), 1953
PBSA, *Papers of the Bibliographical Society of America*
PELICAN, *Works,* general ed. Alfred Harbage (rev. 1-vol. ed.), 1969
PMLA, *Publications of the Modern Language Association of America*
PQ, *Philological Quarterly*
POPE, Alexander, ed., *Works,* 1723–25 (6 vols.); 1728 (8 vols.)
RANN, Joseph, ed., *Works,* 1786–[94] (6 vols.)
REED, Isaac, ed., *Works,* 1803 (21 vols.); 1813 (21 vols.)
RES, *Review of English Studies*
RIDLEY, M. R., ed., *Works* (New Temple), 1935–36 (40 vols.)
RITSON, Joseph, *Remarks, Critical and Illustrative . . . on the Last Edition of Shakespeare,* 1778
RODERICK, Richard, *Remarks on Shakespear* (in Thomas Edwards, *Canons of Criticism,* 6th ed.), 1758
ROWE, Nicholas, ed., *Works,* 1709 (2 eds., 6 vol.); 1714 (8 vols.)
SB, *Studies in Bibliography*
SCHMIDT, Alexander, *Shakespeare-Lexicon* (2 vols., 4th ed., rev.
  G. Sarrazin), 1923
SEL, *Studies in English Literature 1500–1900*
SEYMOUR, E. H., *Remarks . . . upon the Plays of Shakespeare,* 1805 (2 vols.)
SINGER, S. W., ed., *Works,* 1826 (10 vols.); 1855–56 (10 vols.)
SISSON, Charles, ed., *Works,* [1954]
SMOCK ALLEY PROMPT-BOOK (*Hamlet, Macbeth, Othello, King Lear, Twelfth Night, A Midsummer Night's Dream, Henry VIII, 1 Henry IV, The Comedy of Errors, The Merry Wives of Windsor, The Winter's Tale*), Smock Alley Theater, Dublin (see G. B. Evans, ed., *Shakespearean Prompt-Books of the Seventeenth Century,* 1966–96 (vols. IV–VIII)

SP, *Studies in Philology*
SQ, *Shakespeare Quarterly*
S. ST., *Shakespeare Studies*
S. SUR., *Shakespeare Survey*
STAUNTON, Howard, ed., *Works*, 1858–60 (3 vols.)
STEEVENS, George, ed., *Works*, 1773 (with Samuel Johnson, 10 vols.);
    1778 (10 vols.); 1793 (15 vols.)
THEOBALD, Lewis, ed., *Works*, 1733 (7 vols.); 1740 (8 vols.); 1757 (8 vols.)
THIRLBY, Styan (see THEOBALD, *Works*, 1733)
TILLEY, M. P., *A Dictionary of the Proverbs of England in the Sixteenth and
    Seventeenth Centuries*, 1950
TLS, (London) *Times Literary Supplement*
TYRRELL, Henry, ed., *Works*, 1850–53 (4 vols.)
TYRWHITT, Thomas, *Observations and Conjectures upon Some Passages of
    Shakespeare*, 1766
UPTON, John, *Critical Observations on Shakespeare*, 1747
VAUGHAN, Henry H., *New Readings . . . of Shakespeare's Tragedies*,
    1878–86 (3 vols.)
WALKER, William S., *Critical Examination of the Text of Shakespeare*,
    1860 (3 vols.)
WARBURTON, William, ed., *Works*, 1747 (8 vols.)
WELLS, Stanley and Gary Taylor, et al., eds., *William Shakespeare: The
    Complete Works, Original Spelling Edition* (1986)
    William Shakespeare: A Textual Companion (1987)
WHITE, Richard Grant, ed. *Works*, 1857–66 (12 vols.); 1883 (6 vols.)
WILSON, John Dover (with A. Quiller-Couch et al.), ed., *Works*
    (New Shakespeare), 1921–66 (39 vols.)

THE TRAGEDY OF

HAMLET

Prince of Denmark

DRAMATIS PERSONAE

CLAUDIUS, *King of Denmark*
HAMLET, *son to the late King Hamlet, and nephew to the present King*
POLONIUS, *Lord Chamberlain*
HORATIO, *friend to Hamlet*
LAERTES, *son to Polonius*

VOLTEMAND
CORNELIUS
ROSENCRANTZ
GUILDENSTERN ⎬ *Courtiers*
OSRIC
GENTLEMAN

MARCELLUS ⎱ *Officers*
BARNARDO ⎰

FRANCISCO, *a soldier*
REYNALDO, *servant to Polonius*
FORTINBRAS, *Prince of Norway*
NORWEGIAN CAPTAIN
DOCTOR OF DIVINITY
PLAYERS
Two CLOWNS, *grave-diggers*
ENGLISH AMBASSADORS

GERTRUDE, *Queen of Denmark, and mother to Hamlet*
OPHELIA, *daughter to Polonius*

GHOST *of Hamlet's Father*

LORDS, LADIES, OFFICERS, SOLDIERS, SAILORS, MESSENGERS, *and* ATTENDANTS

SCENE: *Denmark*

Act I

SCENE I

Enter BARNARDO *and* FRANCISCO, *two sentinels,* [*meeting*].

BARNARDO Who's there?
FRANCISCO Nay, answer me. Stand and unfold yourself.
BARNARDO Long live the King!
FRANCISCO Barnardo.
BARNARDO He. 5
FRANCISCO You come most carefully upon your hour.
BARNARDO 'Tis now strook twelf. Get thee to bed, Francisco.
FRANCISCO For this relief much thanks. 'Tis bitter cold,
    And I am sick at heart.
BARNARDO Have you had quiet guard?
FRANCISCO   Not a mouse stirring. 10
BARNARDO Well, good night.
    If you do meet Horatio and Marcellus,
    The rivals of my watch, bid them make haste.

Enter HORATIO *and* MARCELLUS.

FRANCISCO I think I hear them. Stand ho! Who is there?
HORATIO Friends to this ground.
MARCELLUS   And liegemen to the Dane. 15
FRANCISCO Give you good night.
MARCELLUS   O, farewell, honest [soldier].
    Who hath reliev'd you?

Words and passages enclosed in square brackets in the text above are either emendations of the copy-text or additions to it. The Textual Notes immediately following the play cite the earliest authority for every such change or insertion and supply the reading of the copy-text wherever it is emended in this edition.

1.1. Location: Elsinore. A guard-platform of the castle.   **2. answer me:** i.e. *you* answer *me.* Francisco is on watch; Barnardo has come to relieve him. **unfold yourself:** make known who you are.   **3. Long . . . King.** Perhaps a password, perhaps simply an utterance to allow the voice to be recognized.   **7. strook twelf:** struck twelve.   **9. sick at heart:** in low spirits.   **13. rivals:** partners.   **15. liegemen . . . Dane:** loyal subjects to the King of Denmark.   **16. Give:** God give.

FRANCISCO   Barnardo hath my place.
   Give you good night.   *Exit Francisco.*
MARCELLUS   Holla, Barnardo!
BARNARDO   Say—
   What, is Horatio there?
HORATIO   A piece of him.
BARNARDO Welcome, Horatio, welcome, good Marcellus.   20
HORATIO What, has this thing appear'd again to-night?
BARNARDO I have seen nothing.
MARCELLUS Horatio says 'tis but our fantasy,
   And will not let belief take hold of him
   Touching this dreaded sight twice seen of us;   25
   Therefore I have entreated him along,
   With us to watch the minutes of this night,
   That if again this apparition come,
   He may approve our eyes and speak to it.
HORATIO Tush, tush, 'twill not appear.
BARNARDO   Sit down a while,   30
   And let us once again assail your ears,
   That are so fortified against our story,
   What we have two nights seen.
HORATIO   Well, sit we down,
   And let us hear Barnardo speak of this.
BARNARDO Last night of all,   35
   When yond same star that's westward from the pole
   Had made his course t' illume that part of heaven
   Where now it burns, Marcellus and myself,
   The bell then beating one—

                          Enter GHOST.

MARCELLUS Peace, break thee off! Look where it comes again!   40
BARNARDO In the same figure like the King that's dead.
MARCELLUS Thou art a scholar, speak to it, Horatio.
BARNARDO Looks 'a not like the King? Mark it, Horatio.
HORATIO Most like; it [harrows] me with fear and wonder.
BARNARDO It would be spoke to.
MARCELLUS   Speak to it, Horatio.   45
HORATIO What art thou that usurp'st this time of night,

---

23. fantasy: imagination.   **29. approve:** corroborate.   **36. pole:** pole star.   **37. his:** its (the commonest form of the neuter possessive singular in Shakespeare's day). **41. like:** in the likeness of.   **42. a scholar:** i.e. one who knows how best to address it.   **43. 'a:** he.   **45. It . . . to.** A ghost had to be spoken to before it could speak. **46. usurp'st.** The ghost, a supernatural being, has invaded the realm of nature.

Together with that fair and warlike form
In which the majesty of buried Denmark
Did sometimes march? By heaven I charge thee speak!
MARCELLUS It is offended.
BARNARDO   See, it stalks away!   50
HORATIO Stay! Speak, speak, I charge thee speak!

Exit Ghost.

MARCELLUS 'Tis gone, and will not answer.
BARNARDO How now, Horatio? you tremble and look pale.
Is not this something more than fantasy?
What think you on't?   55
HORATIO Before my God, I might not this believe
Without the sensible and true avouch
Of mine own eyes.
MARCELLUS   Is it not like the King?
HORATIO As thou art to thyself.
Such was the very armor he had on   60
When he the ambitious Norway combated.
So frown'd he once when in an angry parle
He smote the sledded [Polacks] on the ice.
'Tis strange.
MARCELLUS Thus twice before, and jump at this dead hour,   65
With martial stalk hath he gone by our watch.
HORATIO In what particular thought to work I know not,
But in the gross and scope of mine opinion,
This bodes some strange eruption to our state.
MARCELLUS Good now, sit down, and tell me, he that knows,   70
Why this same strict and most observant watch
So nightly toils the subject of the land,
And [why] such daily [cast] of brazen cannon,
And foreign mart for implements of war,
Why such impress of shipwrights, whose sore task   75
Does not divide the Sunday from the week,

---

48. majesty . . . Denmark: late King of Denmark.   **49. sometimes:** formerly.
57. sensible: relating to the senses. **avouch:** guarantee.   **61. Norway:** King of
Norway.   **62. parle:** parley.   **63. sledded:** using sleds or sledges. Perhaps 'sledged,'
a form of 'leaded' as in 'sledgehammer' (T). **Polacks:** Poles or pole-ax, a weapon,
the smiting of which on the ice seems an action less brutal than the killing of half-
recumbent ('sledded') Polish soldiers (T).   **65. jump:** precisely.   **67–68. In . . .
opinion:** while I have no precise theory about it, my general feeling is that. *Gross* =
wholeness, totality; *scope* = range.   **69. eruption:** upheaval.   **72. toils:** causes
to work. **subject:** subjects.   **74. foreign mart:** dealing with foreign markets.
75. impress: forced service.

What might be toward, that this sweaty haste
Doth make the night joint-laborer with the day:
Who is't that can inform me?
HORATIO   That can I,
At least the whisper goes so: our last king,   80
Whose image even but now appear'd to us,
Was, as you know, by Fortinbras of Norway,
Thereto prick'd on by a most emulate pride,
Dar'd to the combat; in which our valiant Hamlet
(For so this side of our known world esteem'd him)   85
Did slay this Fortinbras, who, by a seal'd compact
Well ratified by law and heraldy,
Did forfeit (with his life) all [those] his lands
Which he stood seiz'd of, to the conqueror;
Against the which a moi'ty competent   90
Was gaged by our king, which had [return'd]
To the inheritance of Fortinbras,
Had he been vanquisher; as by the same comart
And carriage of the article [design'd],
His fell to Hamlet. Now, sir, young Fortinbras,   95
Of unimproved mettle hot and full,
Hath in the skirts of Norway here and there
Shark'd up a list of lawless resolutes
For food and diet to some enterprise
That hath a stomach in't, which is no other,   100
As it doth well appear unto our state,
But to recover of us, by strong hand
And terms compulsatory, those foresaid lands
So by his father lost; and this, I take it,
Is the main motive of our preparations,   105
The source of this our watch, and the chief head
Of this post-haste and romage in the land.
BARNARDO I think it be no other but e'en so.
Well may it sort that this portentous figure

---

77. **toward:** in preparation.   83. **emulate:** emulous, proceeding from rivalry.
87. **law and heraldy:** heraldic law (governing combat). *Heraldy* is a variant of
heraldry.   89. **seiz'd of:** possessed of.   90. **moi'ty:** portion. **competent:** adequate, i.e. equivalent.   91. **gaged:** pledged. **had:** would have.   92. **inheritance:**
possession.   93. **comart:** bargain.   94. **carriage:** tenor. **design'd:** drawn up.
96. **unimproved:** untried (?) or not directed to any useful end (?).   97. **skirts:**
outlying territories.   98. **Shark'd up:** gathered up hastily and indiscriminately.
100. **stomach:** relish of danger (?) or demand for courage (?).   106. **head:** source.
107. **romage:** rummage, bustling activity.   109. **sort:** fit. **portentous:** ominous.

Comes armed through our watch so like the King   110
That was and is the question of these wars.
HORATIO A mote it is to trouble the mind's eye.
In the most high and palmy state of Rome,
A little ere the mightiest Julius fell,
The graves stood [tenantless] and the sheeted dead   115
Did squeak and gibber in the Roman streets.
As stars with trains of fire, and dews of blood,
Disasters in the sun; and the moist star
Upon whose influence Neptune's empire stands
Was sick almost to doomsday with eclipse.   120
And even the like precurse of [fear'd] events,
As harbingers preceding still the fates
And prologue to the omen coming on,
Have heaven and earth together demonstrated
Unto our climatures and countrymen.   125

Enter GHOST.

But soft, behold! lo where it comes again!

It spreads his arms.

I'll cross it though it blast me. Stay, illusion!
If thou hast any sound or use of voice,
Speak to me.
If there be any good thing to be done   130
That may to thee do ease, and grace to me,
Speak to me.
If thou art privy to thy country's fate,
Which happily foreknowing may avoid,
O speak!   135
Or if thou hast uphoarded in thy life
Extorted treasure in the womb of earth,
For which, they say, your spirits oft walk in death,

---

116. One or more lines may have been lost between this line and the next. **118. Disasters:** ominous signs. **moist star:** moon. **119. Neptune's empire stands:** the seas are dependent. **120. sick. . . doomsday:** i.e. almost totally darkened. When the Day of Judgment is imminent, says Matthew 24:29, "the moon shall not give her light." **eclipse.** There were a solar and two total lunar eclipses visible in England in 1598; they caused gloomy speculation. **121. precurse:** foreshadowing. **122. harbingers:** advance messengers. **still:** always. **123. omen:** i.e. the events portended. **125. climatures:** regions. **126. s.d. his:** its. **127. cross it:** cross its path, confront it directly. **blast:** wither (by supernatural means). **134. happily:** haply, perhaps. **138. your:** Colloquial and impersonal; cf. 1.5.167, 4.3.21, 23. Most editors adopt *you* from F1.

Speak of it, stay and speak! *(The cock crows.)* Stop it,
    Marcellus.
MARCELLUS Shall I strike it with my partisan?   140
HORATIO Do, if it will not stand.
BARNARDO   'Tis here!
HORATIO   'Tis here!
MARCELLUS 'Tis gone!   *[Exit Ghost.]*
    We do it wrong, being so majestical,
    To offer it the show of violence,
    For it is as the air, invulnerable,   145
    And our vain blows malicious mockery.
BARNARDO It was about to speak when the cock crew.
HORATIO And then it started like a guilty thing
    Upon a fearful summons. I have heard
    The cock, that is the trumpet to the morn,   150
    Doth with his lofty and shrill-sounding throat
    Awake the god of day, and at his warning,
    Whether in sea or fire, in earth or air,
    Th' extravagant and erring spirit hies
    To his confine; and of the truth herein   155
    This present object made probation.
MARCELLUS It faded on the crowing of the cock.
    Some say that ever 'gainst that season comes
    Wherein our Saviour's birth is celebrated,
    This bird of dawning singeth all night long,   160
    And then they say no spirit dare stir abroad,
    The nights are wholesome, then no planets strike,
    No fairy takes, nor witch hath power to charm,
    So hallowed, and so gracious, is that time.
HORATIO So have I heard and do in part believe it.   165
    But look, the morn in russet mantle clad
    Walks o'er the dew of yon high eastward hill.
    Break we our watch up, and by my advice
    Let us impart what we have seen to-night
    Unto young Hamlet, for, upon my life,   170
    This spirit, dumb to us, will speak to him.
    Do you consent we shall acquaint him with it,

---

140. partisan: long-handled spear. **146. malicious mockery:** mockery of malice,
i.e. empty pretenses of harming it. **150. trumpet:** trumpeter. **154. extravagant:**
wandering outside its proper bounds. **erring:** wandering abroad. **hies:** hastens.
156. object: sight. **probation:** proof. **158. 'gainst:** just before. **162. strike:** exert
malevolent influence. **163. takes:** bewitches, charms. **164. gracious:** blessed.
166. russet: coarse greyish-brown cloth.

As needful in our loves, fitting our duty?
MARCELLUS Let's do't, I pray, and I this morning know
Where we shall find him most convenient.   175

Exeunt.

SCENE 2

Flourish. Enter CLAUDIUS, KING OF DENMARK, GERTRUDE THE
QUEEN; COUNCIL: *as* POLONIUS; *and his son* LAERTES, HAMLET,
cum aliis [including VOLTEMAND *and* CORNELIUS].

KING Though yet of Hamlet our dear brother's death
The memory be green, and that it us befitted
To bear our hearts in grief, and our whole kingdom
To be contracted in one brow of woe,
Yet so far hath discretion fought with nature   5
That we with wisest sorrow think on him
Together with remembrance of ourselves.
Therefore our sometime sister, now our queen,
Th' imperial jointress to this warlike state,
Have we, as 'twere with a defeated joy,   10
With an auspicious, and a dropping eye,
With mirth in funeral, and with dirge in marriage,
In equal scale weighing delight and dole,
Taken to wife; nor have we herein barr'd
Your better wisdoms, which have freely gone   15
With this affair along. For all, our thanks.
Now follows that you know young Fortinbras,
Holding a weak supposal of our worth,
Or thinking by our late dear brother's death
Our state to be disjoint and out of frame,   20
Co-leagued with this dream of his advantage,
He hath not fail'd to pester us with message
Importing the surrender of those lands
Lost by his father, with all bands of law,
To our most valiant brother. So much for him.   25

1.2. Location: The castle.   o.s.d. **Flourish:** trumpet fanfare. **cum aliis:** with others.
2. befitted: would befit.   **4. contracted in:** (1) reduced to; (2) knit or wrinkled
in. **brow of woe:** mournful brow.   **9. jointress:** joint holder.   **10. defeated:** impaired.   **11. auspicious . . . dropping:** cheerful . . . weeping. **15. freely:** fully,
without reservation.   **17. know:** be informed, learn.   **18. supposal:** conjecture,
estimate.   **21. Co-leagued:** joined.   **22. pester . . . message:** trouble me with
persistent messages (the original sense of *pester* is "overcrowd").   **23. Importing:**
having as import.   **24. bands:** bonds, binding terms.

Now for ourself, and for this time of meeting,
Thus much the business is: we have here writ
To Norway, uncle of young Fortinbras—
Who, impotent and bedred, scarcely hears
Of this his nephew's purpose—to suppress   30
His further gait herein, in that the levies,
The lists, and full proportions are all made
Out of his subject; and we here dispatch
You, good Cornelius, and you, Voltemand,
For bearers of this greeting to old Norway,   35
Giving to you no further personal power
To business with the King, more than the scope
Of these delated articles allow.   [*Giving a paper.*]
Farewell, and let your haste commend your duty.
CORNELIUS, VOLTEMAND In that, and all things, will we show our
    duty.   40
KING We doubt it nothing; heartily farewell.
                        [*Exeunt Voltemand and Cornelius.*]
And now, Laertes, what's the news with you?
You told us of some suit, what is't, Laertes?
You cannot speak of reason to the Dane
And lose your voice. What wouldst thou beg, Laertes,   45
That shall not be my offer, not thy asking?
The head is not more native to the heart,
The hand more instrumental to the mouth,
Than is the throne of Denmark to thy father.
What wouldst thou have, Laertes?
LAERTES   My dread lord,   50
Your leave and favor to return to France,
From whence though willingly I came to Denmark
To show my duty in your coronation,
Yet now I must confess, that duty done,
My thoughts and wishes bend again toward France,   55
And bow them to your gracious leave and pardon.
KING Have you your father's leave? What says Polonius?
POLONIUS H'ath, my lord, wrung from me my slow leave
    By laborsome petition, and at last
    Upon his will I seal'd my hard consent.   60

---

29. impotent and bedred: feeble and bedridden.   **31. gait:** proceeding.   **31–33. in
. . . subject:** since the troops are all drawn from his subjects.   **38. delated:** extended,
detailed (a variant of *dilated*).   **41. nothing:** not at all.   **45. lose:** waste.   **47. native:**
closely related.   **48. instrumental:** serviceable.   **51. leave and favor:** gracious permission.   **56. pardon:** permission to depart.   **58. H'ath:** he hath.   **60. hard:** reluctant.

PL. 1 This 1852 painting by Sir John Everett Millais of the drowning Ophelia, calm and free of the tensions of life caused by her father and her love, is the most famous of the many and various illustrations of this scene, which is reported by Gertrude but not otherwise shown on stage.

PL. 2. The swordfight scene from Kenneth Branagh's 1996 film. Branagh had played Laertes on stage in 1984 and knew well the theatrical thrill of this danger- ous moment in the play and on stage. Redgrave as Laertes once accidentally cut the forehead of Olivier. In 1600, the clash of weapons would have been viscerally felt by the audience.

PL. 3 The comedian Bill Murray as Polonius in Michael Almereyda's 2000 film version of the play. While Polonius is often portrayed as comical, Murray created a complex character both authoritarianly patriarchal and paternally sensitive.

I do beseech you give him leave to go.
KING Take thy fair hour, Laertes, time be thine,
   And thy best graces spend it at thy will!
   But now, my cousin Hamlet, and my son—
HAMLET [*Aside.*] A little more than kin, and less than kind.   65
KING How is it that the clouds still hang on you?
HAMLET Not so, my lord, I am too much in the sun.
QUEEN Good Hamlet, cast thy nighted color off,
   And let thine eye look like a friend on Denmark.
   Do not for ever with thy vailed lids   70
   Seek for thy noble father in the dust.
   Thou know'st 'tis common, all that lives must die,
   Passing through nature to eternity.
HAMLET Ay, madam, it is common.
QUEEN   If it be,
   Why seems it so particular with thee?   75
HAMLET Seems, madam? nay, it is, I know not "seems."
   'Tis not alone my inky cloak, [good] mother,
   Nor customary suits of solemn black,
   Nor windy suspiration of forc'd breath,
   No, nor the fruitful river in the eye,   80
   Nor the dejected havior of the visage,
   Together with all forms, moods, [shapes] of grief,
   That can [denote] me truly. These indeed seem,
   For they are actions that a man might play,
   But I have that within which passes show,   85
   These but the trappings and the suits of woe.
KING 'Tis sweet and commendable in your nature, Hamlet,
   To give these mourning duties to your father.
   But you must know your father lost a father,
   That father lost, lost his, and the survivor bound   90
   In filial obligation for some term
   To do obsequious sorrow. But to persever
   In obstinate condolement is a course
   Of impious stubbornness, 'tis unmanly grief,
   It shows a will most incorrect to heaven,   95

---

64. cousin: kinsman (used in familiar address to any collateral relative more distant than a brother or sister; here to a nephew).   **65. A little . . . kind:** closer than a nephew, since you are my mother's husband; yet more distant than a son, too (and not well disposed to you). Less than kind is unnatural.   **67. sun.** With obvious quibble on *son*.   **70. vailed:** downcast.   **72. common:** general, universal.   **75. particular:** individual, personal.   **80. fruitful:** copious.   **92. obsequious:** proper to obsequies.   **93. condolement:** grief.   **95. incorrect:** unsubmissive.

A heart unfortified, or mind impatient,
An understanding simple and unschool'd:
For what we know must be, and is as common
As any the most vulgar thing to sense,
Why should we in our peevish opposition   100
Take it to heart? Fie, 'tis a fault to heaven,
A fault against the dead, a fault to nature,
To reason most absurd, whose common theme
Is death of fathers, and who still hath cried,
From the first corse till he that died to-day,   105
"This must be so." We pray you throw to earth
This unprevailing woe, and think of us
As of a father, for let the world take note
You are the most immediate to our throne,
And with no less nobility of love   110
Than that which dearest father bears his son
Do I impart toward you. For your intent
In going back to school in Wittenberg,
It is most retrograde to our desire,
And we beseech you bend you to remain   115
Here in the cheer and comfort of our eye,
Our chiefest courtier, cousin, and our son.
QUEEN Let not thy mother lose her prayers, Hamlet,
    I pray thee stay with us, go not to Wittenberg.
HAMLET I shall in all my best obey you, madam.   120
KING Why, 'tis a loving and a fair reply.
    Be as ourself in Denmark. Madam, come.
    This gentle and unforc'd accord of Hamlet
    Sits smiling to my heart, in grace whereof,
    No jocund health that Denmark drinks to-day,   125
    But the great cannon to the clouds shall tell,
    And the King's rouse the heaven shall bruit again,
    Respeaking earthly thunder. Come away.
                        Flourish. Exeunt all but Hamlet.
HAMLET O that this too too sallied flesh would melt,
    Thaw, and resolve itself into a dew!   130

---

99. any . . . sense: what is perceived to be commonest. **101. to:** against.
103. absurd: contrary. **107. unprevailing:** unavailing. **111. dearest:** most loving.
112. impart: i.e. impart love. **113. Wittenberg:** historically the university
with which Martin Luther was associated and fictionally to which Christopher
Marlowe's Doctor Faustus, another Catholic opponent, was connected (T).
127. rouse: bumper, drink. **bruit:** loudly declare. **129. sallied:** sullied. See the
Textual Notes. Many editors prefer the F1 reading, *solid.*

Or that the Everlasting had not fix'd
His canon 'gainst [self-]slaughter! O God, God,
How [weary], stale, flat, and unprofitable
Seem to me all the uses of this world!
Fie on't, ah fie! 'tis an unweeded garden   135
That grows to seed, things rank and gross in nature
Possess it merely. That it should come [to this]!
But two months dead, nay, not so much, not two.
So excellent a king, that was to this
Hyperion to a satyr, so loving to my mother   140
That he might not beteem the winds of heaven
Visit her face too roughly. Heaven and earth,
Must I remember? Why, she should hang on him
As if increase of appetite had grown
By what it fed on, and yet, within a month—   145
Let me not think on't! Frailty, thy name is woman!—
A little month, or ere those shoes were old
With which she followed my poor father's body,
Like Niobe, all tears—why, she, [even she]—
O God, a beast that wants discourse of reason   150
Would have mourn'd longer—married with my uncle,
My father's brother, but no more like my father
Than I to Hercules. Within a month,
Ere yet the salt of most unrighteous tears
Had left the flushing in her galled eyes,   155
She married—O most wicked speed: to post
With such dexterity to incestious sheets,
It is not, nor it cannot come to good,
But break my heart, for I must hold my tongue.

Enter HORATIO, MARCELLUS, *and* BARNARDO.

HORATIO Hail to your lordship!
HAMLET   I am glad to see you well.   160
   Horatio—or I do forget myself.

---

132. canon: law.   **134. uses:** customs.   **137. merely:** utterly.   **139. to:** in comparison with.   **140. Hyperion:** the sun-god.   **141. beteem:** allow.   **147. or ere:** before.   **149. Niobe.** She wept endlessly for her children, whom Apollo and Artemis had killed.   **150. wants . . . reason:** lacks the power of reason (which distinguishes men from beasts).   **154. unrighteous:** i.e. hypocritical.   **155. flushing:** redness. **galled:** inflamed.   **157. incestious:** incestuous. The marriage of a man to his brother's widow was so regarded until long after Shakespeare's day. Papal dispensations were not impossible to obtain: cf. Henry VIII and Catherine of Aragon, the widow of Henry's elder brother Arthur (T).

HORATIO The same, my lord, and your poor servant ever.
HAMLET Sir, my good friend—I'll change that name with you.
 And what make you from Wittenberg, Horatio?
 Marcellus.   165
MARCELLUS My good lord.
HAMLET I am very glad to see you. [*To Barnardo.*] Good even, sir.—
 But what, in faith, make you from Wittenberg?
HORATIO A truant disposition, good my lord.
HAMLET I would not hear your enemy say so,   170
 Nor shall you do my ear that violence
 To make it truster of your own report
 Against yourself. I know you are no truant.
 But what is your affair in Elsinore?
 We'll teach you to drink [deep] ere you depart.   175
HORATIO My lord, I came to see your father's funeral.
HAMLET I prithee do not mock me, fellow student,
 I think it was to [see] my mother's wedding.
HORATIO Indeed, my lord, it followed hard upon.
HAMLET Thrift, thrift, Horatio, the funeral bak'd-meats   180
 Did coldly furnish forth the marriage tables.
 Would I had met my dearest foe in heaven
 Or ever I had seen that day, Horatio!
 My father—methinks I see my father.
HORATIO Where, my lord?
HAMLET   In my mind's eye, Horatio.   185
HORATIO I saw him once, 'a was a goodly king.
HAMLET 'A was a man, take him for all in all,
 I shall not look upon his like again.
HORATIO My lord, I think I saw him yesternight.
HAMLET Saw, who?   190
HORATIO My lord, the King your father.
HAMLET   The King my father?
HORATIO Season your admiration for a while
 With an attent ear, till I may deliver,
 Upon the witness of these gentlemen,
 This marvel to you.
HAMLET   For God's love let me hear!   195
HORATIO Two nights together had these gentlemen,
 Marcellus and Barnardo, on their watch,·

163. change: exchange. 164. what . . . from: what are you doing away
from. 169. truant disposition: inclination to play truant. 177. student: student.
181. coldly: when cold. 182. dearest: most intensely hated. 183. Or: ere,
before. 192. Season: temper. admiration: wonder. 193. deliver: report.

In the dead waste and middle of the night,
Been thus encount'red: a figure like your father,
Armed at point exactly, cap-a-pe,   200
Appears before them, and with solemn march
Goes slow and stately by them; thrice he walk'd
By their oppress'd and fear-surprised eyes
Within his truncheon's length, whilst they, distill'd
Almost to jelly with the act of fear,   205
Stand dumb and speak not to him. This to me
In dreadful secrecy impart they did,
And I with them the third night kept the watch,
Where, as they had delivered, both in time,
Form of the thing, each word made true and good,   210
The apparition comes. I knew your father,
These hands are not more like.
HAMLET   But where was this?
MARCELLUS My lord, upon the platform where we watch.
HAMLET Did you not speak to it?
HORATIO   My lord, I did,
But answer made it none. Yet once methought   215
It lifted up it head and did address
Itself to motion like as it would speak;
But even then the morning cock crew loud,
And at the sound it shrunk in haste away
And vanish'd from our sight.
HAMLET   'Tis very strange.   220
HORATIO As I do live, my honor'd lord, 'tis true,
And we did think it writ down in our duty
To let you know of it.
HAMLET Indeed, [indeed,] sirs. But this troubles me.
Hold you the watch to-night?
[MARCELLUS, BARNARDO]   We do, my lord.   225
HAMLET Arm'd, say you?
[MARCELLUS, BARNARDO] Arm'd, my lord.
HAMLET From top to toe?
[MARCELLUS, BARNARDO] My lord, from head to foot.
HAMLET Then saw you not his face.

---

198. waste: empty expanse. **200. at point exactly:** in every particular. **cap-a-pe:** from head to foot. **203. fear-surprised:** overwhelmed by fear. **204. truncheon:** short staff carried as a symbol of military command. **205. act:** action, operation. **207. dreadful:** held in awe, i.e. solemnly sworn. **212. are . . . like:** i.e. do not resemble each other more closely than the apparition resembled him. **216. it:** its. **216–217. address . . . motion:** begin to make a gesture.

HORATIO O yes, my lord, he wore his beaver up.   230
HAMLET What, look'd he frowningly?
HORATIO   A countenance more
    In sorrow than in anger.
HAMLET   Pale, or red?
HORATIO Nay, very pale.
HAMLET   And fix'd his eyes upon you?
HORATIO Most constantly.
HAMLET   I would I had been there.
HORATIO It would have much amaz'd you.   235
HAMLET Very like, [very like]. Stay'd it long?
HORATIO While one with moderate haste might tell a
    hundreth.
BOTH [MARCELLUS, BARNARDO]. Longer, longer.
HORATIO Not when I saw't.
HAMLET   His beard was grisl'd, no?
HORATIO It was, as I have seen it in his life,   240
    A sable silver'd.
HAMLET   I will watch to-night,
    Perchance 'twill walk again.
HORATIO   I warr'nt it will.
HAMLET If it assume my noble father's person,
    I'll speak to it though hell itself should gape
    And bid me hold my peace. I pray you all,   245
    If you have hitherto conceal'd this sight,
    Let it be tenable in your silence still,
    And whatsomever else shall hap to-night,
    Give it an understanding but no tongue.
    I will requite your loves. So fare you well.   250
    Upon the platform 'twixt aleven and twelf
    I'll visit you.
ALL   Our duty to your honor.
HAMLET Your loves, as mine to you; farewell.
                            Exeunt [all but Hamlet].
    My father's spirit—in arms! All is not well,
    I doubt some foul play. Would the night were come!   255
    Till then sit still, my soul. [Foul] deeds will rise,
    Though all the earth o'erwhelm them, to men's eyes.
                                                    Exit.

230. **beaver:** visor.   237. **tell a hundreth:** count a hundred.   239. **grisl'd:** grizzled, mixed with grey.   247. **tenable:** held close.   251. **aleven:** eleven.   255. **doubt:** suspect.

SCENE 3

Enter LAERTES *and* OPHELIA, *his sister.*

LAERTES My necessaries are inbark'd. Farewell.
  And, sister, as the winds give benefit
  And convey [is] assistant, do not sleep,
  But let me hear from you.
OPHELIA   Do you doubt that?
LAERTES For Hamlet, and the trifling of his favor,   5
  Hold it a fashion and a toy in blood,
  A violet in the youth of primy nature,
  Forward, not permanent, sweet, not lasting,
  The perfume and suppliance of a minute—
  No more.
OPHELIA   No more but so?
LAERTES   Think it no more: 10
  For nature crescent does not grow alone
  In thews and [bulk], but as this temple waxes,
  The inward service of the mind and soul
  Grows wide withal. Perhaps he loves you now,
  And now no soil nor cautel doth besmirch   15
  The virtue of his will, but you must fear,
  His greatness weigh'd, his will is not his own,
  [For he himself is subject to his birth:]
  He may not, as unvalued persons do,
  Carve for himself, for on his choice depends   20
  The safety and health of this whole state,
  And therefore must his choice be circumscrib'd
  Unto the voice and yielding of that body
  Whereof he is the head. Then if he says he loves you,
  It fits your wisdom so far to believe it   25
  As he in his particular act and place

1.3. Location: Polonius' quarters in the castle. **1. inbark'd:** embarked, abroad.
3. convey is assistant: means of transport is available. **6. a fashion:** i.e. standard
behavior for a young man. **toy in blood:** idle fancy of youthful passion. **7. primy:**
springlike. **8. Forward:** early of growth. **9. suppliance:** pastime. **11. crescent:**
growing, increasing. **12. thews:** muscles, sinews. **12–14. as . . . withal:** as the body
develops, the powers of mind and spirit grow along with it. **15. soil:** stain. **cautel:** deceit. **16. will:** desire. **17. His greatness weigh'd:** considering his princely
status. **19. unvalued:** of low rank. **20. Carve for himself:** indulge his own
wishes. **23. voice:** vote, approval. **yielding:** consent. **that body:** i.e. the state. Laertes
is either forgetting the elective nature of the Danish monarchy or he assumes that
"most immediate to our throne" (1.2.109) is a promise that guarantees the prince succession (T). **26. in . . . place:** i.e. acting as he must act in the position he occupies.

May give his saying deed, which is no further
Than the main voice of Denmark goes withal.
Then weigh what loss your honor may sustain
If with too credent ear you list his songs,   30
Or lose your heart, or your chaste treasure open
To his unmast'red importunity.
Fear it, Ophelia, fear it, my dear sister,
And keep you in the rear of your affection,
Out of the shot and danger of desire.   35
The chariest maid is prodigal enough
If she unmask her beauty to the moon.
Virtue itself scapes not calumnious strokes.
The canker galls the infants of the spring
Too oft before their buttons be disclos'd,   40
And in the morn and liquid dew of youth
Contagious blastments are most imminent.
Be wary then, best safety lies in fear:
Youth to itself rebels, though none else near.
OPHELIA I shall the effect of this good lesson keep   45
As watchman to my heart. But, good my brother,
Do not, as some ungracious pastors do,
Show me the steep and thorny way to heaven,
Whiles, [like] a puff'd and reckless libertine,
Himself the primrose path of dalliance treads,   50
And reaks not his own rede.
LAERTES   O, fear me not.

Enter POLONIUS.

I stay too long—but here my father comes.
A double blessing is a double grace,
Occasion smiles upon a second leave.
POLONIUS Yet here, Laertes? Aboard, aboard, for shame!   55
The wind sits in the shoulder of your sail,
And you are stay'd for. There—[*laying his hand on
    Laertes' head*] my blessing with thee!
And these few precepts in thy memory
Look thou character. Give thy thoughts no tongue,

---

28. main: general. **goes withal:** accord with.   **30. credent:** credulous.   **35. shot:** range.   **39. canker:** canker-worm.   **40. buttons:** buds. **disclos'd:** opened. **42. blastments:** withering blights.   **44. to:** of.   **47. ungracious:** graceless. **49. puff'd:** bloated.   **51. reaks:** recks, heeds. **rede:** advice. **fear me not:** don't worry about me.   **54. Occasion:** opportunity (here personified, as often). **smiles upon:** i.e. graciously bestows.   **59. character:** inscribe.

Nor any unproportion'd thought his act.   60
Be thou familiar, but by no means vulgar:
Those friends thou hast, and their adoption tried,
Grapple them unto thy soul with hoops of steel,
But do not dull thy palm with entertainment
Of each new-hatch'd, unfledg'd courage. Beware   65
Of entrance to a quarrel, but being in,
Bear't that th' opposed may beware of thee.
Give every man thy ear, but few thy voice,
Take each man's censure, but reserve thy judgment.
Costly thy habit as thy purse can buy,   70
But not express'd in fancy, rich, not gaudy,
For the apparel oft proclaims the man,
And they in France of the best rank and station
[Are] of a most select and generous chief in that.
Neither a borrower nor a lender [be],   75
For [loan] oft loses both itself and friend,
And borrowing dulleth [th'] edge of husbandry.
This above all: to thine own self be true,
And it must follow, as the night the day,
Thou canst not then be false to any man.   80
Farewell, my blessing season this in thee!
LAERTES Most humbly do I take my leave, my lord.
POLONIUS The time invests you, go, your servants tend.
LAERTES Farewell, Ophelia, and remember well
   What I have said to you.
OPHELIA   'Tis in my memory lock'd,   85
   And you yourself shall keep the key of it.
LAERTES Farewell.   *Exit Laertes.*
POLONIUS What is't, Ophelia, he hath said to you?
OPHELIA So please you, something touching the Lord Hamlet.
POLONIUS Marry, well bethought.   90
   'Tis told me, he hath very oft of late
   Given private time to you, and you yourself
   Have of your audience been most free and bounteous.
   If it be so—as so 'tis put on me,

---

60. unproportion'd: unfitting.   **61. familiar:** affable, sociable. **vulgar:** friendly
with everybody.   **62. their adoption tried:** their association with you tested and
proved.   **65. courage:** spirited, young blood.   **67. Bear't that:** manage it in such
a way that.   **69. Take:** listen to. **censure:** opinion.   **74. generous:** noble. **chief:**
eminence (?). But the line is probably corrupt. Perhaps *of a* is intrusive, in which
case *chief* = chiefly.   **77. husbandry:** thrift.   **81. season:** preserve (?) or ripen,
make fruitful (?).   **83. invests:** besieges. **tend:** wait.   **90. Marry:** indeed (originally the name of the Virgin Mary used as an oath).   **94. put on:** told to.

And that in way of caution—I must tell you, 95
You do not understand yourself so clearly
As it behooves my daughter and your honor.
What is between you? Give me up the truth.
OPHELIA He hath, my lord, of late made many tenders
Of his affection to me. 100
POLONIUS Affection, puh! You speak like a green girl,
Unsifted in such perilous circumstance.
Do you believe his tenders, as you call them?
OPHELIA I do not know, my lord, what I should think.
POLONIUS Marry, I will teach you: think yourself a baby 105
That you have ta'en these tenders for true pay,
Which are not sterling. Tender yourself more dearly,
Or (not to crack the wind of the poor phrase,
[Wringing] it thus) you'll tender me a fool.
OPHELIA My lord, he hath importun'd me with love 110
In honorable fashion.
POLONIUS Ay, fashion you may call it. Go to, go to.
OPHELIA And hath given countenance to his speech, my lord,
With almost all the holy vows of heaven.
POLONIUS Ay, springes to catch woodcocks. I do know, 115
When the blood burns, how prodigal the soul
Lends the tongue vows. These blazes, daughter,
Giving more light than heat, extinct in both
Even in their promise, as it is a-making,
You must not take for fire. From this time 120
Be something scanter of your maiden presence,
Set your entreatments at a higher rate
Than a command to parle. For Lord Hamlet,
Believe so much in him, that he is young,
And with a larger teder may he walk 125
Than may be given you. In few, Ophelia,
Do not believe his vows, for they are brokers,

99. **tenders:** offers.   102. **Unsifted:** untried.   106. **tenders.** With play on the sense "money offered in payment" (as in *legal tender*).   107. **Tender:** hold, value. 109. **Wringing:** straining, forcing to the limit. **tender . . . fool:** (1) show me that you are a fool; (2) make me look like a fool; (3) present me with a (bastard) grandchild.   112. **fashion.** See note on line 6.   113. **countenance:** authority. 115. **springes:** snares. **woodcocks.** Proverbially gullible birds.   122–23. **Set . . . parle:** place a higher value on your favors; do not grant interviews simply because he asks for them. Polonius uses a military figure: *entreatments* = negotiations for surrender; *parle* = parley, discuss terms.   124. **so . . . him:** no more than this with respect to him.   125. **larger teder:** longer tether.   127. **brokers:** procurers.

Not of that dye which their investments show,
But mere [implorators] of unholy suits,
Breathing like sanctified and pious bonds,   130
The better to [beguile]. This is for all:
I would not, in plain terms, from this time forth
Have you so slander any moment leisure
As to give words or talk with the Lord Hamlet.
Look to't, I charge you. Come your ways.   135
OPHELIA I shall obey, my lord.   *Exeunt.*

SCENE 4

Enter HAMLET, HORATIO, *and* MARCELLUS.

HAMLET The air bites shrowdly, it is very cold.
HORATIO It is [a] nipping and an eager air.
HAMLET What hour now?
HORATIO   I think it lacks of twelf.
MARCELLUS No, it is strook.
HORATIO Indeed? I heard it not. It then draws near the season   5
Wherein the spirit held his wont to walk.
                                    A flourish of trumpets, and two pieces goes off [within].
What does this mean, my lord?
HAMLET The King doth wake to-night and takes his rouse,
Keeps wassail, and the swagg'ring up-spring reels;
And as he drains his draughts of Rhenish down,   10
The kettle-drum and trumpet thus bray out
The triumph of his pledge.
HORATIO   Is it a custom?
HAMLET Ay, marry, is't,
But to my mind, though I am native here
And to the manner born, it is a custom   15

128. Not . . . show: not of the color that their garments (*investments*) exhibit, i.e. not what they seem. 129. mere: out-and-out. 130. bonds: (lover's) vows or assurances. Many editors follow Theobald in reading *bawds*. "Bawds" is used in a source work, *The Golden Asse* of Apuleius, which offers a parallel triangle of socially superior lover Cupid (Hamlet), vulnerable maiden Psyche (Ophelia), and anxiously self-centered parent concerned about potential embarrassment Venus (Polonius) (T). 133. slander: disgrace. moment: momentary. 135. Come your ways: come along. 1.4. Location: The guard-platform of the castle. 1. shrowdly: shrewdly, wickedly. 2. eager: sharp. 6. s.d. pieces: cannon. 8. doth . . . rouse: i.e. holds revels far into the night. 9. wassail: carousal. up-spring: wild dance. 10. Rhenish: Rhine wine. 12. triumph . . . pledge: accomplishment of his toast (by draining his cup at a single draught). 15. manner: custom (of carousing).

More honor'd in the breach than the observance.
This heavy-headed revel east and west
Makes us traduc'd and tax'd of other nations.
They clip us drunkards, and with swinish phrase
Soil our addition, and indeed it takes   20
From our achievements, though perform'd at height,
The pith and marrow of our attribute.
So, oft it chances in particular men,
That for some vicious mole of nature in them,
As in their birth, wherein they are not guilty   25
(Since nature cannot choose his origin),
By their o'ergrowth of some complexion
Oft breaking down the pales and forts of reason,
Or by some habit, that too much o'er-leavens
The form of plausive manners—that these men,   30
Carrying, I say, the stamp of one defect,
Being nature's livery, or fortune's star,
His virtues else, be they as pure as grace,
As infinite as man may undergo,
Shall in the general censure take corruption   35
From that particular fault: the dram of [ev'l]
Doth all the noble substance of a doubt
To his own scandal.

                    Enter GHOST.

HORATIO   Look, my lord, it comes!
HAMLET Angels and ministers of grace defend us!
Be thou a spirit of health, or goblin damn'd,   40
Bring with thee airs from heaven, or blasts from hell,
Be thy intents wicked, or charitable,
Thou com'st in such a questionable shape

16. More . . . observance: which it is more honorable to break than to observe. **18. tax'd of:** censured by. **19. clip:** clepe, call. **20. addition:** titles of honor. **21. at height:** most excellently. **22. attribute:** reputation. **23. particular:** individual. **24. vicious . . . nature:** small natural blemish. **26. his:** its. **27. By . . . complexion:** by the excess of some one of the humors (which were thought to govern the disposition). **28. pales:** fences. **29. o'er-leavens:** makes itself felt throughout (as leaven works in the whole mass of dough). **30. plausive:** pleasing. **32. Being . . . star:** i.e. whether they were born with it, or got it by misfortune. *Star* means "blemish." **34. undergo:** carry the weight of, sustain. **35. general censure:** popular opinion. **36. dram:** minute amount. **ev'l:** evil, with a pun on *eale*, "yeast" (cf. *o'er-leavens* in line 29). **37. of a doubt:** A famous crux, for which many emendations have been suggested, the most widely accepted being Steevens' *often dout* (i.e. extinguish). **38. To . . . scandal:** i.e. so that it all shares in the disgrace. **40. of health:** wholesome, good. **43. questionable:** inviting talk.

That I will speak to thee. I'll call thee Hamlet,
King, father, royal Dane. O, answer me!   45
Let me not burst in ignorance, but tell
Why thy canoniz'd bones, hearsed in death,
Have burst their cerements; why the sepulchre,
Wherein we saw thee quietly [inurn'd,]
Hath op'd his ponderous and marble jaws   50
To cast thee up again. What may this mean,
That thou, dead corse, again in complete steel
Revisits thus the glimpses of the moon,
Making night hideous, and we fools of nature
So horridly to shake our disposition   55
With thoughts beyond the reaches of our souls?
Say why is this? wherefore? what should we do?
                                        [*Ghost*] *beckons* [*Hamlet*].
HORATIO It beckons you to go away with it,
    As if it some impartment did desire
    To you alone.
MARCELLUS   Look with what courteous action   60
    It waves you to a more removed ground,
    But do not go with it.
HORATIO   No, by no means.
HAMLET It will not speak, then I will follow it.
HORATIO Do not, my lord.
HAMLET   Why, what should be the fear?
    I do not set my life at a pin's fee,   65
    And for my soul, what can it do to that,
    Being a thing immortal as itself?
    It waves me forth again, I'll follow it.
HORATIO What if it tempt you toward the flood, my lord,
    Or to the dreadful summit of the cliff   70
    That beetles o'er his base into the sea,
    And there assume some other horrible form
    Which might deprive your sovereignty of reason,
    And draw you into madness? Think of it.
    The very place puts toys of desperation,   75

---

47. canoniz'd: buried with the prescribed rites. **48. cerements:** grave-clothes. **52. complete steel:** full armor. **53. Revisits.** The *-s* ending in the second person singular is common. **54. fools of nature:** the children (or the dupes) of a purely natural order, baffled by the supernatural. **55. disposition:** nature. **59. impartment:** communication. **65. fee:** worth. **73. deprive . . . reason:** unseat reason from the rule of your mind. **75. toys of desperation:** fancies of desperate action, i.e. inclinations to jump off.

Without more motive, into every brain
That looks so many fadoms to the sea
And hears it roar beneath.
HAMLET   It waves me still.—
Go on, I'll follow thee.
MARCELLUS You shall not go, my lord.
HAMLET   Hold off your hands.   80
HORATIO Be rul'd, you shall not go.
HAMLET   My fate cries out,
And makes each petty artere in this body
As hardy as the Nemean lion's nerve.
Still am I call'd. Unhand me, gentlemen.
By heaven, I'll make a ghost of him that lets me!   85
I say away!—Go on, I'll follow thee.
                                        Exeunt Ghost and Hamlet.
HORATIO He waxes desperate with [imagination].
MARCELLUS Let's follow. 'Tis not fit thus to obey him.
HORATIO Have after. To what issue will this come?
MARCELLUS Something is rotten in the state of Denmark.   90
HORATIO Heaven will direct it.
MARCELLUS   Nay, let's follow him.
                                                    Exeunt.

SCENE 5

Enter GHOST *and* HAMLET.

HAMLET Whither wilt thou lead me? Speak, I'll go no further.
GHOST Mark me.
HAMLET   I will.
GHOST   My hour is almost come
When I to sulph'rous and tormenting flames
Must render up myself.
HAMLET   Alas, poor ghost!
GHOST Pity me not, but lend thy serious hearing   5
To what I shall unfold.
HAMLET   Speak, I am bound to hear.
GHOST So art thou to revenge, when thou shalt hear.
HAMLET What?

77. **fadoms:** fathoms. 82. **artere:** variant spelling of *artery;* here, ligament, sinew. 83. **Nemean lion.** Slain by Hercules as one of his twelve labors. **nerve:** sinew. 85. **lets:** hinders. 91. **it:** i.e. the issue.
1.5. Location: On the battlements of the castle.

GHOST I am thy father's spirit,
    Doom'd for a certain term to walk the night,   10
    And for the day confin'd to fast in fires,
    Till the foul crimes done in my days of nature
    Are burnt and purg'd away. But that I am forbid
    To tell the secrets of my prison-house,
    I could a tale unfold whose lightest word   15
    Would harrow up thy soul, freeze thy young blood,
    Make thy two eyes like stars start from their spheres,
    Thy knotted and combined locks to part,
    And each particular hair to stand an end,
    Like quills upon the fearful porpentine.   20
    But this eternal blazon must not be
    To ears of flesh and blood. List, list, O, list!
    If thou didst ever thy dear father love—
HAMLET O God!
GHOST Revenge his foul and most unnatural murther.   25
HAMLET Murther!
GHOST Murther most foul, as in the best it is,
    But this most foul, strange, and unnatural.
HAMLET Haste me to know't, that I with wings as swift
    As meditation, or the thoughts of love,   30
    May sweep to my revenge.
GHOST   I find thee apt,
    And duller shouldst thou be than the fat weed
    That roots itself in ease on Lethe wharf,
    Wouldst thou not stir in this. Now, Hamlet, hear:
    'Tis given out that, sleeping in my orchard,   35
    A serpent stung me, so the whole ear of Denmark
    Is by a forged process of my death
    Rankly abus'd; but know, thou noble youth,
    The serpent that did sting thy father's life
    Now wears his crown.
HAMLET   O my prophetic soul!   40
    My uncle?

---

11. fast: do penance, hunger. Both Chaucer and Nashe, favorite authors of Shakespeare, describe such punishment (T). **12. crimes:** sins. **17. spheres:** eye-sockets; with allusion to the revolving spheres in which, according to the Ptolemaic astronomy, the stars were fixed. **19. an end:** on end. **20. fearful porpentine:** frightened porcupine. **21. eternal blazon:** revelation of eternal things. **30. meditation:** thought. **33. Lethe:** river of Hades, the water of which made the drinker forget the past. **wharf:** bank. **35. orchard:** garden. **37. forged process:** false account. **38. abus'd:** deceived.

GHOST Ay, that incestuous, that adulterate beast,
With witchcraft of his wits, with traitorous gifts—
O wicked wit and gifts that have the power
So to seduce!—won to his shameful lust   45
The will of my most seeming virtuous queen.
O Hamlet, what [a] falling-off was there
From me, whose love was of that dignity
That it went hand in hand even with the vow
I made to her in marriage, and to decline   50
Upon a wretch whose natural gifts were poor
To those of mine!
But virtue, as it never will be moved,
Though lewdness court it in a shape of heaven,
So [lust], though to a radiant angel link'd,   55
Will [sate] itself in a celestial bed
And prey on garbage.
But soft, methinks I scent the morning air,
Brief let me be. Sleeping within my orchard,
My custom always of the afternoon,   60
Upon my secure hour thy uncle stole,
With juice of cursed hebona in a vial,
And in the porches of my ears did pour
The leprous distillment, whose effect
Holds such an enmity with blood of man   65
That swift as quicksilver it courses through
The natural gates and alleys of the body,
And with a sudden vigor it doth [posset]
And curd, like eager droppings into milk,
The thin and wholesome blood. So did it mine,   70
And a most instant tetter bark'd about,
Most lazar-like, with vile and loathsome crust
All my smooth body.
Thus was I, sleeping, by a brother's hand
Of life, of crown, of queen, at once dispatch'd,   75
Cut off even in the blossoms of my sin,
Unhous'led, disappointed, unanel'd,

42. adulterate: adulterous.   54. shape of heaven: angelic form.   61. secure:
carefree.   62. hebona: ebony (which Shakespeare, following a literary tradition,
and perhaps also associating the word with *henbane,* thought the name of a poison).   68. posset: curdle.   69. eager: sour.   71. tetter: scabby eruption. bark'd:
formed a hard covering, like bark on a tree.   72. lazar-like: leper-like.   75. at
once: all at the same time. dispatch'd: deprived.   77. Unhous'led: without the
Eucharist. disappointed: without (spiritual) preparation. unanel'd: unanointed,
without extreme unction.

No reck'ning made, but sent to my account
With all my imperfections on my head.
O, horrible, O, horrible, most horrible!   80
If thou hast nature in thee, bear it not,
Let not the royal bed of Denmark be
A couch for luxury and damned incest.
But howsomever thou pursues this act,
Taint not thy mind, nor let thy soul contrive   85
Against thy mother aught. Leave her to heaven,
And to those thorns that in her bosom lodge
To prick and sting her. Fare thee well at once!
The glow-worm shows the matin to be near,
And gins to pale his uneffectual fire.   90
Adieu, adieu, adieu! remember me.   [*Exit.*]
HAMLET O all you host of heaven! O earth! What else?
And shall I couple hell? O fie, hold, hold, my heart,
And you, my sinows, grow not instant old,
But bear me [stiffly] up. Remember thee!   95
Ay, thou poor ghost, whiles memory holds a seat
In this distracted globe. Remember thee!
Yea, from the table of my memory
I'll wipe away all trivial fond records,
All saws of books, all forms, all pressures past   100
That youth and observation copied there,
And thy commandement all alone shall live
Within the book and volume of my brain,
Unmix'd with baser matter. Yes, by heaven!
O most pernicious woman!   105
O villain, villain, smiling, damned villain!
My tables—meet it is I set it down
That one may smile, and smile, and be a villain!
At least I am sure it may be so in Denmark.

                                                      [*He writes*]
So, uncle, there you are. Now to my word: 110
It is "Adieu, adieu! remember me."
I have sworn't.
HORATIO [*Within.*] My lord, my lord!
MARCELLUS [*Within.*]   Lord Hamlet!

---

81. **nature:** natural feeling. 83. **luxury:** lust. 89. **matin:** morning. 90. **gins:** begins. 94. **sinows:** sinews. 97. **globe:** head. 98. **table:** writing tablet. 99. **fond:** foolish. 100. **saws:** wise sayings. **forms:** shapes, images. **pressures:** impressions. 110. **word:** i.e. word of command from the Ghost.

Enter HORATIO *and* MARCELLUS.

HORATIO   Heavens secure him!

HAMLET So be it!

MARCELLUS Illo, ho, ho, my lord!   115

HAMLET Hillo, ho, ho, boy! Come, [bird,] come.

MARCELLUS How is't, my noble lord?

HORATIO   What news, my lord?

HAMLET O, wonderful!

HORATIO Good my lord, tell it.

HAMLET   No, you will reveal it.

HORATIO Not I, my lord, by heaven.

MARCELLUS   Nor I, my lord.   120

HAMLET How say you then, would heart of man once think it?—
But you'll be secret?

BOTH [HORATIO, MARCELLUS] Ay, by heaven, [my lord].

HAMLET There's never a villain dwelling in all Denmark
But he's an arrant knave.

HORATIO There needs no ghost, my lord, come from the grave   125
To tell us this.

HAMLET   Why, right, you are in the right,
And so, without more circumstance at all,
I hold it fit that we shake hands and part,
You, as your business and desire shall point you,
For every man hath business and desire,   130
Such as it is, and for my own poor part,
I will go pray.

HORATIO These are but wild and whirling words, my lord.

HAMLET I am sorry they offend you, heartily,
Yes, faith, heartily.

HORATIO   There's no offense, my lord.   135

HAMLET Yes, by Saint Patrick, but there is, Horatio,
And much offense too. Touching this vision here,
It is an honest ghost, that let me tell you.
For your desire to know what is between us,
O'ermaster't as you may. And now, good friends,   140
As you are friends, scholars, and soldiers,
Give me one poor request.

HORATIO What is't, my lord, we will.

HAMLET Never make known what you have seen tonight.

---

116. Hillo . . . come. Hamlet answers Marcellus' halloo with a falconer's cry.
127. circumstance: ceremony.   **138. honest:** true, genuine.   **143. What is't:**
whatever it is.

BOTH [HORATIO, MARCELLUS] My lord, we will not.
HAMLET   Nay, but swear't.
HORATIO   In faith, 145
  My lord, not I.
MARCELLUS   Nor I, my lord, in faith.
HAMLET Upon my sword.
MARCELLUS   We have sworn, my lord, already.
HAMLET Indeed, upon my sword, indeed.

                                        Ghost cries under the stage.
GHOST Swear.
HAMLET Ha, ha, boy, say'st thou so? Art thou there,
  truepenny?   150
  Come on, you hear this fellow in the cellarage,
  Consent to swear.
HORATIO   Propose the oath, my lord.
HAMLET Never to speak of this that you have seen,
  Swear by my sword.
GHOST [*Beneath.*] Swear.   155
HAMLET *Hic et ubique?* Then we'll shift our ground.
  Come hither, gentlemen,
  And lay your hands again upon my sword.
  Swear by my sword
  Never to speak of this that you have heard.   160
GHOST [*Beneath.*] Swear by his sword.
HAMLET Well said, old mole, canst work i' th' earth so fast?
  A worthy pioner! Once more remove, good friends.
HORATIO O day and night, but this is wondrous strange!
HAMLET And therefore as a stranger give it welcome.   165
  There are more things in heaven and earth, Horatio,
  Than are dreamt of in your philosophy.
  But come—
  Here, as before, never, so help you mercy,
  How strange or odd some'er I bear myself—   170
  As I perchance hereafter shall think meet
  To put an antic disposition on—
  That you, at such times seeing me, never shall,
  With arms encumb'red thus, or this headshake,

---

147. Upon my sword: i.e. on the cross formed by the hilt.   **150. truepenny:** trusty
fellow.   **156. Hic et ubique:** here and everywhere.   **163. pioner:** digger, miner
(variant of *pioneer*).   **165. as . . .welcome:** give it the welcome due in courtesy
to strangers.   **167. your.** See note on 1.1.138. **philosophy:** i.e. natural philosophy,
science.   **172. put . . . on:** behave in some fantastic manner, act like a madman.
174. encumb'red: folded.

Or by pronouncing of some doubtful phrase,   175
As "Well, well, we know," or "We could, and if we
    would,"
Or "If we list to speak," or "There be, and if they
    might,"
Or such ambiguous giving out, to note
That you know aught of me—this do swear,
So grace and mercy at your most need help you.   180
GHOST [*Beneath.*] Swear.   [*They swear.*]
HAMLET Rest, rest, perturbed spirit! So, gentlemen,
With all my love I do commend me to you,
And what so poor a man as Hamlet is
May do t' express his love and friending to you,   185
God willing, shall not lack. Let us go in together,
And still your fingers on your lips, I pray.
The time is out of joint—O cursed spite,
That ever I was born to set it right!
Nay, come, let's go together.   *Exeunt.* 190

---

176. and if: if.   **177. list:** cared, had a mind.   **178. note:** indicate.   **187. still:** always.
190. Nay . . . together. They are holding back to let him go first.

Act 2

SCENE I

Enter old POLONIUS *with his man* [REYNALDO].

POLONIUS Give him this money and these notes, Reynaldo.
REYNALDO I will, my lord.
POLONIUS You shall do marvell's wisely, good Reynaldo,
Before you visit him, to make inquire
Of his behavior.
REYNALDO　　　　My lord, I did intend it.　　　　　　5
POLONIUS Marry, well said, very well said. Look you, sir,
Inquire me first what Danskers are in Paris,
And how, and who, what means, and where they keep,
What company, at what expense; and finding
By this encompassment and drift of question　　　10
That they do know my son, come you more nearer
Than your particular demands will touch it.
Take you as 'twere some distant knowledge of him,
As thus, "I know his father and his friends,
And in part him." Do you mark this, Reynaldo?　　15
REYNALDO Ay, very well, my lord.
POLONIUS "And in part him—but," you may say, "not well.
But if't be he I mean, he's very wild,
Addicted so and so," and there put on him
What forgeries you please: marry, none so rank　　20
As may dishonor him, take heed of that,
But, sir, such wanton, wild, and usual slips
As are companions noted and most known
To youth and liberty.
REYNALDO　　　　　As gaming, my lord.
POLONIUS Ay, or drinking, fencing, swearing, quarrelling,　　25
Drabbing—you may go so far.

2.1. Location: Polonius' quarters in the castle.　**3. marvell's:** marvellous(ly).
7. Danskers: Danes.　**8. keep:** lodge.　**10. encompassment:** circuitousness. **drift of question:** directing of the conversation.　**12. particular demands:** direct questions.
20. forgeries: invented charges.　**22. wanton:** sportive.　**26. Drabbing:** whoring.

REYNALDO My lord, that would dishonor him.
POLONIUS Faith, as you may season it in the charge:
  You must not put another scandal on him,
  That he is open to incontinency—   30
  That's not my meaning. But breathe his faults so quaintly
  That they may seem the taints of liberty,
  The flash and outbreak of a fiery mind,
  A savageness in unreclaimed blood,
  Of general assault.
REYNALDO   But, my good lord—   35
POLONIUS Wherefore should you do this?
REYNALDO   Ay, my lord,
  I would know that.
POLONIUS   Marry, sir, here's my drift,
  And I believe it is a fetch of wit:
  You laying these slight sallies on my son,
  As 'twere a thing a little soil'd [wi' th'] working,   40
  Mark you,
  Your party in converse, him you would sound,
  Having ever seen in the prenominate crimes
  The youth you breathe of guilty, be assur'd
  He closes with you in this consequence: 45
  "Good sir," or so, or "friend," or "gentleman,"
  According to the phrase or the addition
  Of man and country.
REYNALDO   Very good, my lord.
POLONIUS And then, sir, does 'a this—'a does—what was I about to say?
  By the mass, I was about to say something.   50
  Where did I leave?
REYNALDO   At "closes in the consequence."
POLONIUS At "closes in the consequence," ay, marry.
  He closes thus: "I know the gentleman.
  I saw him yesterday, or th' other day,
  Or then, or then, with such or such, and as you say,   55
  There was 'a gaming, there o'ertook in 's rouse,

28. **Faith.** Most editors read *Faith, no,* following F1; this makes easier sense. **season:** qualify, temper. **30. open to incontinency:** habitually profligate. **31. quaintly:** artfully. **34. unreclaimed:** untamed. **35. Of general assault:** i.e. to which young men are generally subject. **38. fetch of wit:** ingenious device. **39. sallies:** sullies, blemishes. **40. soil'd ... working:** i.e. shopworn. **43. Having:** if he has. **prenominate crimes:** aforementioned faults. **45. closes:** falls in. **in this consequence:** as follows. **47. addition:** style of address. **56. o'ertook in 's rouse:** overcome by drink.

There falling out at tennis"; or, perchance,
"I saw him enter such a house of sale,"
Videlicet, a brothel, or so forth. See you now,
Your bait of falsehood take this carp of truth,   60
And thus do we of wisdom and of reach,
With windlasses and with assays of bias,
By indirections find directions out;
So by my former lecture and advice
Shall you my son. You have me, have you not?   65
REYNALDO My lord, I have.
POLONIUS   God buy ye, fare ye well.
REYNALDO Good my lord.
POLONIUS Observe his inclination in yourself.
REYNALDO I shall, my lord.
POLONIUS And let him ply his music.
REYNALDO   Well, my lord.   70
POLONIUS Farewell.   *Exit Reynaldo.*

Enter OPHELIA.

How now, Ophelia, what's the matter?
OPHELIA O my lord, my lord, I have been so affrighted!
POLONIUS With what, i' th' name of God?
OPHELIA My lord, as I was sewing in my closet,
Lord Hamlet, with his doublet all unbrac'd,   75
No hat upon his head, his stockins fouled,
Ungart'red, and down-gyved to his ankle,
Pale as his shirt, his knees knocking each other,
And with a look so piteous in purport
As if he had been loosed out of hell   80
To speak of horrors—he comes before me.
POLONIUS Mad for thy love?
OPHELIA   My lord, I do not know,
But truly I do fear it.
POLONIUS   What said he?

---

59. videlicet: that is to say; namely (T). **61. reach:** capacity, understanding.
62. windlasses: roundabout methods. **assays of bias:** indirect attempts (a figure
from the game of bowls, in which the player must make allowance for the curv-
ing course his bowl will take toward its mark). **63. directions:** the way things
are going. **65. have me:** understand me. **66. God buy ye:** good-bye (a contraction of *God be with you*). **68. in:** by. Polonius asks him to observe Laertes
directly, as well as making inquiries. **70. let him ply:** see that he goes on with.
74. closet: private room. **75. unbrac'd:** unlaced. **76. stockins fouled:** stockings
dirty. **77. down-gyved:** hanging down like fetters on a prisoner's legs.

OPHELIA He took me by the wrist, and held me hard,
　　Then goes he to the length of all his arm,　　　　　　　　85
　　And with his other hand thus o'er his brow,
　　He falls to such perusal of my face
　　As 'a would draw it. Long stay'd he so.
　　At last, a little shaking of mine arm,
　　And thrice his head thus waving up and down,　　　　　90
　　He rais'd a sigh so piteous and profound
　　As it did seem to shatter all his bulk
　　And end his being. That done, he lets me go,
　　And with his head over his shoulder turn'd,
　　He seem'd to find his way without his eyes,　　　　　　95
　　For out a' doors he went without their helps,
　　And to the last bended their light on me.
POLONIUS Come, go with me. I will go seek the King.
　　This is the very ecstasy of love,
　　Whose violent property fordoes itself,　　　　　　　　　100
　　And leads the will to desperate undertakings
　　As oft as any passions under heaven
　　That does afflict our natures. I am sorry—
　　What, have you given him any hard words of late?
OPHELIA No, my good lord, but as you did command　　　105
　　I did repel his letters, and denied
　　His access to me.
POLONIUS　　　　　　That hath made him mad.
　　I am sorry that with better heed and judgment
　　I had not coted him. I fear'd he did but trifle
　　And meant to wrack thee, but beshrow my jealousy!　　110
　　By heaven, it is as proper to our age
　　To cast beyond ourselves in our opinions,
　　As it is common for the younger sort
　　To lack discretion. Come, go we to the King.
　　This must be known, which, being kept close, might move　　115
　　More grief to hide, than hate to utter love.
　　Come.　　　　　　　　　　　　　　　　　　*Exeunt.*

---

92. **bulk:** body.　99. **ecstasy:** madness.　100. **property:** quality. **fordoes:** destroys.　109. **coted:** observed.　110. **beshrow:** beshrew, plague take. **jealousy:** suspicious mind.　111. **proper . . . age:** characteristic of men of my age. 112. **cast beyond ourselves:** overshoot, go too far (by way of caution).　115. **close:** secret.　115–16. **move . . . love:** cause more grievous consequences by its concealment than we shall incur displeasure by making it known.

SCENE 2

Flourish. Enter KING *and* QUEEN, ROSENCRANTZ *and*
GUILDENSTERN [*cum aliis*].

KING Welcome, dear Rosencrantz and Guildenstern!
Moreover that we much did long to see you,
The need we have to use you did provoke
Our hasty sending. Something have you heard
Of Hamlet's transformation; so call it,   5
Sith nor th' exterior nor the inward man
Resembles that it was. What it should be,
More than his father's death, that thus hath put him
So much from th' understanding of himself,
I cannot dream of. I entreat you both   10
That, being of so young days brought up with him,
And sith so neighbored to his youth and havior,
That you voutsafe your rest here in our court
Some little time, so by your companies
To draw him on to pleasures, and to gather   15
So much as from occasion you may glean,
Whether aught to us unknown afflicts him thus,
That, open'd, lies within our remedy.
QUEEN Good gentlemen, he hath much talk'd of you,
And sure I am two men there is not living   20
To whom he more adheres. If it will please you
To show us so much gentry and good will
As to expend your time with us a while
For the supply and profit of our hope,
Your visitation shall receive such thanks   25
As fits a king's remembrance.
ROSENCRANTZ   Both your Majesties
Might, by the sovereign power you have of us,
Put your dread pleasures more into command
Than to entreaty.
GUILDENSTERN   But we both obey,
And here give up ourselves, in the full bent,   30
To lay our service freely at your feet,
To be commanded.

2.2. Location: The castle.   **2. Moreover . . . you:** besides the fact that we wanted
to see you for your own sakes.   **6. Sith:** since.   **11. of:** from.   **13. voutsafe your
rest:** vouchsafe to remain.   **21. more adheres:** is more attached.   **22. gentry:**
courtesy.   **24. supply and profit:** support and advancement.   **30. in . . . bent:**
to our utmost.

KING Thanks, Rosencrantz and gentle Guildenstern.
QUEEN Thanks, Guildenstern and gentle Rosencrantz.
    And I beseech you instantly to visit   35
    My too much changed son. Go some of you
    And bring these gentlemen where Hamlet is.
GUILDENSTERN Heavens make our presence and our practices
    Pleasant and helpful to him!
QUEEN   Ay, amen!
        Exeunt Rosencrantz and Guildenstern [with some Attendants].

                    Enter POLONIUS.

POLONIUS Th' embassadors from Norway, my good lord,   40
    Are joyfully return'd.
KING Thou still hast been the father of good news.
POLONIUS Have I, my lord? I assure my good liege
    I hold my duty as I hold my soul,
    Both to my God and to my gracious king;   45
    And I do think, or else this brain of mine
    Hunts not the trail of policy so sure
    As it hath us'd to do, that I have found
    The very cause of Hamlet's lunacy.
KING O, speak of that, that do I long to hear.   50
POLONIUS Give first admittance to th' embassadors;
    My news shall be the fruit to that great feast.
KING Thyself do grace to them, and bring them in.   [*Exit Polonius.*]
    He tells me, my dear Gertrude, he hath found
    The head and source of all your son's distemper.   55
QUEEN I doubt it is no other but the main,
    His father's death and our [o'erhasty] marriage.

            *Enter [*POLONIUS *with* VOLTEMAND *and*
            CORNELIUS, *the] Embassadors.*

KING Well, we shall sift him.—Welcome, my good friends!
    Say, Voltemand, what from our brother Norway?
VOLTEMAND Most fair return of greetings and desires.   60
    Upon our first, he sent out to suppress
    His nephew's levies, which to him appear'd
    To be a preparation 'gainst the Polack;
    But better look'd into, he truly found

---

40. embassadors: ambassadors.   **42. still:** always.   **43. liege:** sovereign.   **47. policy:**
statecraft.   **52. fruit:** dessert.   **55. head.** Synonymous with *source*. **distemper:**
(mental) illness.   **56. doubt:** suspect. **main:** main cause.   **61. Upon our first:** at
our first representation.

It was against your Highness. Whereat griev'd,   65
That so his sickness, age, and impotence
Was falsely borne in hand, sends out arrests
On Fortinbras, which he, in brief, obeys,
Receives rebuke from Norway, and in fine,
Makes vow before his uncle never more   70
To give th' assay of arms against your Majesty.
Whereon old Norway, overcome with joy,
Gives him three thousand crowns in annual fee,
And his commission to employ those soldiers,
So levied, as before, against the Polack,   75
With an entreaty, herein further shown,   [*Giving a paper.*]
That it might please you to give quiet pass
Through your dominions for this enterprise,
On such regards of safety and allowance
As therein are set down.

KING   It likes us well,   80
And at our more considered time we'll read,
Answer, and think upon this business.
Mean time, we thank you for your well-took labor.
Go to your rest, at night we'll feast together.
Most welcome home!

                    Exeunt Embassadors [and Attendants].

POLONIUS   This business is well ended.   85
My liege, and madam, to expostulate
What majesty should be, what duty is,
Why day is day, night night, and time is time,
Were nothing but to waste night, day, and time;
Therefore, [since] brevity is the soul of wit,   90
And tediousness the limbs and outward flourishes,
I will be brief. Your noble son is mad:
Mad call I it, for to define true madness,
What is't but to be nothing else but mad?
But let that go.

QUEEN   More matter with less art.   95

POLONIUS Madam, I swear I use no art at all.
That he's mad, 'tis true, 'tis true 'tis pity,
And pity 'tis 'tis true—a foolish figure,

---

65. griev'd: aggrieved, offended. **67. borne in hand:** taken advantage of. **69. in fine:** in the end. **71. assay:** trial. **79. On . . . allowance:** with such safeguards and provisos. **80. likes:** pleases. **81. consider'd:** suitable for consideration. **86. expostulate:** expound. **90. wit:** understanding, wisdom. **95. art:** i.e. rhetorical art. **98. figure:** figure of speech.

But farewell it, for I will use no art.
Mad let us grant him then, and now remains   100
That we find out the cause of this effect,
Or rather say, the cause of this defect,
For this effect defective comes by cause:
Thus it remains, and the remainder thus.
Perpend.   105
I have a daughter—have while she is mine—
Who in her duty and obedience, mark,
Hath given me this. Now gather, and surmise.

                     [Reads the salutation of the letter.]
"To the celestial and my soul's idol, the most beautified
Ophelia"—   110
That's an ill phrase, a vile phrase, "beautified" is a vile
phrase. But you shall hear. Thus:
"In her excellent white bosom, these, etc."
QUEEN Came this from Hamlet to her?
POLONIUS Good madam, stay awhile. I will be faithful.   115
                                   [Reads the] letter.

         "Doubt thou the stars are fire,
         Doubt that the sun doth move,
         Doubt truth to be a liar,
         But never doubt I love.
O dear Ophelia, I am ill at these numbers. I have not   120
art to reckon my groans, but that I love thee best, O
most best, believe it. Adieu.
      Thine evermore, most dear lady,
        whilst this machine is to him, Hamlet."
This in obedience hath my daughter shown me,   125
And more [above], hath his solicitings,
As they fell out by time, by means, and place,
All given to mine ear.
KING   But how hath she
   Receiv'd his love?
POLONIUS   What do you think of me?

---

103. For . . . cause: for this effect (which shows as a defect in Hamlet's reason) is not merely accidental, and has a cause we may trace.   **105. Perpend:** consider.
109. beautified: beautiful (not an uncommon usage). Perhaps a tongue-in-cheek allusion to Robert Greene's notorious use of the word in his indictment of the up-and-coming Shakespeare, "beautified with our feathers" in *A Groatsworth of Wit* (1592) (T).   **118. Doubt:** suspect.   **120. ill . . . numbers:** bad at versifying.
121. reckon: count (with a quibble on *numbers*).   **124. machine:** body.   **126. more above:** furthermore.

KING As of a man faithful and honorable.   130
POLONIUS I would fain prove so. But what might you think,
    When I had seen this hot love on the wing—
    As I perceiv'd it (I must tell you that)
    Before my daughter told me—what might you,
    Or my dear Majesty your queen here, think,   135
    If I had play'd the desk or table-book,
    Or given my heart a [winking,] mute and dumb,
    Or look'd upon this love with idle sight,
    What might you think? No, I went round to work,
    And my young mistress thus I did bespeak: 140
    "Lord Hamlet is a prince out of thy star;
    This must not be"; and then I prescripts gave her,
    That she should lock herself from [his] resort,
    Admit no messengers, receive no tokens.
    Which done, she took the fruits of my advice;   145
    And he repell'd, a short tale to make,
    Fell into a sadness, then into a fast,
    Thence to a watch, thence into a weakness,
    Thence to [a] lightness, and by this declension,
    Into the madness wherein now he raves,   150
    And all we mourn for.
KING   Do you think ['tis] this?
QUEEN It may be, very like.
POLONIUS Hath there been such a time—I would fain know that—
    That I have positively said, "'Tis so,"
    When it prov'd otherwise?
KING   Not that I know.   155
POLONIUS [*Points to his head and shoulder.*] Take this from this,
        if this be otherwise.
    If circumstances lead me, I will find
    Where truth is hid, though it were hid indeed
    Within the centre.
KING   How may we try it further?
POLONIUS You know sometimes he walks four hours together   160
    Here in the lobby.
QUEEN   So he does indeed.

---

131. fain: willingly, gladly. **136. play'd . . . table-book:** i.e. noted the matter secretly. **137. winking:** closing of the eyes. **138. idle sight:** noncomprehending eyes. **139. round:** straightforwardly. **140. bespeak:** address. **141. star:** i.e. sphere, lot in life. **145. took . . . of:** profited by, i.e. carried out. **146. repell'd:** repulsed. **148. watch:** sleeplessness. **149. lightness:** lightheadedness. **159. centre:** i.e. of the earth (which in the Ptolemaic system is also the centre of the universe).

POLONIUS At such a time I'll loose my daughter to him.
Be you and I behind an arras then,
Mark the encounter: if he love her not,
And be not from his reason fall'n thereon,   165
Let me be no assistant for a state,
But keep a farm and carters.
KING   We will try it.

Enter HAMLET [*reading on a book*].

QUEEN But look where sadly the poor wretch comes reading.
POLONIUS Away, I do beseech you, both away.
I'll board him presently.   *Exeunt King and Queen.*
                    O, give me leave,   170
How does my good Lord Hamlet?
HAMLET Well, God-a-mercy.
POLONIUS Do you know me, my lord?
HAMLET Excellent well, you are a fishmonger.
POLONIUS Not I, my lord.   175
HAMLET Then I would you were so honest a man.
POLONIUS Honest, my lord?
HAMLET Ay, sir, to be honest, as this world goes, is to
be one man pick'd out of ten thousand.
POLONIUS That's very true, my lord.   180
HAMLET For if the sun breed maggots in a dead dog,
being a good kissing carrion—Have you a daughter?
POLONIUS I have, my lord.
HAMLET Let her not walk i' th' sun. Conception is a
blessing, but as your daughter may conceive, friend, look to't. 185
POLONIUS [*Aside.*] How say you by that? still harping on
my daughter. Yet he knew me not at first, 'a said I was
a fishmonger. 'A is far gone. And truly in my youth I
suff'red much extremity for love—very near this. I'll   190
speak to him again.—What do you read, my lord?
HAMLET Words, words, words.

---

163. arras: hanging tapestry.   **165. thereon:** because of that.   **167. s.d. Reading
on a book.** Speculation as to the title of this book includes Erasmus' *The Praise
of Folly*, Horace's *Satires*, 2.3, which includes references to madness, a sacrificed
daughter, and a fishmonger, and Cardan's *De Consolatione* (T).   **170. board:** accost.
presently: at once.   **172. God-a-mercy:** thank you.   **174. fishmonger.** Usually
explained as slang for "bawd," but no evidence has been produced for such a usage
in Shakespeare's day.   **182. good kissing carrion:** flesh good enough for the sun
to kiss.   **184. Conception:** understanding (with following play on the sense "conceiving a child").

POLONIUS What is the matter, my lord?

HAMLET Between who?

POLONIUS I mean, the matter that you read, my lord.   195

HAMLET Slanders, sir; for the satirical rogue says
    here that old men have grey beards, that their faces are
    wrinkled, their eyes purging thick amber and plum-
    tree gum, and that they have a plentiful lack of wit,
    together with most weak hams; all which, sir,   200
    though I most powerfully and potently believe, yet I
    hold it not honesty to have it thus set down, for your-
    self, sir, shall grow old as I am, if like a crab you could
    go backward.

POLONIUS [*Aside.*] Though this be madness, yet there is   205
    method in't.—Will you walk out of the air, my lord?

HAMLET Into my grave.

POLONIUS Indeed that's out of the air. [*Aside.*] How
    pregnant sometimes his replies are! a happiness that
    often madness hits on, which reason and [sanity]   210
    could not so prosperously be deliver'd of. I will leave
    him, [and suddenly contrive the means of meeting be-
    tween him] and my daughter.—My lord, I will take
    my leave of you.

HAMLET You cannot take from me any thing that I   215
    will not more willingly part withal—except my life,
    except my life, except my life.

POLONIUS Fare you well, my lord.

HAMLET These tedious old fools!

Enter GUILDENSTERN *and* ROSENCRANTZ.

POLONIUS You go to seek the Lord Hamlet, there he is.   220

ROSENCRANTZ [*To* POLONIUS] God save you, sir!

[*Exit Polonius.*]

GUILDENSTERN My honor'd lord!

ROSENCRANTZ My most dear lord!

HAMLET My [excellent] good friends! How dost
    thou, Guildenstern? Ah, Rosencrantz! Good lads,   225
    how do you both?

ROSENCRANTZ As the indifferent children of the earth.

---

193. **matter:** subject; but Hamlet replies as if he had understood Polonius to mean
"cause for a quarrel." 202. **honesty:** a fitting thing. 206. **method:** orderly
arrangement, sequence of ideas. **out . . . air.** Outdoor air was thought to be bad for
invalids. 209. **pregnant:** apt. 212. **suddenly:** at once. 227. **indifferent:** average.

GUILDENSTERN Happy, in that we are not [over-] happy, on
Fortune's [cap] we are not the very button.
HAMLET Nor the soles of her shoe?   230
ROSENCRANTZ Neither, my lord.
HAMLET Then you live about her waist, or in the
middle of her favors?
GUILDENSTERN Faith, her privates we.
HAMLET In the secret parts of Fortune? O, most   235
true, she is a strumpet. What news?
ROSENCRANTZ None, my lord, but the world's grown honest.
HAMLET Then is doomsday near. But your news is
not true. [Let me question more in particular. What
have you, my good friends, deserv'd at the hands of   240
Fortune, that she sends you to prison hither?
GUILDENSTERN Prison, my lord?
HAMLET Denmark's a prison.
ROSENCRANTZ Then is the world one.
HAMLET A goodly one, in which there are many con-   245
fines, wards, and dungeons, Denmark being one o' th'
worst.
ROSENCRANTZ We think not so, my lord.
HAMLET Why then 'tis none to you; for there is
nothing either good or bad, but thinking makes it so.   250
To me it is a prison.
ROSENCRANTZ Why then your ambition makes it one. 'Tis
too narrow for your mind.
HAMLET O God, I could be bounded in a nutshell, and
count myself a king of infinite space—were it not that I   255
have bad dreams.
GUILDENSTERN Which dreams indeed are ambition, for the
very substance of the ambitious is merely the shadow
of a dream.
HAMLET A dream itself is but a shadow.   260
ROSENCRANTZ Truly, and I hold ambition of so airy and light
a quality that it is but a shadow's shadow.
HAMLET Then are our beggars bodies, and our monarchs
and outstretch'd heroes the beggars' shadows.
Shall we to th' court? for, by my fay, I cannot reason.   265

234. privates: (1) intimate friends; (2) genitalia. **236. strumpet.** A common
epithet for Fortune, because she grants favors to all men. **246. wards:** cells.
263. bodies: i.e. not shadows (since they lack ambition). **264. outstretch'd:** i.e.
with their ambition extended to the utmost (and hence producing stretched-out
or elongated shadows). **265. fay:** faith.

BOTH [ROSENCRANTZ, GUILDENSTERN] We'll wait upon you.
HAMLET No such matter. I will not sort you with the
rest of my servants; for to speak to you like an honest
man, I am most dreadfully attended.] But in the beaten
way of friendship, what make you at Elsinore?   270
ROSENCRANTZ To visit you, my lord, no other occasion.
HAMLET Beggar that I am, I am [even] poor in thanks
—but I thank you, and sure, dear friends, my thanks
are too dear a halfpenny. Were you not sent for? is it
your own inclining? is it a free visitation? Come, come,   275
deal justly with me. Come, come—nay, speak.
GUILDENSTERN What should we say, my lord?
HAMLET Any thing but to th' purpose. You were sent
for, and there is a kind of confession in your looks,
which your modesties have not craft enough to color.   280
I know the good King and Queen have sent for you.
ROSENCRANTZ To what end, my lord?
HAMLET That you must teach me. But let me conjure
you, by the rights of our fellowship, by the consonancy
of our youth, by the obligation of our ever-preserv'd   285
love, and by what more dear a better proposer
can charge you withal, be even and direct with me,
whether you were sent for or no!
ROSENCRANTZ [Aside to Guildenstern.] What say you?
HAMLET [Aside.] Nay then I have an eye of you!—   290
If you love me, hold not off.
GUILDENSTERN My lord, we were sent for.
HAMLET I will tell you why, so shall my anticipation
prevent your discovery, and your secrecy to the King
and Queen moult no feather. I have of late—but   295
wherefore I know not—lost all my mirth, forgone all
custom of exercises; and indeed it goes so heavily with
my disposition, that this goodly frame, the earth,
seems to me a sterile promontory; this most excellent

266. **wait upon you:** attend you thither.   267. **sort:** associate.   269. **dreadfully:** execrably.   274. **too . . . halfpenny:** too expensive priced at a halfpenny, i.e. not worth much.   276. **justly:** honestly.   278. **but.** Ordinarily punctuated with a comma preceding, to give the sense "provided that it is"; but Q2 has no comma, and Hamlet may intend, or include, the sense "except."   280. **modesties:** sense of shame.   284–85. **consonancy . . . youth:** similarity of our ages.   287. **charge:** urge, adjure. **even:** frank, honest (cf. modern "level with me").   290. **of:** on.   294. **prevent your discovery:** forestall your disclosure (of what the King and Queen have said to you in confidence).   295. **moult no feather:** not be impaired in the least.   297. **custom of exercises:** my usual athletic activities.

canopy, the air, look you, this brave o'erhanging 300
firmament, this majestical roof fretted with golden fire,
why, it appeareth nothing to me but a foul and pestilent
congregation of vapors. What [a] piece of work is a
man, how noble in reason, how infinite in faculties, in
form and moving, how express and admirable in 305
action, how like an angel in apprehension, how like a
god! the beauty of the world; the paragon of animals;
and yet to me what is this quintessence of dust?
Man delights not me—nor women neither, though by
your smiling you seem to say so. 310
ROSENCRANTZ My lord, there was no such stuff in my
thoughts.
HAMLET Why did ye laugh then, when I said, "Man
delights not me"?
ROSENCRANTZ To think, my lord, if you delight not in man, 315
what lenten entertainment the players shall receive
from you. We coted them on the way, and hither are
they coming to offer you service.
HAMLET He that plays the king shall be welcome—
his Majesty shall have tribute on me, the adventer- 320
ous knight shall use his foil and target, the lover shall
not sigh gratis, the humorous man shall end his part in
peace, [the clown shall make those laugh whose lungs
are [tickle] a' th' sere,] and the lady shall say her mind
freely, or the [blank] verse shall halt for't. What 325
players are they?
ROSENCRANTZ Even those you were wont to take such delight
in, the tragedians of the city.
HAMLET How chances it they travel? Their residence,
both in reputation and profit, was better both 330
ways.

---

300. brave: splendid. **301. fretted:** ornamented as with fretwork. **303. piece
of work:** masterpiece. **304–7. how infinite . . . god.** See the Textual Notes for
the different punctuation in F1. **305. express:** exact. **308. quintessence:** finest
and purest extract. **316. lenten entertainment:** meagre reception, especially as
performances were prohibited during Lent (T). **317. coted:** outstripped. **320.
on:** of, from. **320–21. adventerous:** adventurous, i.e. wandering in search of
adventure. **321. foil and target:** light fencing sword and small shield. **322.
gratis:** without reward. **humorous:** dominated by some eccentric trait (like the
melancholy Jaques in *As You Like It*). **324. tickle . . . sere:** i.e. easily made to
laugh (literally, describing a gun that goes off easily; *sere* = a catch in the gunlock;
tickle = easily affected, highly sensitive to stimulus). **325. halt:** limp, come off
lamely (the verse will not scan if she omits indecent words).

ROSENCRANTZ I think their inhibition comes by the means of
the late innovation.
HAMLET Do they hold the same estimation they did
when I was in the city? Are they so follow'd?   335
ROSENCRANTZ No indeed are they not.
[HAMLET How comes it? do they grow rusty?
ROSENCRANTZ Nay, their endeavor keeps in the wonted
pace; but there is, sir, an aery of children, little eyases,
that cry out on the top of question, and are most   340
tyrannically clapp'd for't. These are now the
fashion, and so [berattle] the common stages—so they
call them—that many wearing rapiers are afraid of
goose-quills and dare scarce come thither.
HAMLET What, are they children? Who maintains   345
'em? How are they escoted? Will they pursue the
quality no longer than they can sing? Will they not
say afterwards, if they should grow themselves to
common players (as it is [most like], if their means are
[no] better), their writers do them wrong, to make them   350
exclaim against their own succession?
ROSENCRANTZ Faith, there has been much to do on both
sides, and the nation holds it no sin to tarre them to
controversy. There was for a while no money bid for
argument, unless the poet and the player went to cuffs   355
in the question.

332. inhibition: hindrance (to playing in the city). The word could be used of an official prohibition. See next note.   **333. innovation.** Shakespeare elsewhere uses this
word of a political uprising or revolt, and lines 332–33 are often explained as meaning
that the company had been forbidden to play in the city as the result of some distur-
bance. It is commonly conjectured that the allusion is to the Essex rebellion of 1601,
but it is known that Shakespeare's company, though to some extent involved on account of the special performance of *Richard II* they were commissioned to give on
the eve of the rising, were not in fact punished by inhibition. A second interpretation
explains *innovation* as referring to the new theatrical vogue described in lines 339 ff.,
and conjectures that *inhibition* may allude to a Privy Council order of 1600 restrict-
ing the number of London playhouses to two and the number of performances to
two a week.   **337–62. How . . . too.** This passage refers topically to the "War of the
Theaters" between the child actors and their poet Jonson on the one side, and on
the other the adults, with Dekker, Marston, and possibly Shakespeare as spokesmen,
in 1600–1601.   **339. aery:** nest. **eyases:** unfledged hawks.   **340. cry . . . question:**
cry shrilly above others in controversy.   **341. tyrannically:** outrageously.   **342. be-
rattle:** cry down, satirize. **common stages:** public theaters (the children played at
the Blackfriars and at the small auditorium abutting St. Paul's Cathedral, both private
theaters).   **344. goose-quills:** pens (of satirical playwrights).   **346. escoted:** supported.   **347. quality:** profession (of acting). **no . . . sing:** i.e. only until their voices
change.   **351. succession:** future.   **352. to do:** ado.   **353. tarre:** incite.   **355. argument:** plot of a play.   **356. in the question:** i.e. as part of the script.

HAMLET Is't possible?
GUILDENSTERN O, there has been much throwing about of brains.
HAMLET Do the boys carry it away?   360
ROSENCRANTZ Ay, that they do, my lord—Hercules and his
    load too.]
HAMLET It is not very strange, for my uncle is King of
    Denmark, and those that would make mouths at him
    while my father liv'd, give twenty, forty, fifty, a   365
    hundred ducats a-piece for his picture in little. 'Sblood,
    there is something in this more than natural, if philoso-
    phy could find it out.   *A flourish [for the Players].*
GUILDENSTERN There are the players.
HAMLET Gentlemen, you are welcome to Elsinore.   370
    Your hands, come then: th' appurtenance of welcome
    is fashion and ceremony. Let me comply with you in
    this garb, [lest my] extent to the players, which, I tell
    you, must show fairly outwards, should more appear
    like entertainment than yours. You are welcome; but   375
    my uncle-father and aunt-mother are deceiv'd.
GUILDENSTERN In what, my dear lord?
HAMLET I am but mad north-north-west. When the
    wind is southerly I know a hawk from a hand-saw.

Enter POLONIUS.

POLONIUS Well be with you, gentlemen!   380
HAMLET [*Aside to them.*] Hark you, Guildenstern,
    and you too—at each ear a hearer—that great baby you
    see there is not yet out of his swaddling-clouts.
ROSENCRANTZ Happily he is the second time come to them,
    for they say an old man is twice a child.   385
HAMLET I will prophesy, he comes to tell me of the
    players, mark it. [*Aloud.*] You say right, sir, a'
    Monday morning, 'twas then indeed.

360. carry it away: win.   **361–62. Hercules . . . too.** Hercules in the course of
one of his twelve labors supported the world for Atlas; the children do better, for
they carry away the world and Hercules as well. There is an allusion to the Globe
playhouse, which reportedly had for its sign the figure of Hercules upholding
the world.   **364. mouths:** derisive faces.   **366. 'Sblood:** by God's (Christ's) blood.
372. comply: observe the formalities.   **373. garb:** fashion, manner.   **my extent:** i.e.
the degree of courtesy I show.   **374–75. more . . . yours:** seem to be a warmer reception than I have given you.   **379. hawk, hand-saw.** Both cutting-tools; but also
both birds, if *hand-saw* quibbles on *hernshaw*, "heron," a bird preyed upon by the hawk.
383. swaddling-clouts: swaddling clothes.   **384. Happily:** haply, perhaps.
385. twice: i.e. for the second time.

POLONIUS My lord, I have news to tell you.
HAMLET My lord, I have news to tell you. When   390
Roscius was an actor in Rome—
POLONIUS The actors are come hither, my lord.
HAMLET Buzz, buzz!
POLONIUS Upon my honor—
HAMLET "Then came each actor on his ass"—   395
POLONIUS The best actors in the world, either for trag-
edy, comedy, history, pastoral, pastoral-comical,
historical-pastoral, [tragical-historical, tragical-comi-
cal-historical-pastoral,] scene individable, or poem
unlimited; Seneca cannot be too heavy, nor Plautus   400
too light, for the law of writ and the liberty: these
are the only men.
HAMLET O Jephthah, judge of Israel, what a treasure
hadst thou!
POLONIUS What a treasure had he, my lord?   405
HAMLET Why—
"One fair daughter, and no more,
The which he loved passing well."
POLONIUS [Aside.] Still on my daughter.
HAMLET Am I not i' th' right, old Jephthah?   410
POLONIUS If you call me Jephthah, my lord, I have a
daughter that I love passing well.
HAMLET Nay, that follows not.
POLONIUS What follows then, my lord?
HAMLET Why—   415
"As by lot, God wot,"
and then, you know,
"It came to pass, as most like it was"—
the first row of the pious chanson will show you
more, for look where my abridgment comes.   420

391. **Roscius:** the most famous of Roman actors (died 62 B.C.E.). News about him would be stale news indeed. 393. **Buzz:** exclamation of impatience at someone who tells news already known. 399. **scene individable:** play observing the unity of place. 399–400. **poem unlimited:** play ignoring rules such as the three unities. 400. **Seneca:** Roman writer of tragedies. **Plautus:** Roman writer of come-dies. 401. **for . . . liberty:** for strict observance of the rules, or for freedom from them (with possible allusion to the location of playhouses, which were not built in properties under city jurisdiction, but in the "liberties"—land once monastic and now outside the jurisdiction of the city authorities). 402. **only:** very best (a frequent use). 403. **Jephthah . . . Israel:** title of a ballad, from which Hamlet goes on to quote. For the story of Jephthah and his daughter, see Judges 11. 419. **row:** stanza. **chanson:** song, ballad. 420. **abridgment:** (1) interruption; (2) pastime.

THE TRAGEDY OF HAMLET

Enter the PLAYERS, [*four or five*].

You are welcome, masters, welcome all. I am glad to
see thee well. Welcome, good friends. O, old friend!
why, thy face is valanc'd since I saw thee last; com'st
thou to beard me in Denmark? What, my young lady
and mistress! by' lady, your ladyship is nearer to   425
heaven than when I saw you last, by the altitude
of a chopine. Pray God your voice, like a piece of
uncurrent gold, be not crack'd within the ring.
Masters, you are all welcome. We'll e'en to't like
[French] falc'ners—fly at any thing we see; we'll have   430
a speech straight. Come give us a taste of your
quality, come, a passionate speech.
[1.] PLAYER What speech, my good lord?
HAMLET I heard thee speak me a speech once, but it
was never acted, or if it was, not above once; for the   435
play, I remember, pleas'd not the million, 'twas
caviary to the general, but it was—as I receiv'd it, and
others, whose judgments in such matters cried in the
top of mine—an excellent play, well digested in the
scenes, set down with as much modesty as cunning. I   440
remember one said there were no sallets in the
lines to make the matter savory, nor no matter in the
phrase that might indict the author of affection, but
call'd it an honest method, as wholesome as sweet, and
by very much more handsome than fine. One speech   445
in't I chiefly lov'd, 'twas Aeneas' [tale] to Dido,
and thereabout of it especially when he speaks of
Priam's slaughter. If it live in your memory, begin at
this line—let me see, let me see:
"The rugged Pyrrhus, like th' Hyrcanian beast—"   450

423. **valanc'd:** fringed, i.e. bearded. 424. **beard:** confront boldly (with
obvious pun). 425. **by' lady:** by Our Lady. 427. **chopine:** thick-soled shoe.
428. **crack'd . . . ring:** i.e. broken to the point where you can no longer play
female roles. A coin with a crack extending far enough in from the edge to cross
the circle surrounding the stamp of the sovereign's head was unacceptable in exchange *(uncurrent).* 431. **straight:** straightway. **taste:** sample (T). 432. **quality:**
professional skill. 437. **caviary . . . general:** caviare to the common people, i.e.
too choice for the multitude. 438–39. **cried . . . of:** were louder than, i.e. carried more authority than. 441. **sallets:** salads, i.e. spicy jokes. 442. **savory:** zesty.
443. **affection:** affectation. 445. **fine:** showily dressed (in language). 448. **Priam's
slaughter:** the slaying of Priam (at the fall of Troy). 450. **Pyrrhus:** another name
for Neoptolemus, Achilles' son. **Hyrcanian beast.** Hyrcania in the Caucasus was
notorious for its tigers.

'Tis not so, it begins with Pyrrhus:
"The rugged Pyrrhus, he whose sable arms,
Black as his purpose, did the night resemble
When he lay couched in th' ominous horse,
Hath now this dread and black complexion smear'd   455
With heraldy more dismal: head to foot
Now is he total gules, horridly trick'd
With blood of fathers, mothers, daughters, sons,
Bak'd and impasted with the parching streets,
That lend a tyrannous and a damned light   460
To their lord's murther. Roasted in wrath and fire,
And thus o'er-sized with coagulate gore,
With eyes like carbuncles, the hellish Pyrrhus
Old grandsire Priam seeks."
So proceed you.   465
POLONIUS 'Fore God, my lord, well spoken, with good
accent and good discretion.
[1.] PLAYER   "Anon he finds him
Striking too short at Greeks. His antique sword,
Rebellious to his arm, lies where it falls,   470
Repugnant to command. Unequal match'd,
Pyrrhus at Priam drives, in rage strikes wide,
But with the whiff and wind of his fell sword
Th' unnerved father falls. [Then senseless Ilium,]
Seeming to feel this blow, with flaming top   475
Stoops to his base, and with a hideous crash
Takes prisoner Pyrrhus' ear; for lo his sword,
Which was declining on the milky head
Of reverent Priam, seem'd i' th' air to stick.
So as a painted tyrant Pyrrhus stood   480
[And,] like a neutral to his will and matter,
Did nothing.
But as we often see, against some storm,
A silence in the heavens, the rack stand still,

452. **sable arms:** The Greeks within the Trojan horse had blackened their skin so as to be inconspicuous when they emerged at night.   456. **heraldy:** heraldry. **dismal:** ill-boding.   457. **gules:** red (heraldic term). **trick'd:** adorned.   459. **Bak'd:** caked. **impasted:** crusted. **with . . . streets:** i.e. by the heat from the burning streets. 462. **o'er-sized:** covered over as with a coat of sizing, "a glutinous or viscid wash" (*OED*).   463. **carbuncles:** jewels believed to shine in the dark.   471. **Repugnant:** resistant, hostile.   473. **fell:** cruel.   474. **unnerved:** drained of strength. **senseless:** insensible. **Ilium:** the citadel of Troy.   479. **reverent:** reverend, aged.   481. **like . . . matter:** i.e. poised midway between intention and performance.   483. **against:** just before.   484. **rack:** cloud-mass.

The bold winds speechless, and the orb below 485
As hush as death, anon the dreadful thunder
Doth rend the region; so after Pyrrhus' pause,
A roused vengeance sets him new a-work,
And never did the Cyclops' hammers fall
On Mars's armor forg'd for proof eterne 490
With less remorse than Pyrrhus' bleeding sword
Now falls on Priam.
Out, out, thou strumpet Fortune! All you gods,
In general synod take away her power!
Break all the spokes and [fellies] from her wheel, 495
And bowl the round nave down the hill of heaven
As low as to the fiends!"
POLONIUS This is too long.
HAMLET It shall to the barber's with your beard.
Prithee say on, he's for a jig or a tale of bawdry, or he 500
sleeps. Say on, come to Hecuba.
[1.] PLAYER "But who, ah woe, had seen the mobled
queen"—
HAMLET "The mobled queen"?
POLONIUS That's good, ["[mobled] queen" is good].
[1.] PLAYER "Run barefoot up and down, threat-
'ning the flames 505
With bisson rheum, a clout upon that head
Where late the diadem stood, and for a robe,
About her lank and all o'er-teemed loins,
A blanket, in the alarm of fear caught up—
Who this had seen, with tongue in venom steep'd, 510
'Gainst Fortune's state would treason have pronounc'd.
But if the gods themselves did see her then,
When she saw Pyrrhus make malicious sport
In mincing with his sword her [husband's] limbs,
The instant burst of clamor that she made, 515
Unless things mortal move them not at all,
Would have made milch the burning eyes of heaven,
And passion in the gods."

---

487. region: i.e. air. **489. Cyclops:** giants who worked in Vulcan's smithy, where armor was made for the gods. **490. proof eterne:** eternal endurance. **491. remorse:** pity. **495. fellies:** rims. **496. nave:** hub. **500. jig:** song-and-dance entertainment performed after the main play. **502. mobled:** muffled. **506. bisson rheum:** blinding tears. **clout:** cloth. **508. o'er-teemed:** worn out by childbearing. **511. state:** rule, government. **517. milch:** moist (literally, milky). **518. passion:** grief.

POLONIUS Look whe'er he has not turn'd his color and
  has tears in 's eyes. Prithee no more.   520
HAMLET 'Tis well, I'll have thee speak out the rest
  of this soon. Good my lord, will you see the players
  well bestow'd? Do you hear, let them be well us'd,
  for they are the abstract and brief chronicles of the
  time. After your death you were better have a bad   525
  epitaph than their ill report while you live.
POLONIUS My lord, I will use them according to their
  desert.
HAMLET God's bodkin, man, much better: use every
  man after his desert, and who shall scape whipping?   530
  Use them after your own honor and dignity—the less
  they deserve, the more merit is in your bounty.
  Take them in.
POLONIUS Come, sirs.   [*Exit.*]
HAMLET Follow him, friends, we'll hear a play to-   535
  morrow.   [*Exeunt all the Players but the First.*]
  Dost thou hear me, old friend? Can you play "The
  Murther of Gonzago"?
[1.] PLAYER Ay, my lord.
HAMLET We'll ha't to-morrow night. You could   540
  for need study a speech of some dozen or sixteen
  lines, which I would set down and insert in't, could
  you not?
[1.] PLAYER Ay, my lord.
HAMLET Very well. Follow that lord, and look you   545
  mock him not. [*Exit First Player.*] My good friends,
  I'll leave you [till] night. You are welcome to Elsinore.
ROSENCRANTZ Good my lord!
HAMLET Ay so, God buy to you.
                    Exeunt [Rosencrantz and Guildenstern].
                    Now I am alone.
O, what a rogue and peasant slave am I!   550
Is it not monstrous that this player here,
But in a fiction, in a dream of passion,
Could force his soul so to his own conceit
That from her working all the visage wann'd,
Tears in his eyes, distraction in his aspect,   555

---

519. **Look . . . not:** i.e. note how he has.   523. **bestow'd:** lodged. **us'd:** treated.
529. **God's bodkin:** by God's (Christ's) little body.   541. **for need:** if necessary.
553. **conceit:** imaginative conception.

A broken voice, an' his whole function suiting
With forms to his conceit? And all for nothing,
For Hecuba!
What's Hecuba to him, or he to [Hecuba],
That he should weep for her? What would he do   560
Had he the motive and [the cue] for passion
That I have? He would drown the stage with tears,
And cleave the general ear with horrid speech,
Make mad the guilty, and appall the free,
Confound the ignorant, and amaze indeed   565
The very faculties of eyes and ears. Yet I,
A dull and muddy-mettled rascal, peak
Like John-a-dreams, unpregnant of my cause,
And can say nothing; no, not for a king,
Upon whose property and most dear life   570
A damn'd defeat was made. Am I a coward?
Who calls me villain, breaks my pate across,
Plucks off my beard and blows it in my face,
Tweaks me by the nose, gives me the lie i' th' throat
As deep as to the lungs? Who does me this?   575
Hah, 'swounds, I should take it; for it cannot be
But I am pigeon-liver'd, and lack gall
To make oppression bitter, or ere this
I should 'a' fatted all the region kites
With this slave's offal. Bloody, bawdy villain!   580
Remorseless, treacherous, lecherous, kindless villain!
Why, what an ass am I! This is most brave,
That I, the son of a dear [father] murthered,
Prompted to my revenge by heaven and hell,
Must like a whore unpack my heart with words,   585
And fall a-cursing like a very drab,
A stallion. Fie upon't, foh!
About, my brains! Hum—I have heard
That guilty creatures sitting at a play

556. his whole function: the operation of his whole body. **557. forms:** actions, expressions. **564. free:** innocent. **565. amaze:** confound. **567. muddy-mettled:** dull-spirited. **peak:** mope. **568. John-a-dreams:** a sleepy fellow. **unpregnant of:** unquickened by. **571. defeat:** destruction. **574–75. gives . . . lungs:** calls me a liar in the extremest degree. **576. 'swounds:** by God's (Christ's) wounds. **should:** would certainly. **577. am . . . gall:** i.e. am constitutionally incapable of resentment. That doves were mild because they had no gall was a popular belief. **579. region kites:** kites of the air. **580. offal:** entrails. **581. kindless:** unnatural. **587. stallion:** male whore. Most editors adopt the F1 reading *scullion*, "kitchen menial." **588. About:** to work.

Have by the very cunning of the scene   590
Been strook so to the soul, that presently
They have proclaim'd their malefactions:
For murther, though it have no tongue, will speak
With most miraculous organ. I'll have these players
Play something like the murther of my father   595
Before mine uncle. I'll observe his looks,
I'll tent him to the quick. If 'a do blench,
I know my course. The spirit that I have seen
May be a [dev'l], and the [dev'l] hath power
T' assume a pleasing shape, yea, and perhaps,   600
Out of my weakness and my melancholy,
As he is very potent with such spirits,
Abuses me to damn me. I'll have grounds
More relative than this—the play's the thing
Wherein I'll catch the conscience of the King.   *Exit.* 605

---

591. presently: at once, then and there.   **597. tent:** probe. **blench:** flinch.
602. spirits: states of temperament.   **603. Abuses:** deludes.   **604. relative:** closely
related (to fact), i.e. conclusive, with a pun reminding the audience of the identity
of the still-likely criminal (T).

Act 3

SCENE I

Enter KING, QUEEN, POLONIUS, OPHELIA, ROSENCRANTZ,
GUILDENSTERN, LORDS.

KING An' can you by no drift of conference
Get from him why he puts on this confusion,
Grating so harshly all his days of quiet
With turbulent and dangerous lunacy?
ROSENCRANTZ He does confess he feels himself distracted,   5
But from what cause 'a will by no means speak.
GUILDENSTERN Nor do we find him forward to be sounded,
But with a crafty madness keeps aloof
When we would bring him on to some confession
Of his true state.
QUEEN   Did he receive you well?   10
ROSENCRANTZ Most like a gentleman.
GUILDENSTERN But with much forcing of his disposition.
ROSENCRANTZ Niggard of question, but of our demands
Most free in his reply.
QUEEN   Did you assay him
To any pastime?   15
ROSENCRANTZ Madam, it so fell out that certain players
We o'erraught on the way; of these we told him,
And there did seem in him a kind of joy
To hear of it. They are here about the court,
And as I think, they have already order   20
This night to play before him.
POLONIUS   'Tis most true,
And he beseech'd me to entreat your Majesties

3.1. Location: The castle.   See the Textual Notes for the Q1 version of parts
of this scene.   **1. An':** and. **drift of conference:** leading on of conversation.
7. forward: readily willing. **sounded:** plumbed, probed.   **8. crafty madness:** i.e.
mad craftiness, the shrewdness that mad people sometimes exhibit.   **12. disposition:** inclination.   **13. question:** conversation. **demands:** questions.   **14. assay:**
attempt to win.   **17. o'erraught:** passed (literally, overreached).

To hear and see the matter.
KING With all my heart, and it doth much content me
  To hear him so inclin'd.   25
  Good gentlemen, give him a further edge,
  And drive his purpose into these delights.
ROSENCRANTZ We shall, my lord.
                        Exeunt Rosencrantz and Guildenstern.
KING   Sweet Gertrude, leave us two,
  For we have closely sent for Hamlet hither,
  That he, as 'twere by accident, may here   30
  Affront Ophelia. Her father and myself,
  We'll so bestow ourselves that, seeing unseen,
  We may of their encounter frankly judge,
  And gather by him, as he is behav'd,
  If't be th' affliction of his love or no   35
  That thus he suffers for.
QUEEN   I shall obey you.
  And for your part, Ophelia, I do wish
  That your good beauties be the happy cause
  Of Hamlet's wildness. So shall I hope your virtues
  Will bring him to his wonted way again,   40
  To both your honors.
OPHELIA   Madam, I wish it may.   *[Exit Queen.]*
POLONIUS Ophelia, walk you here.—Gracious, so please you,
  We will bestow ourselves. [*To Ophelia.*] Read on this book,
  That show of such an exercise may color
  Your [loneliness]. We are oft to blame in this—   45
  'Tis too much prov'd—that with devotion's visage
  And pious action we do sugar o'er
  The devil himself.
KING   *[Aside.]* O, 'tis too true!
  How smart a lash that speech doth give my conscience!
  The harlot's cheek, beautied with plast'ring art,   50
  Is not more ugly to the thing that helps it
  Than is my deed to my most painted word.
  O heavy burthen!
POLONIUS I hear him coming. Withdraw, my lord.
                        [Exeunt King and Polonius.]

26. edge: stimulus. **27. into:** on to. **29. closely:** privately. **31. Affront:** meet. **33. frankly:** freely. **44. exercise:** i.e. religious exercise (as the next sentence makes clear). **44–45. color Your loneliness:** make your solitude seem natural. **46. too much prov'd:** too often proved true. **47. action:** demeanor. **51. to . . . it:** in comparison with the paint that makes it look beautiful.

Enter HAMLET.

HAMLET To be, or not to be, that is the question: 55
Whether 'tis nobler in the mind to suffer
The slings and arrows of outrageous fortune,
Or to take arms against a sea of troubles,
And by opposing, end them. To die, to sleep—
No more, and by a sleep to say we end   60
The heart-ache and the thousand natural shocks
That flesh is heir to; 'tis a consummation
Devoutly to be wish'd. To die, to sleep—
To sleep, perchance to dream—ay, there's the rub,
For in that sleep of death what dreams may come,   65
When we have shuffled off this mortal coil,
Must give us pause; there's the respect
That makes calamity of so long life:
For who would bear the whips and scorns of time,
Th' oppressor's wrong, the proud man's contumely,   70
The pangs of despis'd love, the law's delay,
The insolence of office, and the spurns
That patient merit of th' unworthy takes,
When he himself might his quietus make
With a bare bodkin; who would fardels bear,   75
To grunt and sweat under a weary life,
But that the dread of something after death,
The undiscover'd country, from whose bourn
No traveller returns, puzzles the will,
And makes us rather bear those ills we have,   80
Than fly to others that we know not of?
Thus conscience does make cowards [of us all],
And thus the native hue of resolution
Is sicklied o'er with the pale cast of thought,

55–89. See the Textual Notes for the version of this soliloquy in Q1. **56. suffer:** submit to, endure patiently. **62. consummation:** completion, end. **64. rub:** obstacle (a term from the game of bowls). **66. shuffled off:** freed ourselves from. Note variant uses of this term by Claudius at 3.3.61 and 4.7.137. (T). **this mortal coil:** (1) the turmoil of this mortal life; (2) the body, the fleshy material wrapped around the soul (T). **67. respect:** consideration. **68. of . . . life:** so long-lived. **69. time:** the world. **74. his quietus make:** write paid to his account. **75. bare bodkin:** mere dagger. **fardels:** burdens. **78. undiscover'd:** not disclosed to knowledge; about which men have no information. **bourn:** boundary, i.e. region. **79. puzzles:** paralyzes. **82. conscience:** reflection (but with some of the modern sense of moral judgment, too). **83. native hue:** natural (ruddy) complexion. **84. pale cast:** pallor. **thought:** i.e. melancholy thought, brooding.

And enterprises of great pitch and moment   85
With this regard their currents turn awry,
And lose the name of action.—Soft you now,
The fair Ophelia. Nymph, in thy orisons
Be all my sins rememb'red.
OPHELIA   Good my lord,
How does your honor for this many a day?   90
HAMLET I humbly thank you, well, [well, well].
OPHELIA My lord, I have remembrances of yours
That I have longed long to redeliver.
I pray you now receive them.
HAMLET   No, not I,
I never gave you aught.   95
OPHELIA My honor'd lord, you know right well you did,
And with them words of so sweet breath compos'd
As made these things more rich. Their perfume lost,
Take these again, for to the noble mind
Rich gifts wax poor when givers prove unkind.   100
There, my lord.
HAMLET   Ha, ha! are you honest?
OPHELIA My lord?
HAMLET Are you fair?
OPHELIA What means your lordship?   105
HAMLET That if you be honest and fair, [your
honesty] should admit no discourse to your beauty.
OPHELIA Could beauty, my lord, have better commerce
than with honesty?
HAMLET Ay, truly, for the power of beauty will   110
sooner transform honesty from what it is to a bawd
than the force of honesty can translate beauty into
his likeness. This was sometime a paradox, but now
the time gives it proof. I did love you once.
OPHELIA Indeed, my lord, you made me believe so. 115
HAMLET You should not have believ'd me, for virtue
cannot so [inoculate] our old stock but we shall relish of
it. I lov'd you not.
OPHELIA I was the more deceiv'd.
HAMLET Get thee [to] a nunn'ry, why wouldst thou 120
be a breeder of sinners? I am myself indifferent honest,

85. pitch: loftiness (a term from falconry, signifying the highest point of a hawk's flight). **88. orisons:** prayers. **102. honest:** chaste. **113. sometime:** formerly. **paradox:** tenet contrary to accepted belief. **116–18. virtue . . . it:** virtue, engrafted on our old stock (of viciousness), cannot so change the nature of the plant that no trace of the original will remain. **121. indifferent honest:** tolerably virtuous.

but yet I could accuse me of such things that it were
better my mother had not borne me: I am very proud,
revengeful, ambitious, with more offenses at my beck
than I have thoughts to put them in, imagination to   125
give them shape, or time to act them in. What should
such fellows as I do crawling between earth and
heaven? We are arrant knaves, believe none of us. Go
thy ways to a nunn'ry. Where's your father?
OPHELIA At home, my lord.   130
HAMLET Let the doors be shut upon him, that he may
play the fool no where but in 's own house. Farewell.
OPHELIA O, help him, you sweet heavens!
HAMLET If thou dost marry, I'll give thee this plague
for thy dowry: be thou as chaste as ice, as pure as   135
snow, thou shalt not escape calumny. Get thee to a
nunn'ry, farewell. Or if thou wilt needs marry, marry
a fool, for wise men know well enough what monsters
you make of them. To a nunn'ry, go, and quickly too.
Farewell.   140
OPHELIA Heavenly powers, restore him!
HAMLET I have heard of your paintings, well enough.
God hath given you one face, and you make yourselves
another. You jig and amble, and you [lisp,] you nick-
name God's creatures and make your wantonness   145
[your] ignorance. Go to, I'll no more on't, it hath
made me mad. I say we will have no moe marriage.
Those that are married already (all but one) shall live,
the rest shall keep as they are. To a nunn'ry, go.

                                                          Exit.
OPHELIA O, what a noble mind is here o'erthrown!   150
The courtier's, soldier's, scholar's, eye, tongue, sword,
Th' expectation and rose of the fair state,
The glass of fashion and the mould of form,
Th' observ'd of all observers, quite, quite down!
And I, of ladies most deject and wretched,   155
That suck'd the honey of his [music] vows,

138. monsters. Alluding to the notion that the husbands of unfaithful wives grew
horns.   **139. you:** you women.   **144-45. You . . . creatures:** i.e. you walk and
talk affectedly.   **145-46. make . . . ignorance:** excuse your affectation as ignorance.   **147. moe:** more.   **152. expectation:** hope. **rose:** ornament. **fair.** Probably
proleptic: "(the kingdom) made fair by his presence."   **153. glass:** mirror. **mould
of form:** pattern of (courtly) behavior.   **154. observ'd . . . observers.** Shakespeare
uses *observe* to mean not only "behold, mark attentively" but also "pay honor to."

Now see [that] noble and most sovereign reason
Like sweet bells jangled out of time, and harsh;
That unmatch'd form and stature of blown youth
Blasted with ecstasy. O, woe is me   160
T' have seen what I have seen, see what I see!

                                         [*Ophelia withdraws.*]

                      Enter KING *and* POLONIUS.

KING Love? his affections do not that way tend,
    Nor what he spake, though it lack'd form a little,
    Was not like madness. There's something in his soul
    O'er which his melancholy sits on brood,   165
    And I do doubt the hatch and the disclose
    Will be some danger; which for to prevent,
    I have in quick determination
    Thus set it down: he shall with speed to England
    For the demand of our neglected tribute.   170
    Haply the seas, and countries different,
    With variable objects, shall expel
    This something-settled matter in his heart,
    Whereon his brains still beating puts him thus
    From fashion of himself. What think you on't?   175
POLONIUS It shall do well; but yet do I believe
    The origin and commencement of his grief
    Sprung from neglected love.   [*Ophelia comes forward.*]
          How now, Ophelia?
    You need not tell us what Lord Hamlet said,
    We heard it all. My lord, do as you please,   180
    But if you hold it fit, after the play
    Let his queen-mother all alone entreat him,
    To show his grief. Let her be round with him,
    And I'll be plac'd (so please you) in the ear
    Of all their conference. If she find him not,   185
    To England send him, or confine him where
    Your wisdom best shall think.
KING   It shall be so.
    Madness in great ones must not [unwatch'd] go.

                                           Exeunt.

---

159. blown: in full bloom.   **160. Blasted:** withered. **ecstasy:** madness.   **162. affections:** inclinations, feelings.   **166. doubt:** fear. **disclose.** Synonymous with *hatch*; see also 5.1.287.   **178. neglected:** unrequited.   **183. his grief:** what is troubling him. **round:** blunt, outspoken.   **185. find him:** learn the truth about him.

SCENE 2

Enter HAMLET *and three of the* PLAYERS.

HAMLET Speak the speech, I pray you, as I pronounc'd
it to you, trippingly on the tongue, but if you mouth it,
as many of our players do, I had as live the town-crier
spoke my lines. Nor do not saw the air too much with
your hand, thus, but use all gently, for in the very   5
torrent, tempest, and, as I may say, whirlwind of your
passion, you must acquire and beget a temperance that
may give it smoothness. O, it offends me to the soul to
hear a robustious periwig-pated fellow tear a passion to
totters, to very rags, to spleet the ears of the   10
groundlings, who for the most part are capable of noth-
ing but inexplicable dumb shows and noise. I would
have such a fellow whipt for o'erdoing Termagant, it
out-Herods Herod, pray you avoid it.
[1.] PLAYER I warrant your honor.   15
HAMLET Be not too tame neither, but let your own
discretion be your tutor. Suit the action to the word,
the word to the action, with this special observance,
that you o'erstep not the modesty of nature: for any
thing so o'erdone is from the purpose of playing,   20
whose end, both at the first and now, was and is, to
hold as 'twere the mirror up to nature: to show virtue
her feature, scorn her own image, and the very age and
body of the time his form and pressure. Now this over-
done, or come tardy off, though it makes the un-   25
skillful laugh, cannot but make the judicious grieve; the
censure of which one must in your allowance o'er-
weigh a whole theater of others. O, there be players
that I have seen play—and heard others [praise], and
that highly—not to speak it profanely, that,   30

3.2. Location: The castle. **2. mouth:** pronounce with exaggerated distinctness
or declamatory effect. **3. live:** lief, willingly. **10. totters:** tatters. **Spleet:** split.
11. groundlings: those who paid the lowest admission price and stood on the ground
in the "yard" or pit of the theater. **capable of:** able to take in. **12. inexplicable:** incapable of being interpreted. **dumb shows:** silent, often symbolic plot-summarizing
versions of the play that was to follow, as instanced later in this very scene, ll. 135 ff. (T).
13. Termagant: a supposed god of the Saracens, whose role in medieval drama, like
that of Herod (line 14), was noisy and violent. **14. Herod:** the frustrated tetrarch of
Galilee, who failed to have killed the infant Jesus (T). **19. modesty:** moderation.
20. from: contrary to. **23. scorn:** i.e. that which is worthy of scorn. **24. pressure:**
impression (as of a seal), exact image. **25. tardy:** inadequately. **27. censure:** judgment.
which one: (even) one of whom. **allowance:** estimation. **30. profanely:** irreverently.

neither having th' accent of Christians nor the gait of
Christian, pagan, nor man, have so strutted and
bellow'd that I have thought some of Nature's journey-
men had made men, and not made them well, they
imitated humanity so abominably.   35
[1.] PLAYER I hope we have reform'd that indiffer-
ently with us, [sir].
HAMLET O, reform it altogether. And let those that
play your clowns speak no more than is set down for
them, for there be of them that will themselves   40
laugh to set on some quantity of barren spectators to
laugh too, though in the mean time some necessary
question of the play be then to be consider'd. That's
villainous, and shows a most pitiful ambition in the
fool that uses it. Go make you ready.   45

[Exeunt Players.]

Enter POLONIUS, GUILDENSTERN, *and* ROSENCRANTZ.

How now, my lord? Will the King hear this piece of
work?
POLONIUS And the Queen too, and that presently.
HAMLET Bid the players make haste.   *[Exit Polonius.]*
Will you two help to hasten them?   50
ROSENCRANTZ Ay, my lord.   *Exeunt they two.*
HAMLET What ho, Horatio!

Enter HORATIO.

HORATIO Here, sweet lord, at your service.
HAMLET Horatio, thou art e'en as just a man
As e'er my conversation cop'd withal.   55
HORATIO O my dear lord—
HAMLET   Nay, do not think I flatter,
For what advancement may I hope from thee
That no revenue hast but thy good spirits
To feed and clothe thee? Why should the poor be flatter'd?
No, let the candied tongue lick absurd pomp,   60

33–35. some . . . abominably: i.e. they were so unlike men that it seemed
Nature had not made men herself, but had delegated the task to mediocre assis-
tants. 36–37. indifferently: pretty well. 40. of them: some of them. 45. fool:
(1) stupid person; (2) actor playing a fool's role. uses it. See the Textual Notes for an
interesting passage following these words in Ql. 46–47. piece of work: masterpiece
(said jocularly). 48. presently: at once. 54. thou . . . man: i.e. you come as close
to being what a man should be (*just* = exact, precise). 55. my . . . withal: my
association with people has brought me into contact with. 60. candied: sugared,
i.e. flattering. absurd: tasteless (Latin sense).

And crook the pregnant hinges of the knee
Where thrift may follow fawning. Dost thou hear?
Since my dear soul was mistress of her choice
And could of men distinguish her election,
Sh' hath seal'd thee for herself, for thou hast been   65
As one in suff'ring all that suffers nothing,
A man that Fortune's buffets and rewards
Hast ta'en with equal thanks; and blest are those
Whose blood and judgment are so well co-meddled,
That they are not a pipe for Fortune's finger   70
To sound what stop she please. Give me that man
That is not passion's slave, and I will wear him
In my heart's core, ay, in my heart of heart,
As I do thee. Something too much of this.
There is a play to-night before the King,   75
One scene of it comes near the circumstance
Which I have told thee of my father's death.
I prithee, when thou seest that act afoot,
Even with the very comment of thy soul
Observe my uncle. If his occulted guilt   80
Do not itself unkennel in one speech,
It is a damned ghost that we have seen,
And my imaginations are as foul
As Vulcan's stithy. Give him heedful note,
For I mine eyes will rivet to his face,   85
And after we will both our judgments join
In censure of his seeming.
HORATIO   Well, my lord.
If 'a steal aught the whilst this play is playing,
And scape [detecting], I will pay the theft.

> [*Sound a flourish. Danish march.*] *Enter Trumpets and*
> *Kettle-drums,* KING, QUEEN, POLONIUS, OPHELIA,
> [ROSENCRANTZ, GUILDENSTERN, *and other* LORDS *attendant,*
> *with his* GUARD *carrying torches*].

HAMLET They are coming to the play. I must be idle;
   Get you a place.
KING How fares our cousin Hamlet?

61. pregnant: moving readily.   **62. thrift:** thriving, profit.   **69. blood:** passions. **co-meddled:** mixed, blended.   **73. my heart of heart:** the heart of my heart.   **79. very . . . soul:** your most intense critical observation.   **80. occulted:** hidden.   **81. unkennel:** bring into the open.   **82. damned ghost:** evil spirit, devil.   **84. stithy:** forge.   **87. censure . . . seeming:** reaching a verdict on his behavior.   **90. be idle:** act foolish, pretend to be crazy.   **92. fares.** Hamlet takes up this word in another sense.

HAMLET Excellent, i' faith, of the chameleon's dish:
I eat the air, promise-cramm'd—you cannot feed ca-
pons so.   95
KING I have nothing with this answer, Hamlet,
these words are not mine.
HAMLET No, nor mine now. [*To Polonius.*] My lord,
you play'd once i' th' university, you say?
POLONIUS That did I, my lord, and was accounted a good   100
actor.
HAMLET What did you enact?
POLONIUS I did enact Julius Caesar. I was kill'd i' th'
Capitol; Brutus kill'd me.
HAMLET It was a brute part of him to kill so capital a   105
calf there. Be the players ready?
ROSENCRANTZ Ay, my lord, they stay upon your patience.
QUEEN Come hither, my dear Hamlet, sit by me.
HAMLET No, good mother, here's metal more attractive.
                                        [*Lying down at Ophelia's feet.*]
POLONIUS [*To the King.*] O ho, do you mark that?
HAMLET Lady, shall I lie in your lap?
OPHELIA No, my lord.
[HAMLET I mean, my head upon your lap?
OPHELIA Ay, my lord.]   115
HAMLET Do you think I meant country matters?
OPHELIA I think nothing, my lord.
HAMLET That's a fair thought to lie between maids'
legs.
OPHELIA What is, my lord?   120
HAMLET Nothing.
OPHELIA You are merry, my lord.
HAMLET Who, I?
OPHELIA Ay, my lord.
HAMLET O God, your only jig-maker. What should a   125

---

93. chameleon's dish. Chameleons were thought to feed on air. Hamlet says that
he subsists on an equally nourishing diet, the promise of succession. There is probably a pun on *air/heir.* **96. have nothing with:** do not understand. **97. mine:**
i.e. an answer to my question. **104. Brutus killed me.** Something of an in-joke,
as Burbage, who played Brutus in *Julius Caesar* a year previously is now in the role of
Hamlet, who is soon to kill Polonius, played by the same actor who had performed
the role of Caesar (T). **105. part:** action. **116. country matters:** indecency, as
from the vulgar pun on the first syllable (T). **125. only:** very best. **jig-maker:**
one who composed or played in the farcical song-and-dance entertainments that
followed plays.

man do but be merry, for look you how cheerfully my
mother looks, and my father died within 's two hours.
OPHELIA Nay, 'tis twice two months, my lord.
HAMLET So long? Nay then let the dev'l wear black,
for I'll have a suit of sables. O heavens, die two   130
months ago, and not forgotten yet? Then there's hope
a great man's memory may outlive his life half a year,
but, by'r lady, 'a must build churches then, or else shall
'a suffer not thinking on, with the hobby-horse, whose
epitaph is, "For O, for O, the hobby-horse is forgot."   135

The trumpets sounds. Dumb show follows.

*Enter a King and a Queen [very lovingly], the Queen
embracing him and he her. [She kneels and makes show
of protestation unto him.] He takes her up and declines
his head upon her neck. He lies him down upon a bank
of flowers. She, seeing him asleep, leaves him. Anon
come in another man, takes off his crown, kisses it,
pours poison in the sleeper's ears, and leaves him. The
Queen returns, finds the King dead, makes passionate
action. The pois'ner with some three or four [mutes]
come in again, seem to condole with her. The dead
body is carried away. The pois'ner woos the Queen
with gifts; she seems harsh [and unwilling] awhile,
but in the end accepts love.*   [*Exeunt.*]

OPHELIA What means this, my lord?
HAMLET Marry, this' [miching] mallecho, it means mischief.
OPHELIA Belike this show imports the argument of
the play.   140

Enter PROLOGUE.

HAMLET We shall know by this fellow. The players
cannot keep [counsel], they'll tell all.
OPHELIA Will 'a tell us what this show meant?
HAMLET Ay, or any show that you will show him.
Be not you asham'd to show, he'll not shame to tell you   145
what it means.

---

127. 's: this.   **129–30. let . . . sables:** i.e. to the devil with my garments; after so long
a time I am ready for the old man's garb of sables (fine fur).   **134. not thinking
on:** not being thought of, i.e. being forgotten.   **135. For . . . forgot:** line from a popular
ballad lamenting puritanical suppression of such country sports as the May-games,
in which the hobby-horse, a character costumed to resemble a horse, traditionally
appeared.   **137. this' miching mallecho:** this is sneaking mischief.   **139. argument:** subject, plot.   **142. counsel.** secrets.   **145. Be not you:** if you are not.

OPHELIA You are naught, you are naught. I'll mark
    the play.

PROLOGUE For us, and for our tragedy,
    Here stooping to your clemency,   150
    We beg your hearing patiently.   [*Exit.*]

HAMLET Is this a prologue, or the posy of a ring?

OPHELIA 'Tis brief, my lord.

HAMLET As woman's love.

Enter [two Players,] KING *and* QUEEN.

[P.] KING Full thirty times hath Phoebus' cart gone round   155
    Neptune's salt wash and Tellus' orbed ground,
    And thirty dozen moons with borrowed sheen
    About the world have times twelve thirties been,
    Since love our hearts and Hymen did our hands
    Unite comutual in most sacred bands.   160

[P.] QUEEN So many journeys may the sun and moon
    Make us again count o'er ere love be done!
    But woe is me, you are so sick of late,
    So far from cheer and from [your] former state,
    That I distrust you. Yet though I distrust,   165
    Discomfort you, my lord, it nothing must,
    [For] women's fear and love hold quantity,
    In neither aught, or in extremity.
    Now what my [love] is, proof hath made you know,
    And as my love is siz'd, my fear is so.   170
    Where love is great, the littlest doubts are fear;
    Where little fears grow great, great love grows there.

[P.] KING Faith, I must leave thee, love, and shortly too;
    My operant powers their functions leave to do,
    And thou shalt live in this fair world behind,   175
    Honor'd, belov'd, and haply one as kind
    For husband shalt thou—

[P.] QUEEN   O, confound the rest!
    Such love must needs be treason in my breast.
    In second husband let me be accurs'd!

---

147. naught: wicked.   **152. posy . . . ring:** verse motto inscribed in a ring (necessarily short).   **155–73.** See the Textual Notes for the corresponding lines in Q1.   **155. Phoebus' cart:** the sun-god's chariot.   **156. Tellus:** goddess of the earth.   **159. Hymen:** god of marriage.   **160. bands:** bonds.   **165. distrust:** fear for.   **167. hold quantity:** are related in direct proportion.   **169. proof:** experience.   **174. operant:** active, vital. **leave to do:** cease to perform.   **177. confound the rest:** may destruction befall what you are about to speak of—a second marriage on my part.

None wed the second but who kill'd the first.   180
HAMLET [*Aside.*] That's wormwood!
[P. QUEEN] The instances that second marriage move
  Are base respects of thrift, but none of love.
  A second time I kill my husband dead,
  When second husband kisses me in bed.   185
[P.] KING I do believe you think what now you speak,
  But what we do determine, oft we break.
  Purpose is but the slave to memory,
  Of violent birth, but poor validity,
  Which now, the fruit unripe, sticks on the tree,   190
  But fall unshaken when they mellow be.
  Most necessary 'tis that we forget
  To pay ourselves what to ourselves is debt.
  What to ourselves in passion we propose,
  The passion ending, doth the purpose lose.   195
  The violence of either grief or joy
  Their own enactures with themselves destroy.
  Where joy most revels, grief doth most lament;
  Grief [joys], joy grieves, on slender accident.
  This world is not for aye, nor 'tis not strange   200
  That even our loves should with our fortunes change:
  For 'tis a question left us yet to prove,
  Whether love lead fortune, or else fortune love.
  The great man down, you mark his favorite flies,
  The poor advanc'd makes friends of enemies.   205
  And hitherto doth love on fortune tend,
  For who not needs shall never lack a friend,
  And who in want a hollow friend doth try,
  Directly seasons him his enemy.
  But orderly to end where I begun,   210
  Our wills and fates do so contrary run
  That our devices still are overthrown,
  Our thoughts are ours, their ends none of our own:
  So think thou wilt no second husband wed,

---

181. wormwood: a noun used as an adjective, meaning "bitter" (T).   **182. instances:** motives. **move:** give rise to.   **183. respects of thrift:** considerations of advantage.   **189. validity:** strength, power to last.   **192–93. Most . . . debt:** i.e. such resolutions are debts we owe to ourselves, and it would be foolish to pay such debts.   **194. passion:** violent emotion.   **196–97. The violence . . . destroy:** i.e. both violent grief and violent joy fail of their intended acts because they destroy themselves by their very violence.   **199. slender accident:** slight occasion.   **209. seasons:** ripens, converts into.   **212. devices:** devisings, intentions. **still:** always.

But die thy thoughts when thy first lord is dead.   215
[P.] QUEEN Nor earth to me give food, nor heaven light,
    Sport and repose lock from me day and night,
    To desperation turn my trust and hope,
    [An] anchor's cheer in prison be my scope!
    Each opposite that blanks the face of joy   220
    Meet what I would have well and it destroy!
    Both here and hence pursue me lasting strife,
    If once a widow, ever I be wife!
HAMLET If she should break it now!
[P.] KING 'Tis deeply sworn. Sweet, leave me here a while,   225
    My spirits grow dull, and fain I would beguile
    The tedious day with sleep.   [*Sleeps.*]
[P.] QUEEN   Sleep rock thy brain,
    And never come mischance between us twain!   *Exit.*
HAMLET Madam, how like you this play?
QUEEN The lady doth protest too much, methinks.   230
HAMLET O but she'll keep her word.
KING Have you heard the argument? is there no
    offense in't?
HAMLET No, no, they do but jest, poison in jest—no
    offense i' th' world.   235
KING What do you call the play?
HAMLET "The Mouse-trap." Marry, how? tropi-
    cally: this play is the image of a murther done in
    Vienna; Gonzago is the duke's name, his wife,
    Baptista. You shall see anon. 'Tis a knavish piece   240
    of work, but what of that? Your Majesty, and we that
    have free souls, it touches us not. Let the gall'd jade
    winch, our withers are unwrung.

Enter LUCIANUS.

This is one Lucianus, nephew to the king.
OPHELIA You are as good as a chorus, my lord.   245

---

219. anchor's cheer: hermit's fare. **my scope:** the extent of my comforts.
220. blanks: blanches, makes pale (a symptom of grief). **233. offense:** offensive matter (but Hamlet quibbles on the sense "crime"). **234. jest:** i.e. pretend.
237–38. tropically: figuratively (with play on *trapically*—which is the reading of
Q1—and probably with allusion to the children's saying *marry trap,* meaning "now
you're caught"). **238. image:** representation. **242. free souls:** clear consciences.
gall'd jade: chafed horse. **243. winch:** wince. **withers:** ridge between a horse's
shoulders. **unwrung:** not rubbed sore. **245. chorus:** i.e. one who explains the
forthcoming action.

HAMLET I could interpret between you and your love,
if I could see the puppets dallying.
OPHELIA You are keen, my lord, you are keen.
HAMLET It would cost you a groaning to take off
mine edge.   250
OPHELIA Still better, and worse.
HAMLET So you mistake your husbands. Begin,
murtherer, leave thy damnable faces and begin. Come,
the croaking raven doth bellow for revenge.
LUCIANUS Thoughts black, hands apt, drugs fit, and time agreeing, 255
[Confederate] season, else no creature seeing,
Thou mixture rank, of midnight weeds collected,
With Hecat's ban thrice blasted, thrice [infected],
Thy natural magic and dire property
On wholesome life usurps immediately.   260
                              [*Pours the poison in his ears.*]
HAMLET 'A poisons him i' th' garden for his estate.
His name's Gonzago, the story is extant, and written
in very choice Italian. You shall see anon how the
murtherer gets the love of Gonzago's wife.
OPHELIA The King rises.   265
[HAMLET What, frighted with false fire?]
QUEEN How fares my lord?
POLONIUS Give o'er the play.
KING Give me some light. Away!
POLONIUS Lights, lights, lights!   270
                              Exeunt all but Hamlet and Horatio.
HAMLET   "Why, let the strooken deer go weep,
                  The hart ungalled play,
            For some must watch while some
                  must sleep,
            Thus runs the world away."
Would not this, sir, and a forest of feathers—if the rest   275

246–47. I . . . dallying: I could speak the dialogue between you and your lover like a puppet-master (with an indecent jest).   **248. keen:** bitter, sharp.   **251. better, and worse:** i.e. more pointed and less decent.   **252. So:** i.e. "for better, for worse," in the words of the marriage service. **mistake:** i.e. mis-take, take wrongfully. Their vows, Hamlet suggests, prove false.   **253. faces:** facial expressions.   **254. the croaking . . . revenge.** Misquoted from an old play, *The True Tragedy of Richard III.*   **256. Confederate season:** the time being my ally.   **258. Hecat's ban:** the curse of Hecate, goddess of witchcraft.   **266. false fire:** i.e. a blank cartridge.   **271. strooken:** struck, i.e. wounded.   **272. ungalled:** unwounded.   **273. watch:** stay awake.   **275. feathers:** the plumes worn by tragic actors.

of my fortunes turn Turk with me—with [two] Pro-
vincial roses on my raz'd shoes, get me a fellowship
in a cry of players?
HORATIO Half a share.
HAMLET A whole one, I.   280
"For thou dost know, O Damon dear,
    This realm dismantled was
Of Jove himself, and now reigns here
    A very, very"—pajock.
HORATIO You might have rhym'd.   285
HAMLET O good Horatio, I'll take the ghost's word
for a thousand pound. Didst perceive?
HORATIO Very well, my lord.
HAMLET Upon the talk of the pois'ning?
HORATIO I did very well note him.   290
HAMLET Ah, ha! Come, some music! Come, the
recorders!
          For if the King like not the comedy,
          Why then belike he likes it not, perdy.
Come, some music!   295

          Enter ROSENCRANTZ *and* GUILDENSTERN.

GUILDENSTERN Good my lord, voutsafe me a word with
you.
HAMLET Sir, a whole history.
GUILDENSTERN The King, sir—
HAMLET Ay, sir, what of him?   300
GUILDENSTERN Is in his retirement marvellous distemp'red.
HAMLET With drink, sir?
GUILDENSTERN No, my lord, with choler.
HAMLET Your wisdom should show itself more richer
to signify this to the doctor, for for me to put him to   305
his purgation would perhaps plunge him into more
choler.

---

276. turn Turk: i.e. go to the bad. 276–77. Provincial roses: rosettes designed to
look like a variety of French rose. 277. raz'd: with decorating slashing. fellowship: partnership. 278. cry: company. 281. Damon: standard pastoral name for
an ideal friend (T). 282. dismantled: divested, deprived. 284. pajock: peacock
(substituting for an expected rhyme-word ending in -as. (T)). The natural history
of the time attributed many vicious qualities to the peacock. Other birds suggested
include "puttock," a kite-like scavenger (T). 285. might have rhymed. Horatio
is perhaps suggesting "Claudi-ass" (T). 294. perdy: assuredly (French pardieu, "by
God"). 303. choler: anger (but Hamlet willfully takes up the word in the sense
"biliousness"). 305–6. put . . . purgation: i.e. prescribe for what's wrong with him.

GUILDENSTERN Good my lord, put your discourse into some
  frame, and [start] not so wildly from my affair.
HAMLET I am tame, sir. Pronounce.   310
GUILDENSTERN The Queen, your mother, in most great
  affliction of spirit, hath sent me to you.
HAMLET You are welcome.
GUILDENSTERN Nay, good my lord, this courtesy is not of the
  right breed. If it shall please you to make me a   315
  wholesome answer, I will do your mother's commandement; if not, your pardon and my return shall be the
  end of [my] business.
HAMLET Sir, I cannot.
ROSENCRANTZ What, my lord?   320
HAMLET Make you a wholesome answer—my wit's
  diseas'd. But, sir, such answer as I can make, you
  shall command, or rather, as you say, my mother.
  Therefore no more, but to the matter: my mother, you
  say—   325
ROSENCRANTZ Then thus she says: your behavior hath strook
  her into amazement and admiration.
HAMLET O wonderful son, that can so stonish a
  mother! But is there no sequel at the heels of this
  mother's admiration? Impart.   330
ROSENCRANTZ She desires to speak with you in her closet ere
  you go to bed.
HAMLET We shall obey, were she ten times our
  mother. Have you any further trade with us?
ROSENCRANTZ My lord, you once did love me.   335
HAMLET And do still, by these pickers and stealers.
ROSENCRANTZ Good my lord, what is your cause of dis-
  temper? You do surely bar the door upon your own
  liberty if you deny your griefs to your friend.
HAMLET Sir, I lack advancement.   340
ROSENCRANTZ How can that be, when you have the voice of
  the King himself for your succession in Denmark?
HAMLET Ay, sir, but "While the grass grows"—the
  proverb is something musty.

---

309. frame: logical structure. **316. wholesome:** sensible, rational. **317. pardon:**
permission for departure. **327. amazement and admiration:** bewilderment and
wonder. **328. stonish:** astound. **331. closet:** private room. **336. pickers and
stealers:** hands; which, as the Catechism says, we must keep "from picking and
stealing." **344. proverb:** i.e. "While the grass grows, the steed starves." **something
musty:** somewhat stale.

Enter the PLAYERS *with recorders.*

O, the recorders! Let me see one.—To withdraw with   345
you—why do you go about to recover the wind of me,
as if you would drive me into a toil?
GUILDENSTERN O my lord, if my duty be too bold, my love
is too unmannerly.
HAMLET I do not well understand that. Will you play   350
upon this pipe?
GUILDENSTERN My lord, I cannot.
HAMLET I pray you.
GUILDENSTERN Believe me, I cannot.
HAMLET I do beseech you.   355
GUILDENSTERN I know no touch of it, my lord.
HAMLET It is as easy as lying. Govern these ventages
with your fingers and [thumbs], give it breath with
your mouth, and it will discourse most eloquent music.
Look you, these are the stops.   360
GUILDENSTERN But these cannot I command to any utt'rance
of harmony. I have not the skill.
HAMLET Why, look you now, how unworthy a thing
you make of me! You would play upon me, you would
seem to know my stops, you would pluck out the   365
heart of my mystery, you would sound me from my
lowest note to [the top of] my compass; and there is
much music, excellent voice, in this little organ, yet
cannot you make it speak. 'Sblood, do you think I am
easier to be play'd on than a pipe? Call me what   370
instrument you will, though you fret me, [yet] you
cannot play upon me.

Enter POLONIUS.

God bless you, sir.
POLONIUS My lord, the Queen would speak with you,
and presently.   375
HAMLET Do you see yonder cloud that's almost in
shape of a camel?
POLONIUS By th' mass and 'tis, like a camel indeed.
HAMLET Methinks it is like a weasel.
POLONIUS It is back'd like a weasel.   380
HAMLET Or like a whale.

---

346. recover the wind: get to windward. **347. toil:** snare. **357. ventages:**
stops. **368. organ:** instrument. **371. fret:** (1) finger (an instrument); (2)
vex. **375. presently:** at once.

POLONIUS Very like a whale.
HAMLET Then I will come to my mother by and by.
[*Aside.*] They fool me to the top of my bent.—I will
come by and by.   385
[POLONIUS] I will say so.   [*Exit.*]
HAMLET "By and by" is easily said. Leave me,
friends.   [*Exeunt all but Hamlet.*]
'Tis now the very witching time of night,
When churchyards yawn and hell itself [breathes] out
Contagion to this world. Now could I drink hot blood,   390
And do such [bitter business as the] day
Would quake to look on. Soft, now to my mother.
O heart, lose not thy nature! let not ever
The soul of Nero enter this firm bosom,
Let me be cruel, not unnatural;   395
I will speak [daggers] to her, but use none.
My tongue and soul in this be hypocrites—
How in my words somever she be shent,
To give them seals never my soul consent!   *Exit.*

SCENE 3

Enter KING, ROSENCRANTZ, *and* GUILDENSTERN.

KING I like him not, nor stands it safe with us
To let his madness range. Therefore prepare you.
I your commission will forthwith dispatch,
And he to England shall along with you.
The terms of our estate may not endure   5
Hazard so near 's as doth hourly grow
Out of his brows.
GUILDENSTERN We will ourselves provide.
Most holy and religious fear it is
To keep those many many bodies safe
That live and feed upon your Majesty.   10
ROSENCRANTZ The single and peculiar life is bound

---

384. They . . . bent: they make me play the fool to the limit of my ability. **385. by and by:** at once. **388. witching:** i.e. when the powers of evil are at large. **393. nature:** natural affection, filial feeling. **394. Nero.** Murderer of his mother. **398. shent:** rebuked. **399. give them seals:** confirm them by deeds. 3.3. Location: The castle. **1. him:** i.e. his state of mind, his behavior. **3. dispatch:** have drawn up. **5. terms:** conditions, nature. **our estate:** my position (as king). **7. his brows:** the madness visible in his face (?). **8. fear:** concern. **11. single and peculiar:** individual and private.

With all the strength and armor of the mind
To keep itself from noyance, but much more
That spirit upon whose weal depends and rests
The lives of many. The cess of majesty   15
Dies not alone, but like a gulf doth draw
What's near it with it. Or it is a massy wheel
Fix'd on the summit of the highest mount,
To whose [huge] spokes ten thousand lesser things
Are mortis'd and adjoin'd, which when it falls,   20
Each small annexment, petty consequence,
Attends the boist'rous [ruin]. Never alone
Did the King sigh, but [with] a general groan.
KING Arm you, I pray you, to this speedy viage,
For we will fetters put about this fear,   25
Which now goes too free-footed.
ROSENCRANTZ   We will haste us.
            Exeunt Gentlemen [Rosencrantz and Guildenstern].

            Enter POLONIUS.

POLONIUS My lord, he's going to his mother's closet.
Behind the arras I'll convey myself
To hear the process. I'll warrant she'll tax him home,
And as you said, and wisely was it said,   30
'Tis meet that some more audience than a mother,
Since nature makes them partial, should o'erhear
The speech, of vantage. Fare you well, my liege,
I'll call upon you ere you go to bed,
And tell you what I know.
KING   Thanks, dear my lord.   35
                                        Exit [Polonius].

O, my offense is rank, it smells to heaven,
It hath the primal eldest curse upon't,
A brother's murther. Pray can I not,
Though inclination be as sharp as will.
My stronger guilt defeats my strong intent,   40
And, like a man to double business bound,

---

13. noyance: injury.   **15. cess:** cessation, death.   **16. gulf:** whirlpool.   **20. mortis'd:** fixed.   **22. Attends:** accompanies. **ruin:** fall.   **24. Arm:** prepare. **viage:** voyage. **25. fear:** object of fear.   **29. process:** course of the talk. **tax him home:** take him severely to task.   **33. of vantage:** from an advantageous position (?) or in addition (?). **36–72.** See the Textual Notes for the corresponding lines in Q1.   **37. primal eldest curse:** i.e. God's curse on Cain, who also slew his brother.   **39. Though . . . will:** though my desire is as strong as my resolve to do so.   **41. bound:** committed.

I stand in pause where I shall first begin,
And both neglect. What if this cursed hand
Were thicker than itself with brother's blood,
Is there not rain enough in the sweet heavens   45
To wash it white as snow? Whereto serves mercy
But to confront the visage of offense?
And what's in prayer but this twofold force,
To be forestalled ere we come to fall,
Or [pardon'd] being down? then I'll look up.   50
My fault is past, but, O, what form of prayer
Can serve my turn? "Forgive me my foul murther"?
That cannot be, since I am still possess'd
Of those effects for which I did the murther:
My crown, mine own ambition, and my queen.   55
May one be pardon'd and retain th' offense?
In the corrupted currents of this world
Offense's gilded hand may [shove] by justice,
And oft 'tis seen the wicked prize itself
Buys out the law, but 'tis not so above: 60
There is no shuffling, there the action lies
In his true nature, and we ourselves compell'd,
Even to the teeth and forehead of our faults,
To give in evidence. What then? What rests?
Try what repentance can. What can it not?   65
Yet what can it, when one can not repent?
O wretched state! O bosom black as death!
O limed soul, that struggling to be free
Art more engag'd! Help, angels! Make assay,
Bow, stubborn knees, and heart, with strings of steel,   70
Be soft as sinews of the new-born babe!
All may be well.   [He kneels.]

Enter HAMLET.

HAMLET Now might I do it [pat], now 'a is a-praying;
And now I'll do't—and so 'a goes to heaven,
And so am I [reveng'd]. That would be scann'd: 75

43. **neglect:** omit. 46–47. **Whereto . . . offense:** i.e. what function has mercy except when there has been sin. 56. **th' offense:** i.e. the "effects" or fruits of the offense. 57. **currents:** courses. 58. **gilded:** i.e. bribing. 59. **wicked prize:** rewards of vice. 61. **shuffling:** evasion. **the action lies:** the charge comes for legal consideration. 63. **Even . . . forehead:** i.e. fully recognizing their features, extenuating nothing. 64. **rests:** remains. 68. **limed:** caught (as in birdlime, a sticky substance used for catching birds). 69. **engag'd:** entangled. 75. **would be scann'd:** must be carefully considered.

A villain kills my father, and for that
I, his sole son, do this same villain send
To heaven.
Why, this is [hire and salary], not revenge.
'A took my father grossly, full of bread,   80
With all his crimes broad blown, as flush as May,
And how his audit stands who knows save heaven?
But in our circumstance and course of thought
'Tis heavy with him. And am I then revenged,
To take him in the purging of his soul,   85
When he is fit and season'd for his passage?
No!
Up, sword, and know thou a more horrid hent:
When he is drunk asleep, or in his rage,
Or in th' incestious pleasure of his bed,   90
At game a-swearing, or about some act
That has no relish of salvation in't—
Then trip him, that his heels may kick at heaven,
And that his soul may be as damn'd and black
As hell, whereto it goes. My mother stays,   95
This physic but prolongs thy sickly days.   *Exit.*
KING [*Rising.*] My words fly up, my thoughts
    remain below:
Words without thoughts never to heaven go.   *Exit.*

SCENE 4

Enter [QUEEN] GERTRUDE *and* POLONIUS.

POLONIUS 'A will come straight. Look you lay home to him.
    Tell him his pranks have been too broad to bear with,
    And that your Grace hath screen'd and stood between
    Much heat and him. I'll silence me even here;
    Pray you be round [with him].   5
QUEEN I'll [warr'nt] you, fear me not. Withdraw,
    I hear him coming.   [*Polonius hides behind the arras.*]

80. **grossly:** in a gross state; not spiritually prepared.   81. **crimes:** sins. **broad blown:** in full bloom. **flush:** lusty, vigorous.   82. **audit:** account.   83. **in . . . thought:** i.e. to the best of our knowledge and belief.   88. **Up:** into the sheath. **know . . . bent:** be grasped at a more dreadful time. **hent:** hint, meaning occasion, chance, opportunity (T).   92. **relish:** trace.   96. **physic:** (attempted) remedy, i.e. prayer.   3.4. Location: The Queen's closet in the castle.   1. **lay . . . him:** reprove him severely.   2. **broad:** unrestrained.   5. **round:** plain-spoken.   6. **fear me not:** have no fears about my handling of the situation.

Enter HAMLET.

HAMLET Now, mother, what's the matter?
QUEEN Hamlet, thou hast thy father much offended.
HAMLET Mother, you have my father much offended.   10
QUEEN Come, come, you answer with an idle tongue.
HAMLET Go, go, you question with a wicked tongue.
QUEEN Why, how now, Hamlet?
HAMLET   What's the matter now?
QUEEN Have you forgot me?
HAMLET   No, by the rood, not so:
   You are the Queen, your husband's brother's wife,   15
   And would it were not so, you are my mother.
QUEEN Nay, then I'll set those to you that can speak.
HAMLET Come, come, and sit you down, you shall not boudge;
   You go not till I set you up a glass
   Where you may see the [inmost] part of you.   20
QUEEN What wilt thou do? Thou wilt not murther me?
   Help ho!
POLONIUS [*Behind.*] What ho, help!
HAMLET [*Drawing.*]   How now? A rat? Dead, for a ducat,
   dead!   [*Kills Polonius through the arras.*]
POLONIUS [*Behind.*] O, I am slain.
QUEEN   O me, what hast thou done?   25
HAMLET Nay, I know not, is it the King?
QUEEN O, what a rash and bloody deed is this!
HAMLET A bloody deed! almost as bad, good mother,
   As kill a king, and marry with his brother.
QUEEN As kill a king!
HAMLET   Ay, lady, it was my word.   30
                          [*Parts the arras and discovers Polonius.*]
   Thou wretched, rash, intruding fool, farewell!
   I took thee for thy better. Take thy fortune;
   Thou find'st to be too busy is some danger.—
   Leave wringing of your hands. Peace, sit you down,
   And let me wring your heart, for so I shall   35
   If it be made of penetrable stuff,
   If damned custom have not brass'd it so
   That it be proof and bulwark against sense.

11. idle: foolish. **14. rood:** cross. **18. boudge:** budge. **24. for a ducat:** I'll
wager a ducat. A ducat is a gold coin, here indicating Hamlet's confidence in his
judgment as to the fate but not the identity of the victim (T). **33. busy:** officious,
meddlesome. **37. damned custom:** i.e. the habit of ill-doing. **brass'd:** hardened,
literally, plated with brass. **38. proof:** armor. **sense:** feeling.

QUEEN What have I done, that thou dar'st wag thy tongue
In noise so rude against me?
HAMLET   Such an act   40
That blurs the grace and blush of modesty,
Calls virtue hypocrite, takes off the rose
From the fair forehead of an innocent love
And sets a blister there, makes marriage vows
As false as dicers' oaths, O, such a deed   45
As from the body of contraction plucks
The very soul, and sweet religion makes
A rhapsody of words. Heaven's face does glow
O'er this solidity and compound mass
With heated visage, as against the doom;   50
Is thought-sick at the act.
QUEEN   Ay me, what act,
That roars so loud and thunders in the index?
HAMLET Look here upon this picture, and on this,
The counterfeit presentment of two brothers.
See what a grace was seated on this brow: 55
Hyperion's curls, the front of Jove himself,
An eye like Mars, to threaten and command,
A station like the herald Mercury
New lighted on a [heaven-]kissing hill,
A combination and a form indeed,   60
Where every god did seem to set his seal
To give the world assurance of a man.
This was your husband. Look you now what follows:
Here is your husband, like a mildewed ear,
Blasting his wholesome brother. Have you eyes?   65
Could you on this fair mountain leave to feed,
And batten on this moor? ha, have you eyes?
You cannot call it love, for at your age
The heyday in the blood is tame, it's humble,
And waits upon the judgment, and what judgment   70
Would step from this to this? Sense sure you have,

44. blister: brand of shame.   **46. contraction:** the making of contracts, i.e. the assuming of solemn obligation.   **47. religion:** i.e. sacred vows.   **48. rhapsody:** miscellaneous collection, jumble. **glow:** i.e. with anger.   **49. this . . . mass:** i.e. the earth. *Compound* = compounded of the four elements.   **50. as . . . doom:** as if for Judgment Day.   **52. index:** i.e. table of contents. The index was formerly placed at the beginning of a book.   **54. counterfeit presentment:** painted likenesses.   **56. Hyperion's:** the sun-god's. **front:** forehead.   **58. station:** bearing.   **64. ear:** i.e. of grain.   **65. blasting:** infecting (T).   **67. batten:** gorge.   **69. heyday:** excitement.   **71. Sense:** sense perception, the five senses.

Else could you not have motion, but sure that sense
Is apoplex'd, for madness would not err,
Nor sense to ecstasy was ne'er so thrall'd
But it reserv'd some quantity of choice   75
To serve in such a difference. What devil was't
That thus hath cozen'd you at hoodman-blind?
Eyes without feeling, feeling without sight,
Ears without hands or eyes, smelling sans all,
Or but a sickly part of one true sense   80
Could not so mope. O shame, where is thy blush?
Rebellious hell,
If thou canst mutine in a matron's bones,
To flaming youth let virtue be as wax
And melt in her own fire. Proclaim no shame   85
When the compulsive ardure gives the charge,
Since frost itself as actively doth burn,
And reason [panders] will.
QUEEN   O Hamlet, speak no more!
Thou turn'st my [eyes into my very] soul,
And there I see such black and [grained] spots   90
As will [not] leave their tinct.
HAMLET   Nay, but to live
In the rank sweat of an enseamed bed,
Stew'd in corruption, honeying and making love
Over the nasty sty!
QUEEN   O, speak to me no more!
These words like daggers enter in my ears.   95
No more, sweet Hamlet!
HAMLET   A murtherer and a villain!
A slave that is not twentith part the [tithe]
Of your precedent lord, a Vice of kings,
A cutpurse of the empire and the rule,
That from a shelf the precious diadem stole,   100
And put it in his pocket—
QUEEN   No more!

73. apoplex'd: paralyzed.   73–76. madness . . . difference: i.e. madness itself could
not go so far astray, nor were the senses ever so enslaved by lunacy that they did
not retain the power to make so obvious a distinction.   77. cozen'd: cheated.
hoodman-blind: blindman's bluff.   79. sans: without.   81. mope: be dazed.
83. mutine: rebel.   85–88. Proclaim . . . will: do not call it sin when the hot
blood of youth is responsible for lechery, since here we see people of calmer age on
fire for it; and reason acts as procurer for desire, instead of restraining it. *Ardure* =
ardor.   90. grained: fast-dyed, indelible.   91. leave their tinct: lose their color.
92. enseamed: greasy.   97. twentith: twentieth.   98. precedent: former. Vice:
buffoon (like the Vice of the morality plays).

Enter GHOST [*in his night-gown*].

HAMLET A king of shreds and patches—
Save me, and hover o'er me with your wings,
You heavenly guards! What would your gracious figure?
QUEEN Alas, he's mad!   105
HAMLET Do you not come your tardy son to chide,
That, laps'd in time and passion, lets go by
Th' important acting of your dread command?
O, say!
GHOST. Do not forget! This visitation   110
Is but to whet thy almost blunted purpose.
But look, amazement on thy mother sits,
O, step between her and her fighting soul.
Conceit in weakest bodies strongest works,
Speak to her, Hamlet.
HAMLET   How is it with you, lady?   115
QUEEN Alas, how is't with you,
That you do bend your eye on vacancy,
And with th' incorporal air do hold discourse?
Forth at your eyes your spirits wildly peep,
And as the sleeping soldiers in th' alarm,   120
Your bedded hair, like life in excrements,
Start up and stand an end. O gentle son,
Upon the heat and flame of thy distemper
Sprinkle cool patience. Whereon do you look?
HAMLET On him, on him! look you how pale he glares!   125
His form and cause conjoin'd, preaching to stones,
Would make them capable.—Do not look upon me,
Lest with this piteous action you convert
My stern effects, then what I have to do
Will want true color—tears perchance for blood.   130
QUEEN To whom do you speak this?
HAMLET   Do you see nothing there?
QUEEN Nothing at all, yet all that is I see.
HAMLET Nor did you nothing hear?

101 s.d. **night-gown:** dressing gown. **102. of . . . patches:** clownish (alluding to
the motley worn by jesters) (?) or patched-up, beggarly (?). **107. laps'd . . . passion:**
"having suffered time to slip and passion to cool" (Johnson). **108. important:**
urgent. **112. amazement:** utter bewilderment. **114. Conceit:** imagination.
120. in th' alarm: when the call to arms is sounded. **121. excrements:** out-
growths; here, hair (also used of nails). **122. an end:** on end. **124. patience:** self-
control. **126. His . . . cause:** his appearance and what he has to say. **127. capable:**
sensitive, receptive. **128. convert:** alter. **129. effects:** (purposed) actions.
130. want true color: lack its proper appearance.

QUEEN   No, nothing but ourselves.
HAMLET Why, look you there, look how it steals away!
My father, in his habit as he lived!   135
Look where he goes, even now, out at the portal!

Exit Ghost.

QUEEN This is the very coinage of your brain,
This bodiless creation ecstasy
Is very cunning in.
HAMLET   [Ecstasy?]
My pulse as yours doth temperately keep time,   140
And makes as healthful music. It is not madness
That I have utt'red. Bring me to the test,
And [I] the matter will reword, which madness
Would gambol from. Mother, for love of grace,
Lay not that flattering unction to your soul,   145
That not your trespass but my madness speaks;
It will but skin and film the ulcerous place,
Whiles rank corruption, mining all within,
Infects unseen. Confess yourself to heaven,
Repent what's past, avoid what is to come,   150
And do not spread the compost on the weeds
To make them ranker. Forgive me this my virtue,
For in the fatness of these pursy times
Virtue itself of vice must pardon beg,
Yea, curb and woo for leave to do him good.   155
QUEEN O Hamlet, thou hast cleft my heart in twain.
HAMLET O, throw away the worser part of it,
And [live] the purer with the other half.
Good night, but go not to my uncle's bed—
Assume a virtue, if you have it not.   160
That monster custom, who all sense doth eat,
Of habits devil, is angel yet in this,
That to the use of actions fair and good
He likewise gives a frock or livery
That aptly is put on. Refrain [to-]night,   165

---

135. habit: dress. **137–216.** See the Textual Notes for the conclusion of the scene in Ql. **138. ecstasy:** madness. **144. gambol:** start, jerk away. **145. flattering unction:** soothing ointment. **151. compost:** manure. **153. pursy:** puffy, out of condition. **155. curb and woo:** bow and entreat. **161. all . . . eat:** wears away all natural feeling. **162. Of habits devil:** i.e. though it acts like a devil in establishing bad habits. Most editors read (in lines 161–62) *eat/Of habits evil,* following Theobald. **164–65. frock . . . on:** i.e. a "habit" or customary garment, readily put on without need of any decision.

And that shall lend a kind of easiness
To the next abstinence, the next more easy;
For use almost can change the stamp of nature,
And either [. . . .] the devil or throw him out
With wondrous potency. Once more good night,   170
And when you are desirous to be blest,
I'll blessing beg of you. For this same lord,

                               [*Pointing to Polonius.*]

I do repent; but heaven hath pleas'd it so
To punish me with this, and this with me,
That I must be their scourge and minister.   175
I will bestow him, and will answer well
The death I gave him. So again good night.
I must be cruel only to be kind.
This bad begins and worse remains behind.
One word more, good lady.
QUEEN   What shall I do?   180
HAMLET Not this, by no means, that I bid you do:
Let the bloat king tempt you again to bed,
Pinch wanton on your cheek, call you his mouse,
And let him, for a pair of reechy kisses,
Or paddling in your neck with his damn'd fingers,   185
Make you to ravel all this matter out,
That I essentially am not in madness,
But mad in craft. 'Twere good you let him know,
For who that's but a queen, fair, sober, wise,
Would from a paddock, from a bat, a gib,   190
Such dear concernings hide? Who would do so?
No, in despite of sense and secrecy,
Unpeg the basket on the house's top,
Let the birds fly, and like the famous ape,
To try conclusions in the basket creep,   195
And break your own neck down.

---

168. use: habit.   **169.** A word seems to be wanting after *either:* for conjectures see the Textual Notes.   **171. desirous . . . blest:** i.e. repentant.   **175. scourge and minister:** the agent of heavenly justice against human crime. *Scourge* suggests a permissive cruelty (Tamburlaine was the "scourge of God"), but "woe to him by whom the offense cometh"; the scourge must suffer for the evil it performs.   **176. bestow:** dispose of. **answer:** answer for. **179. behind:** to come.   **184. reechy:** filthy.   **190. paddock:** toad. **gib:** tom-cat.   **191. dear concernings:** matters of intense concern.   **193. Unpeg the basket:** open the door of the cage.   **194. famous ape.** The actual story has been lost.   **195. conclusions:** experiments (to see whether he too can fly if he enters the cage and then leaps out).   **196. down:** by the fall.

QUEEN Be thou assur'd, if words be made of breath,
    And breath of life, I have no life to breathe
    What thou hast said to me.
HAMLET I must to England, you know that?
QUEEN   Alack,   200
    I had forgot. 'Tis so concluded on.
HAMLET There's letters seal'd, and my two schoolfellows,
    Whom I will trust as I will adders fang'd,
    They bear the mandate, they must sweep my way
    And marshal me to knavery. Let it work,   205
    For 'tis the sport to have the enginer
    Hoist with his own petar, an't shall go hard
    But I will delve one yard below their mines,
    And blow them at the moon. O, 'tis most sweet
    When in one line two crafts directly meet.   210
    This man shall set me packing;
    I'll lug the guts into the neighbor room.
    Mother, good night indeed. This counsellor
    Is now most still, most secret, and most grave,
    Who was in life a foolish prating knave.   215
    Come, sir, to draw toward an end with you.
    Good night, mother.
                  Exeunt [severally, Hamlet tugging in Polonius].

---

205. **knavery:** some knavish scheme against me.   206. **enginer:** deviser of military "engines" or contrivances.   207. **Hoist with:** blown up by. **petar:** petard, bomb.   210. **crafts:** plots.   211. **packing:** (1) taking on a load; (2) leaving in a hurry.   216. **draw . . . end:** finish my conversation.

Act 4

SCENE I

Enter KING *and* QUEEN *with* ROSENCRANTZ *and*
GUILDENSTERN.

KING There's matter in these sighs, these profound heaves—
You must translate, 'tis fit we understand them.
Where is your son?
QUEEN Bestow this place on us a little while.
                    [*Exeunt Rosencrantz and Guildenstern.*]
Ah, mine own lord, what have I seen to-night!   5
KING What, Gertrude? How does Hamlet?
QUEEN Mad as the sea and wind when both contend
Which is the mightier. In his lawless fit,
Behind the arras hearing something stir,
Whips out his rapier, cries, "A rat, a rat!"   10
And in this brainish apprehension kills
The unseen good old man.
KING   O heavy deed!
It had been so with us had we been there.
His liberty is full of threats to all,
To you yourself, to us, to every one.   15
Alas, how shall this bloody deed be answer'd?
It will be laid to us, whose providence
Should have kept short, restrain'd, and out of haunt
This mad young man; but so much was our love,
We would not understand what was most fit,   20
But like the owner of a foul disease,
To keep it from divulging, let it feed
Even on the pith of life. Where is he gone?
QUEEN To draw apart the body he hath kill'd,
O'er whom his very madness, like some ore   25

4.1. Location: The castle. 11. **brainish apprehension:** crazy notion.
16. **answer'd:** i.e. satisfactorily accounted for to the public. 17. **providence:**
foresight. 18. **short:** on a short leash. **out of haunt:** away from other people.
22. **divulging:** being revealed. 25. **ore:** vein of gold.

Among a mineral of metals base,
Shows itself pure: 'a weeps for what is done.
KING O Gertrude, come away!
The sun no sooner shall the mountains touch,
But we will ship him hence, and this vile deed   30
We must with all our majesty and skill
Both countenance and excuse. Ho, Guildenstern!

Enter ROSENCRANTZ *and* GUILDENSTERN.

Friends both, go join you with some further aid:
Hamlet in madness hath Polonius slain,
And from his mother's closet hath he dragg'd him.   35
Go seek him out, speak fair, and bring the body
Into the chapel. I pray you haste in this.
                                   [*Exeunt Rosencrantz and Guildenstern.*]
Come, Gertrude, we'll call up our wisest friends
And let them know both what we mean to do
And what's untimely done, [. . . .]   40
Whose whisper o'er the world's diameter,
As level as the cannon to his blank,
Transports his pois'ned shot, may miss our name,
And hit the woundless air. O, come away!
My soul is full of discord and dismay.   *Exeunt.* 45

SCENE 2

Enter HAMLET.

HAMLET Safely stow'd.
[GENTLEMEN. *(Within.)* Hamlet! Lord Hamlet!]
[HAMLET] But soft, what noise? Who calls on Ham-
  let? O, here they come.

Enter ROSENCRANTZ *and* [GUILDENSTERN].

ROSENCRANTZ What have you done, my lord, with the dead
  body?   5
HAMLET [Compounded] it with dust, whereto 'tis kin.
ROSENCRANTZ Tell us where 'tis, that we may take it thence,
  And bear it to the chapel.

26. mineral: mine. **40.** Some words are wanting at the end of the line.
Capell's conjecture, *so, haply, slander,* probably indicates the intended sense of
the passage. **42. As level:** with aim as good. **blank:** target. **44. woundless:** incapable
of being hurt. 4.2. Location: The castle.

HAMLET Do not believe it.

ROSENCRANTZ Believe what?   10

HAMLET That I can keep your counsel and not mine
own. Besides, to be demanded of a spunge, what
replication should be made by the son of a king?

ROSENCRANTZ Take you me for a spunge, my lord?

HAMLET Ay, sir, that soaks up the King's counte-   15
nance, his rewards, his authorities. But such officers
do the King best service in the end: he keeps them,
like [an ape] an apple, in the corner of his jaw, first
mouth'd, to be last swallow'd. When he needs what
you have glean'd, it is but squeezing you, and, spunge,   20
you shall be dry again.

ROSENCRANTZ I understand you not, my lord.

HAMLET I am glad of it, a knavish speech sleeps in a
foolish ear.

ROSENCRANTZ My lord, you must tell us where the body is,   25
and go with us to the King.

HAMLET The body is with the King, but the King is
not with the body. The King is a thing—

GUILDENSTERN A thing, my lord?

HAMLET Of nothing, bring me to him. [Hide fox,   30
and all after.]   *Exeunt.*

SCENE 3

Enter KING *and two or three.*

KING I have sent to seek him, and to find the body.
How dangerous is it that this man goes loose!
Yet must not we put the strong law on him.
He's lov'd of the distracted multitude,
Who like not in their judgment, but their eyes,   5
And where 'tis so, th' offender's scourge is weigh'd,

---

12. **demanded of:** questioned by. **spunge:** sponge.   13. **replication:** reply.
15–16. **countenance:** favor.   23. **sleeps:** is meaningless.   27–28. **The body .. .the
body.** Possibly alluding to the legal fiction that the king's dignity is separate from
his mortal body.   30. **Of nothing:** of no account. Cf. "Man is like a thing of
nought, his time passeth away like a shadow" (Psalm 144:4 in the Prayer Book
version). "Hamlet at once insults the King and hints that his days are numbered"
(Dover Wilson).   30–31. **Hide . . . after.** Probably a cry in some game resembling
hide-and-seek, perhaps echoing the comically vivid moment in Chaucer's *Nun's
Priest's Tale* when everyone chases after the all-too-clever fox (T).   4.3. Location:
The castle.   4. **distracted:** unstable.   6. **scourge:** i.e. punishment.

But never the offense. To bear all smooth and even,
This sudden sending him away must seem
Deliberate pause. Diseases desperate grown
By desperate appliance are reliev'd,   10
Or not at all.

Enter ROSENCRANTZ.

How now, what hath befall'n?
ROSENCRANTZ Where the dead body is bestow'd, my lord,
    We cannot get from him.
KING   But where is he?
ROSENCRANTZ Without, my lord, guarded, to know your pleasure.
KING Bring him before us.
ROSENCRANTZ   Ho, bring in the lord.   15

They [HAMLET *and* GUILDENSTERN] *enter.*

KING Now, Hamlet, where's Polonius?
HAMLET At supper.
KING At supper? where?
HAMLET Not where he eats, but where 'a is eaten; a
    certain convocation of politic worms are e'en at   20
    him. Your worm is your only emperor for diet: we
    fat all creatures else to fat us, and we fat ourselves for
    maggots; your fat king and your lean beggar is but var-
    iable service, two dishes, but to one table—that's the
    end.   25
KING Alas, alas!
HAMLET A man may fish with the worm that hath eat
    of a king, and eat of the fish that hath fed of that worm.
KING What dost thou mean by this?
HAMLET Nothing but to show you how a king may go   30
    a progress through the guts of a beggar.
KING Where is Polonius?
HAMLET In heaven, send thither to see; if your
    messenger find him not there, seek him i' th' other
    place yourself. But if indeed you find him not   35

---

7. bear: manage. **8–9. must . . . pause:** i.e. must be represented as a maturely
considered decision. **20. politic:** crafty, prying; "such worms as might breed in a
politician's corpse" (Dowden). **e'en:** even now. **21. for diet:** with respect to what
it eats. "Diet" punningly adds to "politic," "emperor," and "worms" as an allusion to
the Diet of Worms (1521), where Luther defended himself in response to the sum-
mons by the Emperor Charles V (T). **23–24. variable service:** different courses
of a meal. **31. progress:** royal journey of state. **33-4. the other place:** Hell (T).

within this month, you shall nose him as you go up the
stairs into the lobby.
KING   [*To Attendants.*] Go seek him there.
HAMLET 'A will stay till you come.

[*Exeunt Attendants.*]

KING Hamlet, this deed, for thine especial
safety—   40
Which we do tender, as we dearly grieve
For that which thou hast done—must send thee hence
[With fiery quickness]; therefore prepare thyself,
The bark is ready, and the wind at help,
Th' associates tend, and every thing is bent   45
For England.
HAMLET   For England.
KING   Ay, Hamlet.
HAMLET   Good.
KING So is it, if thou knew'st our purposes.
HAMLET I see a cherub that sees them. But come, for
England! Farewell, dear mother.
KING Thy loving father, Hamlet.   50
HAMLET My mother: father and mother is man and
wife, man and wife is one flesh—so, my mother.
Come, for England!   *Exit.*
KING Follow him at foot, tempt him with speed aboard.
Delay it not, I'll have him hence to-night.   55
Away, for every thing is seal'd and done
That else leans on th' affair. Pray you make haste.

[*Exeunt Rosencrantz and Guildenstern.*]

And, England, if my love thou hold'st at aught—
As my great power thereof may give thee sense,
Since yet thy cicatrice looks raw and red   60
After the Danish sword, and thy free awe
Pays homage to us—thou mayst not coldly set
Our sovereign process, which imports at full,
By letters congruing to that effect,
The present death of Hamlet. Do it, England,   65

41. **tender:** regard with tenderness, hold dear. **dearly:** with intense feeling.
44. **bark:** ship (T). **at help:** favorable.   45. **Th':** thy. **tend:** await. **bent:** made ready.
48. **I . . . them:** i.e. heaven sees them.   54. **at foot:** at his heels, close behind.
57. **leans on:** relates to.   58. **England:** King of England.   60. **cicatrice:** scar.
61–62. **thy .. . Pays:** your fear makes you pay voluntarily.   62. **coldly set:**
undervalue, disregard.   63. **process:** command.   64. **congruing to:** in accord
with.   65. **present:** immediate.

159

For like the hectic in my blood he rages,
And thou must cure me. Till I know 'tis done,
How e'er my haps, my joys [were] ne'er [begun].   *Exit.*

SCENE 4

Enter FORTINBRAS *with his army over the stage.*

FORTINBRAS Go, captain, from me greet the Danish king.
Tell him that by his license Fortinbras
Craves the conveyance of a promis'd march
Over his kingdom. You know the rendezvous.
If that his Majesty would aught with us,   5
We shall express our duty in his eye,
And let him know so.
CAPTAIN   I will do't, my lord.
FORTINBRAS Go softly on.   [*Exeunt all but the Captain.*]

Enter HAMLET, ROSENCRANTZ, [GUILDENSTERN,] *et al.*

HAMLET Good sir, whose powers are these?
CAPTAIN They are of Norway, sir.   10
HAMLET How purpos'd, sir, I pray you?
CAPTAIN Against some part of Poland.
HAMLET Who commands them, sir?
CAPTAIN The nephew to old Norway, Fortinbras.
HAMLET Goes it against the main of Poland, sir,   15
Or for some frontier?
CAPTAIN Truly to speak, and with no addition,
We go to gain a little patch of ground
That hath in it no profit but the name.
To pay five ducats, five, I would not farm it;   20
Nor will it yield to Norway or the Pole
A ranker rate, should it be sold in fee.
HAMLET Why then the Polack never will defend it.
CAPTAIN Yes, it is already garrison'd.
HAMLET Two thousand souls and twenty thousand ducats   25
Will not debate the question of this straw.

---

66. **hectic:** continuous fever. 68. **haps:** fortunes. 4.4. Location: The Danish
coast, near the castle. 3. **conveyance of:** escort for. 6. **eye:** presence. 8. **softly:**
slowly. 9. **powers:** forces. 15. **main:** main territory. 20. **To pay:** i.e. for an
annual rent of. **farm:** lease. 22. **ranker:** higher. **in fee:** outright. 26. **Will not
debate:** i.e. will scarcely be enough to fight out.

This is th' imposthume of much wealth and peace,
That inward breaks, and shows no cause without
Why the man dies. I humbly thank you, sir.
CAPTAIN God buy you, sir.   [*Exit.*]
ROSENCRANTZ   Will't please you go, my lord?   30
HAMLET I'll be with you straight—go a little before.
                                      [*Exeunt all but Hamlet.*]
How all occasions do inform against me,
And spur my dull revenge! What is a man,
If his chief good and market of his time
Be but to sleep and feed? a beast, no more.   35
Sure He that made us with such large discourse,
Looking before and after, gave us not
That capability and godlike reason
To fust in us unus'd. Now whether it be
Bestial oblivion, or some craven scruple   40
Of thinking too precisely on th' event—
A thought which quarter'd hath but one part wisdom
And ever three parts coward—I do not know
Why yet I live to say, "This thing's to do,"
Sith I have cause, and will, and strength, and means   45
To do't. Examples gross as earth exhort me:
Witness this army of such mass and charge,
Led by a delicate and tender prince,
Whose spirit with divine ambition puff'd
Makes mouths at the invisible event,   50
Exposing what is mortal and unsure
To all that fortune, death, and danger dare,
Even for an egg-shell. Rightly to be great
Is not to stir without great argument,
But greatly to find quarrel in a straw   55
When honor's at the stake. How stand I then,
That have a father kill'd, a mother stain'd,
Excitements of my reason and my blood,
And let all sleep, while to my shame I see
The imminent death of twenty thousand men,   60

27. **imposthume:** abscess.   32. **inform against:** denounce, accuse.   34. **market:** purchase, profit.   36. **discourse:** reasoning power.   39. **fust:** grow mouldy.   40. **oblivion:** forgetfulness.   41. **event:** outcome.   46. **gross:** large, obvious.   47. **mass and charge:** size and expense.   50. **Makes mouths at:** treats scornfully. **invisible:** i.e. unforeseeable.   54. **Is not to:** i.e. is *not* not to. **argument:** cause.   55. **greatly:** nobly.   58. **Excitements of:** urgings by.

That for a fantasy and trick of fame
Go to their graves like beds, fight for a plot
Whereon the numbers cannot try the cause,
Which is not tomb enough and continent
To hide the slain? O, from this time forth, 65
My thoughts be bloody, or be nothing worth! *Exit.*

SCENE 5

Enter HORATIO, [QUEEN] GERTRUDE, *and a* GENTLEMAN.

QUEEN I will not speak with her.
GENTLEMAN She is importunate, indeed distract.
Her mood will needs be pitied.
QUEEN   What would she have?
GENTLEMAN She speaks much of her father, says she hears
There's tricks i' th' world, and hems, and beats her heart, 5
Spurns enviously at straws, speaks things in doubt
That carry but half sense. Her speech is nothing,
Yet the unshaped use of it doth move
The hearers to collection; they yawn at it,
And botch the words up fit to their own thoughts, 10
Which as her winks and nods and gestures yield them,
Indeed would make one think there might be thought,
Though nothing sure, yet much unhappily.
HORATIO 'Twere good she were spoken with, for she may strew
Dangerous conjectures in ill-breeding minds. 15
[QUEEN] Let her come in. [*Exit Gentleman.*]
[*Aside.*] To my sick soul, as sin's true nature is,
Each toy seems prologue to some great amiss,
So full of artless jealousy is guilt,
It spills itself in fearing to be spilt. 20

---

61. fantasy: caprice. **trick:** trifle.   **63. Whereon ... cause:** which isn't large enough to let the opposing armies engage upon it.   **64. continent:** container.   4.5. Location: The castle.   **1–20.** See the Textual Notes for the lines that replace these in Ql.   **6. Spurns . . . straws:** spitefully takes offense at trifles. **in doubt:** obscurely.   **7. Her speech:** what she says.   **8. unshaped use:** distracted manner.   **9. collection:** attempts to gather the meaning. **yawn at:** gape eagerly (as if to swallow). Most editors adopt the Fl reading *aim at.*   **10. botch:** patch.   **11. Which:** i.e. the words.   **12. thought:** inferred, conjectured.   **15. ill-breeding:** conceiving ill thoughts, prone to think the worst.   **18. toy:** trifle. **amiss:** calamity.   **19. artless jealousy:** uncontrolled suspicion.   **20. spills:** destroys.

Enter OPHELIA [*distracted, with her hair down,*
playing on a lute].

OPHELIA Where is the beauteous majesty of Denmark?
QUEEN How now, Ophelia?
OPHELIA "How should I your true-love know   *She sings.*
    From another one?
    By his cockle hat and staff,   25
    And his sandal shoon."
QUEEN Alas, sweet lady, what imports this song?
OPHELIA Say you? Nay, pray you mark.
    "He is dead and gone, lady,   *Song.*
    He is dead and gone,   30
    At his head a grass-green turf,
    At his heels a stone."
  O ho!
QUEEN Nay, but, Ophelia—
OPHELIA Pray you mark.   35
[SINGS.] "White his shroud as the mountain snow"—

Enter KING.

QUEEN Alas, look here, my lord.
OPHELIA "Larded all with sweet flowers,   *Song.*
    Which be wept to the ground did not go
    With true-love showers."   40
KING How do you, pretty lady?
OPHELIA Well, God dild you! They say the owl was a
  baker's daughter. Lord, we know what we are, but
  know not what we may be. God be at your table!
KING Conceit upon her father.   45
OPHELIA Pray let's have no words of this, but when

23–24. These lines resemble a passage in an earlier ballad beginning "As you came
from the holy land/Of Walsingham." Probably all the song fragments sung by
Ophelia were familiar to the Globe audience, but only one other line (187) is
from a ballad still extant.   **25. cockle hat:** hat bearing a cockle shell, the badge of
a pilgrim to the shrine of St. James of Compostela in Spain. **staff.** Another mark
of a pilgrim.   **26. shoon:** shoes (already an archaic form in Shakespeare's day).
38. Larded: adorned.   **39. not.** Contrary to the expected sense, and unmetrical;
explained as Ophelia's alteration of the line to accord with the facts of Polonius'
burial (see line 84).   **42. dild:** yield, reward. **owl.** Alluding to the legend of a baker's
daughter whom Jesus turned into an owl because she did not respond generously
to his request for bread.   **43. baker's daughter.** There may also be an indeli-
cate suggestion to the immodest reputation of women whose work material was
associated with rising and swelling. A baker's daughter would be similar in ill-
repute to a fishmonger's daughter (T).   **45. Conceit:** fanciful brooding.

they ask you what it means, say you this:
"To-morrow is Saint Valentine's day,   *Song.*
All in the morning betime,
And I a maid at your window,   50
To be your Valentine.
"Then up he rose and donn'd his clo'es,
And dupp'd the chamber-door,
Let in the maid, that out a maid
Never departed more."   55
KING Pretty Ophelia!
OPHELIA Indeed without an oath I'll make an end on't.
[SINGS.]   "By Gis, and by Saint Charity,
Alack, and fie for shame!
Young men will do't if they come to't,   60
By Cock, they are to blame.
"Quoth she, 'Before you tumbled me,
You promis'd me to wed.'"
(He answers.)
"'So would I 'a' done, by yonder sun,   65
And thou hadst not come to my bed.'"
KING How long hath she been thus?
OPHELIA I hope all will be well. We must be patient,
but I cannot choose but weep to think they would lay
him i' th' cold ground. My brother shall know of   70
it, and so I thank you for your good counsel. Come,
my coach! Good night, ladies, good night. Sweet
ladies, good night, good night.   [*Exit.*]
KING Follow her close, give her good watch, I
pray you.   [*Exit Horatio.*]
O, this is the poison of deep grief, it springs   75
All from her father's death—and now behold!
O Gertrude, Gertrude,
When sorrows come, they come not single spies,
But in battalions: first, her father slain;
Next, your son gone, and he most violent author   80
Of his own just remove; the people muddied,
Thick and unwholesome in [their] thoughts and whispers
For good Polonius' death; and we have done but greenly
In hugger-mugger to inter him; poor Ophelia

53. **dupp'd:** opened. 58. **Gis:** contraction of *Jesus.* 61. **Cock:** corruption of *God,* with consequent vulgar pun. 66. **And:** if. 78. **spies:** i.e. soldiers sent ahead of the main force to reconnoiter, scouts. 81. **muddied:** confused. 83. **greenly:** unwisely. 84. **In hugger-mugger:** secretly and hastily.

Divided from herself and her fair judgment,   85
Without the which we are pictures, or mere beasts;
Last, and as much containing as all these,
Her brother is in secret come from France,
Feeds on this wonder, keeps himself in clouds,
And wants not buzzers to infect his ear   90
With pestilent speeches of his father's death,
Wherein necessity, of matter beggar'd,
Will nothing stick our person to arraign
In ear and ear. O my dear Gertrude, this,
Like to a murd'ring-piece, in many places   95
Gives me superfluous death.   *A noise within.*
[QUEEN   Alack, what noise is this?]
KING Attend!
Where is my Swissers? Let them guard the door.

                    Enter a MESSENGER.

What is the matter?
MESSENGER   Save yourself, my lord!
The ocean, overpeering of his list,   100
Eats not the flats with more impiteous haste
Than young Laertes, in a riotous head,
O'erbears your officers. The rabble call him lord,
And as the world were now but to begin,
Antiquity forgot, custom not known,   105
The ratifiers and props of every word,
[They] cry, "Choose we, Laertes shall be king!"
Caps, hands, and tongues applaud it to the clouds,
"Laertes shall be king, Laertes king!"   *A noise within.*
QUEEN How cheerfully on the false trail they cry!   110
O, this is counter, you false Danish dogs!

                    Enter LAERTES *with others.*

KING The doors are broke.
LAERTES Where is this king? Sirs, stand you all without.
ALL No, let 's come in.

---

89. in clouds: i.e. in cloudy surmise and suspicion (rather than the light of fact).   **90. wants:** lacks. **buzzers:** whispering informers.   **92. of matter beggar'd:** destitute of facts.   **93. nothing . . . arraign:** scruple not at all to charge me with the crime.   **95. murd'ring-piece:** cannon firing a scattering charge.   **98. Swissers:** Swiss guards.   **100. overpeering . . . list:** rising higher than its shores.   **102. in . . . head:** with a rebellious force.   **104. as:** as if. **106. word:** pledge, promise.   **111. counter:** on the wrong scent (literally, following the scent backward).

LAERTES   I pray you give me leave.
ALL We will, we will.   115
LAERTES I thank you, keep the door.   [*Exeunt Laertes' followers.*]
                         O thou vile king,
   Give me my father!
QUEEN   Calmly, good Laertes.
LAERTES That drop of blood that's calm proclaims me
   bastard,
   Cries cuckold to my father, brands the harlot
   Even here between the chaste unsmirched brow   120
   Of my true mother.
KING   What is the cause, Laertes,
   That thy rebellion looks so giant-like?
   Let him go, Gertrude, do not fear our person:
   There's such divinity doth hedge a king
   That treason can but peep to what it would,   125
   Acts little of his will. Tell me, Laertes,
   Why thou art thus incens'd. Let him go, Gertrude.
   Speak, man.
LAERTES Where is my father?
KING   Dead.
QUEEN   But not by him.
KING Let him demand his fill.   130
LAERTES How came he dead? I'll not be juggled with.
   To hell, allegiance! vows, to the blackest devil!
   Conscience and grace, to the profoundest pit!
   I dare damnation. To this point I stand,
   That both the worlds I give to negligence,   135
   Let come what comes, only I'll be reveng'd
   Most throughly for my father.
KING   Who shall stay you?
LAERTES My will, not all the world's:
   And for my means, I'll husband them so well,
   They shall go far with little.
KING   Good Laertes,   140
   If you desire to know the certainty
   Of your dear father, is't writ in your revenge
   That, swoopstake, you will draw both friend and foe,

---

119. cuckold: husband betrayed sexually by his wife. **123. fear:** fear for.
125. would: i.e. would like to do. **135. both . . . negligence:** i.e. I don't care
what the consequences are in this world or in the next. **137. throughly:** thoroughly. **138. world's:** i.e. world's will. **143. swoopstake:** sweeping up everything without discrimination (modern *sweepstake*).

Winner and loser?
LAERTES None but his enemies.
KING   Will you know them then?   145
LAERTES To his good friends thus wide I'll ope my arms,
     And like the kind life-rend'ring pelican,
     Repast them with my blood.
KING   Why, now you speak
     Like a good child and a true gentleman.
     That I am guiltless of your father's death,   150
     And am most sensibly in grief for it,
     It shall as level to your judgment 'pear
     As day does to your eye.
                    A noise within: "Let her come in!"
LAERTES How now, what noise is that?

                    Enter OPHELIA.

     O heat, dry up my brains! tears seven times salt   155
     Burn out the sense and virtue of mine eye!
     By heaven, thy madness shall be paid with weight
     [Till] our scale turn the beam. O rose of May!
     Dear maid, kind sister, sweet Ophelia!
     O heavens, is't possible a young maid's wits   160
     Should be as mortal as [an old] man's life?
     [Nature is fine in love, and where 'tis fine,
     It sends some precious instance of itself
     After the thing it loves.]
OPHELIA "They bore him barefac'd on the bier   *Song.* 165
                    [Hey non nonny, nonny, hey nonny,]
               And in his grave rain'd many a tear"—
     Fare you well, my dove!
LAERTES Hadst thou thy wits and didst persuade revenge,
     It could not move thus.   170
OPHELIA You must sing, "A-down, a-down," and you
     call him a-down-a. O how the wheel becomes it! It is
     the false steward, that stole his master's daughter.

---

147. pelican. The pelican was believed to draw blood from its own breast to nourish its young.   **149. good child:** faithful son.   **151. sensibly:** feelingly.   **152. level:** plain.   **156. virtue:** faculty.   **162. fine in:** refined or spiritualized by.   **163. instance:** proof, token. So delicate is Ophelia's love for her father that her sanity has pursued him into the grave.   **169. persuade:** argue logically for.   **171–72. and . . . a-down-a:** "if he indeed agrees that Polonius is 'a-down,' i.e. fallen low" (Dover Wilson).   **172. wheel:** refrain (?) or spinning-wheel, at which women sang ballads (?).

LAERTES This nothing's more than matter.

OPHELIA There's rosemary, that's for remembrance;   175
pray you, love, remember. And there is pansies, that's
for thoughts.

LAERTES A document in madness, thoughts and remembrance fitted.

OPHELIA [*To Claudius.*] There's fennel for you, and   180
columbines. [*To Gertrude.*] There's rue for you, and
here's some for me; we may call it herb of grace
a' Sundays. You may wear your rue with a difference.
There's a daisy. I would give you some violets, but
they wither'd all when my father died. They say 'a
made a good end—

[SINGS.] "For bonny sweet Robin is all my joy."

LAERTES Thought and afflictions, passion, hell itself,
She turns to favor and to prettiness.

OPHELIA   "And will 'a not come again?   *Song.* 190
           And will 'a not come again?
             No, no, he is dead,
             Go to thy death-bed,
           He never will come again.

           "His beard was as white as snow,   195
           [All] flaxen was his pole,
             He is gone, he is gone,
             And we cast away moan,
           God 'a' mercy on his soul!"
And of all Christians' souls, [I pray God]. God buy   200
you.   [*Exit.*]

LAERTES Do you [see] this, O God?

KING Laertes, I must commune with your grief,
Or you deny me right. Go but apart,
Make choice of whom your wisest friends you will,   205
And they shall hear and judge 'twixt you and me.
If by direct or by collateral hand
They find us touch'd, we will our kingdom give,

---

174. matter: lucid speech.   **178. A document in madness:** a lesson contained in
mad talk.   **180, 181. fennel, columbines.** Symbols respectively of flattery and in-
gratitude.   **181. rue.** Symbolic of sorrow and repentance.   **183. with a difference:**
i.e. to represent a different cause of sorrow. *Difference* is a term from heraldry, meaning
a variation in a coat of arms made to distinguish different members of a family.   **184.
daisy, violets.** Symbolic respectively of dissembling and faithfulness. It is not clear
who are the recipients of these.   **187. Robin.** The term sometimes had a lewd association in the 16th century.   **188. Thought:** melancholy.   **189. favor:** grace, charm. **196.
flaxen:** white. **pole:** poll, head.   **207. collateral:** i.e. indirect.   **208. touch'd:** guilty.

Our crown, our life, and all that we call ours,
To you in satisfaction; but if not,   210
Be you content to lend your patience to us,
And we shall jointly labor with your soul
To give it due content.
LAERTES   Let this be so.
His means of death, his obscure funeral—
No trophy, sword, nor hatchment o'er his bones,   215
No noble rite nor formal ostentation—
Cry to be heard, as 'twere from heaven to earth,
That I must call't in question.
KING   So you shall,
And where th' offense is, let the great axe fall.
I pray you go with me.   *Exeunt.* 220

SCENE 6

Enter HORATIO *and others.*

HORATIO What are they that would speak with me?
GENTLEMAN Sea-faring men, sir. They say they
    have letters for you.
HORATIO Let them come in.   [*Exit Gentleman.*]
    I do not know from what part of the world   5
    I should be greeted, if not from Lord Hamlet.

Enter SAILORS.

[1.] SAILOR God bless you, sir.
HORATIO Let him bless thee too.
[1.] SAILOR 'A shall, sir, and['t] please him. There's
    a letter for you, sir—it came from th' embassador   10
    that was bound for England—if your name be
    Horatio, as I am let to know it is.
HORATIO [*Reads.*] "Horatio, when thou shalt have
    overlook'd this, give these fellows some means to the
    King, they have letters for him. Ere we were two   15
    days old at sea, a pirate of very warlike appointment
    gave us chase. Finding ourselves too slow of sail, we
    put on a compell'd valor, and in the grapple I boarded

215. trophy: memorial. **hatchment:** heraldic memorial tablet. **216. formal ostentation:** fitting and customary ceremony. **218. That:** so that. 4.6. Location: The castle. See the Textual Notes for a scene unique to Q1.

them. On the instant they got clear of our ship, so I
alone became their prisoner. They have dealt with   20
me like thieves of mercy, but they knew what they did:
I am to do a [good] turn for them. Let the King have
the letters I have sent, and repair thou to me with as
much speed as thou wouldest fly death. I have words to
speak in thine ear will make thee dumb, yet are   25
they much too light for the [bore] of the matter. These .
good fellows will bring thee where I am. Rosencrantz
and Guildenstern hold their course for England, of
them I have much to tell thee. Farewell.
            [He] that thou knowest thine,   30
                        Hamlet."
Come, I will [give] you way for these your letters,
And do't the speedier that you may direct me
To him from whom you brought them.   *Exeunt.*

SCENE 7

Enter KING *and* LAERTES.

KING Now must your conscience my acquittance seal,
    And you must put me in your heart for friend,
    Sith you have heard, and with a knowing ear,
    That he which hath your noble father slain
    Pursued my life.
LAERTES   It well appears. But tell me   5
    Why you [proceeded] not against these feats
    So criminal and so capital in nature,
    As by your safety, greatness, wisdom, all things else
    You mainly were stirr'd up.
KING   O, for two special reasons,
    Which may to you perhaps seem much unsinow'd,   10
    But yet to me th' are strong. The Queen his mother
    Lives almost by his looks, and for myself—
    My virtue or my plague, be it either which—
    She is so [conjunctive] to my life and soul,
    That, as the star moves not but in his sphere,   15

21. **thieves of mercy:** merciful thieves.   26. **bore:** calibre, size (gunnery term).   4.7.
Location: The castle.   1. **my acquittance seal:** ratify my acquittal, i.e. acknowledge
my innocence in Polonius' death.   6. **feats:** acts.   8. **safety:** i.e. regard for your own
safety.   9. **mainly:** powerfully.   10. **unsinow'd:** unsinewed, i.e. weak.   13. **either**
which: one or the other.   14. **conjunctive:** closely joined.   15. **in his sphere:** by
the movement of the sphere in which it is fixed (as the Ptolemaic astronomy taught).

I could not but by her. The other motive,
Why to a public count I might not go,
Is the great love the general gender bear him,
Who, dipping all his faults in their affection,
Work like the spring that turneth wood to stone,   20
Convert his gyves to graces, so that my arrows,
Too slightly timber'd for so [loud a wind],
Would have reverted to my bow again,
But not where I have aim'd them.
LAERTES And so have I a noble father lost,   25
A sister driven into desp'rate terms,
Whose worth, if praises may go back again,
Stood challenger on mount of all the age
For her perfections—but my revenge will come.
KING Break not your sleeps for that. You must not think 30
That we are made of stuff so flat and dull
That we can let our beard be shook with danger
And think it pastime. You shortly shall hear more.
I lov'd your father, and we love ourself,
And that, I hope, will teach you to imagine—   35

Enter a MESSENGER *with letters.*

[How now? What news?
MESSENGER   Letters, my lord, from Hamlet:]
These to your Majesty, this to the Queen.
KING From Hamlet? Who brought them?
MESSENGER Sailors, my lord, they say, I saw them not.
They were given me by Claudio. He receiv'd them   40
Of him that brought them.
KING   Laertes, you shall hear them.
—Leave us.   [*Exit Messenger.*]
[*Reads.*] "High and mighty, You shall know I am set
naked on your kingdom. To-morrow shall I beg leave
to see your kingly eyes, when I shall, first asking   45
you pardon thereunto, recount the occasion of my
sudden [and more strange] return.
                                        [Hamlet.]"

---

17. count: reckoning.   **18. the general gender:** everybody.   **21. gyves:** fetters.   **26. terms:** condition.   **27. go back again:** i.e. refer to what she was before
she went mad.   **28. on mount:** pre-eminent.   **30. for that:** i.e. for fear of losing
your revenge.   **31. flat:** spiritless.   **32. let . . . shook.** To ruffle or tweak a man's
beard was an act of insolent defiance that he could not disregard without loss
of honor. Cf. 2.2.573. **with:** by.   **44. naked:** destitute.   **46. pardon thereunto:**
permission to do so.

What should this mean? Are all the rest come back?
Or is it some abuse, and no such thing?   50
LAERTES Know you the hand?
KING   'Tis Hamlet's character. "Naked"!
And in a postscript here he says "alone."
Can you devise me?
LAERTES I am lost in it, my lord. But let him come,
It warms the very sickness in my heart   55
That I [shall] live and tell him to his teeth,
"Thus didst thou."
KING   If it be so, Laertes—
As how should it be so? how otherwise?—
Will you be rul'd by me?
LAERTES   Ay, my lord,
So you will not o'errule me to a peace.   60
KING To thine own peace. If he be now returned
As [checking] at his voyage, and that he means
No more to undertake it, I will work him
To an exploit, now ripe in my device,
Under the which he shall not choose but fall;   65
And for his death no wind of blame shall breathe,
But even his mother shall uncharge the practice,
And call it accident.
LAERTES   My lord, I will be rul'd,
The rather if you could devise it so
That I might be the organ.
KING   It falls right.   70
You have been talk'd of since your travel much,
And that in Hamlet's hearing, for a quality
Wherein they say you shine. Your sum of parts
Did not together pluck such envy from him
As did that one, and that, in my regard,   75
Of the unworthiest siege.
LAERTES   What part is that, my lord?
KING A very riband in the cap of youth,
Yet needful too, for youth no less becomes

50. abuse: deceit.   51. character: handwriting.   53. devise me: explain it to
me.   58. As . . . otherwise: How can he have come back? Yet he obviously has.
60. So: provided that.   62. checking at: turning from (like a falcon diverted from
its quarry by other prey).   67. uncharge the practice: adjudge the plot no plot, i.e.
fail to see the plot.   70. organ: instrument, agent.   72. quality: skill.   73. Your . . .
parts: all your (other) accomplishments put together.   76. unworthiest: i.e. least
important (with no implication of unsuitableness). siege: status, position.

172

The light and careless livery that it wears
Than settled age his sables and his weeds,   80
Importing health and graveness. Two months since
Here was a gentleman of Normandy:
I have seen myself, and serv'd against, the French,
And they can well on horseback, but this gallant
Had witchcraft in't, he grew unto his seat,   85
And to such wondrous doing brought his horse,
As had he been incorps'd and demi-natur'd
With the brave beast. So far he topp'd [my] thought,
That I in forgery of shapes and tricks
Come short of what he did.
LAERTES   A Norman was't?   90
KING A Norman.
LAERTES Upon my life, Lamord.
KING   The very same.
LAERTES I know him well. He is the brooch indeed
    And gem of all the nation.
KING He made confession of you,   95
    And gave you such a masterly report
    For art and exercise in your defense,
    And for your rapier most especial,
    That he cried out 'twould be a sight indeed
    If one could match you. The scrimers of their nation   100
    He swore had neither motion, guard, nor eye,
    If you oppos'd them. Sir, this report of his
    Did Hamlet so envenom with his envy
    That he could nothing do but wish and beg
    Your sudden coming o'er to play with you.   105
    Now, out of this—
LAERTES   What out of this, my lord?
KING Laertes, was your father dear to you?
    Or are you like the painting of a sorrow,
    A face without a heart?
LAERTES   Why ask you this?
KING Not that I think you did not love your father,   110

---

80. **weeds:** (characteristic) garb.   81. **Importing . . . graveness:** signifying prosperity and dignity.   84. **can . . . horseback:** are excellent riders.   87. **incorps'd:** made one body. **demi-natur'd:** i.e. become half of a composite animal.   89. **forgery:** mere imagining.   92. **Lamord**. Perhaps suggestive of the French word for death, "*la mort*" (T).   93. **brooch:** ornament (worn in the hat).   95. **made . . . you:** acknowledged your excellence.   100. **scrimers:** fencers.   105. **sudden:** speedy.

But that I know love is begun by time,
And that I see, in passages of proof,
Time qualifies the spark and fire of it.
There lives within the very flame of love
A kind of week or snuff that will abate it,   115
And nothing is at a like goodness still,
For goodness, growing to a plurisy,
Dies in his own too much. That we would do,
We should do when we would; for this "would" changes,
And hath abatements and delays as many   120
As there are tongues, are hands, are accidents,
And then this "should" is like a spendthrift's sigh,
That hurts by easing. But to the quick of th' ulcer:
Hamlet comes back. What would you undertake
To show yourself indeed your father's son   125
More than in words?
LAERTES   To cut his throat i' th' church.
KING No place indeed should murther sanctuarize,
      Revenge should have no bounds. But, good Laertes,
      Will you do this, keep close within your chamber.
      Hamlet return'd shall know you are come home.   130
      We'll put on those shall praise your excellence,
      And set a double varnish on the fame
      The Frenchman gave you, bring you in fine together,
      And wager o'er your heads. He, being remiss,
      Most generous, and free from all contriving,   135
      Will not peruse the foils, so that with ease,
      Or with a little shuffling, you may choose
      A sword unbated, and in a [pass] of practice
      Requite him for your father.
LAERTES   I will do't,
      And for [that] purpose I'll anoint my sword.   140

---

111. time: i.e. a particular set of circumstances. 112. in . . . proof: i.e. by the test of experience, by actual examples. 113. qualifies: moderates. 115. week: wick. 116. nothing . . . still: nothing remains forever at the same pitch of perfection. 117. plurisy: plethora (a variant spelling of *pleurisy,* which was erroneously related to *plus,* stem *plur-,* "more, overmuch." 118. too much: excess. 122. spendthrift's sigh. A sigh was supposed to draw blood from the heart. 123. hurts by easing: injures us at the same time that it gives us relief. 127. sanctuarize: offer asylum to. 129. Will . . . this: if you want to undertake this. 131. put on those: incite those who. 132. double varnish: second coat of varnish. 133. in fine: finally. 134. remiss: careless, overtrustful. 135. generous: noble-minded, free . . . contriving: innocent of sharp practices. 136. peruse: examine. 137. shuffling: cunning exchange. 138. unbated: not blunted. pass of practice: tricky thrust.

I bought an unction of a mountebank,
So mortal that, but dip a knife in it,
Where it draws blood, no cataplasm so rare,
Collected from all simples that have virtue
Under the moon, can save the thing from death   145
That is but scratch'd withal. I'll touch my point
With this contagion, that if I gall him slightly,
It may be death.
KING   Let's further think of this,
Weigh what convenience both of time and means
May fit us to our shape. If this should fail,   150
And that our drift look through our bad performance,
'Twere better not assay'd; therefore this project
Should have a back or second, that might hold
If this did blast in proof. Soft, let me see.
We'll make a solemn wager on your cunnings—   155
I ha't!
When in your motion you are hot and dry—
As make your bouts more violent to that end—
And that he calls for drink, I'll have preferr'd him
A chalice for the nonce, whereon but sipping,   160
If he by chance escape your venom'd stuck,
Our purpose may hold there. But stay, what noise?

Enter QUEEN.

QUEEN One woe doth tread upon another's heel,
So fast they follow. Your sister's drown'd, Laertes.
LAERTES Drown'd! O, where?   165
QUEEN There is a willow grows askaunt the brook,
That shows his hoary leaves in the glassy stream,
Therewith fantastic garlands did she make
Of crow-flowers, nettles, daisies, and long purples
That liberal shepherds give a grosser name,   170
But our cull-cold maids do dead men's fingers call them.

141. unction: ointment. mountebank: travelling quack-doctor. 142. mortal: deadly. 143. cataplasm: poultice. 144. simples: medicinal herbs. virtue: curative power. 147. gall: graze. 150. fit ... shape: i.e. suit our purposes best. 151. drift: purpose. look through: become visible, be detected. 153. back or second: i.e. a second plot in reserve for emergency. 154. blast in proof: blow up while being tried (an image from gunnery). 158. As: i.e. and you should. 159. preferr'd: offered to. Most editors adopt the F1 reading *prepar'd*. 160. nonce: occasion. 161. stuck: thrust (from *stoccado*, a fencing term). 166. askaunt: sideways over. 167. hoary: grey-white. 168. Therewith: i.e. with willow branches. 169. long purples: wild orchids. 170. liberal: free-spoken. 171. cull-cold: chaste.

There on the pendant boughs her crownet weeds
Clamb'ring to hang, an envious sliver broke,
When down her weedy trophies and herself
Fell in the weeping brook. Her clothes spread wide,   175
And mermaid-like awhile they bore her up,
Which time she chaunted snatches of old lauds,
As one incapable of her own distress,
Or like a creature native and indued
Unto that element. But long it could not be   180
Till that her garments, heavy with their drink,
Pull'd the poor wretch from her melodious lay
To muddy death.
LAERTES   Alas, then she is drown'd?
QUEEN Drown'd, drown'd.
LAERTES Too much of water hast thou, poor Ophelia,   185
And therefore I forbid my tears; but yet
It is our trick, Nature her custom holds,
Let shame say what it will; when these are gone,
The woman will be out. Adieu, my lord,
I have a speech a' fire that fain would blaze,   190
But that this folly drowns it.   *Exit.*
KING   Let's follow, Gertrude.
How much I had to do to calm his rage!
Now fear I this will give it start again,
Therefore let's follow.   *Exeunt.*

---

172. **crownet:** made into coronets.   173. **envious sliver:** malicious branch.   177.
lauds: hymns.   178. **incapable:** insensible.   179. **indued:** habituated.   187. **It:** i.e.
weeping. **trick:** natural way.   188. **these:** these tears.   189. **The woman . . . out:**
my womanish traits will be gone for good.   190. **fain:** gladly (T).

Act 5

SCENE I

Enter two CLOWNS [*with spades and mattocks*].

1. CLOWN Is she to be buried in Christian burial when
she willfully seeks her own salvation?
2. CLOWN I tell thee she is, therefore make her grave
straight. The crowner hath sate on her, and finds it
Christian burial.   5
1. CLOWN How can that be, unless she drown'd herself
in her own defense?
2. CLOWN Why, 'tis found so.
1. CLOWN It must be [*se offendendo*], it cannot be else.
For here lies the point: if I drown myself wittingly,   10
it argues an act, and an act hath three branches—it is
to act, to do, to perform; [argal], she drown'd herself
wittingly.
2. CLOWN Nay, but hear you, goodman delver—
1. CLOWN Give me leave. Here lies the water; good.   15
Here stands the man; good. If the man go to this water
and drown himself, it is, will he, nill he, he goes, mark
you that. But if the water come to him and drown him,
he drowns not himself; argal, he that is not guilty of
his own death shortens not his own life.   20
2. CLOWN But is this law?
1. CLOWN Ay, marry, is't—crowner's quest law.
2. CLOWN Will you ha' the truth an't? If this had not
been a gentlewoman, she should have been buried out
a' Christian burial.   25

5.1. Location: A churchyard. o.s.d. **Clowns:** rustics. **2. salvation:** comical error for
'damnation' (T). **4. straight:** immediately. **crowner:** coroner. **9. se offendendo:**
blunder for *se defendendo,* "in self-defense." **12. argal:** blunder for *ergo,* "therefore;"
in the midst of all this logic-chopping, Shakespeare creates a pun on the name of the
Oxford logician (and college actor) John Argall (T). **15–20. Here . . . life.** Alluding
to a very famous suicide case, that of Sir James Hales, a judge who drowned himself
in 1554; it was long cited in the courts. The clown gives a garbled account of the
defense summing-up and the verdict. **17. nill he:** will he not. **22. quest:** inquest.

1. CLOWN Why, there thou say'st, and the more pity
that great folk should have count'nance in this world to
drown or hang themselves, more than their even-
Christen. Come, my spade. There is no ancient
gentlemen but gard'ners, ditchers, and grave-makers;   30
they hold up Adam's profession.
2. CLOWN Was he a gentleman?
1. CLOWN 'A was the first that ever bore arms.
[2. CLOWN Why, he had none.
1. CLOWN What, art a heathen? How dost thou   35
understand the Scripture? The Scripture says Adam
digg'd; could he dig without arms?] I'll put another
question to thee. If thou answerest me not to the purpose,
confess thyself—
2. CLOWN Go to.   40
1. CLOWN What is he that builds stronger than either
the mason, the shipwright, or the carpenter?
2. CLOWN The gallows-maker, for that outlives a
thousand tenants.
1. CLOWN I like thy wit well, in good faith. The gallows   45
does well; but how does it well? It does well to
those that do ill. Now thou dost ill to say the gallows
is built stronger than the church; argal, the gallows
may do well to thee. To't again, come.
2. CLOWN Who builds stronger than a mason, a shipwright,   50
or a carpenter?
1. CLOWN Ay, tell me that, and unyoke.
2. CLOWN Marry, now I can tell.
1. CLOWN To't.
2. CLOWN Mass, I cannot tell.   55

Enter HAMLET *and* HORATIO *[afar off]*.

1. CLOWN Cudgel thy brains no more about it, for
your dull ass will not mend his pace with beating, and
when you are ask'd this question next, say "a grave-maker":
the houses he makes lasts till doomsday. Go
get thee in, and fetch me a sup of liquor.   60
                [Exit Second Clown. First Clown digs.]
"In youth when I did love, did love,   *Song.*
    Methought it was very sweet,

28–29. **even-Christen:** fellow-Christians.   **34. none:** i.e. no coat of arms.
52. unyoke: i.e. cease to labor, call it a day.   **55. Mass:** by the mass.

To contract—O—the time for—a—my behove,
O, methought there—a—was nothing—a—meet."
HAMLET Has this fellow no feeling of his business?   65
'a sings in grave-making.
HORATIO Custom hath made it in him a property of
easiness.
HAMLET 'Tis e'en so, the hand of little employment
hath the daintier sense.   70
1. CLOWN "But age with his stealing steps   *Song.*
    Hath clawed me in his clutch,
    And hath shipped me into the land,
    As if I had never been such."
            [*Throws up a shovelful of earth with a skull in it.*]
HAMLET That skull had a tongue in it, and could sing   75
once. How the knave jowls it to the ground, as if
'twere Cain's jaw-bone, that did the first murder!
This might be the pate of a politician, which this ass
now o'erreaches, one that would circumvent God,
might it not?   80
HORATIO It might, my lord.
HAMLET Or of a courtier, which could say, "Good
morrow, sweet lord! How dost thou, sweet lord?"
This might be my Lord Such-a-one, that prais'd my
Lord Such-a-one's horse when 'a [meant] to beg it,   85
might it not?
HORATIO Ay, my lord.
HAMLET Why, e'en so, and now my Lady Worm's,
chopless, and knock'd about the [mazzard] with a
sexton's spade. Here's fine revolution, and we had   90
the trick to see't. Did these bones cost no more the
breeding, but to play at loggats with them? Mine
ache to think on't.
1. CLOWN "A pickaxe and a spade, a spade,   *Song.*
    For and a shrouding sheet: 95

63. contract . . . behove: shorten, i.e. spend agreeably . . . advantage. The song,
punctuated by the grunts of the clown as he digs, is a garbled version of a poem by
Thomas Lord Vaux, entitled "The Aged Lover Renounceth Love." **67. Custom:**
habit. **67–68. a property of easiness:** i.e. a thing he can do with complete ease
of mind. **70. daintier sense:** more delicate sensitivity. **76. jowls:** dashes. **78.
politician:** schemer, intriguer. **79. o'erreaches:** gets the better of (with play on
the literal sense). **circumvent God:** bypass God's law. **89. chopless:** lacking the
lower jaw. **mazzard:** head. **90. revolution:** change. **and:** if. **91. trick:** knack,
ability. **Did . . . cost:** were . . . worth. **92. loggats:** a game in which blocks of
wood were thrown at a stake.

O, a pit of clay for to be made
For such a guest is meet."
[Throws up another skull.]
HAMLET There's another. Why may not that be the
skull of a lawyer? Where be his quiddities now, his
quillities, his cases, his tenures, and his tricks?   100
Why does he suffer this mad knave now to knock him
about the sconce with a dirty shovel, and will not tell
him of his action of battery? Hum! This fellow might
be in 's time a great buyer of land, with his statutes, his
recognizances, his fines, his double vouchers, his   105
recoveries. [Is this the fine of his fines, and the re-
covery of his recoveries,] to have his fine pate full of
fine dirt? Will [his] vouchers vouch him no more of his
purchases, and [double ones too], than the length and
breadth of a pair of indentures? The very con-   110
veyances of his lands will scarcely lie in this box, and
must th' inheritor himself have no more, ha?
HORATIO Not a jot more, my lord.
HAMLET Is not parchment made of sheep-skins?
HORATIO Ay, my lord, and of calves'-skins too.   115
HAMLET They are sheep and calves which seek out
assurance in that. I will speak to this fellow. Whose
grave's this, sirrah?
1. CLOWN Mine, sir.
[Sings] "[O], a pit of clay for to be made   120
[For such a guest is meet]."
HAMLET I think it be thine indeed, for thou liest in't.
1. CLOWN You lie out on't, sir, and therefore 'tis not
yours; for my part, I do not lie in't, yet it is mine.
HAMLET Thou dost lie in't, to be in't and say it is thine.   125
'Tis for the dead, not for the quick; therefore thou liest.
1. CLOWN 'Tis a quick lie, sir, 'twill away again from
me to you.

99. **quiddities:** subtleties, quibbles.   100. **quillities:** fine distinctions. **tenures:** titles to real estate.   102. **sconce:** head.   104, 105. **statutes, recognizances:** bonds securing debts by attaching land and property.   105, 106. **fines, recoveries:** procedures for converting an entailed estate to freehold.   105. **double vouchers:** documents guaranteeing title to real estate, signed by two persons.   106. **fine:** end.   110. **pair of indentures:** legal document cut into two parts which fitted together on a serrated edge. Perhaps Hamlet thus refers to the two rows of teeth in the skull, or to the bone sutures.   110–11. **conveyances:** documents relating to transfer of property.   111. **this box:** i.e. the skull itself.   112. **inheritor:** owner.   118. **sirrah:** term of address to inferiors.

HAMLET What man dost thou dig it for?   130
1. CLOWN For no man, sir.
HAMLET What woman then?
1. CLOWN For none neither.
HAMLET Who is to be buried in't?
1. CLOWN One that was a woman, sir, but, rest her   135
    soul, she's dead.
HAMLET How absolute the knave is! we must speak
    by the card, or equivocation will undo us. By the Lord,
    Horatio, this three years I have took note of it: the age
    is grown so pick'd that the toe of the peasant   140
    comes so near the heel of the courtier, he galls his kibe.
    How long hast thou been grave-maker?
1. CLOWN Of [all] the days i' th' year, I came to't that
    day that our last king Hamlet overcame Fortinbras.
HAMLET How long is that since?   145
1. CLOWN Cannot you tell that? Every fool can tell
    that. It was that very day that young Hamlet was born
    —he that is mad, and sent into England.
HAMLET Ay, marry, why was he sent into England?
1. CLOWN Why, because 'a was mad. 'A shall recover   150
    his wits there, or if 'a do not, 'tis no great matter
    there.
HAMLET Why?
1. CLOWN 'Twill not be seen in him there, there the
    men are as mad as he.   155
HAMLET How came he mad?
1. CLOWN Very strangely, they say.
HAMLET How strangely?
1. CLOWN Faith, e'en with losing his wits.
HAMLET Upon what ground?   160
1. CLOWN Why, here in Denmark. I have been sexton
    here, man and boy, thirty years.
HAMLET How long will a man lie i' th' earth ere he
    rot?
1. CLOWN Faith, if 'a be not rotten before 'a die—as   165
    we have many pocky corses, that will scarce hold the
    laying in—'a will last you some eight year or nine year.
    A tanner will last you nine year.

---

137. **absolute:** positive. 138. **by the card:** by the compass, i.e. punctiliously.
equivocation: ambiguity. 140. **pick'd:** refined. 141. **galls his kibe:** rubs the
courtier's chilblain. 166. **pocky:** rotten with venereal disease. 166–67. **hold . . .
in:** last out the burial.

HAMLET Why he more than another?

1. CLOWN Why, sir, his hide is so tann'd with his trade   170
that 'a will keep out water a great while, and your
water is a sore decayer of your whoreson dead body.
Here's a skull now hath lien you i' th' earth three and
twenty years.

HAMLET Whose was it?   175

1. CLOWN A whoreson mad fellow's it was. Whose
do you think it was?

HAMLET Nay, I know not.

1. CLOWN A pestilence on him for a mad rogue! 'a
pour'd a flagon of Rhenish on my head once. This same   180
skull, sir, was, sir, Yorick's skull, the King's jester.

HAMLET This?   [*Takes the skull.*]

1. CLOWN E'en that.

HAMLET Alas, poor Yorick! I knew him, Horatio, a
fellow of infinite jest, of most excellent fancy. He   185
hath bore me on his back a thousand times, and now
how abhorr'd in my imagination it is! my gorge rises
at it. Here hung those lips that I have kiss'd I know not
how oft. Where be your gibes now, your gambols,
your songs, your flashes of merriment, that were   190
wont to set the table on a roar? Not one now to mock
your own grinning—quite chop-fall'n. Now get you
to my lady's [chamber], and tell her, let her paint an
inch thick, to this favor she must come; make her
laugh at that. Prithee, Horatio, tell me one thing.   195

HORATIO What's that, my lord?

HAMLET Dost thou think Alexander look'd a' this
fashion i' th' earth?

HORATIO E'en so.

HAMLET And smelt so? pah!   [*Puts down the skull.*] 200

HORATIO E'en so, my lord.

HAMLET To what base uses we may return, Horatio!
Why may not imagination trace the noble dust of
Alexander, till 'a find it stopping a bunghole?

HORATIO 'Twere to consider too curiously, to consider   205
so.

---

192. chop-fall'n: (1) lacking the lower jaw; (2) downcast.   **194. favor:** appearance.   **197. Alexander**: Alexander the Great, Macedonian conqueror of the world (356-323 B.C.E.), like Hamlet a student of Priam, Hecuba, and the Trojan War (T).   **204. bunghole:** opening in a wine cask or beer barrel (T).   **205. curiously:** closely, minutely.

HAMLET No, faith, not a jot, but to follow him thither
with modesty enough and likelihood to lead it: Alexander
died, Alexander was buried, Alexander returneth
to dust, the dust is earth, of earth we make loam,   210
and why of that loam whereto he was converted might
they not stop a beer-barrel?
Imperious Caesar, dead and turn'd to clay,
Might stop a hole to keep the wind away.
O that that earth which kept the world in awe   215
Should patch a wall t' expel the [winter's] flaw!
But soft, but soft awhile, here comes the King,

> Enter KING, QUEEN, LAERTES, and [a DOCTOR OF DIVINITY,
> following] the corse, [with LORDS attendant].

The Queen, the courtiers. Who is this they follow?
And with such maimed rites? This doth betoken
The corse they follow did with desp'rate hand   220
Foredo it own life. 'Twas of some estate.
Couch we a while and mark.   [Retiring with Horatio.]
LAERTES What ceremony else?
HAMLET That is Laertes, a very noble youth. Mark.
LAERTES What ceremony else?   225
DOCTOR Her obsequies have been as far enlarg'd
As we have warranty. Her death was doubtful,
And but that great command o'ersways the order,
She should in ground unsanctified been lodg'd
Till the last trumpet; for charitable prayers,   230
[Shards,] flints, and pebbles should be thrown on her.
Yet here she is allow'd her virgin crants,
Her maiden strewments, and the bringing home
Of bell and burial.
LAERTES Must there no more be done?
DOCTOR   No more be done: 235
We should profane the service of the dead
To sing a requiem and such rest to her
As to peace-parted souls.

---

208. **modesty:** moderation.   210. **loam:** a mixture of moistened clay with sand,
straw, etc.   213. **Imperious:** imperial.   216. **flaw:** gust.   219. **maimed rites:**
lack of customary ceremony.   221. **Foredo:** fordo, destroy. **it:** its. **estate:** rank.
222. **Couch we:** let us conceal ourselves.   227. **doubtful:** i.e. the subject of an
"open verdict."   228. **order:** customary procedure.   229. **should:** would certainly.
230. **for:** instead of.   232. **crants:** garland.   233. **maiden strewments:** flowers
scattered on the grave of an unmarried girl.   233–34. **bringing . . . burial:** i.e.
burial in consecrated ground, with the bell tolling.   237. **requiem:** dirge.

LAERTES   Lay her i' th' earth,
And from her fair and unpolluted flesh
May violets spring! I tell thee, churlish priest,   240
A minist'ring angel shall my sister be
When thou liest howling.
HAMLET   What, the fair Ophelia!
QUEEN [*Scattering flowers.*] Sweets to the sweet,
   farewell!
I hop'd thou shouldst have been my Hamlet's wife.
I thought thy bride-bed to have deck'd, sweet maid,
And not have strew'd thy grave.   245
LAERTES   O, treble woe
Fall ten times [treble] on that cursed head
Whose wicked deed thy most ingenious sense
Depriv'd thee of! Hold off the earth a while,
Till I have caught her once more in mine arms.   250
                                 [*Leaps in the grave.*]
Now pile your dust upon the quick and dead,
Till of this flat a mountain you have made
T' o'ertop old Pelion, or the skyish head
Of blue Olympus.
HAMLET [*Coming forward.*] What is he whose grief
Bears such an emphasis, whose phrase of sorrow   255
Conjures the wand'ring stars and makes them stand
Like wonder-wounded hearers? This is I,
Hamlet the Dane!   [*Hamlet leaps in after Laertes.*]
LAERTES The devil take thy soul!
                                 [*Grappling with him.*]
HAMLET   Thou pray'st not well.
I prithee take thy fingers from my throat.   260
For though I am not splenitive [and] rash,
Yet have I in me something dangerous,
Which let thy wisdom fear. Hold off thy hand!
KING Pluck them asunder.
QUEEN   Hamlet, Hamlet!
ALL   Gentlemen!
HORATIO Good my lord, be quiet.   265
   [*The Attendants part them, and they come out of the grave.*]

---

243. Sweets: flowers.   **248. ingenious:** intelligent.   **253, 254. Pelion, Olympus:** mountains in northeastern Greece.   **255. emphasis, phrase.** Rhetorical terms, here used in disparaging reference to Laertes' inflated language.   **256. Conjures:** puts a spell upon. **wand'ring stars:** planets.   **258. the Dane.** This title normally signifies the King.   **261. splenitive:** impetuous.

HAMLET Why, I will fight with him upon this theme
      Until my eyelids will no longer wag.
QUEEN O my son, what theme?
HAMLET I lov'd Ophelia. Forty thousand brothers
      Could not with all their quantity of love   270
      Make up my sum. What wilt thou do for her?
KING O, he is mad, Laertes.
QUEEN For love of God, forbear him.
HAMLET 'Swounds, show me what thou't do.
      Woo't weep, woo't fight, woo't fast, woo't tear thyself?   275
      Woo't drink up eisel, eat a crocadile?
      I'll do't. Dost [thou] come here to whine?
      To outface me with leaping in her grave?
      Be buried quick with her, and so will I.
      And if thou prate of mountains, let them throw   280
      Millions of acres on us, till our ground,
      Singeing his pate against the burning zone,
      Make Ossa like a wart! Nay, and thou'lt mouth,
      I'll rant as well as thou.
QUEEN   This is mere madness,
      And [thus] a while the fit will work on him;   285
      Anon, as patient as the female dove,
      When that her golden couplets are disclosed,
      His silence will sit drooping.
HAMLET   Hear you, sir,
      What is the reason that you use me thus?
      I lov'd you ever. But it is no matter.   290
      Let Hercules himself do what he may,
      The cat will mew, and dog will have his day.
                                            Exit Hamlet.
KING I pray thee, good Horatio, wait upon him.
                                         [*Exit*] *Horatio.*
[*To Laertes*] Strengthen your patience in our last night's speech,
      We'll put the matter to the present push.—   295

---

274. thou't: thou wilt.   **275. Woo't:** wilt thou.   **276. eisel:** vinegar. **crocadile:** crocodile.   **280. if . . . mountains.** Referring to lines 251–54.   **282. burning zone:** sphere of the sun.   **283. Ossa:** another mountain in Greece, near Pelion and Olympus. **mouth:** talk bombast (synonymous with *rant* in the next line).   **284. mere:** utter.   **286. patient:** calm.   **287. golden couplets:** pair of baby birds, covered with yellow down. **disclosed:** hatched.   **291–92. Let ... day:** i.e. nobody can prevent another from making the scenes he feels he has a right to.   **294–99.** See the Textual Notes for the lines that replace these in Q1.   **294. in:** i.e. by recalling.   **295. present push:** immediate test.

Good Gertrude, set some watch over your son.
This grave shall have a living monument.
An hour of quiet [shortly] shall we see,
Till then in patience our proceeding be.   *Exeunt.*

SCENE 2

Enter HAMLET *and* HORATIO.

HAMLET So much for this, sir, now shall you see the
   other—
   You do remember all the circumstance?
HORATIO Remember it, my lord!
HAMLET Sir, in my heart there was a kind of fighting
   That would not let me sleep. [Methought] I lay   5
   Worse than the mutines in the [bilboes]. Rashly—
   And prais'd be rashness for it—let us know
   Our indiscretion sometime serves us well
   When our deep plots do pall, and that should learn us
   There's a divinity that shapes our ends,   10
   Rough-hew them how we will—
HORATIO   That is most certain.
HAMLET Up from my cabin,
   My sea-gown scarf'd about me, in the dark
   Grop'd I to find out them, had my desire,
   Finger'd their packet, and in fine withdrew   15
   To mine own room again, making so bold,
   My fears forgetting manners, to [unseal]
   Their grand commission; where I found, Horatio—
   Ah, royal knavery!—an exact command,
   Larded with many several sorts of reasons,   20
   Importing Denmark's health and England's too,
   With, ho, such bugs and goblins in my life,

---

297. living: enduring (?) or in the form of a lifelike effigy (?).   5.2. Location: The castle.   **1. see the other:** i.e. hear the other news I have to tell you (hinted at in the letter to Horatio, 4.6.24–25).   **6. mutines:** mutineers (but the term *mutiny* was in Shakespeare's day used of almost any act of rebellion against authority). **bilboes:** fetters attached to a heavy iron bar. **Rashly:** on impulse.   **7. know:** recognize, acknowledge.   **9. pall:** lose force, come to nothing. **learn:** teach.   **10. shapes our ends:** gives final shape to our designs.   **11. Rough-hew them:** block them out in initial form.   **15. Finger'd:** filched, "pinched."   **20. Larded:** garnished.   **21. Importing:** relating to.   **22. bugs . . . life:** terrifying things in prospect if I were permitted to remain alive. *Bugs* = bugaboos.

That, on the supervise, no leisure bated,
No, not to stay the grinding of the axe,
My head should be strook off.
HORATIO   Is't possible?   25
HAMLET Here's the commission, read it at more leisure.
But wilt thou hear now how I did proceed?
HORATIO I beseech you.
HAMLET Being thus benetted round with [villainies],
Or I could make a prologue to my brains,   30
They had begun the play. I sat me down,
Devis'd a new commission, wrote it fair.
I once did hold it, as our statists do,
A baseness to write fair, and labor'd much
How to forget that learning, but, sir, now   35
It did me yeman's service. Wilt thou know
Th' effect of what I wrote?
HORATIO   Ay, good my lord.
HAMLET An earnest conjuration from the King,
As England was his faithful tributary,
As love between them like the palm might flourish,   40
As peace should still her wheaten garland wear
And stand a comma 'tween their amities,
And many such-like [as's] of great charge,
That on the view and knowing of these contents,
Without debatement further, more or less,   45
He should those bearers put to sudden death,
Not shriving time allow'd.
HORATIO   How was this seal'd?
HAMLET Why, even in that was heaven ordinant.
I had my father's signet in my purse,
Which was the model of that Danish seal;   50
Folded the writ up in the form of th' other,
[Subscrib'd] it, gave't th' impression, plac'd it safely,
The changeling never known. Now the next day

23. **supervise:** perusal. **bated:** deducted (from the stipulated speediness).   **24. stay:** wait for.   **30. Or:** before.   **32. fair:** i.e. in a beautiful hand (such as a professional scribe would use).   **33. statists:** statesmen, public officials.   **34. A baseness:** i.e. a skill befitting men of low rank.   **36. yeman's:** yeoman's, i.e. solid, substantial.   **37. effect:** purport, gist. **42. comma:** connective, link.   **43. as's . . . charge:** (1) weighty clauses beginning with *as;* (2) asses with heavy loads.   **47. shriving time:** time for confession and absolution.   **48. ordinant:** in charge, guiding. **50. model:** small copy.   **52. Subscrib'd:** signed.   **53. changeling:** i.e. Hamlet's letter, substituted secretly for the genuine letter, as fairies substituted their children for human children. **never known:** never recognized as a substitution (unlike the fairies' changelings).

Was our sea-fight, and what to this was sequent
Thou knowest already.   55
HORATIO So Guildenstern and Rosencrantz go to't.
HAMLET [Why, man, they did make love to this employment,]
They are not near my conscience. Their defeat
Does by their own insinuation grow.
'Tis dangerous when the baser nature comes   60
Between the pass and fell incensed points
Of mighty opposites.
HORATIO   Why, what a king is this!
HAMLET Does it not, think thee, stand me now upon—
He that hath kill'd my king and whor'd my mother,
Popp'd in between th' election and my hopes,   65
Thrown out his angle for my proper life,
And with such coz'nage—is't not perfect conscience
[To quit him with this arm? And is't not to be
damn'd,
To let this canker of our nature come
In further evil?   70
HORATIO It must be shortly known to him from England
What is the issue of the business there.
HAMLET It will be short; the interim's mine,
And a man's life's no more than to say "one."
But I am very sorry, good Horatio,   75
That to Laertes I forgot myself,
For by the image of my cause I see
The portraiture of his. I'll [court] his favors.
But sure the bravery of his grief did put me
Into a tow'ring passion.
HORATIO   Peace, who comes here?]   80

Enter [young OSRIC,] *a courtier.*

OSRIC Your lordship is right welcome back to
Denmark.

---

56. go to't: i.e. are going to their death. **58. defeat:** ruin, overthrow. **59. insinuation:** winding their way into the affair. **60. baser:** inferior. **61. pass:** thrust. **fell:**
fierce. **63. stand . . . upon:** i.e. rest upon me as a duty. **65. election:** i.e. as
King of Denmark. **66. angle:** hook and line. **proper:** very. **67. coz'nage:** trick-
ery. **68. quit him:** pay him back. **69. canker:** cancerous sore. **69–70. come
In:** grow into. **74. a man's . . . more:** i.e. to kill a man takes no more time.
say "one." Perhaps this is equivalent to "deliver one sword thrust"; see line 280
below, where Hamlet says "One" as he makes the first hit. **77. image:** likeness.
79. bravery: ostentatious expression.

HAMLET I [humbly] thank you, sir.—Dost know this
    water-fly?
HORATIO No, my good lord.
HAMLET Thy state is the more gracious, for 'tis a vice
    to know him. He hath much land, and fertile; let a   85
    beast be lord of beasts, and his crib shall stand at the
    King's mess. 'Tis a chough, but, as I say, spacious in
    the possession of dirt.
OSRIC Sweet lord, if your lordship were at leisure,
    I should impart a thing to you from his Majesty.   90
HAMLET I will receive it, sir, with all diligence of
    spirit. [Put] your bonnet to his right use, 'tis for the
    head.
OSRIC I thank your lordship, it is very hot.
HAMLET No, believe me, 'tis very cold, the wind is   95
    northerly.
OSRIC It is indifferent cold, my lord, indeed.
HAMLET But yet methinks it is very [sultry] and hot
    [for] my complexion.
OSRIC Exceedingly, my lord, it is very sultry—as   100
    'twere—I cannot tell how. My lord, his Majesty bade
    me signify to you that 'a has laid a great wager on your
    head. Sir, this is the matter—
HAMLET I beseech you remember.
                    [*Hamlet moves him to put on his hat.*]
OSRIC Nay, good my lord, for my ease, in good faith.   105
    Sir, here is newly come to court Laertes, believe me, an
    absolute [gentleman], full of most excellent differences,
    of very soft society, and great showing; indeed, to
    speak sellingly of him, he is the card or calendar of
    gentry; for you shall find in him the continent of what   110
    part a gentleman would see.

---

82. water-fly: i.e. tiny, vainly agitated creature. **84. gracious:** virtuous. **85–87. let…
mess:** i.e. if a beast owned as many cattle as Osric, he could feast with the King.
87. chough: jackdaw, a bird that could be taught to speak. **92. bonnet:** hat.
97. indifferent: somewhat. **99. complexion:** temperament. **105. for my ease:**
i.e. I am really more comfortable with my hat off (a polite insistence on main-
taining ceremony). **107. absolute:** complete, possessing every quality a gentleman should have. **differences:** distinguishing characteristics, personal qualities.
108. soft: agreeable. **great showing:** splendid appearance. **109. sellingly:** i.e. like
a seller to a prospective buyer; in a fashion to do full justice. Most editors follow Q3 in reading *feelingly* = with exactitude, as he deserves. **card or calendar:**
chart or register, i.e. compendious guide. **110. gentry:** gentlemanly behavior.
110–11. the continent … part: one who contains every quality.

HAMLET Sir, his definement suffers no perdition in
you, though I know to divide him inventorially
would dozy th' arithmetic of memory, and yet but
yaw neither in respect of his quick sail; but in   115
the verity of extolment, I take him to be a soul of
great article, and his infusion of such dearth and rare-
ness as, to make true diction of him, his semblable is
his mirror, and who else would trace him, his um-
brage, nothing more.   120
OSRIC Your lordship speaks most infallibly of him.
HAMLET The concernancy, sir? Why do we wrap the
gentleman in our more rawer breath?
OSRIC Sir?
HORATIO Is't not possible to understand in another   125
tongue? You will to't, sir, really.
HAMLET What imports the nomination of this gentle-
man?
OSRIC Of Laertes?
HORATIO His purse is empty already: all 's golden   130
words are spent.
HAMLET Of him, sir.
OSRIC I know you are not ignorant—
HAMLET I would you did, sir, yet, in faith, if you did,
it would not much approve me. Well, sir?   135
OSRIC You are not ignorant of what excellence
Laertes is—
HAMLET I dare not confess that, lest I should com-
pare with him in excellence, but to know a man well
were to know himself.   140
OSRIC I mean, sir, for [his] weapon, but in the
imputation laid on him by them, in his meed he's un-
fellow'd.

---

112. perdition: loss.   114. dozy: make dizzy.   115. yaw: keep deviating erratically
from its course (said of a ship). neither: for all that. in respect of: compared
with.   115–16. in . . . extolment: to praise him truly.   117. article: scope (?)
or importance (?). infusion: essence, quality. dearth: scarceness.   118. make
true diction: speak truly. his semblable: his only likeness or equal.   119. who
. . . him: anyone else who tries to follow him.   119–20. umbrage: shadow.
122. concernancy: relevance.   123. more rawer breath: i.e. words too crude to
describe him properly.   125–26. in another tongue: i.e. when someone else is
the speaker.   126. You . . . really: i.e. you can do it if you try.   127. nomination:
naming, mention.   135. approve: commend.   138–39. compare . . . excellence:
i.e. seem to claim the same degree of excellence for myself.   139. but. The sense
seems to require *for*.   140. himself: i.e. oneself.   141–42. in . . . them: i.e. in
popular estimation.   142. meed: merit.

HAMLET What's his weapon?
OSRIC Rapier and dagger.   145
HAMLET That's two of his weapons—but well.
OSRIC The King, sir, hath wager'd with him six Barbary horses, against the which he has impawn'd, as I
take it, six French rapiers and poniards, with their
assigns, as girdle, [hangers], and so. Three of the   150
carriages, in faith, are very dear to fancy, very responsive to the hilts, most delicate carriages, and of
very liberal conceit.
HAMLET What call you the carriages?
HORATIO I knew you must be edified by the margent   155
ere you had done.
OSRIC The [carriages], sir, are the hangers.
HAMLET The phrase would be more germane to the
matter if we could carry a cannon by our sides; I
would it [might be] hangers till then. But on: six   160
Barb'ry horses against six French swords, their
assigns, and three liberal-conceited carriages; that's
the French bet against the Danish. Why is this all
[impawn'd, as] you call it?
OSRIC The King, sir, hath laid, sir, that in a dozen   165
passes between yourself and him, he shall not exceed
you three hits; he hath laid on twelve for nine; and
it would come to immediate trial, if your lordship
would vouchsafe the answer.
HAMLET How if I answer no?   170
OSRIC I mean, my lord, the opposition of your person
in trial.
HAMLET Sir, I will walk here in the hall. If it please
his Majesty, it is the breathing time of day with me.
Let the foils be brought, the gentleman willing,   175
and the King hold his purpose, I will win for him and

148. **impawn'd:** staked. 150. **assigns:** appurtenances. **hangers:** straps on which the
swords hang from the girdle.   151. **carriages:** properly, gun-carriages; here used
affectedly in place of *hangers*. **fancy:** taste.   151–52. **very responsive to:** match-
ing well.   153. **liberal conceit:** elegant design.   155. **must . . . margent:** would
require enlightenment from a marginal note.   165. **laid:** wagered.   166–67. **he . . .
hits.** Laertes must win by at least eight to four (if none of the "passes" or bouts are
draws), since at seven to five he would be only two up.   167. **he . . . nine.** Not
satisfactorily explained despite much discussion. One suggestion is that Laertes
has raised the odds against himself by wagering that out of twelve bouts he will
win nine.   169. **answer:** encounter (as Hamlet's following quibble forces Osric to
explain in his next speech).   174. **breathing . . . me:** my usual hour for exercise.

I can; if not, I will gain nothing but my shame and the
odd hits.

OSRIC Shall I deliver you so?

HAMLET To this effect, sir—after what flourish your   180
nature will.

OSRIC I commend my duty to your lordship.

HAMLET Yours. [*Exit Osric.*] ['A] does well to commend it himself, there are no tongues else for 's turn.

HORATIO This lapwing runs away with the shell on his   185
head.

HAMLET 'A did [comply], sir, with his dug before 'a
suck'd it. Thus has he, and many more of the same
breed that I know the drossy age dotes on, only got the
tune of the time, and out of an habit of encounter,   190
a kind of [yesty] collection, which carries them
through and through the most [profound] and [winnow'd]
opinions, and do but blow them to their trial, the bub-
bles are out.

Enter a LORD.

LORD My lord, his Majesty commended him to   195
you by young Osric, who brings back to him that you
attend him in the hall. He sends to know if your
pleasure hold to play with Laertes, or that you will
take longer time.

HAMLET I am constant to my purposes, they follow   200
the King's pleasure. If his fitness speaks, mine is ready;
now or whensoever, provided I be so able as now.

LORD The King and Queen and all are coming
down.

HAMLET In happy time.   205

LORD The Queen desires you to use some gentle
entertainment to Laertes before you fall to play.

---

180. after what flourish: with whatever embellishment of language.   **182. commend my duty:** offer my dutiful respects (but Hamlet picks up the phrase in the sense "praise my manner of bowing").   **185. lapwing:** a foolish bird which upon hatching was supposed to run with part of the eggshell still over its head. (Osric has put his hat on at last.)   **187. comply . . . dug:** bow politely to his mother's nipple.   **189. drossy:** i.e. worthless.   **190. tune . . . time:** i.e. fashionable ways of talk. **habit of encounter:** mode of social intercourse.   **191. yesty:** yeasty, frothy. **collection:** i.e. anthology of fine phrases.   **192. winnow'd:** sifted, choice. **193. opinions:** judgments. **blow . . . trial:** test them by blowing on them, i.e. make even the least demanding trial of them.   **194. out:** blown away (?) or at an end, done for (?).   **201. If . . . ready:** i.e. if this is a good moment for him, it is for me also.   **206–7. gentle entertainment:** courteous greeting.

HAMLET She well instructs me.   [*Exit Lord.*]
HORATIO You will lose, my lord.
HAMLET I do not think so; since he went into France   210
  I have been in continual practice. I shall win at the
  odds. Thou wouldst not think how ill all's here about
  my heart—but it is no matter.
HORATIO Nay, good my lord—
HAMLET It is but foolery, but it is such a kind of   215
  [gain-]giving, as would perhaps trouble a woman.
HORATIO If your mind dislike any thing, obey it. I will
  forestall their repair hither, and say you are not fit.
HAMLET Not a whit, we defy augury. There is special
  providence in the fall of a sparrow. If it be [now],   220
  'tis not to come; if it be not to come, it will be now; if
  it be not now, yet it [will] come—the readiness is all.
  Since no man, of aught he leaves, knows what is't to
  leave betimes, let be.

  A table prepar'd, [and flagons of wine on it. Enter] Trumpets,
  Drums, and Officers with cushions, foils, daggers; KING, QUEEN,
  LAERTES, [OSRIC,] *and all the State.*

KING Come, Hamlet, come, and take this hand from me.   225
                    [*The King puts Laertes' hand into Hamlet's.*]
HAMLET Give me your pardon, sir. I have done you wrong,
  But pardon't as you are a gentleman.
  This presence knows,
  And you must needs have heard, how I am punish'd
  With a sore distraction. What I have done   230
  That might your nature, honor, and exception
  Roughly awake, I here proclaim was madness.
  Was't Hamlet wrong'd Laertes? Never Hamlet!
  If Hamlet from himself be ta'en away,
  And when he's not himself does wrong Laertes,   235
  Then Hamlet does it not, Hamlet denies it.
  Who does it then? His madness. If't be so,
  Hamlet is of the faction that is wronged,
  His madness is poor Hamlet's enemy.
  [Sir, in this audience,]   240

---

216. gain-giving: misgiving.   **219–20. special . . . sparrow.** See Matthew
10:29.   **222. the readiness is all.** See Matthew 24:44, "Be ye also ready" (T).
223. of aught: i.e. whatever.   **223–24. knows . . . betimes:** knows what is the
best time to leave it.   **224. s.d. State:** nobles.   **228. presence:** assembled court.
229. punish'd: afflicted.   **231. exception:** objection.

Let my disclaiming from a purpos'd evil
Free me so far in your most generous thoughts,
That I have shot my arrow o'er the house
And hurt my brother.
LAERTES   I am satisfied in nature,
Whose motive in this case should stir me most   245
To my revenge, but in my terms of honor
I stand aloof, and will no reconcilement
Till by some elder masters of known honor
I have a voice and president of peace
To [keep] my name ungor'd. But [till] that time   250
I do receive your offer'd love like love,
And will not wrong it.
HAMLET   I embrace it freely,
And will this brothers' wager frankly play.
Give us the foils. [Come on.]
LAERTES   Come, one for me.
HAMLET I'll be your foil, Laertes; in mine ignorance   255
Your skill shall like a star i' th' darkest night
Stick fiery off indeed.
LAERTES   You mock me, sir.
HAMLET No, by this hand.
KING Give them the foils, young Osric. Cousin
Hamlet,
You know the wager?
HAMLET   Very well, my lord.   260
Your Grace has laid the odds a' th' weaker side.
KING I do not fear it, I have seen you both;
But since he is [better'd], we have therefore odds.
LAERTES This is too heavy; let me see another.
HAMLET This likes me well. These foils have all a
length?   [Prepare to play.] 265
OSRIC Ay, my good lord.
KING Set me the stoups of wine upon that table.

---

241. my . . . evil: my declaration that I intended no harm.   **242. Free:** absolute.   **244. in nature:** so far as my personal feelings are concerned.   **246. in . . . honor:** i.e. as a man governed by an established code of honor.   **249–50. have . . . ungor'd:** can secure an opinion backed by precedent that I can make peace with you without injury to my reputation.   **253. brothers':** i.e. amicable, as if between brothers. **frankly:** freely, without constraint.   **255. foil:** thin sheet of metal placed behind a jewel to set it off.   **257. Stick . . . off:** blaze out in contrast.   **261. laid the odds:** i.e. wagered a higher stake (horses to rapiers).   **263. is better'd:** has perfected his skill. **odds:** i.e. the arrangement that Laertes must take more bouts than Hamlet to win.   **265. likes:** pleases. **a length:** the same length.   **267. stoups:** tankards.

If Hamlet give the first or second hit,
Or quit in answer of the third exchange,
Let all the battlements their ord'nance fire.   270
The King shall drink to Hamlet's better breath,
And in the cup an [union] shall he throw,
Richer than that which four successive kings
In Denmark's crown have worn. Give me the cups,
And let the kettle to the trumpet speak,   275
The trumpet to the cannoneer without,
The cannons to the heavens, the heaven to earth,
"Now the King drinks to Hamlet." Come begin;
                              Trumpets the while.
And you, the judges, bear a wary eye.
HAMLET Come on, sir.
LAERTES   Come, my lord.
                    [*They play and Hamlet scores a hit.*]
HAMLET   One.
LAERTES   No.
HAMLET   Judgment.   280
OSRIC A hit, a very palpable hit.
LAERTES   Well, again.
KING Stay, give me drink. Hamlet, this pearl is thine,
    Here's to thy health! Give him the cup.
            *Drum, trumpets [sound] flourish. A piece goes
            off [within].*
HAMLET I'll play this bout first, set it by a while.
    Come. [*They play again.*] Another hit; what say you?   285
LAERTES [A touch, a touch,] I do confess't.
KING Our son shall win.
QUEEN   He's fat, and scant of breath.
    Here, Hamlet, take my napkin, rub thy brows.
    The Queen carouses to thy fortune, Hamlet.
HAMLET Good madam!
KING   Gertrude, do not drink.   290
QUEEN I will, my lord, I pray you pardon me.
KING [*Aside.*] It is the pois'ned cup, it is too late.
HAMLET I dare not drink yet, madam; by and by.
QUEEN Come, let me wipe thy face.
LAERTES My lord, I'll hit him now.

269. quit . . . exchange: pays back wins by Laertes in the first and second bouts by taking the third. **270. ord'nance:** cannon (T). **272. union:** an especially fine pearl. **275. kettle:** kettle-drum. **285. napkin:** handkerchief (T). **287. fat:** sweaty. **289. carouses:** drinks a toast.

KING   I do not think't.   295
LAERTES [*Aside.*] And yet it is almost against my conscience.
HAMLET Come, for the third, Laertes, you do but dally.
    I pray you pass with your best violence;
    I am sure you make a wanton of me.
LAERTES Say you so? Come on.   [*They play.*] 300
OSRIC Nothing, neither way.
LAERTES Have at you now!
    [*Laertes wounds Hamlet; then, in scuffling, they
    change rapiers.*]
KING   Part them, they are incens'd.
HAMLET Nay, come again.
                    [*Hamlet wounds Laertes. The Queen falls.*]
OSRIC   Look to the Queen there ho!
HORATIO They bleed on both sides. How is it, my lord?
OSRIC How is't, Laertes?   305
LAERTES Why, as a woodcock to mine own springe,
    Osric:
    I am justly kill'd with mine own treachery.
HAMLET How does the Queen?
KING   She sounds to see them bleed.
QUEEN No, no, the drink, the drink—O my dear
    Hamlet—
    The drink, the drink! I am pois'ned.   [*Dies.*] 310
HAMLET O villainy! Ho, let the door be lock'd!
    Treachery! Seek it out.
LAERTES It is here, Hamlet. [Hamlet,] thou art slain.
    No med'cine in the world can do thee good;
    In thee there is not half an hour's life.   315
    The treacherous instrument is in [thy] hand,
    Unbated and envenom'd. The foul practice
    Hath turn'd itself on me. Lo here I lie,
    Never to rise again. Thy mother's pois'ned.
    I can no more—the King, the King's to blame.   320
HAMLET The point envenom'd too!
    Then, venom, to thy work.   [*Hurts the King.*]
ALL Treason! treason!
KING O, yet defend me, friends, I am but hurt.
HAMLET Here, thou incestious, [murd'rous], damned Dane,   325

---

299. make . . . me: i.e. are holding back, in order to let me win, as one does
with a spoiled child *(wanton)*.   **306. woodcock.** See note on 1.3.115 (T). **springe:**
snare.   **308. sounds:** swoons.   **317. Unbated:** not blunted. **foul practice:** vile
plot.   **322 s.d. Hurts:** wounds.

Drink [off] this potion! Is [thy union] here?
Follow my mother!   [*King dies.*]
LAERTES   He is justly served,
It is a poison temper'd by himself.
Exchange forgiveness with me, noble Hamlet.
Mine and my father's death come not upon thee,   330
Nor thine on me!   [*Dies.*]
HAMLET   Heaven make thee free of it! I follow thee.
I am dead, Horatio. Wretched queen, adieu!
You that look pale, and tremble at this chance,
That are but mutes or audience to this act,   335
Had I but time—as this fell sergeant, Death,
Is strict in his arrest—O, I could tell you—
But let it be. Horatio, I am dead,
Thou livest. Report me and my cause aright
To the unsatisfied.
HORATIO   Never believe it;   340
I am more an antique Roman than a Dane.
Here's yet some liquor left.
HAMLET   As th' art a man,
Give me the cup. Let go! By heaven, I'll ha't!
O God, Horatio, what a wounded name,
Things standing thus unknown, shall I leave behind me!   345
If thou didst ever hold me in thy heart,
Absent thee from felicity a while,
And in this harsh world draw thy breath in pain
To tell my story.   *A march afar off* [*and a shot within*].
What warlike noise is this?
                              [*Osric goes to the door and returns.*]
OSRIC   Young Fortinbras, with conquest come from Poland,   350
To th' embassadors of England gives
This warlike volley.
HAMLET   O, I die, Horatio,
The potent poison quite o'er-crows my spirit.
I cannot live to hear the news from England,
But I do prophesy th' election lights   355
On Fortinbras, he has my dying voice.
So tell him, with th' occurrents more and less

---

328. temper'd: mixed.   **332. make thee free:** absolve you.   **335. mutes or audience:** silent spectators.   **336. fell:** cruel. **sergeant:** sheriff's officer.   **341. antique Roman:** i.e. one who will commit suicide on such an occasion.   **353. o'er-crows:** triumphs over (a term derived from cockfighting). **spirit:** vital energy.   **356. voice:** nomination, vote.   **357. occurrents:** occurrences.

Which have solicited—the rest is silence.   [*Dies.*]
HORATIO Now cracks a noble heart. Good night, sweet prince,
And flights of angels sing thee to thy rest!   360
                             [*March within.*]
Why does the drum come hither?

    Enter FORTINBRAS *with the* [ENGLISH] EMBASSADORS,
        [*with Drum, Colors, and Attendants*].

FORTINBRAS Where is this sight?
HORATIO   What is it you would see?
If aught of woe or wonder, cease your search.
FORTINBRAS This quarry cries on havoc. O proud death,
What feast is toward in thine eternal cell,   365
That thou so many princes at a shot
So bloodily hast strook?
[1.] EMBASSADOR The sight is dismal,
And our affairs from England come too late.
The ears are senseless that should give us hearing,
To tell him his commandment is fulfill'd,   370
That Rosencrantz and Guildenstern are dead.
Where should we have our thanks?
HORATIO   Not from his mouth,
Had it th' ability of life to thank you.
He never gave commandement for their death.
But since so jump upon this bloody question,   375
You from the Polack wars, and you from England,
Are here arrived, give order that these bodies
High on a stage be placed to the view,
And let me speak to [th'] yet unknowing world
How these things came about. So shall you hear   380
Of carnal, bloody, and unnatural acts,
Of accidental judgments, casual slaughters,
Of deaths put on by cunning and [forc'd] cause,
And in this upshot, purposes mistook
Fall'n on th' inventors' heads: all this can I   385
Truly deliver.
FORTINBRAS   Let us haste to hear it,
And call the noblest to the audience.
For me, with sorrow I embrace my fortune.

---

358. solicited: instigated.   **364. This . . . havoc:** this heap of corpses proclaims
a massacre.   **365. toward:** in preparation.   **372. his:** i.e. the King's.   **375. jump:**
precisely, pat. **question:** matter.   **378. stage:** platform.   **382. judgments:** retribu-
tions. **casual:** happening by chance.   **383. put on:** instigated.

I have some rights, of memory in this kingdom,
Which now to claim my vantage doth invite me.   390
HORATIO Of that I shall have also cause to speak,
And from his mouth whose voice will draw [on] more.
But let this same be presently perform'd
Even while men's minds are wild, lest more mischance
On plots and errors happen.
FORTINBRAS   Let four captains   395
Bear Hamlet like a soldier to the stage,
For he was likely, had he been put on,
To have prov'd most royal; and for his passage,
The soldiers' music and the rite of war
Speak loudly for him.   400
Take up the bodies. Such a sight as this
Becomes the field, but here shows much amiss.
Go bid the soldiers shoot.
        Exeunt [marching; after the which a peal of ordinance are shot off].

---

389. of memory: unforgotten.   **390. my vantage:** i.e. my opportune presence
at a moment when the throne is empty.   **392. his . . . more:** the mouth of
one (Hamlet) whose vote will induce others to support your claim.   **393. presently:** at once.   **394. wild:** distraught.   **397. put on:** put to the test (by becoming
king).   **398. passage:** death.   **402. Becomes . . . amiss:** befits the battlefield, but
appears very much out of place here.

NOTE ON THE TEXT

Hamlet offers a textual situation too complicated to permit here more
than a sketch of the principal problems involved.

There are three early and significant editions of *Hamlet:* First Quarto
(Q1), 1603; Second Quarto (Q2), 1604/5; First Folio (F1), 1623. Three
more quartos, stemming from Q2, appeared before the Restoration: Q3
(1611); Q4 (undated); Q5 (1637). The first of several Players' Quartos (Bet-
terton's acting version) was printed in 1676.

Q1, approximately half the length of Q2, is one of the so-called "bad"
quartos, i.e., a memorially reconstructed version, in this case, one based
most probably on a much shortened text prepared by Shakespeare's company for provincial touring, the principal reporter, it is generally agreed,
being the actor who doubled in the roles of Marcellus, Lucianus (the villain in the play-within-the-play who represents Hamlet's uncle, Claudius),
and perhaps, Voltemand. Thus, although in one sense a substantive text,
Q1 is without any real textual authority, but its stage directions and very
occasionally its readings are valuable in supplementing, corroborating, or

correcting Q2 and F1. It also contains one scene (see Textual Notes, 4.6) not found in Q2–4 or F1. Recently, a few critics, whose views have received almost no acceptance, have resurrected the long outmoded theory that Q1 represents Shakespeare's first draft of *Hamlet*.

Since the pioneer work of John Dover Wilson in 1934, the position of Q2 as the basic copy-text for a critical edition has, until very recently (see below), gone unchallenged. Wilson was able to show with near certainty that Q2 was printed from some form of Shakespeare's autograph, most probably the "foul papers," containing among other evidence of authorial origin occasional "first" shots (e.g., 2.2.73, 541; 3.2.166, 168, 223). One qualification of this view, however, is now generally admitted: Act 1, as Greg had earlier suggested, was set in good part not from the manuscript but from a copy of Q1 corrected and enlarged by collation with the manuscript. This qualification has important bearings on the relative authority of the Q2 text in Act 1 where its readings agree with Q1 against those of F1. Another influential theory advanced by Wilson—that Q2 was badly printed because the work was set up by a young and inexperienced compositor—must now be abandoned. Fredson Bowers and J. R. Brown have proved that two compositors set Q2 and that the printing errors and supposed omissions, etc., are pretty evenly distributed between them. Such a view suggests that at least some words and passages found only in F1 were probably not accidentally omitted by Wilson's hypothetical inexperienced compositor but were not present in Shakespeare's manuscript when it served as copy for Q2. This suggestion, if accepted, raises one of several questions about the provenience of the F1 text.

The exact status of the F1 text has become increasingly uncertain in recent years. The theory that F1 was printed from a copy of Q2 which had been brought into some measure of conformity (by verbal substitutions, deletion of some 230 lines, and addition of some 83 lines) with a playhouse manuscript has been generally discounted. Textual critics now agree that F1 was set up, with occasional reference to Q2–4, from some kind of manuscript at one or more removes from Shakespeare's "foul papers," but whether the provenience of such a manuscript was promptcopy, at one point theater related, or scribal or authorial "fair copy" remains debatable. Such a theory allows the F1 text an independent authority apart from Q2 and strengthens the authority of readings in which F1 and Q2 agree. F1 also contains a number of substantive readings which reflect early stage usage, as is shown by the quite frequent agreement, against Q2, between F1 and Q1 (e.g., 17 in 2.2). This would appear to suggest a date for the F1 text of sometime shortly before the publication of Q1 in 1603. On the other hand, Q1 also shares a substantial number of readings with Q2, which differ in their turn from F1 readings (e.g., 43 in 2.2). This divergence in Q1 readings suggests, I believe, that a distinction must be drawn between the manuscript underlying the reported Q1 text (as suggested above, probably an official abridgement by Shakespeare's company) and the manuscript that served as printer's copy for the F1 text, which should in all likelihood, though not necessarily, be dated sometime after 1602–3. In other words the manuscript from which F1 was set must have undergone at least one more transcription, thus differing in many readings from the manuscript from which the abridgement underlying Q1's reported text had been derived, in order to account for Fl's variant readings in those places where Q1 had agreed with Q2 against F1. Whether such F1 readings (as well as some of the additions in F1) represent possible Shakespearean revision (the major additions, unless, as some have argued, they were accidentally omitted when Q2 was set from Shakespeare's "foul papers," probably do) or actors' or bookholder's changes must in the present state of our knowledge remain uncertain, though Jenkins argues that the F1 text shows definite signs of contamination from actors' adlibbing. The present text has been influenced by Jenkins's suggestion.

It was noted above that, since 1934, Q2 has been accepted (as in the present edition) as the basic copy-text for *Hamlet*. In the last few years, however, there has been a reversion by Taylor/Wells *(Complete Works, Oxford, 1986)* and Hibbard (Oxford, 1987) to F1 as the basic copy-text (for substantive readings) on the unprovable assumption that Shakespeare himself was responsible for all or most of the additions, omissions (see below), and multiple word substitutions which distinguish F1 from Q2, surely a questionable decision considering its extremely uncertain provenience. This reversion to F1 is, of course, the outgrowth of two further assumptions: (a) the recently fashionable view that Shakespeare was an inveterate reviser (see Werstine for a critical analysis of privileging either Q2 or F1); and (b) the dangerous premise that an editor should prefer an acting text (despite the obvious fact that such a text would inevitably change over the years, even from performance to performance) instead of what is described as a "literary" text such as Q2.

A reader who wishes to reconstruct the main outlines of the F1 text as it differs from that of Q2 may do so (a) by noting those passages found only in F1, which in the present text are enclosed in square brackets, and (b) by marking the following F1 omissions (single words and phrases are generally not included; agreement with Q1 omissions is indicated by *(Q1)* following each F1 omission): 1.1.108–25 *(Q1);* 1.2.58–60 ("wrung ... consent."), partly in Q1; 1.4.17–38 (" ...scandal.") *(Q1),* 75–8 (" ...beneath.") *(Q1);* 2.2.17 *(Q1),* 444–5 ("as wholesome ... fine."), partly in Ql, 465 ("So proceed you."), equivalent in Ql; 3.2.171–2 *(Q1),* 218–9 *(Q1);* 3.4.71–6 ("Sense ... difference.") *(Q1),* 78–81 (" ... mope.") *(Q1),* 161–5 (" ... on.") *(Q1),* 167–70 ("the next more ... potency.") *(Q1),* 180 ("One ... lady.") *(Q1),* 202–10) *(Q1);* 4.1.4 *(Q1),* 41–4 (" ... air.") *(Q1);* 4.3.26–8 *("King.* Alas ... worm."), equivalent in Q1; 4.4.9–66 *(Q1,* except 1. 14); 4.5.76 ("and now behold!") *(Q1),* 97 ("Attend!") *(Q1);* 4.7.59 ("Ay, my lord.") *(Q1),* 68–81 ("My ... graveness.") *(Q1,* except for a variant reading of 1.68), 100–02 ("The scrimers ... them.") *(Q1),* 114–23 *(Q1);*

5.1.264 ("Gentlemen!") *(Q1)*; 5.2.106 ("Sir ..")-43, except F1 retains a compacted version of 11. 136–7 and part of 1. 141 (all omitted, *Q1*), 155–6 *(Q1)*.

Since the textual situation in *Hamlet* is so intricate, the Textual Notes offer as complete a picture of the interrelations between Q2, F1, and Q1 as considerations of space allow. All significant variants between Q2–4 and F1, as well as additions and omissions, are listed, together with a record of Q1's concurrence or disagreement with Q2 and F1 in these and some other readings. *(Q1)* immediately after the square bracket or following other sigla indicates that Q1 here agrees with Q2 or with the other editions listed. The absence of citation of Q1 in any entry indicates that the reading of the lemma occurs in a passage which in Q1 is either omitted or so differently worded that it offers no recognizable equivalent. To help the reader in appreciating the debased nature of the Q1 text, especially where it differs most markedly from Q2–4 and F1, some longer passages (including the Q1 version of "To be, or not to be," 3.1.55–89) are given in the Textual Notes (see 1.3.135–6, 2.2.546–8, 3.1 opening, 3.2.45, 155–73, 3.3.36–72, 3.4.137, 4.5 opening and line 96, 4.6, 4.7.140, 5.1.294–9, 5.2.165–9).

Der bestrafte Brudermord, oder Prinz Hamlet aus Dännemark (Fratricide Punished), referred to occasionally in the Textual Notes, is a German adaptation of *Hamlet* played by visiting English comedians in the early years of the seventeenth century. It shows several interesting points of contact with Q1, but it is ultimately derived from Shakespeare's text as it appears in Q2, or possibly through performance of the officially shortened text which underlies Q1's reported text.

For further information, see: J. D. Wilson, *The Manuscript of Shakespeare's "Hamlet,"* 2 vols. (Cambridge, 1934), and ed., New Shakespeare *Hamlet* (Cambridge, 1934, rev. ed., 1948); T. M. Parrott and Hardin Craig, eds., *The Tragedy of Hamlet* (Madison, Wisc., 1938); G. I. Duthie, *The "Bad" Quarto of "Hamlet," A Critical Study* (Cambridge, 1941); Alice Walker, *Textual Problems of the First Folio* (Cambridge, 1953); W. W. Greg, *The Shakespeare First Folio* (Oxford, 1955); J. R. Brown, "The Compositors of Hamlet Q2 and *The Merchant of Venice*," *SB*, VII (1955), 17–40; F. T. Bowers, "The Printing of Hamlet, Q2," *SB* VII (1955) 41–50; Harold Jenkins, "The Relation between the Second Quarto and the Folio Text of Hamlet," *SB*, VII (1955), 69–83, "Playhouse Interpolations in the Folio Text of Hamlet," *SB*, XIII (1960), 31–47, and ed., New Arden *Hamlet* (London, 1982); J. M. Nosworthy, *Shakespeare's Occasional Plays* (London, 1965); J. K. Walton, *The Quarto Copy for the First Folio of Shakespeare* (Dublin, 1971); Gary Taylor, "The Folio Copy for Hamlet, King Lear, and Othello," *SQ*, XXXIV (1983), 44–61; Philip Edwards, ed., New Cambridge *Hamlet, Prince of Denmark* (Cambridge, 1985); G. R. Hibbard, ed., New Oxford *Hamlet* (Oxford, 1987); Stanley Wells, Gary Taylor, et al., *William Shakespeare: A Textual Companion* (Oxford, 1987); Paul Werstine, "The Textual Mystery of Hamlet," *SQ*, XXXIX (1988), 1–26; Thomas Clayton, *ed., The "Hamlet"*

First Published (Q1, 1603): Origins, Form, Intertextualities (Newark, N.J., 1992). See also Y.S. Bains, "The Incidence of Corrupt Passages in the First Quarto of Shakespeare's *Hamlet*," *Notes & Queries* 40 (1993), 186–92; Bernice Kliman, ed., "The Enfolded *Hamlet*," *SNL* (1996), 1–44; Ann Thompson and Neil Taylor, "'O that this too too XXXXX text would melt:' *Hamlet* and the Indecisions of Modern Editors and Publishers," *TEXT*, 10 (1997), 221–36; Jesús Tronch-Pérez, ed., *A Synoptic* Hamlet (Valencia, 2002); Paul Bertram and Bernice Kliman, eds., *The Three-Text* Hamlet: *Parallel Texts of the First and Second Quartos and First Folio*, 2nd ed. (New York, 2003); Ann Thompson and Neil Taylor, eds., Arden *Hamlet*, 3rd Series (London, 2006) (updated T, 2011).

TEXTUAL NOTES

Title: The . . . Denmark] *F1;* The Tragicall Historie of Hamlet, Prince of Denmarke. By William Shakespeare. Newly imprinted and enlarged to almost as much againe as it was, according to the true and perfect Coppie. *Q2 (title-page);* The Tragicall Historie of Hamlet Prince of Denmarke By William Shake-speare. As it hath beene diuerse times acted by his Highnesse seruants in the Cittie of London: as also in the two Vniuersities of Cambridge and Oxford, and else-where *Q1 (title-page)*

Dramatis personae: *subs. as first given in Q (1676)*

Act-scene division: *none in Q1–4; F1 marks l.1-3, Act 2, ll.2; other act-scene divisions from Q (1676), Rowe, and later editors (see first note to each scene); present act-scene division as a whole first established by Capell*

I.I

1.1] *F1*

Location: *Alexander (after Rowe)*

o.s.d. meeting] *ed.; Q1 s.d. reads:* Enter two Centinels. *(with s.pp. distinguishing Barnardo and Francisco only as 1. and 2.)*

4 **Barnardo.]** Barnardo? *F1*
7 **twelf]** twelue *Q3–4, F1*
14 **ho! Who is]** who's *F1;* who is *Q1*
16 **soldier]** *F1 (Q1);* souldiers *Q2–4*
17 **hath my]** *(Q1);* ha's my *F1*
21 s.p. **Hor.] Mar.** *F1 (Q1)*
33 **have two nights]** *(Q1);* two Nights haue *F1*

40 **off]** *Q3–4 (Q1):* of *Q2, F1*
41 **figure]** figure, *F1*
43 **'a]** it *F1 (Q1)*
44 **harrows]** *F1;* horrowes *Q2–4;* horrors *Q1*
45 **Speak to]** Question *F1 (Q1)*
51 s.d. **Exit Ghost.]** *placed as in F1; after* offended, /. *50, Q2–4*
55 **you on't]** *F1 (Q1);* you-ont *Q2;* you of it *Q3–4*
61 **he]** *(Q1);* om. *F1*
61 **the]** *(Q1);* th'] *F1*
63 **smote]** *Q3–4;* smot *Q2, F1 (Q1)*
63 **sledded]** *F1;* sleaded *Q2–4 (Q1)*
63 **Polacks]** *Malone;* pollax *Q2–4, F1 (Q1)*
65 **jump]** *(Q1);* iust *F1*
68 **mine]** my *F1 (Q1)*
73 **why]** *F1 (Q1);* with *Q2–4*
73 **cast]** *F1;* cost *Q2–4 (Q1)*
79 **I,]** *F1 (Q1);* I. *Q2–4*
87 **heraldy]** Heraldrie *F1, Q3–4 (Q1)*
88 **those]** *F1 (Q1);* these *Q2–4*
89 **of]** *(Q1);* on *F1*
91 **return'd]** *F1;* returne *Q2–4*
93 **comart]** Cou'nant *F1*
94 **design'd]** *F2;* desseigne *Q2–4, F1*
98 **lawless]** *(Q1);* Landlesse *F1*
101 **As]** And *F1*
103 **compulsatory]** Compulsatiue *F1*
108–25 **I . . . countrymen.]** *om. F1 (Q1)*
108 **e'en so]** *Collier;* enso *Q2;* euen so *Q3–4*
112 **mote]** *Q4;* moth *Q2–3*
115 **tenantless]** *Q3–4;* tennatlesse *Q2*
116 **streets.]** *Theobald (subs.);* streets *Q2–4*
121 **fear'd]** *Collier conj.;* feare *Q2;* fearce *Q3;* fierce *Q4*

125 s.d. **Ghost**] Ghost againe *F1*
126 **again!**] *F1 (subs.)*; againe *Q2–4;* againe, *Q1*
126 s.d. **It . . . arms.**] *om. F1 (Q1)*
138 **your**] you *F1 (Q1)*
139 s.d. **The cock crows.**] *placed as in Cambridge; after l. 138, Q2–4; om. F1 (Q1)*
140 **it**] at ir *F1*
142 s.d. **Exit Ghost.**] *F1 (Q1)*
150 **morn**] day *F1*; morning *Q1*
151 **shrill-sounding**] *hyphen, F1*; shrill crowing *Q1*
158 **say**] *(Q1)*; sayes *F1*
160 **This**] The *F1 (Q1)*
161 **dare stir**] can walke *F1*; dare walke *Q1*
163 **takes**] *(Q1)*; talkes *F1*
164 **that**] *(Q1)*; the *F1*
167 **eastward hill.**] *Q3–4 (subs.)*; Eastward hill *Q2*; Easterne Hill, *F1*; mountaine top, *Q1*
168 **advice**] *F1*; aduise *Q2–4(Q1)*
175 **convenient**] conueniently *F1 (Q1)*

I.2

1.2] *F1*
Location: *Capell (subs., after Rowe)*
o.s.d. **Flourish. . . . aliis**] Enter Claudius King of Denmarke, Gertrude the Queene, Hamlet, Polonius, Laertes, and his Sister Ophelia, Lords Attendant. *F1*; Enter King, Queene, Hamlet, Leartes, Corambis, and the two Ambassadors, with Attendants. *Q1 (Leartes for Laertes and Corambis for Polonius throughout; cf. Corambus in Der bestrafte Brudermord)*
o.s.d. **Gertrude**] *F1 (throughout)*; Gertrad *Q2–4 (or Gertrard throughout, except Gertrud at 2.2.54 in Q3–4)*; Gertred *Q1 (or Gerterd throughout)* o.s.d. including . . . Cornelius] *from Q1 (see above): F1 brings in the Ambassadors at l. 25*
8 **sometime**] sometimes *F1*
9 **to**] of *F1*
11 **an . . . a**] one . . . one *F1*
16 **all,**] *Pope*; all *Q2–4, F1*
17 **follows**] follows, *F1*
21 **Co-leagued**] *Capell*; Coleagued *Q2*; Colegued *Q3*; Colleagued *Q4*; Colleagued *F1*
21 **this**] the *F1*
22 **pester**] *F1, Q3–4*; pestur *Q2* 24 bands] Bonds *F1*
29 **bedred**] *cf. Love's Labor's Lost, 1.1.138, and Lucrece, l. 975)*; bedrid *F1*; bed-rid *Q1*

34 **Cornelius**] Cornelia *Q1*
34 **Voltemand**] *F1*; Valtemand *Q2–4*; Voltemar *Q1 (throughout)*
35 **bearers**] *(Q1)*; bearing *F1* **38** **delated**] dilated *F1*; related *Q1* **38** s.d. **Giving a paper.**] *Collier MS (subs., after Capell)*
40 s.p. **Cor., Vol.**] Volt. *F1*
41 s.d. **Exeunt . . . Cornelius.**] *F1* (Exit . . .)
50 **My dread**] Dread my *F1*; My gratious *Q1*
55 **toward**] towards *F1*; for *Q1*
58 **H'ath**] *ed.*; Hath *Q2*; He hath *Q3–4. F1(Q1)*
58–60 **wrung . . . consent.**] *om. F1*; wrung from me a forced graunt, *Q1*
58 **wrung**] *Q3–4 (Q1)*; wroung *Q2*
65 s.d. **Aside.**] *Theobald*
67 **so**] *F1*; so much *Q2–4* **67 in the**] i' th' *F1*
67 **sun**] *F1*; sonne *Q2–4*
68 **nighted**] nightly *F1*
72 **common,**] *F1*; common *Q2–4*
77 **good mother**] *F1*; coold mother *Q2*; could smother *Q3–4*
82 **shapes**] *Q3–4*; chapes *Q2*; shewes *F1*
83 **denote**] *F1*; deuote *Q2–3*; deuoute *Q4*
85 **passes**] passeth *F1*
96 **or**] a *F1*
97 **unschool'd:**] *F1*; vnschoold *Q2*; vnschoold, *O-J-4*
105 **cone**] *Capell*; course *Q2–4*, Coarse *F1*
112 **toward**] towards *F1*
112 **you.**] *F1*; you *Q2–4* ; **114 retrograde**] *F1*; retrogard *Q2–3*; retrograd *Q4*
119 **pray thee**] prythee *F1*
126 **tell,**] *F1*; tell. *Q2–4*, tell *Q1*
127 **rouse**] *Malone*; rowse *Q2–4 (Q1)*: Rouce *F1*
127 **heaven**] Heauens *F1*
128 s.d. **Flourish**] *om. F1 (Q1)*
128 s.d. **Exeunt . . . Hamlet.**] *(Q1)*; Exeunt Manet Hamlet. *F1*
129 **sallied**] *cf. sallies at 2.1.39 and vnsallied in Love's Labor's Lost, 5.2.352*; solid *F1*; I grieu'd and sallied *Q1*
132 **self-slaughter**] *F1*; seale slaughter *Q2–4*
132 **God, God,**] God, O God! *F1*
133 **weary**] *F1*; wary *Q2–4*
134 **Seem**] Seemes *F1*
135 **ah fie**] Oh fie, fie *F1*
137 **merely. That**] *F1*; meerely that *Q2–4*
137 **to this**] *F1*; thus *Q2–4*
140 **satyr**] *F4*; satire *Q2–3*; Satyre *F1*, *Q4*
141 **beteem**] beteene *F1*

143 **Why,**] Pope; why *Q2–4, F1*
143 **should**] would *F1(Q1)*
147 **month, or**] *F1;* month or *Q2;*
month. Or *Q3–4*
149 **even she**] *F1*
150 **God**] *(Q1).* Heauen *F1* ;
151 **my**] mine *F1 (Q1)*
155 **in**] *(Q1);*of *F1*
156 **married—O**] *ed.;* married, ô *Q2;*
married Oh! *Q3–4;* married. O *F1;*
married, well *Q1*
156 **speed:**] *ed.;* speed; *Q2–4;* speed,
F1 (Q1)
157 **incestious**] Incestuous *F1 (Q1)*
158 **good,**] good. *F1;* good: *Q1*
159 s.d. **Barnardo**] *Wilson;* Bernardo
Q2–4; Barnard *F1;* Q1 *s.d. om. Barnardo*
167 s.d. **To Barnardo.**] *Cambridge*
170 **hear**] haue *F1*
171 **my**] mine *F1*
174 **Elsinore**] *Malone;* Elsonoure *Q2–4;*
Elsenour *F1;* Elseneoure *Q1*
175 **to drink deep**] *F1 (Q1);* for to
drinke *Q2–4*
177 **prithee**] pray thee *F1;* O I pre
thee *Q1*
177 **studient**] *(Q1);* Student *F1, Q3–4*
178 **see**] *F1 (Q1)*
183 **Or . . . had**] Ere I had euer *F1;* Ere
euer I had *Q1*
185 **Where**] *(Q1);* Oh where *F1*
186 **'a**] he *F1(Q1) (the usual F1 form)*
187 **'A**] He *F1 (Q1)*
191 **lord,**] *F1 (Q1);* Lord *Q2–4*
195 **God's**] *(Q1);* Heauens *F1*
198 **waste**] *F2;* wast *Q2–3, F1;* vast
Q4 (Q1)
200 **Armed at point**] Arm'd at all points
F1; Armed to poynt *Q1*
200 **point exactly, cap-a-pe**] *F1*
(points); poynt, exactly Capapea *Q2*
(Q1); poynt, exactly Cap apea *Q3–4*
203 **fear-surprised**] *hyphen, F1;* feare
oppressed *Q1*
204 **distill'd**] bestil'd *F1;* distilled *Q1*
209 **Where, as**] *Q5;* Whereas *Q2–4, F1;*
Where as *Q1*
213 **watch**] watcht *F1;* watched *Q1*
224 **indeed**] *F1(Q1)*
225, 227, 228 s.pp. **Mar., Bar.**] *Capell*
(after F1 Both.); All. *Q2–4(Q1)*
231 **What, look'd**] *F1;* What look't *Q2–4;*
How look't *Q1 (with a comma after he)*
236 **very like**] *F1 (Q1)*
237 **hundreth**] hundred *F1 (Q1)*
238 s.p. **Mar., Bar.**] *Capell; F1* s.p. All.;
Q1 s.p. Mar.

239 **grisl'd**] *Warburton;* grissl'd *Q2–5,*
grisseld *Q4;* grisly *F1;* grisleld *Q1*
241 **I will**] *(Q1);* Ile *F1*
241 **to-night**] *F1, Q3–4 (Q1);* to nigh *Q2*
242 **warr'nt**] *Kittredge (after Wilson);* warn't
Q2–4; warrant you *F1;* warrant *Q1*
247 **tenable**] treble *F1;* tenible *Q1*
248 **whatsomever**] *Wilson;* what
someuer *Q2;* what what soeuer *Q3;*
whatsoeuer *F1, Q4 (Q1)*
250 **fare**] *F1, Q3–4 (Q1);* farre *Q2*
250 **you**] *(Q1);* ye *F1*
251 **aleven**] *ed.;* a leauen *Q2–3;* eleuen
F1, Q4 (Q1)
251 **twelf**] twelue *Q3–4, F1(Q1)*
253 **Your loves**] Your loue *F1;* O your
loues, your loues *Q1*
253 s.d. **all but Hamlet**] *Cambridge (after*
Capell); s.d. after *l. 252, Q2–4, F1 (Q1);*
placed as in *Capell*
256 **Foul**] *F1, Q3–4 (Q1);* fonde *Q2*

I.3

1.3] *F1*
Location: *ed. (after Pope)*
o.s.d. **Ophelia**] Ofelia *Q1 (throughout)*
o.s.d. **his sister**] *om. F1 (Q1)*
1 **inbark'd**] *(Q1);* imbark't *F1, Q4*
3 **convey**] *ed.;* conuay, *Q2–4;* Conuoy *F1*
3 **is**] *F1;* in *Q2–4*
5 **favor**] fauours *F1*
8 **Forward**] Froward *F1*
9 **perfume and**] *om. F1 (Q1)*
9 **minute—**] *F2 (subs.);* minute *Q2–4;*
minute? *F1*
10 **so?**] *Rowe;* so. *Q2–4, F1*
12 **bulk**] *F1;* bulkes *Q2–4*
12 **this**] his *F1*
16 **will**] feare *F1*
18 **For . . . birth:**] *F1*
21 **safety**] sanctity *F1*
21 **this whole**] the weole *F1;* the
whole *F2*
26 **particular . . . place**] peculiar Sect
and force *F1*
34 **you in**] within *F1;* 36, 38, 39] *Q2–4*
mark these lines with gnomic quotes
37 **moon.**] *Q1;* Moone *Q2–4;*
Moone: *F1*
40 **their**] the *F1* 46 **watchman**]
watchmen *F1*
49 **Whiles**] Whilst *F1*
49 **like**] *F1 (Q1)*
51 **reaks**] recks *Q1*
51 s.d. **Enter Polonius.**] *placed as in F1;*
after rede. *l. 51, Q2–4;* Enter Corambis.
Q1 (after l. 54)

57 **stay'd**] *F1 (Q1)*; stayed *Q2–4*
57 **for. There—**] *Theobald;* for, there
  Q2–4 (Q1); for there: *F1* 57 s.d.
  laying . . . head] *Theobald*
57 **thee**] *(Q1)*; you *F1*
59 **Look**] See *F1*
62 **Those**] *(Q1)*; The *F1*
63 **unto thy soul**] to thy Soule *F1;* to
  thee *Q1*
65 **new-hatch'd**] *hyphen, Pope;* vnhatch't
  F1; new *Q1*
65 **courage**] *(Q1);* Comrade *F1*
68 **thy ear**] thine eare *F1*
74 **Are**] *F1, Q4 (Q1);* Or *Q2;* Ar *Q3*
74 **generous**] *F1;* generous, *Q2–4;*
  generall *Q1*
74 **chief**] *(Q1),* cheff *F1*
75 **be**] *F1;* boy *Q2–4*
76 **loan**] *F1* (lone); loue *Q2–4*
77 **dulleth th' edge**] *Q3–4 (reading* the);
  dulleth edge *Q2,* duls the edge *F1*
83 **invests**] inuites *F1*
97–8 **honor. What**] *F1;* honor,/
  What *Q2–4*
98 **you?**] *Q5;* you *Q2–4,* you, *F1*
105 **I will**] Ile *F1*
106 **these**] his *F1*
109 **Wringing**] *Theobald;* Wrong *Q2–4;*
  Roaming *F1;* tendring *Q1*
114 **almost . . . vows**] all the vowes *F1;*
  Q1 reads the line: And withall, such
  earnest vowes.
115 **springes**] *F1, Q3–4 (Q1);*
  springs *Q2*
117 **Lends**] *(Q1);* Giues *F1*
120 **fire. From**] *Q3–4 (subs.);* fire, from
  Q2; fire. For *F1*
120 **time**] time Daughter *F1*
121 **something**] somewhat *F1*
123 **parle**] parley *F1*
125 **teder**] *Q3–4;* tider *Q2,* tether *F1*
128 **that dye**] the eye *F1*
129 **implorators**] *F1, Q3–4;*
  imploratotors *Q2*
131 **beguile**] *F1, Q3–4;* beguide *Q2*
135–6 **Come . . . lord.**] *Q1 ends*
  the scene with the following lines:
  Cor. Ofelia, receiue none of his
  letters,/"For louers lines are snares
  to intrap the heart;/"Refuse his
  tokens, both of them are keyes/
  To vnlocke Chastitie vnto Desire;/
  Come in *Ofelia,* such men often
  proue,/"Great in their wordes, but
  little in their loue. (*the final couplet*
  seems to be a recollection of Twelfth
  Night, *2.4. 117–8*)

1.4

1.4] *Capell*
Location: *Alexander (after Rowe)*
  1 **shrowdly**] shrewdly *F1;* shrewd *Q1*
  1 **it . . . cold.**] is it very cold? *F1*
  2 **a**] *F1;* An *Q1*
  3 **twelf**] twelue *F1, Q3–4 (Q1)*
  5 **It then**] then it *F1*
  6 s.d. **off**] *Q3–4;* of *Q2;* s.d. *om. F1; Q1*
  gives Sound Trumpets, *after l. 3*
  6 s.d. **within**] *Rowe*
  9 **wassail**] *(Q1);* wassels *F1*
  14 **But**] And *F1*
  17–38 **This . . . scandal.**] *om. F1(Q1)* 17
  heavy-headed] *hyphen, Q3-4*
  17 **revel**] *Q3–4;* reueale *Q2*
  18 **traduc'd**] *Q3* (tradu'cd) *-4;* tradust *Q2*
  18 **tax'd**] *Pope;* taxed *Q2–4*
  23 **So,**] *Theobald;* So *Q2–4*
  36 **ev'l**] *ed. (after Keightley);* eale *Q2;*
  ease *Q3–4*
  42 **intents**] euents *F1* **45 Dane. O**] *F1*
  (Dane: Oh, oh); Dane, ô *Q2–4*
  48 **cerements**] cerments *F1;*
  ceremonies *Q1*
  49 **inurn'd**] *F1* (enurn'd); interr'd
  Q2–4 (Q1)
  56 **the**] *(Q1);* thee; *F1*
  57 s.d. **Ghost beckons Hamlet.**] *F1;*
  Beckins *Q2–4*
  61 **waves**] *(Q1);* wafts *F1*
  63 **I will**] will I *F1(Q1)*
  70 **summit**] *Rowe;* somnet *Q2–4;*
  Sonnet *F1*
  70 **cliff**] *F1;* cleefe *Q2–4*
  71 **beetles**] *F1;* bettles *Q2;* bettels *Q3–4;*
  beckles *Q1*
  72 **assume**] *(Q1);* assumes *F1*
  75–8 **The . . . beneath.**] *om. F1(Q1)*
  78 **waves**] wafts *F1*
  80 **hands**] hand *F1*
  82 **artere**] *Wilson;* arture *Q2;* artyre
  Q3; attire *Q4;* artery *Q5;* Artire *F1;*
  Artiue *Q1*
  83 **Nemean**] *Q3–4;* Nemeon *Q2 (Q1);*
  Nemian *F1*
  86 s.d. **Exeunt**] *F1;* Exit *Q2–4*
  87 **imagination**] *F1, Q3–4 (Q1);*
  imagion *Q2*

1.5

1.5] *Capell*
Location: *Alexander*
  1 **Whither**] *Q1;* Whether *Q2–4;*
  Where *F1*
  3 **sulph'rous**] *Kittredge (after Q3–4*
  sulphrous); sulphrus *Q2;* sulphurous *F1*

TEXTUAL NOTES

18 **knotted**] (*Q1*); knotty *F1*
20 **fearful**] fretfull *F1*(*Q1*)
22 **List . . . list!**] list *Hamlet*, oh list, *F1*; Hamlet, *Q1*
24 **God**] (*Q1*); Heauen *F1*
29 **Haste . . . that I**] Hast, hast me to know it/That *F1*; Haste me to knowe it that *Q1*
33 **roots**] (*Q1*); rots *F1*
35 **'Tis**] (*Q1*); It's *F1*
35 **my**] (*Q1*); *mine F1*
38 **know,**] *F4*; knowe *Q2–4*, *F1*(*Q1*)
41 **My uncle?**] mine Vncle? *F1*; my vncle! my vncle! *Q1*
43 **with traitorous gifts—**] *Pope* (*subs.*, *after Rowe*); with trayterous gifts, *Q2–4*; hath Traitorous guifts. *F1*; with gifts, *Q1*
45 **to his**] (*Q1*); to to this *F1* 47 a] *F1*
47 **falling-off**] *hyphen, Capell*
55 **lust**] *F1* (*Q1*); but *Q2–4*
55 **angel**] *F1*, Angle *Q2–4* (*Q1*)
56 **sate**] *F1*; sort *Q2–4*; fate *Q1*
58 **morning**] Mornings *F1* (*Q1*)
59 **my**] (*Q1*); *mine F1*
60 **of**] in *F1* (*Q1*)
62 **hebona**] (*Q1*); Hebenon *F1*
62 **vial**] (*Q1*);Violl *F1*
63 **my**] (*Q1*); *mine F1*
64 **leprous**] (*Q1*); leaperous *F1*
67 **alleys**] *Hanmer*; allies *Q2–4*, *F1*
68 **posset**] *F1*; possesse *Q2–4*
69 **eager**] (*Q1*);Aygre *F1*
71 **bark'd**] bak'd *F1*; barked *Q1*
75 **of queen**] (*Q1*); and Queene *F1*
77 **Unhous'led**] *ed.* (*after Theobald*); Vnhuzled *Q2*; Vnnuzled *Q3–4*; Vnhouzzled *F1*
77 **unanel'd**] *Pope*; vnanueld *Q2*; vn-anueld *Q3–4*; vnnaneld *F1*
79 **With all**] *F1*, *Q3–4* (*Q1*);Withall *Q2*
84 **howsomever**] howsoeuer *F1*(*Q1*)
84 **pursues**] pursuest *F1*
91 **adieu, adieu!**] adue, *Hamlet: F1*; *Q1 reads the line:* Hamlet adue, adue, adue: remember me.
91 **s.d. Exit.**] *F1*
93 **hold,**] *om. F1* (*Q1*)
94 **sinows**] sinnewes *F1*
95 **stiffly**] *F1*; swiftly *Q2–4*
96 **whiles**] while *F1*
102 **commandement**] Commandment *F1*
104 **Yes**] yes, yes *F1* (*Q1*)
101 **My tables—**] *Pope*; My tables, *Q2–4*; My Tables, my Tables; *F1*; (My tables) *Q1*
109 **I am**] (*Q1*); I'm *F1*

109 s.d. **He writes.**] *Rowe* (*subs.*)
113 s.p. **Hor.**] Hor. & Mar. *F1*
113 s.dd. **Within.**] *F1 gives the first, Capell the second*
113 s.d. **Enter . . . Marcellus.**] *placed by ed.; after l. 112, Q2–4; after* lord! *l. 113, F1; opposite l. 113, Q1*
113 **Heavens**] (*Q1*); Heauen *F1*
114 s.p. **Ham.**] Mar. *F1*
115 s.p. **Mar.**] Hor. *F1* (*Q1*)
116 **boy! Come, bird,**] *F1* (*subs.*); boy come, and *Q2–4*; so, come boy, *Q1*
119 **you will**] you'l *F1* (*Q1*)
121 **it?**] *F1* (*Q1*); it, *Q2–4*
122 **secret?**] *F1*; secret. *Q2–4* (*Q1*)
122 s.p. **Hor., Mar.**] *Capell*
122 **my lord**] *F1* (*Q1*)
123 **never**] (*Q1*); nere *F1*
126 **in the**] (*Q1*); i' th' *F1*
129 **desire**] desires *F1* (*Q1*)
130 **hath**] (*Q1*); ha's *F1*
131 **my**] (*Q1*); *mine F1*
132 **I will**] Looke you, Ile *F1*; ile *Q1*
133 **whirling**] *Theobald*; whurling *Q2–4*; hurling *F1*; wherling *Q1*
134 **I am**] (*Q1*); I'm *F1*
136 **Horatio**] (*Q1*); my Lord *F1*
137 **too.**] *Q5* (*subs.*); to, *Q2–4*; too, *F1* (*Q1*)
140 **O'ermaster't**] *F1*, *Q3–4*; Oremastret *Q2*; Or'emaister it *Q1*
145 s.p. **Hor., Mar.**] *Capell*
150 **Ha**] (*Q1*);Ah *F1*
151 **on, you hear**] one you here *F1*; you here, *Q1*
151 **cellarage**] *Johnson*; Sellerige *Q2* (*Q1*); selleredge *F1*
155, 161, 181 s.dd. **Beneath.**] *Capell*
156 **ubique?**] *F1*; vbique, *Q2–4*(*Q1*)
156 **our**] (*Q1*); for *F1*
159 **Swear . . . sword,**] *follows l. 160, F1* (*Q1*)
161 **by his sword**] *om. F1* (*Q1*)
162 **i' th'**] *F1*; it'h *Q2–4*; in the *Q1*
162 **earth**] (*Q1*); ground *F1*
167 **your**] (*Q1*); our *F1*
170–8 **How . . . note**] *F1* (*subs.*); (How . . . note) *Q2–4*
170 **some'er**] *Wilson*; so mere *Q2–4*; so ere *F1*; soere *Q1*
173 **times**] (*Q1*); time *F1*
174 **this**] (*Q1*); thus, *F1*
176 **Well, well,**] (*Q1*); well, *F1*
177 **they**] (*Q1*); there *F1*
179 **do swear,**] not to doe: *F1*
180 **you.**] you:/Sweare. *F1* (*Q1*)
181 s.d. **They swear.**] *Globe* (*after l. 182*); *placed as in Kittredge*

207

183 **With all**] *F1, Q3–4;* Withall *Q2;* In
all *Q1*
187 **pray.**] *Rowe;* pray, *Q2–4, F1 (Q1)*

2.1

2.1] *Q (1676);* Actus Secundus. *F1*
Location: *ed. (after Rowe)*
o.s.d. **with . . . Reynaldo**] *from Q2–4, F1*
s.dd.: with his man or two *Q2–4;* and
Reynoldo *F1; Q1 s.d. reads:* Enter
Corambis, and Montano.
1 **this**] his *F1;* this same *Q1* 1
Reynaldo] Reynoldo *F1 (throughout);*
Montano *Q1 (throughout)*
3 **marvell's**] *Dyce;* meruiles *Q2;*
maruelous *Q3–4;* maruels *F1*
4 **to make inquire**] you make inquiry
F1; To inquire *Q1*
6 **Marry**] *F1, Q4;* Mary *Q2–3*
14 **As**] *(Q1);* And *F1*
18 **if't**] *F1;* y'ft *Q2–4*
28 **Faith,**] Faith no, *F1;* I faith not a
whit, no not a whit, *Q1*
34 **unreclaimed**] *Q4;* vnreclamed
Q2–3; vnreclaim'd *F1*
38 **wit**] warrant *F1*
39 **sallies**] *see 1.2.129;* sullies *Q3–4;*
sulleyes *F1*
40 **wi' th'**] *ed.;* with *Q2–4;* i' th' *F1*
43 **seen**] seene. *F1*
43 **prenominate**] *F1, Q4;* prenominat
Q2–3
47 **or**] and *F1*
47 **addition**] *F1, Q3–4;* addistion *Q2*
49 **'a . . . 'a**] he . . . he *F1*
49 **this—. . . does—**] *Capell (after Rowe);*
this, . . . doos, *Q2;* this, . . . doos: *Q3–4;*
this? . . . does: *F1*
50 **By the mass**] *om. F1 (Q1)*
51 **consequence.**] consequence:/At
friend, or so, and Gentleman. *F1*
53 **closes thus:**] closes with you thus.
F1; closeth with him thus, *Q1*
54 **th' other**] tother *F1 (Q1)*
55 **or such**] and such *F1*
56 **'a**] he *F1*
56 **gaming, there o'ertook**] *F1;*
gaming there, or tooke *Q2–4*
58 **sale**] saile *F1;* lightnes *Q1*
59 **forth.**] *F1;* forth, *Q2–4*
60 **take**] takes *F1*
60 **carp**] Cape *F1*
64 **advice**] *F1;* aduise *Q2–4*
66 **ye . . . ye**] you . . . you *F1*
71 s.d. **Exit Reynaldo.**] *placed as in Dyce*
(after Singer); after l. 70, Q2–4; Exit. *F1*
(Q1) (after l. 70)

71 s.d. **Enter Ophelia.**] *placed as in*
Singer; after 1.70, Q2–4, F1 (Q1)
72 **O . . . I**] Alas, my Lord, I *F1*
73 **i' th'**] in the *F1*
73 **God**] Heauen *F1*
74 **closet**] Chamber *F1*
76 **stocking**] stockings *F1*
77 **down-gyved**] *hyphen, F2*
88 **'a**] he *F1*
92 **As**] That *F1*
94 **shoulder**] *(Q1);* shoulders *F1*
96 **a' doors**] *Q3* (a doores); adoores
Q2; of doores *Q4 (Q1);* adores *F1*
96 **helps**] helpe *F1(Q1)*
98 **Come**] *om. F1 (Q1)*
102 **passions**] passion *F1*
103 **sorry—**] *Capell;* sorry, *Q2–4, F1*
108 **heed**] speed *F1*
109 **coted**] quoted *F1*
109 **fear'd**] feare *F1*
111 **By heaven**] It seemes *F1,*
By heau'n *Q1*
117 **Come.**] om. *F1 (Q1)*

2.2

2.2] *F1*
Location: *Capell (after Rowe)*
o.s.d. **Flourish.**] *om. F1 (Q1)*
o.s.d. **Rosencrantz**] *Malone;* Rosencraus
Q2–4 (so generally throughout,
except Rosencrans *at 2.2.34);*
Rosincrane *F1 (also* Rosencrance
and Rosincran *elsewhere):*
Rossencraft *Q1*
o.s.d. **Guildenstern**] Guyldensterne *Q2–4*
(also Guyldersterne *elsewhere), F1;*
Gilderstone *Q1*
o.s.d. **cum aliis**] *F1*
5 **so**] so I *F1*
6 **Sith nor**] Since not *F1*
10 **dream**] deeme *F1*
12 **sith**] since *F1*
12 **neighbored**] *Q3–4;* nabored *Q2;*
Neighbour'd *F1*
12 **havior**] humour *F1*
13 **voutsafe**] vouchsafe *F1, Q4*
16 **occasion**] Occasions *F1*
17 **Whether . . . thus,**] *om. F1 (Q1)*
20 **is**] are *F1*
29 **But**] *om. F1 (Q1)*
31 **service**] Seruices *F1*
36 **you**] ye *F1*
37 **these**] the *F1*
39 **Ay**] *Capell;* I *Q2–4; om. F1 (Q1)*
39 s.d. **with some Attendants**]
Capell; F1 s.d. is Exit,
(after him! l. 39)

43 **I assure]** (*Q1*); Assure you, *F1* **45 and]**
(*Q1*); one *F1* **48 it hath]** I haue *F1;* it
had *Q1* **50 do I]** I do *F1*
52 **fruit]** Newes *F1*
53 s.d. **Exit Polonius.]** *Rowe*
54 **dear Gertrude]** *Q5;* deere Gertrard
Q2; decree: Gertrud *Q3–4;* sweet
Queene, that *F1*
57 **o'erhasty]** *F1;* hastie *Q2–4*
57 s.d. **Polonius . . . the]** *F1* (*subs.,*
reading Voltumand)
58 **my]** *om. F1* (*Q1*)
63, 75 **Polack]** (*Q1*); Poleak *F1*
73 **three]** *F1* (*Q1*); threescore *Q2–4*
76 **shown]** *F1* (shewne) (*Q1*); shone
Q2–4
76 s.d. **Giving a paper.]** *Malone* (*after*
Capell)
78 **this]** his *F1;* that *Q1*
85 s.d. **Exeunt Embassadors]** (*Q1*
subs.); Exit. Ambass. *F1*
85 s.d. **and Attendants]** *Alexander*
85 **well]** very well *F1*
90 **since]** *F1*
97 **he's]** he is *F1*
98 **'tis 'tis]** it is *F1*
104 **thus.]** *F1;* thus *Q2–4*
106 **while]** (*Q1*); whil'st *F1*
108 s.d. **Reads .. . letter.]** *ed.;* The
Letter. *F1*
111 **vile . . . vile]** vilde . . . vilde *F1*
112 **hear. Thus:]** *Jennens* (*subs.*); heare:
thus *Q2–4* (*Polonius' comments are*
given as part of the letter in Q2–4); heare
these *F1*
113 **etc.]** *om. F1* (*Q1*)
115 s.d. **Reads the]** *Rowe*
125 **This]** *F1; Pol.* This *Q2–4* (*repeated s.p.*)
125 **shown]** shew'd *F1*
126 **above]** *F1;* about *Q2–4* **126**
solicitings] soliciting *F1*
137 **winking,]** *F1;* working *Q2–4*
142 **prescripts]** Precepts *F1*
143 **his]** *F1, Q3–4;* her *Q2*
145 **advice]** *F1;* aduise *Q2–4*
146 **repell'd]** repulsed *F1*
148 **watch]** *F1, Q3–4;* wath *Q2*
149 **a]** *F1*
150 **wherein]** whereon *F1*
151 **mourn]** waile *F1*
151 **'tis]** *F1* (*Q1*)
152 **be,]** *Capell;* be *Q2–4, F1*
152 **like]** likely *F1*
153 **I would]** I'*de F1;* I would very *Q1*
156 s.d. **Points . . . shoulder.]** *Theobald*
161 **does]** ha's *F1*
167 **But]** And *F1*

167 s.d. **reading on a book]** *F1; in Q1*
the King describes the entrance of Hamlet
poring vppon a booke; Q1 (*like Der*
bestrafte Brudermord) *inserts at this*
point its version of 3.1.43–175
169 **you,]** *F1;* you *Q2–4*
170 s.d. **Exeunt]** *Rowe;* Exit *Q2–4, F1; s.d.*
placed as in F1; after l. 169, Q2–4
174 **Excellent]** Excellent, excellent *F1;*
Yea very *Q1*
174 **you are]** y'are *F1*(*Q1*)
177 **lord?]** *F1;* Lord. *Q2–4*
178–9 **Ay . . . thousand.]** *as prose, F1; as*
verse, Q2–4(*Q1*)
179 **ten]** (*Q1*); two *F1*
184–6 **Let . . . to't.]** *as prose, F1; as*
verse, Q2–4
185 **but]** but not *F1*
187 s.d. **Aside.]** *Capell*
188 **'a]** he *Fl* (*Q1*)
189 **'A]** he *F1*
189 **gone]** gone, farre gone *F1*
195 **that]** *om. F1* (*Q1*)
195 **read]** (*Q1*); meane *F1*
196 **rogue]** slaue *F1;* Satyre *Q1*
198 **and]** or *F1*
199 **lack]** locke *F1*
200 **most]** *om. F1;* pittifull *Q1*
202 **yourself]** (*Q1*): you your selfe *F1*
203 **shall grow]** should be *F1;* shalbe *Q1*
205 s.d. **Aside.]** *Johnson*
208 **that's . . . the]** (*Q1*); that is out
o' th' *F1*
208 s.d. **Aside.]** *Capell*
210 **sanity]** *F1;* sanctity *Q2–4* **212–13**
and . . . him] *F1*
213 **lord . . . take]** (*Q1*); Honourable
Lord, I will most humbly / Take *F1*
215 **cannot . . . thing]** cannot Sir . . .
thing *F1;* can take nothing from me
sir *Q1*
216 **not]** *om. F1* (*Q1*)
216–7 **withal—. . . life.]** withall, except
my life, my life. *F1*
219 s.d. **Enter . . . Rosencrantz.]** *placed*
as in Capell; after l. 217, Q2–4; after
l. 220, F1; after l. 214, Q1
220 **the]** my *F1*
221 s.d. **To Polonius.]** *Malone*
221 s.d. **Exit Polonius.]** *Q1* (exit.)
222 **My]** Mine *F1*
224 **excellent]** *F1, Q4;* extent *Q2;*
exelent *Q3*
225 **Ah]** *Q5;* A *Q2–4;* Oh *F1*
226 **you]** ye *F1*
228 **over-happy,]** *F1* (ouer-happy:); euer
happy *Q2–4*

TEXTUAL NOTES

229 cap] *F1;* lap *Q2–4*
230 shoe?] *F1;* shooe. *Q2–4* 233 favors]
  fauour *F1*
236 What] What's the *F1*
237 but] but that *F1* 239–69 Let . . .
  attended.] *F1*
266 s.p. Ros., Guil.] *Capell*
270 Elsinore] *Malone;* Elsonoure *Q2–4;*
  Elsonower *F1;* Elsanoure *Q1*
272 even] *F1;* euer *Q2–4* 275 come] *om.*
  F1 (Q1)
278 Any thing] Why any thing. *F1*
279 of] *(Q1); om. F1* 287 can] could *F1*
289 s.d. Aside to Guildenstern.] *Globe*
  (after Theobald)
290 s.d. Aside.] *Steevens* 294 and] of *F1*
297 exercises] exercise *F1*
297 heavily] heauenly *F1*
301 firmament] *om. F1 (Q1)*
302 appeareth . . . but] appeares no
  other thing to me then *F1*
303 a] *F1*
304–7 how infinite . . . god:] how infinite
  in faculty? in forme and mouing how
  expresse and admirable? in Action,
  how like an Angel? in apprehension,
  how like a God? *F1 (c) (the uncorrected*
  state has no pointing after God)
309 nor] no, nor *F1 (Q1)*
309 women] Woman *F1, Q3–4 (Q1)*
313 ye] you *F1 (Q1)*
313 then] *(Q1); om. F1*
317 coted] coated *F1;* boorded *Q1*
320 on] of *F1 (Q1)*
323–4 the . . . sere,] *F1 (Q1, in part)*
324 tickle] *Staunton conj.;* tickled *F1 (Q1)*
325 blank] *F1, Q3–4 (Q1);* black *Q2*
327 such] *om. F1 (Q1)*
329 travel] *Q1;* trauaile *Q2–4, F1*
336 are they] they are *F1*
337–62 Ham. How . . . too.] *F1*
339 eyases] *Theobald;* Yases *F1*
342 berattle] *F3* (be-rattle); be-ratled *F1;*
  be ratle *F2*
349 most like] *Pope;* like most *F1*
350 no] *Rowe;* not *F1 (the t is uncertain), F2*
363 very] *om. F1 (Q1)*
364 mouths at him] mowes at him *F1;*
  mops and moes / At my vncle *Q1*
365 fifty] *om. F1 (Q1)*
365 a] *(Q1);* an *F1*
366 'Sblood] *om. F1 (Q1)*
368 s.d. for the Players] *F1; Q1 s.d. reads:*
  The Trumpets sound 371 hands,
  come then:] *F1 (which om.* then);
  hands come then, *Q2;* hands, Come
  then *Q3–4*

373 this] the *F1*
373 lest my] *F1;* let me *Q2;* let my *Q3–4*
374 outwards] outward *F1*
379 hand-saw] *Q3–4;* handsaw *Q2;*
  Handsaw *F1*
381 s.d. Aside to them.] *Neilson*
383 swaddling-clouts] *(Q1):* swathing
  clouts *F1*
384 he is] he's *F1*
387 s.d. Aloud.] *Neilson*
387 a'] *(Q1);* for a *F1*
388 then] so *F1(Q1)* 391 was] *(Q1); om.*
  F1
394 my] mine *F1*
395 "Then . . . ass"] *quotes, Johnson conj.*
395 came] can *F1*
397–8 pastoral-comical, historical-
  pastoral] hyphens, *Q3–4;* Pastoricall-
  Comicall-Historicall-Pastorall/*F1;*
  Pastorall, Historicall, Historicall,
  Comicall *Q1*
398–9 tragical- . . . -pastoral,] *F1;*
  Comicall historicall, Pastorall, Tragedy
  historicall: *Q1*
400 Seneca] *F1, Q3–4 (Q1);* Sceneca *Q2*
403, 410, 411 Jephthah] *Hanmer;* Ieptha
  Q2–4; Iephta *F1;* Iepha *Q1 (om. l. 410)*
407–8 One . . . well.] *as verse, F1 (Q1); as*
  prose, Q2–4; quotes, Pope
409 s.d. Aside.] *Capell*
416–8 "As . . . was"] *as partly quoted verse,*
  Malone (after Pope); as prose, Q2–4,
  F1; as irregular verse, Q1, reading: Why
  by lot, or God wot, or as it came to
  passe,/And so it was,
419 pious chanson] Pons Chanson *F1*
  (in italics); godly Ballet *Q1*
420 abridgment comes] *(Q1);*
  Abridgements come *F1*
420 s.d. four or five] *F1 (before* Players)
421 You] *F1 (reading* Y'); Ham. You *Q2–4*
  (repeated s.p.); s.p. and You are *om. Q1*
422 old] my olde *F1 (Q1)*
423 why] *om. F1 (Q1)*
423 valanc'd] *Q3–4;* valanct *Q2;* valiant
  F1; vallanced *Q1;* my Ladie *Q4;* Byrlady
  F1; burlady *Q1* 425 by' lady] *ed.;*
  by lady *Q2–3;* my Ladie *Q4;* Byrlady
  F1; burlady *Q1*
425 to] *om. F1 (Q1)*
429 e'en to't] *F1;* ento't *Q2–4;* euen
  too't *Q1*
430 French] *F1 (Q1);* friendly *Q2–4*
430 falc'ners] *Q3–4* (Faukners); Fankners
  Q2; Faulconers *F1(Q1)*
433, 468, 502, 505 s.pp. l. Play.] *F1;*
  Player. *or* Play. *Q2–4;* Players *Q1*
  (later Play.)

210

433 **good**] (*Q1*); *om. F1*
438 **judgments**] (*Q1*); iudgement *F1*
441 **were**] was *F1* (*Q1*)
443 **affection**] affectation *F1*
444–45 **as wholesome . . . fine.**] *om.*
 F1 (*Q1, in part*)
445 **speech**] (*Q1*); cheefe Speech *F1*
446 **tale**] *F1* (*Q1*); talke *Q2–4*
447 **thereabout**] *F1;* there about *Q2–4;*
 then *Q1* (*om.* of it)
447 **when**] (*Q1*); where *F1*
450 **"The . . . beast"**] *as verse, Q1, Capell;*
 as prose, Q2–4, F1
450 **Hyrcanian**] *F1;* ircanian *Q2–4;*
 arganian *Q1*
451 **'Tis**] It is *F1; No* t'is *Q1*
454 **th'**] the *F1*
456 **heraldy**] Heraldry *F1* (*Q1*)
456 **dismal:**] *F1;* dismall *Q2–4;* dismall, *Q1*
457 **total gules**] to take Geulles *F1;* totall
 guise *Q1*
460 **and a**] and *F1*
461 **lord's murther**] (*apostrophe, Steveens*);
 vilde Murthers *F1*
462 **o'ersized**] *F1;* ore-cised *Q2–4*
465 **So proceed you.**] *om. F1;* So goe
 on. *Q1*
469 **antique**] *Pope;* anticke *Q2–4, F1*(*Q1*)
471 **match'd**] match *F1*
474 **Then senseless Ilium,**] *F1*
475 **this**] his *F1*
481 **And**] *F1*
488 **a-work**] *F1;.* a worke *Q2–4*
490 **Mars's armor**] *Capell;* Marses Armor
 Q2–4; Mars his Armours *F1*
495 **fellies**] *F4;* follies *Q2;* folles *Q3;*
 fellowes *Q4;* Fallies *F1*
499 **to the**] (*Q1*); to'th *F1*
502 **ah woe**] *Q5;* a woe *Q2–4;* O who
 F1(*Q1*)
502, 503 **mobled**] (*Q1, l. 502; om. l. 503*);
 inobled *F1*
504 **mobled . . . good**] *F2;* Inobled . . .
 good *F1; Q1 reads the line:* Mobled
 Queene is good, faith very good.
505 **flames**] flame *F1*
506 **bisson rheum**] *F1; Bison* rehume *Q2;*
 Bison rhume *Q3–4*
506 **clout upon**] clout about *F1;* kercher
 on *Q1* 509 **alarm**] Alarum *F1*(*Q1*)
 514 **husband's**] *F1, Q3–4* (*Q1*);
 husband *Q2*
519 **whe'er**] *Theobald* (*subs*); where *Q2–4*
 F1; if *Q1*
520 **Prithee**] Pray you *F1;* no more good
 heart *Q1*
522 **of this**] *om. F1* (*Q1*)

523 **you**] ye *F1*
524 **abstract**] Abstracts *F1*(*Q1*) 526 **live**]
 (*Q1*); liued *F1*
529 **bodkin**] bodykins *F1*
529 **much**] *om. F1;* farre *Q1*
530 **shall**] should *F1* (*Q1*)
534 s.d. **Exit.**] *F1* (*Q1*); *Q2–4 give exit for*
 Polonius and Players after l. 545
536 s.d. **Exeunt . . . First.**] *Dyce*
539, 544 s.pp. **l. Play.**] *Capell;* Play. *Q2–4.*
 F1; players *Q1*
540 **ha't**] *F1;* hate *Q2;* hau't *Q3–4*
541 **need**] a need *F1*(*Q1*) 541 **dozen or**]
 F1 (*Q1*); dosen lines, or *Q2–4*
543 **you**] ye *F1*
546 s.d. **Exit First Player.**] *Dyce*
546–8 **My . . . lord!**] Gentlemen, for your
 kindnes I thanke you, / And for a
 time I would desire you leaue me. /
 Gil. Our loue and duetie is at your
 commaund. *Q1*
547 **till**] *F1, Q3–4;* tell *Q2*
547 **Elsinore**] *Malone;* Elsonoure *Q2–4;*
 Elsonower *F1*
549 **Ay so,**] *F1* (I so,), *Q3–4;* I so *Q2*
549 **to**] *om. F1* (*Q1*)
549 **you.**] *pointing after F1* ('ye:);
 you, *Q2–4*
549 s.d. **Rosencrantz and**
 Guildenstern] *Capell; s.d. placed as in*
 Globe; after l. 548, Q2–4, F1 (*Q1*)
553 **own**] whole *F1*
554 **the**] his *F1*
554 **wann'd**] *Steevens* (*after Warburton*);
 wand *Q2–4;* warm'd *F1*
555 **in his**] in's *F1*
556 **an'**] *ed.;* an *Q2;* and *F1, Q3–4*
559 **Hecuba**] *F1* (*Q1*); her *Q2–4*
561 **the cue**] *F1:* that *Q2–4; Q1 reads l.*
 561 as; and if he had my losse?
564 **appall**] *Rowe;* appale *Q2;* appeale
 Q3–4; apale *F1*
566 **faculties**] faculty *F1*
567 **muddy-mettled**] *hyphen, F1*
576 **'swounds**] Why *F1;* Sure *Q1*
577 **pigeon-liver'd**] *hyphen, F1*
579 **'a'**] *ed.;* a *Q2* (*Q1*); haue *F1, Q3–4*
580 **offal. Bloody,**] *Q5* (*subs.*); offall,
 bloody, *Q2–4;* Offall, bloudy: a *F1;*
 offell, this *Q1* (*substituting* damned
 villaine *for* 'bawdy villain)
581 **villain!**] villaine! / Oh Vengeance! *F1*
582 **Why,**] Who? *F1*
582 **This**] I sure, this *F1*
583 **a dear father**] *Q3–4;* a deere *Q2;* the
 Deere *F1;* my deare father *Q1*
587 **stallion**] Scullion *F1;* scalion *Q1*

588 About,] *Theobald;* About *Q2–4, F1*
    (*Q1*)
588 brains] *Q2* (c), *Q3–4,* braues *Q2* (*u*);
    Braine *F1* (*Q1*)
588 Hum] om. *F1* (*Q1*)
597 If 'a do] If he but *F1;* And if he doe
    not *Q1*
599 a dev'l . . . dev'l] *ed.:* a deale . . .
    deale *Q2;* a diuell . . . diuell *Q3–4;* the
    Diuell . . . Diuel *F1;* the Diuell, *Q1*

3.1

3.1] Q (1676)
Location: *Capell (subs., after Rowe) Cf. the*
    following version of this scene in Q1 (see
    note at l. 43 s.d. below): Enter, the King,
    Queene, and Lordes. / King Lordes, can
    you by no meanes finde / The cause
    of our sonne Hamlets lunacie? / You
    being so neere in loue, euen from
    his youth, / Me thinkes should gaine
    more than a stranger should. / Gil. My
    lord, we haue done all the best we
    could, / To wring from him the cause
    of all his griefe, / But still he puts vs
    off, and by no meanes / Would make
    an answere to that we exposde. / Ross.
    Yet was he something more inclin'd
    to mirth / Before we left him, and I
    take it, / He hath giuen order for a
    play to night, / At which he craues
    your highnesse company. / King With
    all our heart, it likes vs very well: /
    Gentlemen, seeke still to increase
    his mirth, / Spare for no cost, our
    coffers shall be open, / And we vnto
    your selues will still be thankefull. /
    Both In all wee can, be sure you
    shall commaund. / Queene Thankes
    gentlemen, and what the Queene of
    Denmarke / May pleasure you, be sure
    you shall not want. / Gil. Weele once
    againe vnto the noble Prince. / King
    Thanks to you both: Gertred you'l see
    this play. / Queene My lord I will, and
    it ioyes me at the soule / He is inclin'd
    to any kinde of mirth. / Cor. Madame,
    I pray be ruled by me: / And my
    good Soueraigne, giue me leaue to
    speake, / We cannot yet finde out the
    very ground / Of his distemperance,
    therefore / I holde it meete, if so it
    please you, / Else they shall not meete,
    and thus it is. / King What i'st Corambis
    ? / Cor. Mary my good lord this, soone
    when the sports are done, / Madam,
    send you in haste to speake with

him, / And I myselfe will stand behind
    the Arras, / There question you the
    cause of all his griefe, / And then in
    loue and nature vnto you, hee'le tell
    you all: / My Lord, how thinks you
    on't? / King It likes vs well, Gerterd,
    what say you? / Queene With all my
    heart, soone will I send for him. /
    Cor. My selfe will be that happy
    messenger, / Who hopes his griefe will
    be reueal'd to her. *exeunt omnes*
1 An'] *ed.;* An *Q2;* And *F1, Q3–4*
1 conference] circumstance *F1;*
    meanes *Q1*
6 'a] he *F1*
17 o'er-raught] ore-wrought *F1*
19 here] om. *F1* (*Q1*)
27 into] on / To *F1*
28 s.d. **Exeunt . . . Guildenstern.]**
    Exeunt. *F1* **28 two]** too *F1* **30 here]**
    there *F1*
31–2 myself, We'll] my selfe (lawful
    espials) / Will *F1*
41 s.d. **Exit Queen.]** *Theobald*
42 please you] please ye *F1*
43 s.d. **To Ophelia.]** *Johnson; the Q1*
    version of ll. 43–175 appears in 2.2
    following l. 167 **45 loneliness]** *F1;*
    lowlines *Q2–4*
47 sugar] surge *F1*
48 s.d. **Aside.]** *Capell (after Pope, at l. 49)*
48 too] om. *F1* (*Q1*)
54 Withdraw] let's withdraw *F1*
54 s.d. **Exeunt]** *F1*
54 s.d. **King and Polonius]** *Capell*
54 s.d. **Enter Hamlet.]** *placed as in F1;*
    after l. 53, Q2–4
55–89 To . . . rememb'red.] *This*
    soliloquy appears in the following form in
    Q1: To be, or not to be, I there's the
    point, / To Die, to sleepe, is that all? I
    all: / No, to sleepe, to dreame, I mary
    there it goes, / For in that dreame
    of death, when wee awake, / And
    borne before an euerlasting ludge, /
    From whence no passenger euer
    retur'nd, / The vndiscouered country,
    at whose sight / The happy smile,
    and the accursed damn'd. / But for
    this, the ioyfull hope of this, / Whol'd
    beare the scornes and flattery of the
    world, / Scorned by the right rich,
    the rich cursสed of the poore? / The
    widow being oppressed, the orphan
    wrong'd, / The taste of hunger, or a
    tirants raigne, / And thousand more
    calamities besides, / To grunt and

sweate vnder this weary life,/When
that he may his full *Quietus* make,/
With a bare bodkin, who would this
indure,/But for a hope of something
after death?/Which pusles the braine,
and doth confound the sence,/
Which makes vs rather beare those
euilles we haue,/Than flie to others
that we know not of./I that, O this
conscience makes cowardes of vs all,/
Lady in thy orizons, be all my sinnes
remembred. (*Q1 places this soliloquy,
and the interview between Hamlet and
Ophelia which follows, in 2.2 after the
equivalent of ll. 169–70; Der bestrafte
Brudermord, though it omits the
soliloquy, also places the Hamlet-Ophelia
interview essentially as in Q1*)
59 **them.**] *F1, Q3–4 (subs.)*; them, *Q2*
59 **die,**] *F1 (Q1)*; die *Q2–4*
59 **sleep—**] *Pope;* sleepe *Q2–4, F1;*
sleepe, *Q1*
63 **wish'd.**] *F1;* wisht *Q2–4*
63 **die,**] *Globe (after Pope);* die
Q2–4, F1
70 **proud**] poore *F1*
71 **despis'd**] dispriz'd *F1*
74 **quietus**] *F1, Q4 (Q1);* quietas *Q2–3*
75 **fardels**] these Fardles *F1*
78 **bourn**] *Capell (after Pope);* borne
Q2–4, F1
82 **of us all**] *F1 (Q1)*
84 **sicklied**] *F1;* sickled *Q2–4*
85 **pitch**] pith *F1*
86 **awry**] away *F1*
91 **well, well**] *F1*
94 **No, not I**] No, no *F1*
96 **you know**] I know *F1*
98 **these**] the *F1*
98 **rich. Their**] *Q3–4 (subs.);* rich, their
Q2; rich, then *Q1*
98 **lost,**] left: *F1*
106–7 **your honesty**] *F1;* you *Q2–4;* Your
beauty *Q1*
108–9 **Could . . . honesty?**] *as prose, F1;
as verse, Q2–4 (Q1)*
109 **with**] *(Q1);* your *F1*
117 **inoculate**] *F1;* euocutat *Q2;* euacuat
Q3; euacuate *Q4*
120 **to**] *F1 (Q1)*
127–8 **earth and heaven**] Heauen and
Earth *F1 (Q1)*
128 **knaves**] Knaues all *F1 (Q1)*
131–2 **Let . . . Farewell!**] *as prose, F1; as
verse, Q2–4 (Q1)* 132 **where**] *(Q1);*
way *F1* 137 **nunn'ry,**] Nunnery.
Go, *F1 (Q1)*

141 **Heavenly powers**] O heavenly
Powers *F1;* Pray God *Q1*
142 **paintings**] pratlings too *F1;* paintings
too *Q1*
143 **hath . . . face**] *(Q1);* has . . . pace *F1*
143 **yourselves**] *Q4 (Q1);* your selfes
Q2–3; your selfe *F1*
144 **jig and**] gidge, you *F1;* fig, and
you *Q1*
144 **lisp, you**] *from F1* lispe, and; list
you *Q2–4*
146 **your**] *F1 (Q1)*
147 **moe marriage**] more Marriages
F1 (Q1)
152 **expectation**] expectansie *F1*
155 **And**] Haue *F1*
156 **music**] *F1, Q4;* musickt *Q2–3*
157 **that**] *F1,* what *Q2–4*
158 **time**] tune *F1*
159 **stature**] Feature *F1*
161 s.d. **Ophelia withdraws.**] *ed.
(after Wilson);* Exit. *Q2-4 (Q1)*
162 **Love?**] *F1 (Q1);* Loue, *Q2;* Loue:
Q3–4
167 **for**] *om. F1 (Q1)*
173 **something-settled**] *hyphen, Warburton*
177 **his**] this *F1*
178 s.d. **Ophelia comes forward.**] *Wilson*
183 **grief**] Greefes *F1*
188 **unwatch'd**] *F1;* vnmatcht *Q2–4*

3.2

3.2] *Capell*
Location: *Alexander (after Capell)*
o.s.d. **three . . . Players**] two or three of
the Players *F1;* the Players *Q1*
1 **pronounc'd**] *F1, Q3–4;* pronoun'd
Q2
3 **our**] your *F1 (Q1)*
4 **spoke**] had spoke *F1*
4 **with**] *(Q1); om. F1*
6 **torrent,**] *F1;* torrent *Q2–4*
6 **whirlwind of your**] the
Whirle-winde of *F1*
9 **hear**] *(Q1);* see *F1*
9 **periwig-pated**] *F1 (subs.);*
perwig-pated *Q2–4;* periwig *Q1*
10 **totters**] *(Q1);* tatters *F1*
10 **spleet**] split *F1 (Q1)* 12 **would**] *(Q1);*
could *F1*
14 **out-Herods**] *hyphen, F1;* out,
Herodes *Q1*
15, 36 s.pp. **I. Play.**] *Capell;* Player, *or*
Play. *Q2–4, F1;* players *Q1*
19 **o'erstep**] ore-stop *F1*
20 **o'erdone**] ouer-done *F1*
23 **feature**] owne Feature *F1*

25 **makes**] make *F1*
27 **which**] the which *F1*
29 **praise**] *F1*; praysd *Q2–4*
32 **nor man**] or Norman *F1*;
Nor Turke *Q1*
35 **abominably**] *Q3–4*; abhominably
Q2, F1; abhominable *Q1*
37 **sir**] *F1*
45 **uses it.**] *Following these words Q1
reads:* And then you haue some agen,
that keepes one sute/Of ieasts, as
a man is knowne by one sute of/
Apparell, and Gentlemen quotes
his ieasts downe/In their tables,
before they come to the play, as
thus:/Cannot you stay till I eate
my porrige? and, you owe me/A
quarters wages: and, my coate wants
a cullison:/And, your beere is sowre:
and, blabbering with his lips,/And
thus keeping in his cinkapase of
ieasts,/When, God knows, the warme
Clowne cannot make a iest/Vnlesse
by chance, as the blinde man catcheth
a hare:/Maisters tell him of it.
45 s.d. **Exeunt Players.**] *F1* (Exit) (*Q1*)
45 s.d. **Enter . . . Rosencrantz.**] *placed
as in F1; after l. 48, Q2–4*
49 s.d. **Exit Polonius.**] *F1*
51 **Ros. Ay**] *Both.* We will *F1*
51 s.d. **they two**] *om. F1; Q1 om. the
entrance of Rosencrantz, Guildenstern,
and Polonius at l. 45*
52 **ho**] *F4;* howe *Q2–4;* hoa *F1* 60 **lick**]
like *F1*
62 **fawning**] faining *F1*
63 **her**] my *F1*
65 **Sh' hath**] *Wilson;* S'hath *Q2;* S hath
Q3; Shath *Q4;* Hath *F1*
68 **Hast**] Hath *F1*
69 **co-meddled**] co-mingled *F1*
78 **afoot**] *F1* (*Q1*); a foote *Q2–4*
79 **thy**] my *F1*
80 **my**] mine *F1* 84 **stithy**] Stythe *F1*
84 **heedful**] needfull *F1*
87 **In**] To *F1*
88 **'a**] he *F1*
89 **detecting**] *F1;* detected *Q2–4*
89 s.d. **Sound . . . march.**] *F1*
(*at end of s.d.*)
89 s.d. **Rosencrantz . . . torches**] *F1;
Q1 s.d. reads:* Enter King, Queene,
Corambis, and other Lords.
93–9 **Excellent . . . say?**] *as prose, F1; as
verse, Q2–4*
94 **promise-cramm'd**] *hyphen, F1, Q3–4;*
Promiscram'd *Q2;* capon cramm'd *Q1*

98 **mine now.**] *Johnson;* mine now
Q2–4; mine. Now *F1*
98 s.d. **To Polonius.**] *Rowe*
100 **did I**] I did *F1* (*Q1*)
102 **What**] (*Q1*); And what *F1*
103–6 **I . . . ready?**] *as prose, F1* (*Q1, in
part*); *as verse, Q2–4*
108 s.p. **Queen.**] *F1* (*Q1*); Ger. *Q2–4*
108 **dear**] good *F1*
109 **metal**] *Q5;* mettle *Q2–4, F1* (*Q1*)
110 s.d. **Lying . . . feet.**] *Rowe*
111 s.d. **To the King.**] *Capell*
114–5 **Ham. I . . . lord.**] *F1* (*Q1, in part*)
116 **country**] contrary *Q1*
129 **dev'l**] *ed.;* deule *Q2;* diuell *Q3–4;*
Diuel *F1*
133 **by'r**] *F1;* ber *Q2–4*
133–4 **'a . . . 'a**] he . . . he *F1* (*Q1*)
135 s.d. **The trumpets sounds.**]
Hoboyes play. *F1*
135 s.d. **Dumb show follows.**] The
dumbe shew enters. *F1; Q1 s.d. reads:*
Enter in a Dumbe Shew, the King
and the Queene, he sits downe in an
Arbor, she leaues him: Then enters
Lucianus with poyson in a Viall, and
powres it in his eares, and goes away:
Then the Queene commeth and
findes him dead: and goes away with
the other.
135 s.d. **a Queen**] Queene *F1*
135 s.d. **very lovingly**] *F1*
135 s.d. **and he her**] *om. F1*
135 s.d. **She . . . him.**] *F1*
135 s.d. **he lies**] Layes *F1*
135 s.d. **come**] comes *F1, Q3–4*
135 s.d. **another man**] a Fellow *F1*
135 s.d. **pours**] and powres *F1*
135 s.d. **sleeper's . . . him**] Kings
eares, and Exits *F1*
135 s.d. **makes**] and makes *F1*
135 s.d. **pois'ner . . . pois'ner**]
poysoner . . . poisoner *F1, Q3–4*
135 s.d. **three or four**] two or three *F1*
135 s.d. **mutes**] *F1*
135 s.d. **come**] comes *F1, Q3–4*
135 s.d. **seem to condole**] seeming to
lament *F1*
135 s.d. **harsh**] loath *F1*
135 s.d. **and unwilling**] *F1*
135 s.d. **love**] his loue *F1*
135 s.d. **Exeunt.**] *F1*
137 **this'**] *ed.;* this *Q2;* tis *Q3;* it is *Q4;*
this is *F1* (*Q1*)
137 **miching**] *F1* (*Q1*); munching
Q2–4 (miching *is a Middle
English variant of* munching)

137 **mallecho**] *Malone;* Mallico
Q2–4 (Q1); Malicho F1
137 **it**] that F1 (Q1)
140 s.d. **Enter Prologue.**] *placed as in
Theobald; after* fellow. *l. 141, Q2–4; after
l. 148, F1; after l. 136, Q1*
141–2 **We . . . all.**] *as prose, F1; as
verse, Q2–4; Q1 reduces to:* you
shall heare anone, this fellow
will tell you all.
141 **this fellow**] (Q1); these Fellowes F1
142 **counsel**] F1 (Q1)
143 **'a**] they F1; he Q1
144 **you will**] you'l F1 (Q1)
151 s.d. **Exit.**] *Globe*
152 **posy**] Poesie F1 (Q1)
154 s.d. **two Players,**] *Globe;* Q1 s.d.
reads: Enter the Duke and Dutchesse.
155 etc. s.pp. **P. King.**] *Steevens;* King.
Q2–4, F1; Duke Q1
155–73] *Cf. the following version of these lines
in Q1: Duke* Full fortie yeares are past,
their date is gone,/Since happy time
ioyn'd both our hearts as one:/And
now the blood that fill'd my youthfull
veines,/Runnes weakely in their pipes,
and all the straines/Of musicke, which
whilome pleasde mine eare,/Is now a
burthen that Age cannot beare:/And
therefore sweete Nature must pay his
due,/To heauen must I, and leaue the
earth with you./*Dutchesse* O say not
so, lest that you kill my heart,/When
death takes you, let life from me depart.
156 **orbed**] F1; orb'd the Q2–4
161 etc. s.pp. **P. Queen.**] *Steevens:* Quee.
Q2–4; Bap. F1 (*except* Qu. *at l.* 227);
Dutchesse Q1
164 **your**] F1, Q3–4; our Q2
166] *In Q2–4 this line is followed by what
appears to be a first draft of l. 167:* For
women feare too much, euen as they
loue, (*note the absence of a rhyming line,
and see note on l. 168 below*)
167 **For**] F1; And Q2–4
167 **hold**] holds F1
168 **In neither aught**] *an apparent first
draft of these words precedes them in
Q2–4:* Eyther none, (*cf. l. 166 above*)
168 **aught**] *Malone;* ought Q2–4, F1
169 **love**] F1; Lord Q2–4
170 **siz'd**] F1; ciz'd Q2; ciz'st Q3–4
171–2 **Where . . . there.**] *om.* F1 (Q1)
174 **their**] my F1 181 s.d. **Aside.**] *Capell*
181 **That's wormwood!**] Wormwood,
Wormwood. F1; O wormewood,
wormewood! Q1

182 s.p. **P. Queen.**] *Steevens (after Rowe);
om.* Q2–4; Bapt. F1 190 **the fruit**] like
Fruite F1
196 **either**] other F1
197 **enactures**] ennactors F1
199 **joys**] F1; ioy Q2–4
199 **grieves**] F1; griefes Q2–4
204 **favorite**] fauourites F1
212 **devices**] F1, Q3–4; deuises Q2;
demises Q1
216 **me give**] giue me F1
218–9 **To . . . scope!**] *om.* F1 (Q1)
219 **An**] *Theobald;* And Q2–4
223 **once . . . wife**] F1 (Q1); once I be a
widdow, euer I be a wife Q2–4
227 s.d. **Sleeps.**] F1 (*after l.* 227); *placed as
in Rowe*
228 s.d. **Exit.**] F1; Exeunt. Q2–4; exit
Lady Q1
230 **doth protest**] protests F1 (Q1)
237 **Marry**] F1; mary Q2–4 (Q1)
237–8 **how? tropically:**] F1; how
tropically, Q2–4; how trapically: Q1
239 **Vienna**] guyana Q1
239 **Gonzago**] Albertus Q1
241 **of that**] o'that F1; A that Q1
243 **unwrung**] Q3–4; vnwrong Q2;
vnrung F1
243 s.d. **Enter Lucianus.**] *placed as in* F1;
after l. 244, Q2–4
245 **as good as a**] (Q1); a good F1
246–7 **I . . . dallying.**] *as prose,* F1 (Q1); *as
verse,* Q2–4 250 **mine**] my F1
252 **mistake**] must take Q1
252 **your**] (Q1); *om.* F1
253 **leave**] Pox, leaue F1; a poxe, leaue Q1
256 **Confederate**] F1 (Q1); Considerat
Q2–3; Considerate Q4
258 **ban**] bane Q1
258 **infected**] F1, Q3–4 (Q1); inuected Q2
260 **usurps**] (Q1); vsurpe F1
260 s.d. **Pours . . . ears.**] F1
261 **'A**] He F1 (Q1)
261 **for his**] (Q1); for's F1
262 **name's**] F1; names Q2–4 262–3
written in very] writ in F1 266
Ham. What . . . fire?] F1 (Q1,
reading fires)
270 s.p. **Pol.**] All. F1; Cor. Q1 (*thus
supporting* Q2)
271 **Why,**] *Theobald;* Why Q2–4, F1; Then
Q1
271 **strooken**] strucken F1; stricken Q1
274 **Thus**] (Q1); So F1 276 **two**] F1
278 **players?**] Players sir. F1
284 **very—**] *Warburton;* very Q2–4, F1
291 **Ah**] Oh F1

296 **voutsafe**] vouchsafe *F1*
303 **with**] rather with *F1*
305 **the**] his *F1*
306 **more**] farre more *F1*
309 **start**] *F1;* stare *Q2–4*
318 **my**] *F1*
320 s.p. **Ros.**] Guild. *F1*
322 **answer**] answers *F1*
323 **as**] *om. F1 (Q1, which om. ll. 298–330,
338–350* (You do . . . that.))
328 **stonish**] astonish *F1*
330 **impart.**] *om. F1 (Q1)*
336 **And**] So I *F1*
338 **surely**] freely *F1*
338 **upon**] of *F1*
343 **sir**] *om. F1 (Q1)*
344 s.d. **the . . . recorders**] one with a
Recorder *F1; s.d. placed as in F1; after l.
342, Q2–4*
345 **recorders**] Recorder *F1*
345 **one.—**] *Capell (after Rowe);* one,
*Q2–4; om.
F1 (Q1)*
357 **It is**] 'Tis *F1*
358 **fingers**] finger *F1*
358 **thumbs**] *Wilson;* the vmber *Q2;* the
thumb *Q3–4;* thumbe *F1*
359 **eloquent**] excellent *F1;* delicate *Q1*
367 **the top of**] *F1*
369 **it speak. 'Sblood**] it. Why *F1;*
Zownds *Q1*
369 **think**] *(Q1);* thinke, that *F1*
371 **fret**] can fret *F1 (Q1)*
371 **yet**] *Q1;* not *Q2—4; om. F1*
372 s.d. **Enter Polonius.**] *placed as in
Capell; after l. 373, Q2–4, F1 (Q1)*
376 **yonder**] *(Q1);* that *F1*
377 **of**] *(Q1);* like *F1*
378 **mass**] Misse *F1*
378 **'tis,**] it's *F1;* T'is *Q1*
383 s.p. **Ham**] *from catchword in Q2; om. in
text proper*
383–5 **Then . . . by.**] *as prose, Pope; as verse
Q2–4, F1 (Q1)*
383 **I will**] will I *F1;* i'le *Q1*
384 s.d. **Aside.**] *Staunton*
386 **Pol. I will say so.**] *F1; Q2–4 read*
I will, say so. *and continue the line to
Hamlet. The Q2 arrangement (see also l.
387 below) is perhaps what Shakespeare
originally intended; l. 386 as pointed in
Q2 and spoken by Hamlet means: "Yes,
I will come. Say so." and should be
taken as addressed to Polonius, who has
lingered after the others have gone out in
obedience to Hamlet's* Leave me, friends,
(immediately preceding l. 386 in Q2).

*Q1, significantly perhaps, gives Corambis
(i.e. Polonius) no exit line, suggesting
that the F1 arrangement may be a later
sophistication.*
386 s.d. **Exit.**] *F1;* exit Coram. *Q1
(after l. 383)*
387 **Leave me, friends.**] *placed as in F1;
after* by and by. *l. 385, Q2–4*
387 s.d. **Exeunt . . . Hamlet.**]
Capell (subs.)
389 **breathes**] *F1;* breakes *Q2–4*
391 **bitter . . . the**] *F1;* busines as the
bitter *Q2–4*
396 **daggers**] *F1 (Q1);* dagger *Q2–4*
399 s.d. **Exit.**] *(Q1); om. F1*

3.3

3.3] *Capell Location: Alexander (after
Capell)*
6 **near 's**] dangerous *F1*
7 **brows**] Lunacies *F1*
14 **weal**] spirit *F1*
15 **many. The**] *Q5;* many, the *Q2–4, F1*
15 **cess**] cease *F1*
17 **Or**] *om. F1 (Q1, see ll. 36–72 below)*
18 **summit**] *Rowe;* somnet *Q2–4, F1
(see 1.4.70)*
19 **huge**] *F1, Q4;* hough *Q2;* hugh *Q3*
22 **ruin**] *F1;* raine *Q2–4*
23 **with**] *F1*
24 **viage**] Voyage *F1*
25 **about**] vpon *F1*
26 s.p. **Ros.**] Both. *F1*
26 s.d. **Gentlemen**] *Warburton;* Gent.
Q2–4, F1
26 s.d. **Rosencrantz and
Guildenstern**] *Hanmer*
33 **speech,**] *Theobald;* speech *Q2–4, F1*
35 s.d. **Exit Polonius.**] *Capell;* Exit.
Q2–4 (after know. *l. 35)*
36–72] *Q1, om. everything before, begins
the scene with Claudius' soliloquy,
which reads as follows: King* O that
this wet that falles vpon my face/
Would wash the crime cleere from
my conscience!/When I looke vp
to heauen, I see my trespasse,/The
earth doth still crie out vpon my
fact,/Pay me the murder of a brother
and a king,/And the adulterous
fault I haue committed:/O these
are sinnes that are vnpardonable:/
Why say thy sinnes were blacker then
is ieat,/Yet may contrition make
them as white as snowe:/I but still
to perseuer in a sinne,/It is an act
gainst the vniuersall power,/Most

216

wretched man, stoope, bend thee to
thy prayer,/Aske grace of heauen to
keepe thee from despaire./*hee kneeles.
enters Hamlet*
39 **will.**] *F1* (*subs.*); will, *Q2–4*
43 **neglect.**] *F1, Q3–4* (*subs.*);
neglect, *Q2*
50 **pardon'd**] *F1;* pardon *Q2–4*
58 **shove**] *F1;* showe *Q2–4*
66 **can not**] *Capell;* cannot *Q2–4, F1*
69 **engag'd**] *F1;* ingaged *Q2–4*
69 **angels! Make**] *Theobald* (*subs.*);
Angels make *Q2;* Angles make *Q3–4;*
Angels, make *F1*
72 s.d. **He kneels.**] *Q1*
73 **it pat**] *F1;* it, but *Q2–4*
73 **'a**] he *F1*
73 **a-praying**] praying *F1*
74 **'a**] he *F1*
75 **reveng'd**] *Ft;* reuendge *Q2–3;*
revenged *Q4* (*Q1*)
77 **sole**] foule *F1*
79 **Why**] Oh *F1*
79 **hire and salary**] *F1;* base and silly
Q2–4; a benefit *Q1*
80 **'A**] *He F1* (*Q1*)
81 **With all**] *F1;* Withall *Q2–4*
81 **flush**] fresh *F1*
89 **drunk asleep**] *F1;* drunke, a sleepe
Q2–4; drinking drunke *Q1*
90 **incestious**] incestuous *F1* (*Q1*)
91 **game a-swearing**] *ed.* (*after
Cambridge*); game a swearing *Q2;*
game, a swearing *Q3–4;* gaming,
swearing *F1:* game swaring *Q1*
97 s.d. **Rising.**] *Capell*

3.4

3.4] *Capell* Location: *Steevens*
1 **'A**] He *F1*
4 **I'll . . . here**] I'le shrowde my selfe
behinde the Arras, *exit Cor. Q1*
4 **even**] e'ene *F1*
5 **with him**] *F1*
5 **him**] him./*Ham. within.* Mother,
mother, mother. *F1; Q1 reads: Ham.*
Mother, mother, O are you here?
6 **warr'nt**] *Wilson* (*subs.*); wait *Q2–4;*
warrant *F1*
7 s.d. **Polonius . . . arras.**] *Rowe,
supported by the Q1 reading quoted at l. 4
above*
7 s.d. **Enter Hamlet.**] *placed as in F1;
after round l. 5, Q2–4*
12 **wicked**] idle *F1*
16 **And would it**] But would you *F1*
20 **inmost**] *F1;* most *Q2–4*

22 **Help ho**] *Q3–4* (*Q1*); Helpe how *Q2;*
Helpe, helpe, hoa *F1*
23 s.d. **Behind.**] *Rowe* (*subs.*)
23 **What ho, help**] *Q3–4* (*subs.*); What
how helpe *Q2;* What hoa, helpe,
helpe, helpe *F1;* Helpe for the
Queene *Q1*
24 s.d. **Drawing.**] *Malone* (*after* rat?);
placed as in Globe
24 s.d. **Kills Polonius**] *F1* (*after* slain. *l. 25*);
placed as in Warburton
24 s.d. **through the arras**] *Capell*
25 s.d. **Behind.**] *Capell*
30 **it was**] 'twas *F1*
30 s.d. **Parts . . . Polonius.**] *Capell*
(*subs., after l. 25*); *placed as in Dyce*
32 **better**] (*Q1*); Betters *F1*
37 **brass'd**] braz'd *F1*
38 **be**] is *F1*
42 **off**] *F1;* of *Q2–4*
44 **sets**] makes *F1*
48 **does**] doth *F1*
49 **O'er**] Yea *F1*
50 **heated**] tristfull *F1*
50 **doom;**] *ed.;* doome *Q2–4;* doome, *F1*
51 **thought-sick**] hyphen, *F1, Q3–4*
51 **act.**] *Q3–4, F1;* act *Q2*
52 **That . . . index?**] *continued to
Queen, F1; assigned to Hamlet, Q2–4*
55 **this**] his *F1*
57 **and**] or *F1*
59 **heaven-kissing**] *F1;* heaue, a
kissing *Q2–4*
65 **brother**] breath *F1*
71–6 **Sense . . . difference.**] *om. F1* (*Q1*)
76 **was't**] *F1;* wast *Q2–4*
77 **hoodman-blind**] *F1;* hodman blind
Q2; hodman-blind *Q3–4;* hob-man
blinde *Q1*
78–81 **Eyes . . . mope.**] *om. F1* (*Q1*)
88 **And**] As *F1*
88 **panders**] *F1;* pardons *Q2–4*
89 **turn'st my**] turn'st mine *F1*
89 **eyes . . . very**] *F1;* very eyes into
my *Q2–4*
90 **grained**] *F1;* greeued *Q2–4*
91 **not leave**] *F1;* leaue there *Q2–4*
92 **enseamed**] *F1;* inseemed *Q2;*
incestuous *Q3–4; cf. Q1:* To liue in the
incestuous pleasure of his bed ?
93 **Stew'd**] *F1;* Stewed *Q2–4*
97 **twentith part**] twentieth patt *F1*
97 **tithe**] *F1;* kyth *Q2–4*
101 s.d. **in his nightgown**] *Q1*
104 **your**] you *F1*
117 **you do**] you *F1;* thus you *Q1*
118 **th' incorporal**] their corporall *F1*

131 whom] who *F1*
137] *The greatly abridged and variant conclusion of this scene in Q1 begins at the equivalent of this line and is interesting in view of Gertrude's active role in aiding Hamlet against Claudius in the sources and her attitude in the Q1 text of 4.6 (see Textual Notes): Queene Alas, it is the weakenesse of thy braine,/ Which makes thy tongue to blazon thy hearts griefe:/But as I haue a soule, I sweare by heauen,/I neuer knew of this most horride murder:/ But Hamlet, this is onely fantasie,/ And for my loue forget these idle fits./Ham. Idle, no mother, my pulse doth beate like yours,/It is not madnesse that possesseth Hamlet./ O mother, if euer you did my deare father loue,/Forbeare the adulterous bed to night,/And win your selfe by little as you may,/In time it may be you wil lothe him quite:/And mother, but assist mee in revenge,/And in his death your infamy shall die./Queene Hamlet, I vow by that maiesty,/That knowes our thoughts, and lookes into our hearts,/I will conceale, consent, and doe my best,/What stratagem soe're thou shall deuise. [The last two lines seem to be a recollection of Kyd's Spanish Tragedy, 4.1.46–7.]/Ham. It is enough, mother good night:/Come sir, Fie prouide for you a graue,/Who was in life a foolish prating knaue./ Exit Hamlet with the dead body.*
139 Ecstasy?] *F1*
143 I] *F1*
145 that] a *F1*
148 Whiles] Whil'st *F1*
151 on] or *F1*
152 ranker] ranke *F1*
153 these] this *F1*
158 live] *F1*; leaue *Q2–4*
160 Assume] *F1, Q3–4*; Assune *Q2*
161–5 That . . . on.] *om. F1 (Q1)*
161–2 eat, . . . this,] *Q5*; eate . . . this *Q2–4*
165 on. Refrain to-night] *F1 (om. through on.; see above, ll. 161–5)*; on to refraine night *Q2–4*; Forbeare the adulterous bed to night *Q1*
167–70 the next more . . . potency.] *om. F1 (Q1)*
169 either. . . . the devil] *a word apparently om. Q2; many emendations suggested:* master *(Q3–4),* curb *(Malone),* quell *(Singer),* shame

(Hudson), etc.; C. J. Monro (in Cambridge) suggests reading entertain *in place of* either, *a reading strongly argued for by A. S. Cairncross in SQ, IX (1958)*
170 wondrous] *Q4*; wonderous *Q2–3*
172 you. For] *F1*; you, for *Q2–4* **172** *s.d.* **Pointing to Polonius.**] *Rowe*
179 This] Thus *F1*
180 One . . . lady.] *om. F1 (Q1)*
182 bloat] *Warburton*; blowt *Q2–4*; blunt *F1*
186 ravel] *F1*; rouell *Q2–4*
188 mad] made *F1*
188 craft. 'Twere] *F1*; craft, t'were *Q2–4*
190 paddock] *F1*; paddack *Q2–4*
200 that?] *F1*; that. *Q2*; that, *Q3–4*
202–10 There's . . . meet.] *om. F1 (Q1)*
210 meet.] *Q5*; meete, *Q2–4*
215 foolish] *F1 (Q1)*; most foolish *Q2–4*
217 *s.d.* **Exeunt . . . Polonius.**] *F1 (Capell adding severally); Exit. Q2–4; Exit Hamlet with the dead body. Q1*

4.1

4.1] *Q (1676); Q2–4, F1, Q1 indicate no scene or act break here, the Queen remaining on stage to meet Claudius (see 3.4. 217 s.d.); Q2–4, however, also re-enter the Queen as for a new scene*
Location: *Alexander (after Rowe)*
o.s.d. **Enter . . . Guildenstern.**] Enter King. *F1*; Enter the King and Lordes. *Q1 (Lordes being Rosencrantz and Guildenstern)*
1 matter] matters *F1*
1 heaves—] *Rowe (subs.)*; heaues, *Q2–4*; heaues *F1*
4 Bestow . . . while.] *om. F1 (Q1); note that Rosencrantz and Guildenstern are absent in F1*
4 *s.d.* **Exeunt . . . Guildenstern.**] *Capell*
5 mine own] my good *F1*
7 sea] *(Q1)*; Seas *F1*
8 mightier.] *Rowe (subs.)*; mightier, *Q2, F1*; mightier *Q3–4*
9 something] *F1*; some thing *Q2–4*
10 Whips . . . rapier,] He whips his Rapier out, and *F1*; but whips me / Out his rapier, and *Q1*
11 this] his *F1 (Q1)*
22 let] let's *F1*
27 'a] He *F1*
30 vile] vilde *F1*
32 *s.d.* **Enter . . . Guildenstern.**] *placed as in Dyce; after l. 31, Q2–4; after* excuse. l. 32, *F1*

35 **mother's closet**] Mother Clossets *F1*
35 **dragg'd**] *F1, Q3–4;* dreg'd *Q2*
37 s.d. **Exeunt . . . Guildenstern.**]
Rowe; Exit Gent. *F1;* Exeunt
Lordes. *Q1*
39 **And**] To *F1*
40 **done,. . . .**] *apparently the last part of*
this line is missing in Q2–4 (om. F1, Q1
as part of a cut); Capell suggests reading
so, haply, slander,
41–4 **Whose . . . air.**] *om. F1 (Q1)*

4.2

4.2] Pope
Scene om. Q1
Location: *Alexander (after Capell)*
o.s.d. **Enter Hamlet.**] *F1;* Enter Hamlet
Rosencraus, and others. *Q2–4*
2 **Gentlemen. (Within.) Hamlet!**
Lord Hamlet!] *F1*
3 s.p. **Ham.**] *F1*
3 **But soft**] *om. F1*
4 s.d. **Enter . . . Guildenstern.**] *F1;*
for Q2–4, see o.s.d. above
6 **Compounded**] *F1, Q3–4;*
Compound *Q2*
18 **like ... apple**] *Farmer conj.;* like an
apple *Q2–4;*
like an Ape *F1;* as an Ape
doth nuttes *Q1*
28 **thing—**] *F1;* thing. *Q2–4*
30–1 **Hide . . . after.**] *F1*

4.3

4.3] *Pope*
Location: *Alexander (after Capell)*
o.s.d. **Enter . . . three.**] Enter King. *F1*
6 **weigh'd**] *F1;* wayed *Q2–4*
7 **never**] neerer *F1*
11 s.d. **Enter Rosencrantz.**] *F1*
(Rosincrane); Enter Rosencraus and
all the rest. *Q2–4;* Enter Hamlet and
the Lordes. *Q1*
11 **How**] *F1; King.* How *Q2–4*
(repeated s.p.)
15 **Ho, . . . lord.**] *Q3–4;* How, . . . Lord.
Q2; Hoa, Guildensterne? Bring in my
Lord. *F1*
15 s.d. **Hamlet and Guildenstern**] *F1*
19 **'a**] he *F1 (Q1)*
20 **convocation**] *F1, Q4;* conuacation
Q2–3; company *Q1*
20 **politic**] *(Q1); om. F1*
22 **ourselves**] our selfe *F1*
24 **two**] *(Q1);* to *F1*
26–8 **King. Alas . . . worm.**] *om. F1;*
Looke you, a man may fish with that

worme/That hath eaten of a King,/
And a Beggar eate that fish,/Which
that worme hath caught. *Q1*
29 s.p. **King.**] *F1, Q3–4 (Q1);* King.
King. *Q2*
34 **there**] *F1, Q3–4 (Q1);* thrre *Q2*
35 **if indeed**] indeed, if *F1;* if *Q1*
36 **within**] *om. F1 (Q1)*
38 s.d. **To Attendants.**] *Capell (subs.)*
39 **'A will**] He will *F1;* hee'le *Q1*
39 **you**] *(Q1);* ye *F1*
39 s.d. **Exeunt Attendants.**] *Capell*
40 **deed,**] deed of thine, *F1*
43 **With fiery quickness**] *F1*
45 **is**] at *F1*
48–9 **I . . . mother.**] *as prose, F1; as*
verse, Q2–4
48 **them**] him *F1*
51–3 **My . . . England!**] *as prose, F1; as*
verse, Q2–4 (Q1)
52 **so**] and so *F1 (Q1)*
57 s.d. **Exeunt . . . Guildenstern.**]
Theobald
64 **congruing**] coniuring *F1*
68 **were ne'er begun**] *F1;* will nere
begin *Q2–4*

4.4

4.4] *Pope*
Location: *ed. (after Pelican)*
o.s.d. **Enter . . . stage.**] Enter
Fortenbrasse, Drumme and
Souldiers. *Q1*
3 **Craves**] *(Q1);* Claimes *F1*
8 **softly**] safely *F1*
8 s.d. **Exeunt . . . Captain.**] *Kittredge*
(after Theobald); Exit. *F1;* Exeunt all.
Q1
8 s.d. **Guildenstern,**] *Theobald; s.d. om.*
F1 (Q1)
9–66 **Ham. Good . . . worth!**] *om. F1*
(Q1), except l. 14 in Q1
19 **name.**] *Pope;* name *Q2–4;* name, *Q5*
30 s.d. **Exit.**] *Capell*
31 s.d. **Exeunt . . . Hamlet**] *Rowe (subs.)*

4.5

4.5] *Pope*
Location: *Alexander (after Rowe)*
o.s.d., 1–20] *For this passage in Q2–4, F1,*
the following lines are substituted in Q1:
enter King and Queene./King Hamlet
is ship't for England, fare him well,/I
hope to heare good newes from
thence ere long,/If euery thing fall
out to our content, / As I doe make
no doubt but so it shall./Queene

God grant it may, heau'ns keep my
Hamlet safe:/But this mischance of
olde *Corambis* death,/Hath piersed
so the yong *Ofeliaes* heart,/That
she, poore maide, is quite bereft her
wittes./*King* Alas deere heart! And on
the other side,/We vnderstand her
brother's come from *France,*/And he
hath halfe the heart of all our Land,
/ And hardly hee'le forget his fathers
death,/Vnlesse by some meanes he be
pacified./*Qu.* O see where the yong
Ofelia is! *[There are some vague echoes
here of ll. 74–94 below.]*

o.s.d. **a Gentleman.**] *om. F1 (which assigns
his speeches to Horatio)*

2, 4 s.pp. **Gent.**] Hor. *F1*

9 yawn] ayme *F1*

12 might] would *F1*

15 ill-breeding] *hyphen, Rowe*

15 minds.] *F1;* mindes, *Q2–4*

16 s.p. **Queen.**] *from F1 at l. 14 (F1 gives
ll. 14–20 to Queen); Q2–4 continue l. 16
to Horatio*

16 s.d. **Exit Gentleman.**] *Hanmer*

17 s.d. **Aside.**] *Capell*

17–20 To . . . spilt.] *marked with gnomic
quotes, Q2–4*

20 s.d. **distracted . . . lute**] *from F1
(distracted) and Q1, which reads:*
playing on a Lute, and her haire
downe singing.; *Q2–4 s.d. follows l. 16;
placed as in F1*

23 true-love] *hyphen, Capell*

23 s.d. **She sings.**] *om. F1 (see l. 20 s.d.
for Q1)*

26 sandal] *F1 (Q1);* Sendall *Q2–4*

28 you?] *F1;* you, *Q2–4*

29 etc. s.dd. **Song.**] *om. F1 (Q1)
(throughout scene; in F1 the songs
are in italics)*

33 O ho!] *om. F1 (Q1)*

36, 58 s.dd. **Sings.**] *Capell*

36 s.d. **Enter King.**] *after l. 32, F1*

38 all] *om. F1 (Q1)*

39 bewept] *F1 (Q1);* beweept *Q2–4*

39 ground] graue *F1 (Q1)*

40 true-love] *F1;* true loue *Q2–4;* true
louers *Q1*

41 do you] do ye *F1;* i'st with you *Q1*

42 God] *F1 (Q1);* good *Q2–4*

46 Pray] Pray you *F1 (Q1)*

48–66 "To-morrow . . . more."] *Q1
transfers this song so that it follows l.
173 below. It is thus heard by Laertes, on
whom its implications might be expected
to have an especially powerful effect in*

*arousing him further against Hamlet; Q1
also transfers the song at ll. 190–9, making
it follow Ophelia's first song at ll. 23–32.*

52 clo'es] *Wilson;* close *Q2–4;* clothes
F1 (Q1)

57 Indeed] Indeed la? *F1*

64 (He answers.)] *om. F1 (Q1)*

65 'a'] *Kittredge;* a *Q2–4 (Q1);* ha *F1*

67 thus] this *F1*

69 would] should *F1*

72–3 Good . . . night.] *pointing from
Q2–4, which, however, read God and god
for Good and good;* Goodnight Ladies:
Goodnight sweet Ladies: Goodnight,
goodnight. *F1;* God be with you
Ladies, God be with you. *Q1*

73 s.d. **Exit.**] *F1 (Q1)*

74 s.d. **Exit Horatio.**] *Theobald*

76 and now behold!] *om. F1 (Q1)*

78 come,] comes, *F1*

79 battalions] *Q (1676);* battalians *Q2–4;*
Battaliaes *F1* **82 their**] *F1*

89 Feeds] Keepes *F1* **89 this**] his *F1*

92 Wherein] Where in *F1*

93 person] persons *F1*

96 Queen. **Alack . . . this?**] *F1;* How
now, what noyse is that? *Q1 (spoken
by the King and preceded by four lines
found only in Q1: king A pretty wretch!
this is a change indeede:/O Time,
how swiftly runnes our ioyes away ?/
Content on earth was neuer certaine
bred,/To day we laugh and liue, to
morrow dead.)*

97 Attend!] *om. F1 (Q1)*

98 is] are *F1*

98 Swissers] Switzers *F1*

98 s.d. **Enter a Messenger.**] *placed as in
Capell; after death. l. 96, Q2–4, F1*

107 They] *F1;* The *Q2–4*

109 with others] *om. F1 (Q1); Laertes'
followers do not enter in Q1*

113 this] the *F1*

116 s.d. **Exeunt Laertes' followers.**]
Kittredge (after Theobald)

116 vile] vilde *F1 (Q1)*

118 that's calm] that calmes *F1*

128 Where is] Where's *F1 (Q1)*

133–4 pit! . . . damnation.] *F1 (subs.);*
pit . . . damnation, *Q2–4*

138 world's] *Pope;* worlds *Q2–4;*
world *F1 (Q1)*

142 father] Fathers death *F1*

142 is't] *Q5;* i'st *Q2–4;* if *F1*

143 swoopstake] *from Q1*
Swoop-stake-like; soopstake *Q2;*
soope-stake *Q3;* soopstake *Q4, F1*

144 **loser?**] Q5; looser. Q2–4, F1; all? Q1
147 **pelican**] Politician F1
151 **sensibly**] sensible F1, Q4;
sencible Q3
152 **'pear**] Johnson; peare Q2–4; pierce F1
153 s.d. **"Let . . . in!"**] as F1; given to
Laertes, Q2–4
154 s.d. **Enter Ophelia.**] placed as in
Theobald; before Laertes' speech in Q2–4,
F1 (see preceding note)
157 **paid with**] payed by F1
158 **Till**] F1, Q3–4; Tell Q2
158 **turn**] turnes F1
161 **an old**] F1 (Q1); a poore Q2–4
162–4 **Nature . . . loves.**] F1
165 **barefac'd**] F1, Q3–4; bare-faste Q2
166 **Hey . . . nonny,**] F1
167 **in**] on F1
167 **rain'd**] raines F1
171–3 **You . . . daughter.**] as prose, F1; as
verse, Q2–4 (Q1) 171–2 **"A-down,
a-down,"** . . . **a-down-a.**] hyphens,
F1 (but reading downe a-downe,);
a downe, And you a downe a, Q1;
quotes, Wilson (after Capell)
176 **you**] om. F1 (Q1)
176 **pansies**] Johnson; Pancies Q2–4;
Paconcies F1; pansey Q1
180 s.d. **To Claudius.**] Wilson
181 s.d. **To Gertrude.**] Wilson
182 **herb of grace**] Herb-Grace F1;
hearb a grace Q1
183 **You may**] Oh you must F1; you
must Q1 185 **'a**] he F1
187 s.d. **Sings.**] Capell
188 **afflictions**] (Q1); Affliction F1
190–1 **'a . . . 'a**] he . . . he F1 (Q1)
195 **was**] om. F1 (Q1)
196 **All**] F1 (Q1)
199 **God 'a' mercy**] Kittredge; God a
mercy Q2–4 (Q1); Gramercy F1
200 **Christians'**] ed.; Christians Q2–4;
Christian F1; christen Q1
200 **I pray God**] F1 (Q1)
200–1 **buy you**] buy ye F1; buy yous
Q3–4; be with you Q1
201 s.d. **Exit.**] F1 (Q1)
202 **see**] F1
202 **O God**] you Gods F1; O God, O
God Q1
203 **commune**] common F1
201 **collateral**] F1; colaturall Q2–4
214 **funeral**] buriall F1
215 **trophy**] Q5; Trophee F1; trophe Q2;
trophae Q3–4
216 **rite**] F1; right Q2–4
218 **call't**] call F1

4.6

4.6] Capell
Location: *Alexander (after Capell)*
*Scene om. Q1, which at this point contains
the following scene not found in Q2–4
or F1: Enter Horatio and the Queene. /
Hor. Madame, your sonne is safe
arriv'de in Denmarke, / This letter
I euen now re-ceiv'd of him, /
Whereas he writes how he escap't
the danger, / And subtle treason that
the king had plotted, / Being crossed
by the contention of the windes, / He
found the Packet sent to the king of
England, / Wherein he saw himselfe
betray'd to death, / As at his next
conuersion with your grace, / He will
relate the circumstance at full. / Queene
Then I perceiue there's treason in
his lookes / That seem'd to sugar o're
his villanie: / But I will soothe and
please him for a time, / For murderous
mindes are alwayes jealous, / But know
not you Horatio where he is ? / Hor.
Yes Madame, and he hath appoynted
me / To meete him on the east side
of the Cittie / To morrow morning. /
Queene O faile not, good Horatio, and
withal), commend me / A mothers
care to him, bid him a while / Be wary
of his presence, lest that he / Faile in
that he goes about. / Hor. Madam,
neuer make doubt of that: / I thinke
by this the news be come to court: /
He is arriv'de, obserue the king, and
you shall / Quickely finde, Hamlet
being here, / Things fell not to his
minde. / Queene But what became
of Gilderstone and Rossen-craft ? /
Hor. He being set ashore, they went
for England, / And in the Packet
there writ down that doome / To
be perform'd on them poynted for
him: / And by great chance he had
his fathers Seale, / So all was done
without discouerie. / Queene Thankes
be to heauen for blessing of the
prince, / Horatio once againe I take
my leaue, / With thowsand mothers
blessings to my sonne. / Horat. Madam
adue. (four of Horatio's lines seem to echo
passages in 4.6 and 5.2)*
o.s.d. **and others**] with an Attendant F1
2 **Gentleman. Sea-faring men**]
Ser. Saylors F1
4 s.d. **Exit Gentleman.**] Hanmer
6 **greeted,**] F1; greeted. Q2–4

6 s.d. **Sailors**] Saylor *F1*
7, 9 s.pp. l. **Sail.**] *Capell;* Say. *Q2–4, F1*
9 **'A**] Hee *F1*
9 **and't**] *F;* and *Q2–4*
10 **came**] comes *F1*
11 **embassador**] Ambassadours *F1*
13 s.d. **Reads.** | *F1* (Reads the Letter.)
16 **warlike**] Warlicke *F1*
18 **and**] *om. F1*
22 **good**] *F1*
24 **speed**] hast *F1*
25 **thine**] your *F1*
26 **bore**] *F1;* bord *Q2–4*
30 **He**] *F1;* So *Q2–4*
30 **thine,**] *F1;* thine *Q2–4*
32 **Come**] *F1; Hor.* Come *Q2–4*
(*repeated s.p.*)
32 **give**] *F1; om.* Q2; make *Q3–4*

4.7

4.7] *Capell.* Location: *Alexander*
(*after Capell*)
6 **proceeded**] *F1;* proceede *Q2–4*
7 **criminal**] crimefull *F1*
8 **greatness**] *om. F1* (*Q1, om. everything
down to about l. 50*)
10 **unsinow'd**] vnsinnowed *F1*
11 **But**] And *F1*
11 **th' are**] *Alexander;* tha'r *Q2–4;* they
are *F1*
14 **She is**] She's *F1*
14 **conjunctive**] *F1;* concliue *Q2–4*
22 **loud a wind**] *F1;* loued Arm'd *Q2;*
loued armes *Q3–4*
24 **But . . . have aim'd**] And . . . had
arm'd *F1*
26 **desp'rate**] *ed.;* desprat *Q2;* desperate
F1, Q3–4
27 **Whose worth**] Who was *F1*
29 **perfections—**] *Pope;* perfections,
Q2–4; perfections. *F1*
34 **lov'd**] *F1, Q3–4;* loued *Q2*
35 **imagine—**] *F1 (subs.);*
imagine. *Q2–4*
35 s.d. **with letters**] *om. F1 (Q1)*
36 **How . . . Hamlet:**] *F1*
37 **These**] This *F1*
40 **receiv'd**] *F1;* receiued *Q2–4*
41 **Of . . . them.**] *om. F1 (Q1)*
42 s.d. **Exit Messenger.**] *F1*
43 s.d. **Reads.**] *Capell*
46 **you**] your *F1*
46 **pardon thereunto,**] *F1 (subs.);*
pardon, there-vnto *Q2–4*
46 **the occasion**] th'Occasions *F1*
47 **and more strange**] *F1*
48 **Hamlet.**] *F1*

49 **What**] *F1; King.* What *Q2–4*
(*repeated s.p.*)
50 **and**] Or *F1*
53 **devise**] aduise *F1*
54 **I am**] I'm *F1*
56 **shall**] *F1 (Q1)*
57 **didst**] diddest *F1*
59 **Ay, my lord,**] *om. F1 (Q1)*
60 **So you will**] If so you'l *F1*
62 **checking at**] *F1;* the King at *Q2–3;*
liking not *Q4*
64 **device**] *F1;* deuise *Q2–4*
68–81 **Laer. My . . . graveness.**] *om. F1*
(*Q1, except for a variant version of l. 68*)
71 **travel**] *Q4;* trauaile *Q2–3*
11 **riband**] *Q3–4;* ribaud *Q2*
81 **Two months since**] Some two
Monthes hence *F1*
83 **I have**] I'ue *F1*
83 **against,**] *Hanmer;* against *Q2–4, F1*
84 **can**] ran *F1*
85 **unto**] into *F1*
88 **topp'd**] past *F1*
88 **my**] *F1;* me *Q2–4*
90 **was't**] *F1;* wast *Q2–4*
92 **Lamord**] Lamound *F1*
94 **the**] our *F1*
95 **made**] mad *F1*
98 **especial**] especially *F1*
100–2 **The . . . them.**] *om. F1 (Q1)*
100 **scrimers**] *Q3–4;* Scrimures *Q2*
105 **you**] him *F1*
106 **What out of**] Why out of *F1;* And
how for *Q1*
114–23 **There . . . ulcer:**] *om. F1 (Q1)*
121 **accidents**] *Q4;* accidents *Q2–3*
122 **spendthrift's**] *Q3–4 (subs.);* spend
thirfts *Q2;* spend-thrift *Q5*
125 **indeed . . . son**] your Fathers sonne
indeed *F1*
127 **sanctuarize**] Sancturize *F1*
129 **chamber.**] *Steevens;* chamber, *Q2, F1;*
chamber *Q3–4*
133 **Frenchman**] *F1, Q4;* french
man *Q2–3*
134 **o'er**] on *F1*
138 **pass**] *F1;* pace *Q2–4*
139 **Requite**] Requit *F1*
140] *In Q1 and Der bestrafte Brudermord
the suggestion for poisoning Laertes' sword
comes from Claudius. In Q1 the King
says:* . . . now this being granted,/
When you are hot in midst of all
your play,/Among the foyles shall a
keene rapier lie,/Steeped in a mixture
of deadly poyson,/That if it drawes
but the least dramme of blood,/

In any part of him, he cannot liue:/
This being done will free you from
suspition,/And not the deerest friend
that *Hamlet* lov'de/Will euer haue
Leartes in suspect.
140 **that**] *F1*
142 **that, but dip**] I but dipt *F1*
149 **Weigh**] *F1, Q4;* Wey *Q2–3*
150 **shape. If . . . fail,**] *Rowe;* shape
if . . . fayle, *Q2–4;* shape, if . . .
faile; *F1;* And lest that all
should miss, *Q1*
154 **did**] should *F1*
155 **cunnings**] commings *F1*
156 **ha't**] *F1;* hate *Q2;* hau't *Q3–4*
158 **that**] the *F1*
159 **preferr'd**] *Q3–4;* prefard *Q2;*
prepar'd *F1*
162 **But . . . noise?**] how sweet
Queene. *F1;* How now Gertred, why
looke you heauily? *Q1*
164 **they**] they'l *F1*
166 **askaunt the**] aslant a *F1;* by a *Q1*
167 **hoary**] hore *F1*
168 **Therewith . . . make**] There with . . .
come *F1*
171 **cull-cold**] cold *F1*
172 **crownet**] *Wilson;* cronet *Q2;*
Coronet *F1, Q3–4*
174 **her**] the *F1*
177 **snatches . . . lauds**] snatches of old
tunes *F1;* olde sundry tunes *Q1*
181 **their**] (*Q1*); her *F1*
182 **lay**] buy *F1*
183 **she is**] (*Q1*); is she *F1*
190 **a'**] of *F1*
191 **drowns**] doubts *F1*

5.1

5.1] *Q (1676)*
Location: *Capell (after Rowe)*
o.s.d. **with mattocks**] *Q (1676)*
1 s.p. **1. Clo.**] *Rowe;* Clowne. *Q2–4, F1*
(*Q1*) (*throughout*)
1–2 when she] that *F1*
3 s.p. **2. Clo.**] *Rowe;* Other. *Q2–4, F1*
(*throughout*); 2. *Q1*
3 therefore] and therefore *F1*
9 se offendendo] *F1;* so offended
Q2–4
12 to act] an Act *F1*
12 do] doe and *F1*
12 perform; argal,] *F1 (subs.);*
performe, or all; *Q2–4;* Ergo *Q1*
14 goodman] *F1;* good man *Q2–4*
16 good.] *F1 (subs.);* good, *Q2–4*
17 himself] himsele *F1*

18 that. But] *Q5 (subs.);* that, but *Q2–4;*
that? But *F1*
23 an't] on't *F1*
25 a'] of *F1*
28 even-Christen] *hyphen, Furness;*
euen Christian *F1*
33 'A] He *F1*
34–7 2. Clo. Why . . . arms?] *F1 (s.p.*
Other)
39 thyself—] *F1;* thy selfe. *Q2–4*
43 that] (*Q1*); that Frame *F1*
55 s.d. **afar off**] *F1;* s.d. *after 1.64, Q2–4*
(*Q1*); placed as in *F1*
59 houses] (*Q1*); Houses that *F1*
59 lasts] last *Q4 (Q1)*
60 in, and] to Yaughan *F1*
60 sup] *Kermode conj. (privately);* scope
Q2–4; stoupe *F1;* stope *Q1*
60 s.d. **Exit . . . digs.**] *Rowe (subs.)*
61 s.d. **Song.**] Sings. *F1*
64 a—was nothing—a—meet.] was
nothing meete. *F1;* most meete. *Q1*
66 'a . . . grave-making] that he sings
at Graue-making *F1;* That is thus
merry in making of a graue *Q1*
70 daintier] *F1, Q3–4;* dintier *Q2*
71, 94 s.dd. **Song.**] sings *F1*
72 clawed] caught *F1*
73 into] intill *F1*
74 s.d. **Throws . . . it.**] *ed., from Q1*
and Capell; Q1 reads: he throwes vp a
shouel.
77 'twere] it were *F1*
78 This] It *F1*
79 now o'erreaches] o're Offices *F1*
79 would] could *F1*
83 sweet] good *F1*
85 'a] he *F1 (Q1)*
85 meant] *F1, Q3–4 (Q1);* went *Q2*
88 Worm's,] *F1 (subs.);* wormes *Q2–4*
89 chopless] *Wilson;* Choples *Q2–4;*
Chap-lesse *F1*
89 mazzard] *F1;* massene *Q2;* mazer
Q3–4
90 and] if *F1*
92 them] 'em *F1*
94 pickaxe] (*Q1*); Pickhaxe *F1*
97 s.d. **Throws . . . skull.**] *Capell*
98 may] might *F1 (Q1)*
99 of] of of *F1*
99 quiddities] Quiddits *F1;* Quirkes *Q1*
100 quillities] *Q3–4;* quillites *Q2;*
Quillets *F1*
100 tenures] *F1, Q4;* tenurs *Q2–3*
101 mad] rude *F1*
106–7 Is . . . recoveries,] *F1*
108 his] *F1*

109 **double ones too**] *F1;* doubles *Q2–4*
111 **scarcely**] hardly *F1;* scarse *Q1*
115 **calves'-skins**] *(Q1);* Calue-skinnes *F1, Q3–4*
116 **which**] that *F1*
118 **sirrah**] Sir *F1; Q1 reads the line:* Now my friend, whose graue is this ?
120 s.d. **Sings.**] *Capell*
120 **O**] *F1;* or *Q2–4*
121 **For . . . meet.**] *F1*
123 **'tis**] it is *F1*
124 **yet**] and yet *F1*
125 **it is**] 'tis *F1*
139 **this three**] these three *F1;* this seauen *Q1*
139 **I . . . of**] I haue taken note of *F1;* haue I noted *Q1*
141 **heel . . . courtier**] *(Q1);* heeles of our Courtier *F1*
142 **been**] been a *F1*
143 **all**] *F1*
144 **overcame**] o'recame *F1*
147 **that very**] the very *F1*
148 **is**] was *F1;* 's *Q1*
150 **'a**] he *F1*
150–1 **'A . . . 'a**] hee . . . he *F1 (Q1)*
151 **'tis**] *(Q1);* it's *F1*
154 **him there,**] him, *F1*
161–2 **I . . . thirty years.**] *Q1 om. this passage which makes Hamlet thirty years old; see ll. 173–4 below.*
161 **sexton**] sixteene *F1*
165 **Faith**] Ifaith *F1 (Q1)*
165 **'a . . . 'a**] he . . . he *F1 (Q1)*
166 **corses**] *(Q1);* Coarses now adaies *F1*
167 **'a**] he *F1 (Q1)*
171 **'a**] he *F1;* it *Q1*
173–4 **hath . . . years.**] *Q2–4* (23. yeeres); this Scul, has laine in the earth three & twenty years. *F1;* hath bin here this dozen yeare, *Q1 (Q1 thus makes Hamlet a very young man; see ll. 161–2 above)*
179 **pestilence**] pestlence *F1;* plague *Q1*
180–1 **This same skull, sir**] *repeated. F1*
181 **sir, Yorick's**] *Wilson;* sir Yoricks *Q2–4;* Yoricks *F1;* one Yorickes *Q1*
182 s.d. **Takes the skull.**] *Capell*
184 **Alas**] Let me see. Alas *F1;* I prethee let me see it, alas *Q1*
186 **bore**] borne *F1;* caried *Q1*
186 **now**] *(Q1); om. F1*
187 **in . . . it**] my Imagination *F1*
191 **Not**] No *F1*
192 **grinning**] leering *F1*
193 **chamber**] *F1 (Q1);* table *Q2–4*
197 **a'**] o' *F1*

200 **so? pah**] *Q5;* so pah *Q2;* so: pah *Q3–4;* so? Puh *F1*
200 s.d. **Puts . . . skull.**] *Collier*
204 **'a**] he *F1*
208 **it:**] it; as thus. *F1;* as thus of *Q1*
210 **to**] into *F1*
213 **imperious**] *(Q1);* Imperiall. *F1*
216 **winter's**] *F1;* waters *Q2–4*
217 **awhile**] aside *F1*
217 s.d. **Enter . . . attendant.**] *based on Q2–4, F1; Q1 s.dd.:* Enter K. Q. Laertes and the corse. *Q2–4;* Enter King, Queene, Laertes, and a Coffin, with Lords attendant. *F1;* Enter King and Queene, Leartes, and other lordes, with a Priest after the coffin. *Q1* (a Doctor of Divinity *from Wilson;* following *from Q1* after)
220 **desp'rate**] disperate *F1*
221 **of**] *om. F1 (Q1)*
222 s.d. **Retiring with Horatio.**] *Capell*
226, 235 s.pp. **Doctor.**] *Priest. F1 (Q1, l. 226)*
227 **warranty**] warrantis *F1*
229 **been**] *(Q1);* haue *F1*
230 **prayers**] praier *F1*
231 **Shards**] *F1*
232 **allow'd**] allowed *F1*
232 **crants**] Rites *F1*
237 **a**] sage *F1*
243 s.d. **Scattering flowers.**] *Johnson*
243 **Sweets . . . sweet,**] *(Q1);* Sweets, . . . sweet *F1*
246 **have**] t'haue *F1*
246 **treble woe**] terrible woer *F1*
247 **treble**] *F1;* double *Q2–4*
249 **Depriv'd**] *F1;* Depriued *Q2–4*
250 s.d. **Leaps . . . grave.**] *F1 (Q1 subs.)*
254 s.d. **Coming forward.**] *Collier MS (subs.)*
254 **grief**] griefes *F1*
256 **Conjures**] *(Q1);* Coniure *F1*
257 **wonder-wounded**] *hyphen, F1*
258 s.d. **Hamlet . . . Laertes.**] *Q1*
259 s.d. **Grappling with him.**] *Rowe*
261 **For**] Sir *F1*
261 **and**] *F1*
262 **in me something**] something in me *F1 (Q1)*
263 **wisdom**] *(Q1);* wisenesse *F1 (c);* wisensse *F1 (u)*
263 **Hold off**] *(Q1);* Away *F1*
264 **All. Gentlemen!**] *om. F1 (Q1)*
265 s.p. **Hor.**] Gen. *F1*
265 s.d. **The . . . grave.**] *Capell (subs.)*
269 **lov'd**] *F1, Q3–4 (Q1);* loued *Q2*
274 **'Swounds**] Come *F1*

274 **thou't**] *Q5;* th'owt *Q2;* th'out *Q3–4;*
  thou'lt *F1;* thou wilt *Q1*
275 **woo't fast,**] *om. F1;* wilt fast *Q1*
276 **eisel**] *Theobald;* Esill *Q2–4;* Esile *F1;*
  vessels *Q1*
276 **crocadile**] *(Q1);* Crocodile *F1 (c);*
  Crocadile *F1 (u)*
277 **thou**] *F1 (Q1)*
284 s.p. **Queen.**] Kin. *F1;* King. *Q1*
285 **thus**] *F1;* this *Q2–4*
287 **couplets**] Cuplet *F1*
292, 293 s.dd. **Exit Hamlet., Exit
  Horatio.**] *as in F1 and Pope; Q2–4
  combine these in one s.d.* Exit Hamlet/
  and Horatio, *opposite ll. 292, 293
  (so Q1 after l. 292, om. l. 293)*
293 **thee**] you *F1*
294–9] *Q1 substitutes the following lines:*
  Queene. Alas, it is his madnes makes
  him thus,/And not his heart, *Leartes./
  King.* My lord, t'is so: but wee'le no
  longer trifle,/This very day shall
  Hamlet drinke his last,/For presently
  we meane to send to him,/Therfore
  Leartes be in ready-nes./*Lear.* My lord,
  till then my soule will not bee quiet./
  King. Come *Gertred,* wee'l haue
  Leartes, and our sonne,/Made friends
  and Louers, as befittes them both,/
  Euen as they tender vs, and loue their
  countrie./*Queene* God grant they
  may. *exeunt omnes.*
294 s.d. **To Laertes.**] *Rowe*
294 **your**] you *F1*
298 **shortly**] *F1;* thirtie *Q2 (u);* thereby
  Q2 (c), Q3–4
298 **see,**] *Q5;* see *Q2–4;* see; *F1*
299 **Till**] *F1.* Tell *Q2–4*

5.2

5.2] *Rowe* Location: *Alexander
  (after Theobald)*
1 **shall you**] let me *F1; Q1 om. ll. 1–74*
3 **lord!**] *Capell;* Lord. *Q2–4;* Lord? *F1*
5 **Methought**] *F1, Q3–4;* my
  thought *Q2*
6 **bilboes**] *F1, Q3–4;* bilbo *Q2*
7 **prais'd**] praise *F1*
8 **sometime**] sometimes *F1, Q4*
9 **deep**] deare *F1*
9 **pall**] *Q2 (u);* fall *Q2 (c), Q3–4;*
  paule *F1*
9 **learn**] teach *F1*
11 **Rough-hew**] *hyphen, F1*
13 **me,**] *Q5;* me *Q2–4, F1*
16–7 **bold, . . . manners,**] *F1 (subs.);*
  bold . . . manners *Q2–4*

17 **unseal**] *F1;* vnfold *Q2–4*
19 **Ah**] *Delias conj.;* A *Q2–4;* Oh *F1*
20 **reasons**] reason *F1*
22 **ho**] *Pope;* hoe *Q2–4;* hoo *F1*
27 **now**] me *F1*
29 **villainies**] *Capell,* villaines *Q2–4, F1*
30 **Or**] Ere *F1*
36 **yeman's**] *F3;* yemans *Q2–3;* Yeomans
  F1, Q4
37 **Th' effect**] The effects *F1*
40 **like**] as *F1*
40 **might**] should *F1*
43 **as's**] *Rowe;* as sir *Q2–4;* Assis *F1*
44 **knowing**] know *F1*
46 **those**] the *F1*
47 **allow'd**] *Q4;* alow'd *Q2–3;* allowed *F1*
48 **ordinant**] ordinate *F1*
51 **in the**] in *F1*
52 **Subscrib'd**] *F1, Q3–4;* Subscribe *Q2*
54 **sequent**] sement *F1*
55 **knowest**] know'st *F1*
57 **Why . . . employment,**] *F1*
58 **defeat**] debate *F1*
59 **Does**] Doth *F1*
63 **think**] thinks *F1*
63 **upon—**] *Boswell;* vppon? *Q2–4;*
  vpon *F1*
67 **coz'nage—**] *Boswell (subs.);* cusnage,
  Q2; cosnage, *Q3–4;* coozenage, *F1*
68–80 **To . . . here?**] *F1; ll. 75–78 in
  substance in Q1*
78 **court**] *Rowe;* count *F1*
80 s.d. **young Osric**] *F1; s.d. in Q1 reads:*
  Enter a Bragart Gentleman.
81, 89, etc. s.pp. **Osr.**] *F1;* Cour. *Q2–4;*
  Gent. *Q1*
82 **humbly**] *Q3–4, F1;* humble *Q2*
87 **say**] saw *F1*
89 **lordship**] friendship *F1*
91 **sir**] *(Q1); om. F1*
91 **with all**] *F1, Q3–4;* withall *Q2*
92 **Put**] *F1*
94 **it is**] 'tis *F1*
98 **But yet**] *om. F1 (Q1)*
98 **sultry**] *F1, Q3–4* (soultry); sully *Q2*
99 **for**] *F1;* or *Q2–4*
100 **sultry**] *F1, Q3–4* (soultry); soultery
  Q2; swoltery *Q1*
101 **My**] but my *F1*
102 **'a**] he *F1*
102 **laid**] *F1;* layed *Q2–4*
103 **matter—**] *Rowe;* matter. *Q2–4, F1*
104 s.d. **Hamlet . . . hat.**] *Johnson*
105 **good my lord**] in good faith *F1*
105 **my**] mine *F1*
106–43 **Sir . . . unfellow'd.**] *om. F1, except
  for:* Sir, you are not ignorant of what

excellence *Laertes* is at / his weapon.;
om. Q1
107 gentleman] *Q3–4;* gentlemen *Q2*
109 sellingly] *Q2 (u);* Fellingly *Q2 (c);*
feelingly *Q3–4*
114 dozy] *Kittredge;* dosie *Q2 (u);* dazzie
Q2 (c); dizzie *Q3–4*
115 yaw] *Q2 (u);* raw *Q2 (c), Q3–4*
122 sir? Why] *Capell;* sir, why *Q2–4*
126 to't] too't *Q2 (u);* doo't *Q2 (c),*
Q3–4
135 me. Well, sir?] *Globe (after Theobald);*
me, well sir. *Q2–4*
141 his] *Q5;* this *Q2–4*
142 them, . . . meed] *Steevens;* them . . .
meed, *Q2–4*
147 King, sir] sir King *F1;* sweete
Prince *Q1*
147 hath wager'd] ha's wag'd *F1;* hath
layd a wager *Q1*
148 against] *F1, Q3–4 (Q1);* againgst *Q2*
148 has impawn'd] impon'd *F1*
150 hangers] *F1;* hanger *Q2–4*
150 and] or *F1*
155–6 Hor. I . . . done.] *om. F1 (Q1)*
157 carriages] *F1;* carriage *Q2–4*
158 germane] *F1* (Germaine); Ierman
Q2; German *Q3–4;* cosin
german *Q1*
159 matter] matter: *F1;* phrase, *Q1*
159 a] *om. F1;* the *Q1*
160 might be] *F1, Q3–4;* be might *Q2*
(c); be *Q2(u)*
160 on:] *Pope;* on, *Q2–4;* on *F1*
161 Barb'ry] Barbary *F1*
162 liberal-conceited] *hyphen, Pope*
163 bet] but *F1*
163–4 all impawn'd, as] *Wilson (after*
Malone); all *Q2–4;* impon'd as *F1*
165–9 Osr. The . . . answer.] *Q1 gives*
two statements on the wager; the first in
4.7: King. Mary Leartes thus: I'le lay
a wager,/Shalbe on *Hamlets* side, and
you shall giue the oddes,/The which
will draw him with a more desire,/
To try the maistry, that in twelue
venies/You gaine not three of him:;
the second, here: Gent. Mary sir, that
yong Leartes in twelue venies/At
Rapier and Dagger do not get three
oddes of you,/And on your side the
King hath laide,/And desires you to
be in readinesse.
165 laid, sir,] laid *F1 (Q1)*
166 yourself] you *F1*
167 laid on] one *F1*
167 nine] mine *F1*

168 it] that *F1*
173 hall.] *F1 (subs.);* hall, *Q2–4*
174 it is] 'tis *F1*
176 purpose,] *Theobald;* purpose;
Q2–4, F1
176 him and] him if *F1*
177 I will] Ile *F1*
179 deliver you] redeliuer you ee'n *F1;*
Q1 reads the line: I shall deliuer your
most sweet answer.
183 Yours.] *Jennens (after Capell);* Yours
Q2–4; Yours, yours; *F1*
183 s.d. Exit Osric.] *Capell;* exit. *Q1*
183 'A] *ed. (Parrott-Craig conj.);* hee *F1;*
om. Q2–4
184 turn] tongue *F1*
187 'A . . . 'a] He . . . hee *F1*
187 comply] *F1; om. Q2 (u);* so *Q2 (c),*
Q3–4
188 has] had *F1*
188 many] mine *F1*
189 breed] Beauy *F1*
190 out of an] outward *F1*
191 yesty] *F1;* histy *Q2;* misty *Q3–4*
192 profound] *Bailey conj. (in Cambridge);*
prophane *Q2–4;* fond *F1; Warburton*
conj. (in Hanmer), fann'd
192 winnow'd] *F1* (winnowed);
trennowed *Q2;* trennowned *Q3–4*
193 trial] tryalls *F1*
194 s.d., 195–208 Enter . . . me.] *om. F1*
(Q1, except ll. 203–4)
196 Osric] *from the regular F1 form;*
Ostricke *Q2–4 (subs., throughout, except*
Osrick *at l. 349 s.d.)*
208 s.d. Exit Lord.] *Theobald*
209 lose] lose this wager *F1*
212 Thou wouldst] but thou
wouldest *F1*
212 ill all's] all *F1*
216 gain-giving] *F1;* gamgiuing *Q2;*
game-giuing *Q3–4*
217 it] *om. F1 (Q1)*
218 forestall] *F1, Q3–4;* forstal *Q2*
219 There is] there's a *F1 (Q1)*
220 now] *F1 (Q1)*
222 will] *F1, Q3–4;* well *Q2*
222 all.] *Rowe (subs.);* all, *Q2–4, F1*
223–4 of . . . be.] ha's ought of what
he leaues. What is't to leaue
betimes? *F1*
224 s.d. A . . . state.] *from Q2–4 and*
F1 s.dd.: A table prepard, Trumpets,
Drums, and officers with Cushions,
King, Queene, and all the state, Foiles,
daggars, and Laertes. *Q2–4;* Enter
King, Queene, Laertes and Lords,

with other Attendants with Foyles,
and Gauntlets, a Table and Flagons of
Wine on it. *F1; Q1 reads:* Enter King,
Queene, Leartes, Lordes.
224 s.d. **Osric**] *Theobald*
225 s.d. **The . . . Hamlet's.**] *Johnson*
226 **I have**] I'ue *F1* 230 **a**] *om. F1 (Q1)*
230 **distraction. What**] *Q3–4 (subs.);*
distraction, what *Q2;* distraction?
What *F1*
231 **nature, honor,**] nature honour *F1*
233 **Was't . . . wrong'd**] *F1;* Wast . . .
wronged *Q2–4*
238 **wronged**] wrong'd *F1*
240 **Sir . . . audience,**] *F1*
244 **brother**] *(Q1);* Mother *F1*
250 **keep**] *F1*
250 **ungor'd**] vngorg'd *F1*
250 **till**] *F1;* all *Q2–4*
252–3 **I . . . play.**] *as verse, F1; as prose, Q2–4*
252 **I**] I do *F1*
253 **brothers'**] *M. Edel (privately);*
brothers *Q2–4, F1*
254 **Come on.**] *F1*
257 **off**] *F1;*of *Q2–4*
261 **has**] hath *F1 (Q1)*
261 **laid**] *F1, Q3–4 (Q1);* layed *Q2*
263 **better'd**] *F1;* better *Q2–4*
265 s.d. **Prepare to play.**] *F1*
267 **stoups**] *Johnson;* stoopes *Q2–4;*
Stopes *F1*
270 **ord'nance**] Ordinance *F1*
272 **union**] *F1;* Vnice *Q2 (u);* Onixe *Q2*
(c), *Q3–4*
275 **trumpet**] Trumpets *F1*
278 s.d. **Trumpets the while.**] *om. F1 (Q1)*
279 s.d. **They . . . hit.**] *from F1 and Q1:*
They play. *F1;* a hit./Heere they play:
Q1 (although a hit *is in italics and is
separated from Hamlet's concluding words*
come on sir:, *it is perhaps part of his
speech)*
280 **my lord**] on sir *F1*
283 s.d. **sound flourish**] *ed. (after F1 and
placed as in F1);* and shot./Florish,
Q2–4 (after l. 281); F1 s.d. reads:
Trumpets sound, and shot goes off.
283 s.d. **within**] *Capell*
284 **it**] *(Q1); om. F1*
285 **Come.**] *F1 (subs.);* Come, *Q2–4*
285 s.d. **They play again.**] *F1*
286 **A touch, a touch,**] *F1 (Q1)*
286 **confess't**] *Q (1676),* confest *Q2–4;*
confesse *F1;* grant *Q1*
288 **Here . . . my**] *(Q1);* Heere's a *F1*
292, 296 s.dd. **Aside.**] *Rowe*
296 **it . . . against**] 'tis almost 'gainst *F1*

297 **do**] *om. F1 (Q1)*
299 **sure**] affear'd *F1*
300 s.d. **They play.**] *F1* (Play.)
302 s.d. **Laertes . . . rapiers.**] *Rowe
(incorporating F1* In scuffling they
change Rapiers.)*; They catch one
anothers Rapiers, and both are
wounded, Leartes falles downe, the
Queene falles downe and dies. *Q1;
the s.d. in* Der bestrafte Brudermord
is interesting at this point: Dieser [i.e.
Leonhardus-Laertes] lässt das Rappier
fallen, und ergreift den vergifteten
Degen welcher parat lieget, und stosst
dem Prinzen die Quarte in den Arm.
Hamlet pariret auf Leonhardo, dass sie
beyde die Gewehre fallen lassen. Sie
laufen ein jeder nach dem Rappier.
Hamlet bekommt den vergifteten
Degen, und sticht Leonhardus todt.
[i.e. He lets his foil fall and seizes the
poisoned sword, which is lying ready,
and deals him a thrust in the left arm.
Hamlet parries, so that both drop
their weapons. They each run to pick
up a foil. Hamlet takes the poisoned
sword and kills Leonhardus (lit. sticks
Leonhardus dead).]*
303 **come**] come, *F1*
303 s.d. **Hamlet wounds Laertes.**] *Rowe
(as end of s.d. at l. 302); placed as in
Sisson*
303 s.d. **The Queen falls.**] *Capell after
Q1 (see l. 302 s.d.)*
303 **ho**] *Q3–4* (hoe); howe *Q2;* hoa *F1*
304 **is it**] is't *F1*
306 **own**] *om. F1 (Q1)*
310 **pois'ned**] poyson'd *F1*
310 s.d. **Dies.**] *Rowe after Q1
(see l. 302 s.d.)*
311 **Ho**] *Q3–4* (hoe); how *Q2;* How? *F1*
313 **Hamlet,**] *F1*
314 **med'cine**] Medicine *F1;* medecine *Q4*
315 **hour's**] *Q (1676),* houres *Q2–4;*
houre of *F1 (Q1)*
316 **thy**] *F1 (Q1);* my *Q2–4*
319 **pois'ned**] *(Q1);* poyson'd *F1*
322 s.d. **Hurts the King.**] *F1* 325 **Here**]
F1, Q3–4; Heare *Q2*
325 **incestious**] incestuous *F1*
325 **murd'rous**] *F1*
326 **off**] *F1;*of *Q2–4*
326 **thy union**] *F1 (Q1);* the Onixe *Q2–4*
327 s.d. **King dies.**] *F1 (Q1* The king
dies.)*
328 **temper'd**] temp'red *F1*
331 s.d. **Dies.**] *F1 (Q1* Leartes dies.)*

337 **strict]** strick'd *F1*
339 **cause aright]** *Q3–4;* cause a right
Q2; causes right *F1*
341 **antique]** *Q5;* anticke Q2; Antike
F1, Q3–4
343 **ha't]** *Capell;* hate Q2–4; haue't *F1*
344 **God]** good *F1;* fie *Q1*
345 **I leave]** Hue *F1;* thou leaue *Q1*
349 s.d. **and . . . within]** *F1* (shout),
Steevens (shot)
349 s.d. **Osric . . . returns.]** *ed., based
on* Enter Osrick. *at this point in
Q2–4, F1*
358 **silence.]** silence. O, o, o, o. *F1*
358 s.d. **Dies.]** *F1* (*Q1* Ham. dies.)
359 **cracks]** cracke *F1*
360 s.d. **March within.]** *Capell*
361 s.d. **English]** *F1* (*Q1* from England)
361 s.d. **Embassadors]** (*Q1, subs.*);
Ambassador *F1*
361 s.d. **with . . . Attendants]** *F1; Q1
s.d. reads:* Enter Voltemar and the
Ambassadors from England, enter
Fortenbrasse with his traine.
362 **you]** ye *F1*

364 **This]** His *F1*
364 **proud]** *F1, Q3–4;* prou'd Q2;
imperious *Q1*
366 **a shot]** a shoote *F1;* one draft *Q1*
367 s.p. **l. Emb.]** *Capell;* Embas. *Q2–4;*
Amb. *F1* (*Q1*)
374 **commandement]** command'ment *F1*
376 **Polack]** FJ; Pollack Q2; Pollock
Q3–4; Polake *F1*
379 **th']** *F1, Q3–4*
383 **forc'd]** *F1;* for no Q2–4
389 **rights,]** Rites *F1;* rights *Q1*
390 **now to]** (*Q1*); are ro *F1*
391 **also]** alwayes *F1*
392 **on]** *F1;* no Q2–4
394 **while]** whiles *F1*
395 **plots]** plots, *F1*
398 **prov'd]** *F1* (*Q1*); prooued Q2–4
398 **royal]** (*Q1*); royally *F1*
399 **rite]** *Wilson;* right Q2–4; rites *F1*
401 **bodies]** body *F1* (*Q1*)
403 s.d. **Exeunt]** Exeunt./FINIS. Q2–4;
Exeunt . . . off./FINIS. *F1* (*see
following note*); FINIS. *Q1*
403 s.d. **marching . . . off** *F1*

SOURCES AND CONTEXTS

From *HISTORIAE DANICAE*

Saxo Grammaticus

Translated by Oliver Elton (1894)

This twelfth century history preserves the ninth century narrative of the sagas and is itself the source of Belleforest's expanded French version. There is no evidence that Shakespeare himself had read Saxo.

BOOK 3

AT THIS time Horwendil and Feng, whose father Gerwendil had been governor of the Jutes, were appointed in his place by Rorik to defend Jutland. But Horwendil held the monarchy for three years, and then, to win the height of glory, devoted himself to roving. Then Koll, King of Norway, in rivalry of his great deeds and renown, deemed it would be a handsome deed if by his greater strength in arms he could bedim the far-famed glory of the rover; and, cruising about the sea, he watched for Horwendil's fleet and came up with it. There was an island lying in the middle of the sea, which each of the rovers, bringing his ships up on either side, was holding. The captains were tempted by the pleasant look of the beach, and the comeliness of the shores led them to look through the interior of the spring-tide woods, to go through the glades, and roam over the sequestered forests. It was here that the advance of Koll and Horwendil brought them face to face without any witness. Then Horwendil endeavoured to address the king first, asking him in what way it was his pleasure to fight, and declaring that one best which needed the courage of as few as possible. For, said he, the duel was the surest of all modes of combat for winning the meed of bravery, because it relied only upon native courage, and excluded all help from the hand of another. Koll marvelled at so brave a judgment in a youth, and said: 'Since thou hast granted me the choice of battle, I think it is best to employ that kind which needs only the endeavours of two, and is free from all the tumult. Certainly it is more venturesome, and allows of a speedier award of the victory. This thought we share, in this opinion we agree of our own accord. But since the issue remains doubtful, we must pay some regard to gentle dealing, and must not give way so far to our inclinations as to leave the last offices undone. Hatred is in our hearts; yet let piety be there also, which in its due time may take the place of rigour. For the rights of nature reconcile us, though we are parted by differences of purpose; they link us together, howsoever rancour estrange our spirits. Let us, therefore, have this pious stipulation, that the conqueror shall give funeral rites to the conquered. For all allow that these are the last duties of human kind, from which no righteous man shrinks. Let each army lay aside its sternness and perform this function in harmony. Let jealousy depart at death, let the feud be buried in the tomb. Let us not show such an example of cruelty as to persecute one another's dust, though hatred has come between us in our lives. It will be a boast for the victor if he has borne his beaten foe in a lordly funeral. For the man who pays the rightful dues over his dead enemy wins the goodwill of the survivor; and whoso devotes gentle dealing to him who is no more, conquers the living by his kindness. Also there is another disaster, not less lamentable, which sometimes befalls the living—the loss of some part of their body; and I think that succour is due to this just as much as to the worst hap that may befall. For often those who fight keep their lives safe, but suffer maiming; and this lot is commonly thought more dismal than any death; for death cuts off memory of all things, while the living cannot forget the devastation of his own body. Therefore this mischief also must be helped somehow; so let it be agreed, that the injury of either of us by the other shall be made good with ten tablets [marks] of gold. For if it be righteous to have compassion on the calamities of another, how much more is it to pity one's own? No man but obeys nature's prompting; and he who slights it is a self-murderer.'

After mutually pledging their faiths to these terms, they began the battle. Nor were their strangeness in meeting one another, nor the sweetness of that spring-green spot, so heeded as to prevent them from the fray. Horwendil, in his too great ardour, became keener to attack his enemy than to defend his own body; and, heedless of his shield, had grasped his sword with both hands; and his boldness did not fail. For by his rain of blows he destroyed Koll's shield and deprived him of it, and at last hewed off his foot and drove him lifeless to the ground. Then, not to fail of his compact, he buried him royally, gave him a howe of lordly make and pompous obsequies. Then he pursued and slew Koller's sister Sela, who was a skilled warrior and experienced in roving.

He had now passed three years in valiant deeds of war; and, in order to win higher rank in Rorik's favour, he assigned to him the best trophies and the pick of the plunder. His friendship with Rorik enabled him to woo and win in marriage his daughter Gerutha, who bore him a son Amleth.

Such great good fortune stung Feng with jealousy, so that he resolved treacherously to waylay his brother, thus showing that goodness is not safe even from those of a man's own house. And behold, when a chance came to murder him, his bloody hand sated the deadly passion of his soul. Then he took the wife of the brother he had butchered, capping unnatural murder[1] with incest. For whoso yields to one iniquity, speedily falls an easier victim to the next, the first being an incentive to the second. Also the man veiled the monstrosity of his deed with such hardihood of cunning, that he made up a mock pretence of goodwill to excuse his crime, and glossed over fratricide with a show of righteousness. Gerutha, said he, though so gentle that she would do no man the slightest hurt, had been visited with her husband's extremest hate; and it was all to save her that he had slain his brother; for he thought it shameful that a lady so meek and unrancorous should suffer the heavy disdain of her husband. Nor did his smooth words fail in their intent; for at courts, where fools are sometimes favoured and backbiters preferred, a lie lacks not credit. Nor did Feng keep from shameful embraces the hands that had slain a brother; pursuing with equal guilt both of his wicked and impious deeds.

Amleth beheld all this, but feared lest too shrewd a behaviour might make his uncle suspect him. So he chose to feign dulness, and pretend an utter lack of wits. This cunning course not only concealed his intelligence but ensured his safety. Every day he remained in his mother's house utterly listless and unclean, flinging himself on the ground and bespattering his person with foul and filthy dirt. His discoloured face and visage smutched with slime denoted foolish and grotesque madness. All he said was of a piece with these follies; all he did savoured of utter lethargy. In a word, you would not have thought him a man at all, but some absurd abortion due to a mad fit of destiny. He used at times to sit over the fire, and, raking up the embers with his hands, to fashion wooden crooks, and harden them in the fire, shaping at their tips certain barbs, to make them hold more tightly to their fastenings. When asked what he was about, he said that he was preparing sharp javelins to avenge his father. This answer was not a little scoffed at, all men deriding his idle and ridiculous pursuit; but the thing helped his purpose afterwards. Now it was his craft in this matter that first awakened in the deeper observers a suspicion of his cunning. For his skill in a trifling art betokened the hidden talent of the craftsman; nor could they believe the spirit dull where the hand had acquired so cunning a workmanship. Lastly, he always watched with the most punctual care

---

1. Unnatural murder] These words of the Ghost in *Hamlet*, 1.5.25, exactly translate *parricidium*, which (with *parricida*) occurs constantly in this narrative, and has been variously rendered by 'slaying of kin', 'fratricide', etc. [E]

over his pile of stakes that he had pointed in the fire. Some people, therefore, declared that his mind was quick enough, and fancied that he only played the simpleton in order to hide his understanding, and veiled some deep purpose under a cunning feint. His wiliness (said these) would be most readily detected, if a fair woman were put in his way in some secluded place, who should provoke his mind to the temptations of love; all men's natural temper being too blindly amorous to be artfully dissembled, and this passion being also too impetuous to be checked by cunning. Therefore, if his lethargy were feigned, he would seize the opportunity, and yield straightway to violent delights. So men were commissioned to draw the young man in his rides into a remote part of the forest, and there assail him with a temptation of this nature. Among these chanced to be a foster-brother of Amleth, who had not ceased to have regard to their common nurture; and who esteemed his present orders less than the memory of their past fellowship. He attended Amleth among his appointed train, being anxious not to entrap, but to warn him; and was persuaded that he would suffer the worst if he showed the slightest glimpse of sound reason, and above all if he did the act of love openly. This was also plain enough to Amleth himself. For when he was bidden mount his horse, he deliberately set himself in such a fashion that he turned his back to the neck and faced about, fronting the tail; which he proceeded to encompass with the reins, just as if on that side he would check the horse in its furious pace. By this cunning thought he eluded the trick, and overcame the treachery of his uncle. The reinless steed galloping on, with the rider directing its tail, was ludicrous enough to behold.

Amleth went on, and a wolf crossed his path amid the thicket. When his companions told him that a young colt had met him, he retorted, that in Feng's stud there were too few of that kind fighting. This was a gentle but witty fashion of invoking a curse upon his uncle's riches. When they averred that he had given a cunning answer, he answered that he had spoken deliberately: for he was loth to be thought prone to lying about any matter, and wished to be held a stranger to falsehood; and accordingly he mingled craft and candour in such wise that, though his words did lack truth, yet there was nothing to betoken the truth and betray how far his keenness went.

Again, as he passed along the beach, his companions found the rudder of a ship which had been wrecked, and said they had discovered a huge knife. 'This', said he, 'was the right thing to carve such a huge ham;' by which he really meant the sea, to whose infinitude, he thought, this enormous rudder matched. Also, as they passed the sandhills, and bade him look at the meal, meaning the sand, he replied that it had been ground small by the hoary tempests of the ocean. His companions praising his answer, he said that he had spoken it wittingly. Then they purposely left him, that he might pluck up more courage to practise wantonness. The woman whom his uncle had dispatched met him in a dark spot, as though she had crossed him by chance; and he took her and would have ravished her, had not his foster-brother, by a secret device, given him an inkling of the trap. For this man, while pondering the fittest way to play privily the prompter's part, and forestall the young man's hazardous lewdness, found a straw on the ground and fastened it underneath the tail of a gadfly that was flying past; which he then drove towards the particular quarter where he knew Amleth to be: an act which served the unwary prince exceedingly well. The token was interpreted as shrewdly as it had been sent. For Amleth saw the gadfly, espied with curiosity the straw which it wore embedded in its tail, and perceived that it was a secret warning to beware of treachery. Alarmed, scenting a trap, and fain to possess his desire in greater safety, he caught up the woman in his arms and dragged her off to a distant and impenetrable fen. Moreover, when they had lain together, he conjured her earnestly to disclose the matter to none, and the promise of silence was accorded as heartily as it was asked. For both of them had been under the same fostering in their childhood; and this early rearing in common had brought Amleth and the girl into great intimacy.

So, when he had returned home, they all jeeringly asked him whether he had given way to love, and he avowed that he had ravished the maid. When he was next asked where he did it, and what had been his pillow, he said that he had rested upon the hoof of a beast of burden, upon a cockscomb, and also upon a ceiling. For, when he was starting into temptation, he had gathered fragments of all these things, in order to avoid lying. And though his jest did not take aught of the truth out of the story, the answer was greeted with shouts of merriment from the bystanders. The maiden, too, when questioned on the matter, declared that he had done no such thing; and her denial was the more readily credited when it was found that the escort had not witnessed the deed. Then he who had marked the gadfly in order to give a hint, wishing to show Amleth that to his trick he owed his salvation, observed that latterly he had been singly devoted to Amleth. The young man's reply was apt. Not to seem forgetful of his informant's service, he said that he had seen a certain thing bearing a straw flit by suddenly, wearing a stalk of chaff fixed on its hinder parts. The cleverness of this speech, which made the rest split with laughter, rejoiced the heart of Amleth's friend.

Thus all were worsted, and none could open the secret lock of the young man's wisdom. But a friend of Feng, gifted more with assurance than judgment,[1] declared that the unfathomable cunning of such a mind could not be detected by any vulgar plot, for the man's obstinacy was so great that it ought not to be assailed with any mild measures; there were many sides to his wiliness, and it ought not to be entrapped by any one method. Accordingly, said he, his own profounder acuteness had hit on a more delicate way, which was well fitted to be put in practice, and would effectually discover what they desired to know. Feng was purposely to absent himself, pretending affairs of great import. Amleth should be closeted alone with his mother in her chamber; but a man should first be commissioned to place himself in a concealed part of the room and listen heedfully to what they talked about. For if the son had any wits at all he would not hesitate to speak out in the hearing of his mother, or fear to trust himself to the fidelity of her who bore him. The speaker, loth to seem readier to devise than to carry out the plot, zealously proffered himself as the agent of the eavesdropping. Feng rejoiced at the scheme, and departed on pretence of a long journey. Now he who had given this counsel repaired privily[2] to the [room where Amleth was shut up with his mother,] and lay down skulking in the straw.[3] But Amleth had his antidote for the treachery. Afraid of being overheard by some eavesdropper, he at first resorted to his usual imbecile ways, and crowed like a noisy cock, beating his arms together to mimic the flapping of wings. Then he mounted the straw and began to swing his body and jump again and again, wishing to try if aught lurked there in hiding. Feeling a lump beneath his feet, he drove his sword into the spot, and impaled him who lay hid. Then he dragged him from his concealment and slew him. Then, cutting his body into morsels, he seethed it in boiling water, and flung it through the mouth of an open sewer for the swine to eat, bestrewing the stinking mire with his hapless limbs. Having in this wise eluded the snare, he went back to the room. Then his mother set up a great wailing, and began to lament her son's folly to his face; but he said: 'Most infamous of women! dost thou seek with such lying lamentations to hide thy most heavy guilt? Wantoning like a harlot, thou hast entered a wicked and abominable state of wedlock, embracing with incestuous bosom thy husband's slayer, and wheedling with filthy lures of blandishment him who had slain the father of thy son. This, forsooth, is the way that the mares couple with the vanquishers of their mates; for brute beasts are naturally incited to pair indiscriminately; and it would seem that thou, like them, hast clean forgot thy first husband. As for me, not idly do I wear the mask of folly; for I

---

1. Cf. *Hamlet,* 3.4: 'Thou wretched, rash, intruding fool. . .'   2. 'ambobus inscius', unknown to both of them.   3. 'Stramentum', possibly a straw mattress.

doubt not that he who destroyed his brother will riot as ruthlessly in the blood of his kindred. Therefore it is better to choose the garb of dulness than that of sense, and to borrow some protection from a show of utter frenzy. Yet the passion to avenge my father still burns in my heart; but I am watching the chances, I await the fitting hour. There is a place for all things; against so merciless and dark a spirit must be used the deeper devices of the mind. And thou, who hadst been better employed in lamenting thine own disgrace, know it is superfluity to bewail my witlessness; thou shouldst weep for the blemish in thine own mind, not for that in another's. On the rest see thou keep silence.' With such reproaches he rent the heart of his mother and redeemed her to walk in the ways of virtue,[1] teaching her to set the fires of the past above the seductions of the present.

When Feng returned, nowhere could he find the man who had suggested the treacherous espial; he searched for him long and carefully, but none said they had seen him anywhere. Amleth, among others, was asked in jest if he had come on any trace of him, and replied that the man had gone to the sewer, but had fallen through its bottom and been stifled by the floods of filth, and that he had then been devoured by the swine that came up all about that place. This speech was flouted by those who heard; for it seemed senseless, though really it expressly avowed the truth.

Feng now suspected that his stepson was certainly full of guile, and desired to make away with him, but durst not do the deed for fear of the displeasure, not only of Amleth's grand-sire Rorik, but also of his own wife. So he thought that the King of Britain should be employed to slay him, so that another could do the deed, and he be able to feign innocence. Thus, desirous to hide his cruelty, he chose rather to besmirch his friend than to bring disgrace on his own head. Amleth, on departing, gave secret orders to his mother to hang the hall with knotted tapestry, and to perform pretended obsequies for him a year thence; promising that he would then return. Two retainers of Feng then accompanied him, bearing a letter graven on wood[2]—a kind of writing material frequent in old times; this letter enjoined the king of the Britons to put to death the youth who was sent over to him. While they were reposing, Amleth searched their coffers, found the letter, and read the instructions therein. Whereupon he erased all the writing on the surface, substituted fresh characters, and so, changing the purport of the instructions, shifted his own doom upon his companions. Nor

---

1. '*talis convicis laceratam matrem ad excolendum virtutis habitum revocavit*'; 'With such a reproach did he recall his wounded mother to cultivate the habit of virtue.' Cf. 3.4.160-5. 2. Carved with runic letters.

was he satisfied with removing from himself the sentence of death and passing the peril on to others, but added an entreaty that the King of Britain would grant his daughter in marriage to a youth of great judgment whom he was sending to him. Under this was falsely marked the signature of Feng.

Now when they had reached Britain, the envoys went to the king, and proffered him the letter which they supposed was an implement of destruction to another,[1] but which really betokened death to themselves . . .

Narrative and Dramatic Sources of Shakespeare by Geoffrey Bullough, Vol. 7, Rutledge & Columbia University Presses, 1973, 60–67.

1. No doubts about their being accomplices!

From THE HYSTORIE OF HAMBLET (1608)

François de Belleforest

François de Belleforest's expanded and heavily misogynistic French version of Saxo was available in English translation earlier than this 1608 anonymous translation that itself shows some familiarity with Shakespeare's Hamlet.

CHAP. I

How Horvendile and Fengon were made Governours of the Province of Ditmarse, and how Horvendile marryed Geruth, the daughter to Roderick, chief K. of Denmark, by whom he had Hamblet: and how after his marriage his brother Fengon slewe him trayterously, and marryed his brothers wife, and what followed. . . .

Now the greatest honor that men of noble birth could at that time win and obtaine, was in exercising the art of piracie upon the seas, assayling their neighbours, and the countries bordering upon them; and how much the more they used to rob, pill, and spoyle other provinces, and ilands far adjacent, so much the more their honours and reputation increased and augmented: wherein Horvendile obtained the highest place in his time, beeing the most renouned pirate[1] that in those dayes scoured the seas and havens of the north parts: whose great fame so mooved the heart of Collere, king of Norway, that he was much grieved to heare that Horvendile surmounting him in feates of armes, thereby obscuring the glorie by him alreadie obtained upon the seas: (honor more than covetousnesse of riches (in those dayes) being the reason that provoked those barbarian princes to overthrow and vanquish one the other, not caring to be slaine by the handes of a victorious person). This valiant and hardy king[2] having challenged Horvendile to fight with him body to body, the combate was by him accepted, with conditions, that hee which should be vanquished should loose all the riches he had in his ships, and that the vanquisher should cause the body of the vanquished (that should bee slaine in the combate) to be honourably buried, death being the prise and reward of him that should loose the battaile: and to conclude, Collere, king of Norway (although a valiant, hardy, and couragious prince) was in the end vanquished and slaine by Horvendile, who presently caused a tombe to be erected, and therein (with all honorable obsequies fit for a prince) buried the body of king Collere, according

---

1. *In margin:* 'Horvendile a king and a pirate.'   2. 'ambitious Norway.' 1.1.61,82–95.

to their auncient manner and superstitions in these dayes, and the conditions of the combate, bereaving the kings shippes of all their riches; and having slaine the kings sister, a very brave and valiant warriour, and over runne all the coast of Norway, and the Northern Ilands, returned home againe layden with much treasure,[1] sending the most part thereof to his soveraigne, king Rodericke, thereby to procure his good liking, and so to be accounted one of the greatest favourites about his majestie.

The king, allured by those presents, and esteeming himselfe happy to have so valiant a subject, sought by a great favour and courtesie to make him become bounden unto him perpetually, giving him Geruth his daughter to his wife, of whom he knew Horvendile to bee already much inamored. And the more to honor him, determined himselfe in person to conduct her into Jutie, where the marriage was celebrated according to the ancient manner: and to be briefe, of this marriage proceeded Hamblet, of whom I intend to speake, and for his cause have chosen to renew this present hystorie.[2]

Fengon, brother to this prince Horvendile, who [not] onely fretting and despighting in his heart at the great honor and reputation wonne by his brother in warlike affaires,[3] but solicited and provoked by a foolish jealousie to see him honored with royall aliance, and fearing thereby to bee deposed from his part of the government, or rather desiring to be onely governour,[4] thereby to obscure the memorie of the victories and conquests of his brother Horvendile, determined (whatsoever happened) to kill him; which hee effected in such sort, that no man once so much as suspected him,[5] every man esteeming that from such and so firme a knot of alliance and consanguinitie there could proceed no other issue then the full effects of vertue and courtesie: but (as I sayd before) the desire of bearing soveraigne rule and authoritie respecteth neither blood nor amitie, nor caring for vertue, as being wholly without respect of lawes, or majestie devine; for it is not possible that hee which invadeth the countrey and taketh away the riches of an other man without cause or reason, should know or feare God. Was not this a craftie and subtile counsellor? but he might have thought that the mother, knowing her husbands case, would not cast her sonne into the danger of death. But Fengon, having secretly assembled certain men, and perceiving himself strong enough to execute his interprise, Horvendile his brother being at a banquet with his friends, sodainely set upon him,[6] where he slewe him as traiterously, as cunningly he purged himselfe of so detestable a murther to his

---

1. Hence 1.1.82–95.   **2.** *In margin:* 'Hamlet sonne to Horvendile.'   **3.** *In margin:* 'Fengon, his conspiracie against his brother.'   **4.** 3.3.55.   **5.** I.e. of plotting.   **6.** *In margin:* 'Fengon killeth his brother.' Not secretly as in *Ham.* 1.5.59–74.

subjects; for that before he had any violent or bloody handes, or once committed parricide upon his brother, hee had incestuously abused his wife, whose honour hee ought as well to have sought and procured as traiterously he pursued and effected his destruction.[1] And it is most certaine, that the man that abandoneth himselfe to any notorious and wicked action, whereby he becometh a great sinner, he careth not to commit much more haynous and abhominable offences, and covered his boldnesse and wicked practise with so great subtiltie and policie, and under a vaile of meere simplicitie, that beeing favoured for the honest love that he bare to his sister in lawe, for whose sake, hee affirmed,[2] he had in that sort murthered his brother, that his sinne found excuse among the common people, and of the nobilitie was esteemed for justice: for that Geruth, being as courteous a princesse as any then living in the north parts, and one that had never once so much as offended any of her subjects, either commons or courtyers, this adulter and infamous murtherer, slaundered his dead brother, that hee would have slaine his wife, and that hee by chance finding him upon the point ready to do it, in defence of the lady had slaine him, bearing off the blows, which as then he strooke at the innocent princesse, without any other cause of malice whatsoever. Wherein hee wanted no false witnesses to approove his act,[3] which deposed in like sort, as the wicked calumniator himselfe protested, being the same persons that had born him company, and were participants of his treason;[4] so that instead of pursuing him as a parricide and an incestuous person, al the courtyers admired and flattered him in his good fortune, making more account of false witnesses and detestable wicked reporters, and more honouring the calumniators, then they esteemed of those that seeking to call the matter in question, and admiring the vertues of the murthered prince, would have punished the massacrers and bereavers of his life. Which was the cause that Fengon, boldned and incouraged by such impunitie, durst venture to couple himselfe in marriage with her whom hee used as his concubine during good Horvendiles life, in that sort spotting his name with a double vice,[5] and charging his conscience with abhominable guilt, and two-fold impietie, as incestuous adulterie and parricide murther: and that the unfortunate and wicked woman, that had received the honour to bee the wife of one of the valiantest and wiseth princes in the north, imbased her selfe[6] in such vile sort, as to falsifie her faith unto him, and which is worse, to marrie him, that had bin the tyranous murtherer of her lawfull

1. So in 1.5.42-6.   2. B. has 'for the love of whom'.   3. Shakespeare's Denmark is not so corrupt.   4. *In margin:* 'Slanderers more honoured in court then vertuous persons.'   5. *In margin:* 'The incestuous marriage of Fengon with his brothers wife.'   6. Cf. 1.5.47: 'What a falling off was there.'

husband; which made divers men thinke that she had beene the causer
of the murther, thereby to live in her adultery without controle.[1] But
where shall a man finde a more wicked and bold woman, then a great
parsonage once having loosed the bands of honor and honestie? This
princesse, who at the first, for her rare vertues and courtesses was honored of al men and beloved of her husband, as soone as she once gave
eare to the tyrant Fengon, forgot both the ranke she helde among the
greatest names, and the dutie of an honest wife on her behalfe. But I
will not stand to gaze and mervaile at women, for that there are many
which seeke to blase and set them foorth, in which their writings
they spare not to blame them all for the faults of some one, or few
women. But I say, that either nature ought to have bereaved man of
that opinion to accompany with women, or els to endow them with
such spirits, as that they may easily support the crosses they endure,
without complaining so often and so strangely, seeing it is their owne
beastlinesse that overthrowes them.[2] For if it be so, that a woman is so
imperfect a creature as they make her to be, and that they know this
beast to bee so hard to bee tamed as they affirme, why then are they
so foolish to preserve them, and so dull and brutish as to trust their
deceitfull and wanton imbraceings? But let us leave her in this extream-
itie of laciviousnesse, and proceed to shewe you in what sort the yong
prince Hamblet behaved himselfe, to escape the tyranny of his uncle.[3]

CHAP. 2

*How Hamblet counterfeited the mad man, to escape the tyrannie of his uncle,
and how he was tempted by a woman (through his uncles procurement) who
thereby thought to undermine the Prince, and by that meanes to finde out
whether he counterfeited madnesse or not: and how Hamblet would by no
meanes bee brought to consent unto her, and what followed.*

GERUTH having (as I sayd before) so much forgotten herself, the prince
Hamblet perceiving himself to bee in danger of his life, as beeing
abandoned of his owne mother, and forsaken of all men,[4] and assur-
ing himselfe that Fengon would not detract the time to send him
the same way his father Horvendile was gone, to beguile the tyrant
in his subtilties (that esteemed him to bee of such a minde that if
he once attained to mans estate he wold not long delay the time to
revenge the death of his father) counterfeiting the mad man with such

---

1. Hence 3.4.28-9.   2. *In margin:* 'If a man be deceived by a woman, it is his owne
beastlinesse.' But Cf. 3.1.140-1.   3. This sentence is not in B.   4. Hamlet makes
his own solitude.

craft and subtill practises, that hee made shewe as if hee had utterly lost his wittes: and under that vayle hee covered his pretence, and defended his life from the treasons and practises of the tyrant his uncle. And all though hee had beene at the schoole of the Romane Prince, who, because hee counterfeited himselfe to bee a foole, was called Brutus,[1] yet hee imitated his fashions, and his wisedom. For every day beeing in the queenes palace, (who as then was more carefull to please her whoremaster, then ready to revenge the cruell death of her husband, or to restore her sonne to his inheritance), hee rent and tore his clothes, wallowing and lying in the durt and mire,[2] his face all filthy and blacke, running through the streets[3] like a man distraught, not speaking one worde, but such as seemed to proceede of madnesse and meere frenzie; all his actions and jestures beeing no other than the right countenances of a man wholly deprived of all reason and understanding, in such sort, that as then hee seemed fitte for nothing but to make sport to the pages and ruffling courtiers that attended in the court of his uncle and father-in-law. But the yong prince noted them well enough, minding one day to bee revenged in such manner, that the memorie thereof should remaine perpetually to the world.

Beholde, I pray you, a great point of a wise and brave spirite in a yong prince, by so great a shewe of imperfection in his person for advancement, and his owne imbasing and despising, to worke the meanes and to prepare the way for himselfe to bee one of the happiest kings in his age. In like sort, never any man was reputed by any of his actions more wise and prudent then Brutus[4] dissembling a great alteration in his minde, for that the occasion of such his devise of foolishnesse proceeded onely of a good and mature counsell and deliberation, not onely to preserve his goods, and shunne the rage of the proude tyrant, but also to open a large way to procure the banishment and utter ruine of wicked Tarquinius, and to infranchise the people (which were before oppressed) from the yoake of a great and miserable servitude. And so, not onely Brutus, but this man and worthy prince, to whom wee may also adde king David that counterfeited the madde man among the petie kings of Palestina to preserve his life from the subtill practises of those kings. I shew this example unto such, as beeing offended with any great personage, have not sufficient meanes to prevaile in their intents, or revenge the injurie by them received. But when I speake of revenging any injury received upon a great personage or superior, it must be understood by such an one as

---

1. L. J. Brutus. See Livy tr. Philemon Holland, 1600.   2. B. 'in the sweepings and dirt of the house.'   3. B. 'rubbing his face with the mud of the streets through which he ran...'   4. *In margin:* 'Brutus esteemed wise for counterfeiting the foole. Read Titus Livius and Halicarnassus.'

is not our soveraigne, againste whome wee maie by no means resiste, nor once practise anie treason nor conspiracie against his life:[1] and hee that will followe this course must speake and do all things what-soever that are pleasing and acceptable to him whom hee meaneth to deceive, practise his actions, and esteeme him above all men, cleane contrarye to his owne intent and meaning; for that is rightly to playe and counterfeite the foole, when a man is constrained to dissemble and kisse his hand, whome in hearte hee could wishe an hundred foote depth under the earth, so hee mighte never see him more, if it were not a thing wholly to bee disliked in a christian, who by no meanes ought to have a bitter gall, or desires infected with revenge. Hamblet, in this sorte counterfeiting the madde man, many times did divers actions of great and deepe consideration, and often made such and so fitte answeres, that a wise man would soone have judged from what spirite so fine an invention mighte proceede,[2] for that stand-ing by the fire and sharpning sticks like poynards and prickes, one in smiling manner asked him wherefore he made those little staves so sharpe at the points? I prepare (saith he) piersing dartes and sharpe ar-rowes to revenge my fathers death.[3] Fooles, as I said before, esteemed those his words as nothing; but men of quicke spirits, and such as hadde a deeper reache began to suspect somewhat, esteeming that under that kinde of folly there lay hidden a greate and rare subtilty, such as one day might bee prejudiciall to their prince, saying, that under colour of such rudenes he shadowed a crafty pollicy, and by his devised simplicitye, he concealed a sharp and pregnant spirit:[4] for which cause they counselled the king to try and know, if it were pos-sible, how to discover the intent and meaning of the yong prince; and they could find no better nor more fit invention to intrap him, then to set some faire and beawtifull woman in a secret place, that with flattering speeches and all the craftiest meanes she could use, should purposely seek to allure his mind to have his pleasure of her: for the nature of all young men, (especially such as are brought up wantonlie)[5] is so transported with the desires of the flesh, and entreth so greedily into the pleasures therof, that it is almost impossible to cover the foul affection, neither yet to dissemble or hyde the same by art or industry, much lesse to shunne it.[6] What cunning or subtilty so ever they use to cloak theire pretence, seeing occasion offered, and that in secret, especially in the most inticing sinne that rayneth in man, they cannot chuse (being constrayned by voluptuousnesse) but fall to naturall

---

1. *In margin:* 'Rom. 8.21.' **2.** As Claudius soon does. **3.** *In margin:* 'A subtill answere of Prince Hamlet.' **4.** Polonius sees no danger. 2.2.210-13. **5.** B. 'à son aise', in luxury. **6.** *In margin:* 'Nature corrupted in man.'

effect and working.[1] To this end certaine courtiers were appointed to leade Hamblet into a solitary place within the woods,[2] whether they brought the woman, inciting him to take their pleasures together, and to imbrace one another,[3] subtill practises used in these our daies, not to try if men of great account bee extract out of their wits, but rather to deprive them of strength, vertue and wisedome, by meanes of such devilish practitioners, and infernall spirits, their domestical servants, and ministers of corruption.[4] And surely the poore prince at this assault had bin in great danger, if a gentleman (that in Horvendiles time had been nourished with him) had not showne himselfe more affectioned to the bringing up he had received with Hamblet, then desirous to please the tirant, who by all meanes sought to intangle the sonne in the same nets wherein the father had ended his dayes. This gentleman bare the courtyers (appointed as aforesaide of this treason) company, more desiring to give the prince instruction what he should do, then to intrap him, making full account that the least showe of perfect sence and wisedome that Hamblet should make would be suf-ficient to cause him to loose his life: and therefore by certain signes, he gave Hamblet intelligence in what danger hee was like to fall, if by any meanes hee seemed to obaye, or once like the wanton toyes and vicious provocations of the gentlewoman sent thither by his uncle. Which much abashed the prince, as then wholy beeing in affection to the lady,[5] but by her he was likewise informed of the treason, as being one that from her infancy loved and favoured him, and would have been exceeding sorrowfull for his misfortune, and much more to leave his companie without injoying the pleasure of his body, whome shee loved more than herselfe. The prince in this sort having both deceived the courtiers, and the ladyes expectation,[6] that affirmed and swore that hee never once offered to have his pleasure of the woman, although in subtilty hee affirmed the contrary, every man there upon assured themselves that without all doubt he was distraught of his sences,[7] that his braynes were as then wholly void of force, and incapable of rea-sonable apprehension, [so that as then Fengons practise took no effect. but for al that he left not off, still seeking by al meanes to finde out Hamblets subtilty, as in the next chapter you shall perceive.][8]

1. Contrast *Hamlet*, 2.2.314-16.   2. *In margin:* 'Subtilties used to discover Hamblet's madnes.'   3. 1608 inserts 'but the'.   4. *In margin:* 'Corrupters of yong gentlemen in princes courts and great houses.'   5. B. 'esmeu de la beauté de la fille'. Not in love with her, but 'moved by her beauty'.   6. A mistranslation based on an awk-ward comma in B.1582. 'ayant le jeune seigneur trompé les courtisans, et la fille, soustenans qu'il ne s'estoit ayancé en sorte aucune à la violer...' In *1572* etc. the girl affirmed that he had never tried to ravish her. It is left uncertain whether he had in fact enjoyed her. [Stabler]   7. Hamlet's rejection of Ophelia convinces Claudius otherwise, 3.1.165.   8. The passage within brackets is not in B.

CHAP. 3

How Fengon, uncle to Hamblet, a second time to intrap him in his politick madnes, caused one of his counsellors to be secretly hidden in the queenes chamber, behind the arras, to heare what speeches passed between Hamblet and the Queen; and how Hamblet killed him, and escaped that danger, and what followed. . . .

Narrative and Dramatic Sources of Shakespeare by Geoffrey Bullough, Vol. 7, Routledge & Columbia University Presses, 1973, 85–93.

From *Of Ghostes and Spirites Walking By Night*

Lavater

Lavater's 1572 Protestant interpretation of ghosts and their origins is one of several perspectives on spirits held at the time.

I

FROM LEWES [Ludwig] Lavater, *Of Ghostes and Spirites Walking by Night*, trans. R. H. (1572), ed. J. Dover Wilson and Mary Yardley (1929), pp. 53, 71-4, 91, 160-1, 167, 195-6.

Albeit many melancholic, mad, fearful, and weak-sensed men do oftentimes imagine many things which in very deed are not, and are likewise deceived sometime by men or by brute beasts, and moreover mistake things which proceed of natural causes to be bugs and spirits,. . . . . .yet it is most certain and sure that all those   5
things which appear unto men are not always natural things nor always vain terrors to affray men, but that spirits do often appear and many strange and marvellous things do sundry times chance. . . . . . .
    Some man walketh alone in his house and, behold, a spirit   10
appeareth in his sight; yea, and sometimes the dogs also perceive them and fall down at their masters' feet and will by no means depart fro them, for they are sore afraid themselves too. Some man goeth to bed and layeth him down to rest, and by and by there is some thing pinching him or pulling off the clothes; sometimes it   15
sitteth on him or lieth down in the bed with him, and many times it walketh up and down in the chamber. There have been many times men seen, walking on foot, or riding on horseback, being of a fiery shape, known unto divers men, and such as died not long before. And it hath come to pass likewise that some either slain in   20
the wars, or otherwise dead naturally, have called unto their acquaintance being alive and have been known by their voice.
    Many times in the night season there have been certain spirits heard softly going, or spitting, or groaning, who being asked what

they were have made answer that they were the souls of this or that   25
man, and that they now endure extreme torments. . . . . . .And
hereby it may be well proved that they were not always priests, or
other bold and wicked men, which have feigned themselves to be
souls of men deceased, as I have before said, insomuch that even in
those men's chambers, when they have been shut, there have   30
appeared such things when they have with a candle diligently
searched before whether any thing have lurked in some corner or
no. Many use at this day to search and sift every corner of the
house before they go to bed that they may sleep more soundly, and
yet nevertheless they hear some crying out and making a   35
lamentable noise, etc.

It hath many times chanced that those of the house have verily
thought that some body have overthrown the pots, platters, tables, and trenchers, and tumbled them down the stairs, but after
it waxed day, they have found all things orderly set in their places   40
again. It is reported that some spirits have thrown the door off
from the hooks and have troubled and set all things in the house
out of order, never setting them in their due place again, and that
they have marvellously disquieted men with rumbling and making
a great noise.   45

Pioners or diggers for metal do affirm that in many mines there
appear strange shapes and spirits, who are appareled like unto
other labourers in the pit. These wander up and down in caves
and underminings and seem to bestir themselves in all kind of
labour,. . . . . .They very seldom hurt the labourers (as they say)   50
except they provoke them by laughing and railing at them. . . . . . .

I heard of a grave and wise man, which was a magistrate in the
territory of Tigurie, who affirmed that, as he and his servant went
through the pastures in the summer very early, he espied one
whom he knew very well wickedly defiling himself with a mare,   55
wherewith, being amazed, he returned back again and knocked at
his house whom he supposed he had seen, and there understood
for a certainty that he went not one foot out of his chamber that
morning. And in case he had not diligently searched out the matter,
the good and honest man had surely been cast in prison   60
and put on the rack. I rehearse this history for this end, that
judges should be very circumspect in these cases, for the Devil by
these means doth oftentimes circumvent the innocent. . . . . . .

You will say, I hear and understand very well that these things
are not men's souls, which continually remain in their appointed   65
places; I pray you then what are they? To conclude in few words: if
it be not a vain persuasion proceeding through weakness of the

senses, through fear, or some such like cause, or if it be not deceit
of men or some natural thing,. . . . . .it is either a good or evil
angel, or some other forewarning sent by God,. . . . . .Angels for   70
the most part take upon them the shapes of men, wherein they
appear. . . . . . .

But it is no difficult matter for the Devil to appear in divers
shapes, not only of those which are alive, but also of dead
men,. . . . . .yea, and (which is a less matter) in the form of beasts   75
and birds, etc., as to appear in the likeness of a black dog, a horse,
an owl, and also to bring incredible things to pass, it is a thing
most manifest. . . . . . .

We ought, not without great cause, to suspect all spirits and
other apparitions. For, albeit God doth use the help and service   80
of good angels for the preservation of his elect, yet notwithstanding in these our days they appear unto us very seldom.

NOTES

5 *bugs* bugbears, hobgoblins.

13 *fro* from.

16 *sitteth*. . . . . .*with him* a reference to the 'nightmare' or succubus
demon which was believed to have sexual relations with a man. The
male equivalent was known as an 'incubus'.

23 *certain spirits* Lavater would not admit that these are the actual souls
of the dead individuals but good or evil angels that have assumed
their forms.

24 *going* walking.

27 *priests* Lavater's Protestant prejudice shows itself.

37-45 Lavater seems to be referring to poltergeists.

46 *Pioners* (i.e. pioneers) miners. Compare Hamlet's reference to the
Ghost ('this fellow in the cellarage') as 'old mole' and 'worthy pioner'
(*Hamlet*, 1.5.151, 162-3).

53 *Tigurie* Zurich, Switzerland.

61 *rack* instrument of torture on which individuals were 'stretched' and
their joints dislocated.

73-5 *Devil*. . . . . .*men* Compare Hamlet's reaction to the Ghost of the
elder Hamlet (*Hamlet*, 1.4. 40-1; see also 1.5.92-3).

79 *not*. . . . . .*cause* i.e. for very good reasons.

Elizabethan-Jacobean Drama, G. Blakemore Evans, A&C Black 1988, 275-77.

From *A Treatise of Melancholie*

Timothy Bright

*The four humors or fluids in the body (blood, phlegm, choler and black bile)
helped to determine personality. Although melancholy had some positive aspects (e.g., it could lead to creativity), in its extreme forms it could produce a
disabling disposition. Bright's 1586 book on the subject is one that Shakespeare
read.*

From Timothy Bright, *A Treatise of Melancholie* (1586), chap. 9, pp. 33–8.

How melancholy worketh fearful passions in the mind

Before I declare unto you how this humour afflicteth the
mind, first it shall be necessary for you to understand what
the familiarity is betwixt mind and body; how it affecteth it,
and how it is affected of it again. You know God first created all things subject to the course of times and corruption   5
of the Earth, after that He had distinguished the confused mass
of things into the heavens and the four elements. This Earth
He had endued with a fecundity of infinite seeds of all things,
which He commanded it, as a mother, to bring forth, and, as it
is most agreeable to their nature, to entertain with nourishment   10
that which it had borne and brought forth; whereby, when He
had all the furniture of this inferior world, of these creatures
some He fixed there still and maintaineth the seeds till the end
of all things and that determinate time which He hath ordained
for the emptying of those seeds of creatures, which He first   15
endued the Earth withal. Other some, that is to say the animals,
He drew wholly from the Earth at the beginning and planted
seed in them only, and food from other creatures: as beasts, and
man in respect of his body. The difference only this: that likely
it is man's body was made of purer mould, as a most precious   20
tabernacle and temple, wherein the image of God should af-
terward be enshrined, and being formed, as it were, by God's
proper hand received a greater dignity of beauty and proportion, and stature erect, thereby to be put in mind whither to
direct the religious service of his Creator.   25

This tabernacle thus wrought, as the gross part yielded a mass for the proportion to be framed of, so had it by the blessing of God, before inspired, a spiritual thing of greater excellency than the red earth, which offered itself to the eye only. This is that which philosophers call the spirit, which spirit so prepareth that work to the receiving of the soul, that, with more agreement, the soul and body have grown into acquaintance, and is ordained of God, as it were, a true-love knot to couple heaven and earth together; yea, a more divine nature than the heavens with a base clod of earth, which otherwise would never have grown into society; and hath such indifferent affection unto both that it is both equally affected and communicateth the body and corporal things with the mind, and spiritual and intelligible things after a sort with the body. . . . . . This spirit is the chief instrument, and immediate, whereby the soul bestoweth the exercises of her faculty in her body, that passeth to and fro in a moment, nothing in swiftness and nimbleness being comparable thereunto, which when it is depraved by any occasion, either rising from the body or by other means, then becometh it an instrument unhandsome for performance of such actions as require the use thereof; and so the mind seemeth to be blameworthy, wherein it is blameless; and fault of certain actions imputed thereunto, wherein the body and this spirit are rather to be charged, things corporal and earthly: the one, in substance, and the other in respect of that mixture wherewith the Lord tempered the whole mass in the beginning. . . . . . .

Now, although these spirits rise from earthly creatures, yet are they more excellent than earth, or the earthy parts of those natures from which they are drawn, and rise from that divine influence of life and are not of themselves earthy; neither yet comparable in pureness and excellency unto that breath of life wherewith the Lord made Adam a living soul, which proceeded not from any creature that He had before made, as the life of beasts and trees, but immediately from Himself, representing in some part the character of his image. So then these three we have in our nature to consider distinct for the clearer understanding of that I am to entreat of: the body of earth; the spirit from virtue of that Spirit which did, as it were, hatch that great egg of Chaos; and the soul inspired from God, a nature eternal and divine, not fettered with the body, as certain philosophers have taken it, but handfasted therewith by that golden clasp of the spirit, whereby one (till the predestinate time be expired and the body become unmeet for so pure a spouse) joyeth at and taketh liking of the other.

NOTES

1 *this humour* i.e. melancholy; here used to mean both the humour itself and the disease known as melancholy.

2 *familiarity* intimate intercourse.

3 *it affecteth it* the melancholy humour influences the mind.

3-4 *how......again* how the melancholy humour is in turn influenced by the mind.

4-18 *God first created......body* Bright's account of the creation is the usual amalgam of the biblical story in Genesis and the neo-Platonic conception of the Great Chain of Being, Which, as Pope put it, 'with God began' (i.e. God—pure actuality; angels—pure intellect; man—reason; animals—sense; plants—growth; inanimate matter—mere being). God created either by 'fiat' ('let there be') or by emanation (the nature of good (i.e. God) is naturally diffusive), and in creating He created all possible forms (the Platonic doctrine of plenitude, i.e. 'infinite seeds', 1. 8), each link in the descending chain being connected to the link above and below (the Aristotelian doctrine of continuity, a continuity that was broken with the Fall of Man). This is, of course, a simplification of a very involved and complicated concept (see A. O. Lovejoy, *The Great Chain of Being,* 1961).

8 *seeds of all things* i.e. *rationes seminales,* the seeds, implanted by God, from which all things are generated as by universal causes (see W. C. Curry, *Shakespeare's Philosophical Patterns* (1959), 2nd edn, pp. 38-9). See *Macbeth,* 4.1.59, 'nature's germains'.

11 *furniture* furnishing.

11-12 *inferior world* the Earth.

12-14 *some He......creatures* Bright seems to be referring, not very clearly, to the belief that God, in creating all possible forms at the time of creation (plenitude), arranged to have certain 'seeds' reserved and only to be made operative at his own 'determinate time'. 'creatures'=all created things, either animate or inanimate.

19 *man's......mould* Such a view would accord with man's position in the Great Chain, 'a creature of middle nature betwixt Angels and Beasts' (Bright, p. 30).

23 *stature erect* That man walked upright, unlike the beasts, with his head pointed at heaven, was taken as another characteristic distinguishing him from the rest of the animal creation.

25 *gross part* i.e. the body.

27 *before inspired* earlier breathed in.

29 *the spirit* not to be confused with the soul, also 'inspired' by God. Bright, unlike most authorities, writes of a single 'spirit' (pp. 46-7), but three kinds were usually distinguished: natural, vital and animal. The 'natural' were produced in the liver; the 'vital' were produced in the heart from the natural spirits; and the 'animal' 'formed of the

vital, brought up to the brain, and diffused by the nerves, to the subordinate members, give sense and motion to them all' (Robert Burton, *The Anatomy of Melancholy,* ed. A. R. Shilleto (1896), I, 170).

30 *work* i.e. the body.

32 *true-love knot* complicated, ornamental knot symbolic of true love.

35 *indifferent* impartial, neutral.

37 *intelligible* capable of being apprehended only by the understanding (not by the senses).

37-8 *after a sort* in a certain way.

39-40 *soul. . . . . .body* Bright (pp. 42-4) discusses the soul as having 'one universal and simple faculty', but the usual view postulated three distinct faculties: vegetal, the nutritive, generational faculty, which, in the chain of being; it shares with plants and beasts; sensible, relating to the inward senses' (common sense, phantasy, memory) and the 'outward senses' (touch, hearing, smell, taste, sight), which it shares with the beasts; and rational, with its two 'powers' (understanding and will), which is the special prerogative of man and links him, in the chain, with the faculty of intellection [knowing without the need of logical reasoning], the distinguishing attribute of the angels (see Burton, I, 176-92). Man was thus usually thought of as possessing a 'tripartite soul'.

51 *spirits. . . . . .creatures* i.e. the spirits were generated through the nourishment furnished to man by the flora and fauna ('earthly creatures').

59 *character* stamp, imprint.

62 *egg of Chaos* Compare Genesis 1:2 (Geneva, 1560): 'And the earth was without form and void, and darkness was upon the deep, and the Spirit of God moved upon the waters.'

64 *handfasted* spiritually betrothed, joined.

67 *spouse* i.e. the soul.

Elizabethan-Jacobean Drama, G. Blakemore Evans, A&C Black 1988, 330–32.

From THE COMPLETE WORKS OF THOMAS NASHE

Thomas Nashe

Among Shakespeare's contemporaries, no one was so verbally close to being his equal as Thomas Nashe (1567-1601), a writer whose work Shakespeare continually turned to in order to jumpstart his own imagination and flesh out with concrete instances motifs already derived from other narrative and dramatic sources. Here we note sources for Hamlet's "dram of eale" speech (1.4.17ff.), his graveyard meditation on the dust to which even the mightiest return (5.1.197ff.), something of his "scourge and minister" soliloquy (3.4.173ff.), and Polonius' longwinded exposition on the nature of Hamlet's 'madness' (2.2.96ff.).

From *Pierce Penilesse* (1592).

A mightie deformer of mens manners and features, is this vnnecessary vice of all other. Let him bee indued with neuer so many vertues, and haue as much goodly proportion and fauour as nature can bestow vppon a man: yet if hee be thirstie after his owne destruction, and hath no   5
ioy nor comfort, but when he is drowning his soule in a gallon pot, that one beastly imperfection will vtterlie obscure all that is commendable in him; and all his good qualities sinke like lead down to the bottome of his carrowsing cups, where they will lie, like lees and dregges, dead and   10
vnregarded of any man. . . [205].

From *Christ's Tears Over Jerusalem* (1593, 94)

Of thys kind of honour is thys Elfe (we call Ambition) compacted. . . . *Julius Caesar*. . . . sent men skild in Geometry to measure the whole world, that whereas he intended to conquer it all, he might know howe long he should be in ouer-running it. . . .   15
In this discouery 30. yeeres were spent, from his Consulshyp to the Consulshyp of *Saturninus,* when godwote, poore man, twenty yeeres good before they returned, he was all to bepoynyarded in the Senate house, and had the dust of his bones in a Brasen vrne (no bigger then a boule) barreld vp, whom   20

252

THOMAS NASHE

(if he had lyued) all the Sea and Earth and ayre woulde haue
beene to little for. . . .

Let the ambitious man stretch out hys lymbes neuer so, he
taketh vp no more ground (being dead) then the Begger. . . .

What a thing is the hart of man, that it should swell so   25
bigge as the whole world. *Alexander* was but a lyttle man,
yet if there had beene a hundred Worlds to conquer, hys
hart would haue comprised them. Dyd men consider
whereof they were made, and that the dust was theyr
great Grand-mother, they would be more humi-liate and   30
deiected; Of a britler mettall then Glasse is this we call
Ambition made, and to mischaunces more subiect. Glasse
with good vsage may be kept and continue many ages.
The dayes of man are numbred, threescore and tenne is
his terme; if he lyue any longer, it is but labour and   35
sorrow. . . .

From the rich to the poore (in euery street in *London*)
there is ambition, or swelling aboue theyr states: the rich
Cittizen swells against the pryde of the prodigall Courtier;
the prodigal Courtier swels against the welth of the Cittizen [82–83].   40

From *The Unfortunate Traveller (1594)*

Revenge in our tragedies is continually raised from hell:
of hell doe I esteeme better than heauen, if it afford me
revenge. There is no heauen but revenge. I tel thee, I would
not haue vndertoke so much toile to gaine heauen, as I   45
haue done in pursuing thee for revenge. Diuine revenge,
of which (as of $\stackrel{e}{y}$ ioies aboue) there is no fulnes or satietie [324].

Revenge is the glorie of armes, & the highest performance of
valure: revenge is whatsoeuer we call law or iustice. The farther
we wade in revenge, the neerer come we to $\stackrel{e}{y}$ throne of the   50
almightie. To his scepter it is properly ascribed; his scepter he
lends vnto man, when he lets one man scourge an other. All true
Italians imitate me in reuenging constantly and dying valiantly [326].

From *Have with you to Saffron-Walden (1596)*

Respond: As though the cause and the effect (more than   55
the superficies and the substance) can bee separated, when
in manie things *causa sine qua non* is both the cause and
the effect, the common distinction of *potentia non actu*
approuing it selfe verie crazed and impotent herein, since
the premisses necessarily beget the conclusion, and so   60
contradictorily the conclusion the premisses; a halter

including desperation, and so desperation concluding in a halter; without which fatall conclusion and priuation it cannot truly bee termed desperation, since nothing is said to bee till it is borne, and despaire is neuer fully borne till it ceaseth to bee, and hath depriu'd him of beeing that first bare it and brought it forth. So that herein it is hard to distinguish which is most to be blamed, of the cause or the effect; the Cause without the effect beeing of no effect, and the effect without the cause neuer able to haue been. Carnead: *I beseech you, trouble him not (anie more) with these impertinent Parentheses* [59-60].

65
70

The Complete Works of Thomas Nashe edited by R. B. McKerrow, five volumes 1904-1910, A.H. Bullen; entries from Vols. 1 (*Pierce Penilesse*), 2 (*Christ's Tears Over Jerusalem* and *The Unfortunate Traveller*), and 3 (*Have With You to Saffron Walden*).

OF CONSCIENCE

Montaigne

Translated by John Florio

Scholars agree that by the time of King Lear *and certainly by the time of* The Tempest, *Shakespeare borrowed ideas and expressions from Florio's 1603 translation of Montaigne's* Essais. *It is likely that Shakespeare had access to Florio's work in prepublication form during the time of the composition of* Hamlet.

MY BROTHER the Lord of *Brouze* and my selfe, during the time of our civill warres, travelling one day together, we fortuned to meet upon the way with a Gentleman, in outward semblance, of good demeanour: He was of our contrarie faction, but forasmuch as he counterfeited himselfe otherwise; I knew it not. And the worst of these tumultuous intestine broyles, is, that the cards are so shuffled (your enemie being neither by language nor by fashion, nor by any other apparent marke distinguished from you; nay, which is more, brought up under the same lawes and customes, and breathing the same ayre) that it is a very hard matter to avoid confusion and shun disorder. Which consideration, made me not a little fearefull to meet with our troopes, especially where I was not knowne, lest I should be urged to tell my name, and haply doe worse. As other times before it had befalne me; for, by such a chance, or rather mistaking, I fortuned once to lose all my men and horses, and hardly escaped my selfe: and amongst other my losses, and servants that were slaine, the thing that most grieved me, was the untimely and miserable death of a young Italian Gentleman, whom I kept as my Page, and very carefully brought up, with whom dyed, as forward, as budding and as hopeful a youth as ever I saw. But this man seemed so fearfully-dismaid, and at every encounter of horsemen, and passage, by, or thorow any Towne that held for the King, I observed him to be so strangely distracted, that in the end I perceived, and ghessed they were but guilty alarums that his conscience gave him. It seemed unto this seely man, that all might apparently, both through his blushing selfe-accusing countenance, and by the crosses he wore upon his upper garments, read the secret intentions of his faint heart. Of such marvailous-working power is the sting of conscience: which often induceth us to bewray, to accuse, and to combat our selves; and for want of other evidences shee produceth our selves against our selves.

Occultum quatiente animo tortore flagellum.
—Juven. *Sat.* 13. 195.

Their minde, the tormentor of sinne,
Shaking an unseene whip within.

The storie of *Bessus* the Pœnian is so common, that even children have it in their mouths, who being found fault withall, that in mirth he had beaten downe a nest of young Sparrowes, and then killed them, answered, he had great reason to doe it; forsomuch as those young birds ceased not falsly to accuse him to have murthered his father, which parricide was never suspected to have beene committed by him; and untill that day had layen secret; but the revengefull furies of the conscience, made the same partie to reveale it, that by all right was to doe penance for so hatefull and unnaturall a murther. *Hesiodus* correcteth the saying of *Plato*, That punishment doth commonly succeed the guilt, and follow sinne at hand: for, he affirmeth, that it rather is borne at the instant, and together with sinne it selfe, and they are as twinnes borne at one birth together. *Whosoever expects punishment, suffereth the same, and whosoever deserveth it, he doth expect it. Impietie doth invent, and iniquitie doth frame torments against it selfe.*

Malum consilium consultori pessimum.
—Eras. *Chil.* 1. cent. 2. ad. 14.

Bad counsell is worst for the counseller that gives the counsell.

Even as the Waspe stingeth and offendeth others, but her selfe much more; for, in hurting others, she loseth her force and sting for ever.

—*itasque in ulnere ponunt.*
—Virg. *Georg.* 4. *238.*

They, while they others sting,
Death to themselves doe bring.

The *Cantharides* have some part in them, which by a contrarietie of nature serveth as an antidot or counterpoison against their poison: so likewise, as one taketh pleasure in vice, there is a certaine contrarie displeasure engendred in the conscience, which by sundry irksome and painful imaginations, perplexeth and tormenteth us, both waking and asleepe.

Quippe ubi se multi per somnia saepe loquentes,
Aut morbo delirantes procraxe ferantur,
Et celata diu in medium peccata dedisse.—Lucr. 5. 1168.

Many in dreames oft speaking, or unhealed,
In sicknesse raving have themselves revealed,
And brought to light their sinnes long time concealed.

Apollodorus dreamed he saw himselfe first flead by the Scythians, and then boyled in a pot, and that his owne heart murmured, saying; I only have caused this mischiefe to light upon thee. *Epicurus* was wont to say, that no lurking hole can shroud the wicked; for, they can never assure themselves to be sufficiently hidden, sithence conscience is ever ready to disclose them to themselves.

—*prima est haec ultio, quod se*
Judice nemo nocens absolvitur.
                    —JUVEN. *Sat.* 13. 2.

This is the first revenge, no guilty mind
Is quitted, though it selfe be judge assign'd.

Which as it doth fill us with feare and doubt, so doth it store us with assurance and trust. And I may boldly say, that I have waded thorow many dangerous hazards, with a more untired pace, only in consideration of the secret knowledge I had of mine owne will, and innocence of my desseignes.

Conscia mens ut cuique sua est, ita concipit intra
Pectora pro facto spemque metumque suo.
                    —OVID, *Fast.* 1.485.

As each mans minde is guiltie, so doth he
Inlie breed hope and feare, as his deeds be.

Of examples, there are thousands: It shall suffice us to alleage three only, and all of one man. *Scipio* being one day accused before the Roman people, of an urgent and capitall accusation; in stead of excusing himselfe, or flattering the Judges; turning to them, he said. It will well beseeme you to undertake to judge of his head; by whose meanes you have authoritie to judge of all the world. The same man, another time, being vehemently urged by a *Tribune* of the people, who charged him with sundry imputations, in liew of pleading or excusing his cause, gave him this sudden and short answer. Let us goe (quoth he) my good Citizens; let us forthwith goe (I say) to give hartie thankes unto the Gods for the victorie, which even upon such a day as this is, they gave me against the Carthaginians. And therewith advancing himselfe to march before the people, all the assembly, and even his accuser himselfe did undelayedly follow him towards the Temple. After

that, *Petilius* having beene animated and stirred up by *Cato* to solicite
and demand a strict accompt of him, of the money he had managed,
and which was committed to his trust, whilst he was in the Province
of *Antioch; Scipio* being come into the Senate-house, of purpose to
answer for himselfe, pulling out the booke of his accompts from under
his gowne, told them all, that that booke contained truly, both the
receipt and laying out thereof; and being required to deliver the same
unto a Clarke to register it, he refused to doe it, saying he would not
doe himselfe that wrong or indignitie; and thereupon with his owne
hands, in presence of all the Senate, tore the booke in peeces. I cannot
apprehend or beleeve, that a guiltie-cauterized conscience could possibly dissemble or counterfet such an undismayed assurance: His heart,
was naturally too great, and enured to overhigh fortune (saith *Titus
Livius)* to know how to be a criminall offender, and stoopingly to
yeeld himselfe to the basenesse, to defend his innocencie. Torture and
racking are dangerous inventions, and seeme rather to be trials of patience than Essayes of truth. And both he that can, and he that cannot
endure them, conceale the truth. For wherefore shall paine or smart,
rather compell me to confesse that, which is so indeed, than force me
to tell that which is not? And contrariwise, if he who hath not done
that whereof he is accused, is sufficiently patient to endure those torments; why shall not he be able to tolerate them, who hath done it,
and is guilty indeed; so deare and worthy a reward as life being proposed unto him? I am of opinion, that the ground of his invention,
proceedeth from the consideration of the power and facultie of the
conscience. For, to the guilty, it seemeth to give a kinde of further-
ance to the torture, to make him confesse his fault, and weakneth and
dismayeth him: and on the other part, it encourageth and strengthneth
the innocent against torture. To say truth, it is a meane full of uncer-
tainty and danger. What would not a man say; nay, what not doe, to
avoid so grievous paines, and shun such torments?

Etiam innocentes cogit mentiri dolor.
—SEN. *Prover.*

Torment to lye sometimes will drive,
Ev'n the most innocent alive.

Whence it followeth, that he whom the Judge hath tortured, because
he shall not dye an innocent, he shall bring him to his death, both
innocent and tortured. Many thousands have thereby charged their
heads with false confessions. Amongst which I may well place *Phylotas,*
considering the circumstances of the endictment that *Alexander* framed
against him, and the progresse of his torture. But so it is, that (as men

say) it is the least evill humane weaknesse could invent: though, in my conceit, very inhumanely, and therewithall most unprofitably. Many Nations lesse barbarous in that, than the Græcian, or the Romane, who terme them so, judge it a horrible and cruell thing, to racke and torment a man for a fault whereof you are yet in doubt. Is your ignorance long of him? What can he doe withall? Are not you unjust, who because you will not put him to death without some cause, you doe worse than kill him? And that it is so, consider but how often he rather chuseth to dye guiltlesse, than passe by this information, much more painfull, than the punishment or torment; and who many times, by reason of the sharpnesse of it, preventeth, furthereth, yea, and executeth the punishment. I wot not whence I heard this story, but it exactly hath reference unto the conscience of our Justice. A countrie woman accused a souldier before his Generall, being a most severe Justicer, that he, with violence, had snatched from out her poore childrens hands, the small remainder of some pap or water-gruell, which shee had onely left to sustaine them, forsomuch as the Army had ravaged and wasted all. The poore woman had neither witnesse nor proofe of it; It was but her yea, and his no; which the Generall perceiving, after he had summoned her to be well advised what shee spake, and that shee should not accuse him wrongfully; for, if shee spake an untruth, shee should then be culpable of his accusation: But shee constantly persisting to charge him, he forthwith, to discover the truth, and to be throughly resolved, caused the accused Souldiers belly to be ripped, who was found faulty, and the poore woman to have said true; whereupon shee was discharged. A condemnation instructive to others.

Montaigne's Essays, Florio's 1603 translation as it appears in the early 20th century Tudor Translations, Grant Richards, London, 1908. Bk. 2, 48–54.

From BIATHANATOS

John Donne

Suicide, like tyrannicide and even revenge itself, was a topic that fascinated the Elizabethans, one that had no universally agreed upon responses such that each issue and each instance of each issue asked for consideration of motive, method, or context or individual circumstance. Shakespeare's slightly younger contemporary, John Donne, a great frequenter of playhouses and an admirer of Shakespeare's work, in his maturity wrote a lengthy study of the moral and theological complexities of suicide in his Biathanatos, composed around 1608, but significantly not published until several years after his death. Hamlet reveals a clear interest in the subject of suicide from the Prince's own reference in his first soliloquy to the Lord's "canon [a]gainst self-slaughter" (1.2.132) to Horatio in the last scene of the play wanting to be 'more an antique Roman than a Dane' (5.2.341). And right in the middle of the play (as V. F. Petronella has observed) in the fourth of his seven soliloquies, there is the flourishing of the issue of not only whether some forms of injustice should be met by philosophical passivity rather than by vengeful action but also of the relief-producing attractiveness of suicide.

PREFACE TO BIATHANATOS

Declaring the Reasons, the Purpose, the way, and the end of the author.

BEZA, A man as eminent and illustrious, in the full glory and Noone of Learning, as others were in the dawning, and Morning, when any, the least sparkle was notorious, confesseth of himself, that only for the anguish of a Scurffe, which over-ranne his head, he had once drown'd himselfe from the Miller's bridge in Paris, if his Uncle by chance had not then come that way; I have often such a sickly inclination. And, whether it be, because I had my first breeding and conversation with men of suppressed and afflicted Religion, accustomed to the despite of death, and hungry of an imagin'd Martyrdome; Or that the common Enemie find that doore worst locked against him in mee; Or that there bee a perplexitie and flexibility in the doctrine it selfe; Or because my Conscience ever assures me, that no rebellious grudging at Gods gifts, nor other sinfull concurrence accompanies these thoughts in me, or that a brave scorn, or that a faint cowardlinesse beget it, whensoever any affliction assails me, mee thinks I have the keyes of my prison in mine owne hand, and no remedy presents it selfe so soone to my heart, as mine own sword. Often Meditation of this hath wonne me to a charitable interpretation of their action, who dy so: and provoked me a little to watch and exagitate their reasons, which pronounce so peremptory judgements upon them.

A devout and godly man, hath guided us well, and rectified our uncharitablenesse in such cases, by this remembrance, [Scis lapsum etc. *Thou knowest this mans fall, but thou knowest not his wrastling; which perchance was such, that almost his very fall is justified and accepted of God.*] For, to this end, saith one, [*God hath appointed us tentations, that we might have some excuse for our sinnes, when he calls us to account.*]

The Complete Poems and Selected Prose of John Donne, edited by John Hayward. Nonsuch Press, 1929, 420–21.

"OF REVENGE," From
ESSAYS CIVIL AND MORAL
Francis Bacon

Revenge is built into the ethical codes of earlier cultures, and it is not totally foreign to Christian societies, as Shakespeare knew well. The tension between biblical prohibition and the visceral desire to 'get back one's own' lies at the heart of the popularity of the 'revenge tragedy' in the late sixteenth and early seventeenth century theater. Here is Bacon's celebrated definition of the term in 1625.

R EVENGE IS a kinde of Wilde¹ Iustice; which the more Mans Nature runs to, the more ought Law to weed it out. For as for the first Wrong, it doth but offend the Law; but the *Revenge* of that wrong, putteth the Law out of Office. Certainly, in taking *Revenge*, A Man is but euen with his Enemy; But in passing it ouer, he is Superiour: For it is a Princes part to Pardon. And *Salomon*,² I am sure, saith, *It is the Glory of a Man to passe by an offence.* That which is past, is gone, and Irreuocable; And wise Men haue Enough to doe, with things present, and to come: Therefore, they doe but trifle with themselues, that labour in past matters. There is no man, doth a wrong, for the wrongs sake; But therby to purchase himselfe, Profit, or Pleasure, or Honour, or the like. Therfore why should I be angry with a Man, for louing himselfe better then mee? And if any Man should do wrong, meerely out of ill nature, why? yet it is but like the Thorn, or Bryar, which prick, and scratch, because they can doe no other. The most Tolerable Sort of *Revenge*, is for those wrongs which there is no Law to remedy: But then, let a man take heed, the *Revenge* be such as there is no law to punish: Else, a Mans Enemy, is still before hand, And it is two for one. Some, when they take *Revenge*, are Desirous the party should know, whence it commeth: This is the more Generous. For the Delight seemeth to be, not so much in doing the Hurt, as in Making the Party repent: But Base and Crafty Cowards, are like the Arrow,³ that flyeth in the Darke. *Cosmus* Duke of *Florence*,⁴ had a Desperate Saying, against Perfidious or Neglecting Friends, as if those wrongs were vnpardonable: *You shall reade* (saith he) *that we are commanded to forgiue our Enemies; But you neuer read, that wee are commanded, to forgive our Friends.*

But yet the Spirit of *Iob*,[5] was in a better tune; *Shall wee* (saith he) *take good at Gods Hands, and not be content to take euill also?* And so of Friends in a proportion.[6] This is certaine; That a Man that studieth *Revenge*, keepes his owne Wounds greene, which otherwise would heale, and doe well. Publique *Revenges*, are, for the most part, Fortunate;[7] As that for the Death of *Caesar*; For the Death of *Pertinax*; for the Death of *Henry* the Third of France; And many more. But in priuate *Revenges* it is not so. Nay rather, Vindicatiue Persons liue the Life of Witches; who as they are Mischieuous, So end they Infortunate.

OF REVENGE (1625)

1 *Wilde* uncultivated.
2 *Salomon* in Proverbs, 19:11, though not in these words.
3 *the Arrow* Psalm, 91: 5,6.
4 *Cosmus* Cosimo de'Medici (1519–74). There is an Italian proverb, 'From them I trust, God preserve me; from them I do not trust I will preserve myself.'
5 *Job* Job, 2:10.
6 *in a proportion* to a proportionate extent. God, our Creator and Ruler, may treat us as He will; our friends have less power to help us and less right to give us pain.
7 *Fortunate* Augustus, Severus and Henry IV, the avengers, proved to be competent and good rulers. Avengers in private stations have no such success; as they are vindictive, so do they come to misfortune.

Francis Bacon selected and edited by Arthur Johnston. London: B.T. Batsford Ltd. 1965, 6–7. Used by permission of Oxford University Press.

"HAMLET," From NOTES ON SHAKESPEARE'S PLAYS

Samuel Johnson

Samuel Johnson (1709-1784) was a lexicographer and sixth editor of Shakespeare's plays. His Preface to his edition discussing the strengths and weaknesses in Shakespeare remains well worth reading.

IF THE dramas of Shakespeare were to be characterised, each by the particular excellence which distinguishes it from the rest, we must allow to the tragedy of *Hamlet* the praise of variety. The incidents are so numerous, that the argument of the play would make a long tale. The scenes are interchangeably diversified with merriment and solemnity; with merriment that includes judicious and instructive observations, and solemnity, not strained by poetical violence above the natural sentiments of man. New characters appear from time to time in continual succession, exhibiting various forms of life and particular modes of conversation. The pretended madness of Hamlet causes much mirth, the mournful distraction of Ophelia fills the heart with tenderness, and every personage produces the effect intended, from the apparition that in the first act chills the blood with horror, to the fop in the last, that exposes affectation to just contempt.

The conduct is perhaps not wholly secure against objections. The action, is indeed for the most part in continual progression, but there are some scenes which neither forward nor retard it. Of the feigned madness of Hamlet there appears no adequate cause, for he does nothing which he might not have done with the reputation of sanity. He plays the madman most, when he treats Ophelia with so much rudeness, which seems to be useless and wanton cruelty.

Hamlet is, through the whole play, rather an instrument than an agent. After he has, by the stratagem of the play, convicted the King, he makes no attempt to punish him, and his death is at last effected by an incident which Hamlet has no part in producing.

The catastrophe is not very happily produced; the exchange of weapons is rather an expedient of necessity, than a stroke of art. A scheme might easily have been formed, to kill Hamlet with the dagger, and Laertes with the bowl.

The poet is accused of having shewn little regard to poetical justice, and may be charged with equal neglect of poetical probability. The apparition left the regions of the dead to little purpose; the revenge which he demands is not obtained but by the death of him that was required to take it; and the gratification which would arise from the destruction of an usurper and a murderer, is abated by the untimely death of Ophelia, the young, the beautiful, the harmless, and the pious.

Johnson on Shakespeare, edited by Bertrand H. Bronson with Jean M. O'Meara, Yale University Press: New Haven & London, 1986, Volume 2, 1010–11.

"HAMLET," From COLERIDGE ON SHAKESPEARE: THE TEXT OF THE LECTURES 1811-12

Samuel Taylor Coleridge

Samuel Taylor Coleridge (1772-1834), the most influential of poet-critics, argues for the importance of organic form at the heart of Shakespeare's achievement.

THE LECTURER then passed to Hamlet, in order, as he said, to obviate some of the general prejudices against Shakespeare in reference to the character of the hero. Much had been objected to, which ought to have been praised, and many beauties of the highest kind had been neglected, because they were somewhat hidden.

The first question was, what did Shakespeare mean when he drew the character of Hamlet? Coleridge's belief was that a poet regarded his story before he began to write in much the same light that a painter looked at his canvas before he began to paint. What was the point to which Shakespeare directed himself? He meant to portray a person in whose view the external world, and all its incidents and objects, were comparatively dim and of no interest in themselves, and which began to interest only when they were reflected in the mirror of his mind. Hamlet beheld external objects in the same way that a man of vivid imagination, who shuts his eyes, sees what has previously made an impression upon his organs.

Shakespeare places him in the most stimulating circumstances that a human being can be placed in: he is the heir apparent of the throne; his father dies suspiciously; his mother excludes him from the throne by marrying his uncle. This was not enough, but the Ghost of the murdered father is introduced to assure the son that he was put to death by his own brother. What is the result? Endless reasoning and urging—perpetual solicitation of the mind to act, but as constant an escape from action—ceaseless reproaches of himself for his sloth, while the whole energy of his resolution passes away in those reproaches. This, too, not from cowardice, for he is made one of the bravest of his time—not from want of forethought or quickness of apprehension, for he sees through the very souls of all who surround him,—but merely from that aversion to action which prevails among such as have a world within themselves.

How admirable is the judgment of the poet! Hamlet's own fancy has not conjured up the Ghost of his father; it has been seen by others; he is by them prepared to witness its appearance, and when he does see it he is not brought forward as having long brooded on the subject. The moment before the Ghost enters, Hamlet speaks of other matters in order to relieve the weight on his mind; he speaks of the coldness of the night, and observes that he has not heard the clock strike, adding, in reference to the custom of drinking, that it is

> More honour'd in the breach, than the observance.

From the tranquil state of his mind he indulges in moral reflections. Afterwards the Ghost suddenly enters:

> HORATIO   Look, my lord, it comes.
> HAMLET   Angels and Ministers of grace defend us!

The same thing occurs in *Macbeth:* in the dagger scene, the moment before he sees it, he has his mind drawn to some indifferent matters: thus the appearance has all the effect of abruptness, and the reader is totally divested of the notion that the vision is a figure in the highly wrought imagination.

Here Shakespeare adapts himself to the situation so admirably, and as it were puts himself into the situation, that through poetry, his language is the language of nature: no words, associated with such feelings, can occur to us but those which he has employed, especially the highest, the most august, and the most awful subject that can interest a human being in this sentient world. That this is no mere fancy, Coleridge undertook to show from Shakespeare himself. No character he has drawn could so properly express himself as in the language put into his mouth.

There was no indecision about Hamlet; he knew well what he ought to do, and over and over again he made up his mind to do it: the moment the Players, and the two spies set upon him, have withdrawn, of whom he takes leave with the line, so expressive of his contempt,

> Ay so; good bye you.—Now I am alone,

he breaks out into a delirium of rage against himself for neglecting to perform the solemn duty he had undertaken, and contrasts the artificial feelings of the player with his own apparent indifference:

> What's Hecuba to him, or he to Hecuba,
> That he should weep for her ?

Yet the player did weep for her, and was in an agony of grief at her sufferings, while Hamlet could not rouse himself to action that he might do the bidding of his Father, who had come from the grave to incite him to revenge:

> This is most brave,
> That I, the son of a dear father murdered,
> Prompted to my revenge by heaven and hell,
> Must, like a whore, unpack my heart with words
> And fall a cursing, like a very drab,
> A scullion.

It is the same feeling, the same conviction of what is his duty, that makes Hamlet exclaim in a subsequent part of the tragedy:

> How all occasions do inform against me,
> And spur my dull revenge! What is a man,
> If his chief good and market of his time
> *Be but to sleep and feed?* A beast, no more . . .
>   . . . I do not know
> Why yet live I to say—'this thing's to do',
> Sith I have cause and will and strength and means
> To do't.

Yet with all this sense of duty, this resolution arising out of conviction, nothing is done: this admirable and consistent character, deeply acquainted with his own feelings, painting them with such wonderful power and accuracy, and just as strongly convinced of the fitness of executing the solemn charge committed to him, still yields to the same retiring from all reality, which is the result of having what we express by the term 'a world within himself'.

Such a mind as this is near akin to madness: Dryden has said,[1]
> Great wit to madness, nearly is allied

and he was right; for he means by wit that greatness of genius, which led Hamlet to the perfect knowledge of his own character, which with all strength of motive was so weak as to be unable to carry into effect his most obvious duty.

Still, with all this, he has a sense of imperfectness, which becomes obvious while he is moralising on the skull in the churchyard: something is wanted to make it complete—something is deficient, and he is therefore described as attached to Ophelia. His madness is assumed when he discovers that witnesses have been placed behind the arras

1. *Dryden has said*] 'Great Wits are sure to madness near alli'd', *Absalom and Achitophel*, 1,163 (so Raysor).

to listen to what passes, and when the heroine has been thrown in his way as a decoy.

Another objection has been taken by Dr Johnson,[1] and has been treated by him very severely. I refer to the scene in the third act, where Hamlet enters and finds his Uncle praying, and refuses to assail him excepting when he is in the height of his iniquity: to take the King's life at such a moment of repentance and confession, Hamlet declares,

Why this is hire and salary, not revenge.

He therefore forbears, and postpones his Uncle's death until he can take him in some act

That has no relish of salvation in't.

This sentiment Dr Johnson has pronounced to be so atrocious and horrible as to be unfit to be put into the mouth of a human being (See Malone's Shakespeare, vii. 382).[2] The fact is that the determination to allow the King to escape at such a moment was only part of the same irresoluteness of character. Hamlet seizes hold of a pretext for not acting, when he might have acted so effectually. Therefore he again defers the revenge he sought, and declares his resolution to accomplish it at some time

When he is drunk, asleep, or in his rage,
Or in th'incestuous pleasures of his bed.

This, as Coleridge repeated, was merely the excuse Hamlet made to himself for not taking advantage of this particular moment to accomplish his revenge.

Dr Johnson[3] further states that, in the voyage to England, Shakespeare merely followed the novel as he found it, as if he had no other motive for adhering to his original; but Shakespeare never followed a novel but where he saw the story contributed to tell or explain some great and general truth inherent in human nature. It was unquestionably an incident in the old story, and there it is used merely as an incident, but Shakespeare saw how it could be applied to his own great purpose, and how it was consistent with the character of Hamlet, that after still

1. *Dr Johnson*] see *Johnson on Shakespeare*, ed. Sherbo, VIII, 990; Johnson said the speech 'is too horrible to be read or to be uttered'. 2. The reference in brackets is interlined, and must have been added after 1821, when Malone's edition of Shakespeare in 21 volumes was published. The page reference fits this edition. 3. *Dr Johnson*] Johnson says nothing of the kind, but a note in Reed's edition of 1803, which Coleridge was apparently using (see above, p. 121 and n.), XVIII, 270, on the speech of Claudius at the end of 4, 3, states 'The circumstances mentioned as including the King to send the prince to England, rather than elsewhere, are likewise found in the *Hystory of Hamblet.*' See also Raysor, II, 197 (154).

resolving, and still refusing, still determining to execute, and still post-poning the execution, he should finally give himself up to his destiny, and, in the infirmity of his nature, at last hopelessly place himself in the power and at the mercy of his enemies.

Even after the scene with Osrick, we see Hamlet still indulging in reflection, and thinking little of the new task he has just undertaken; he is all meditation, all resolution as far as words are concerned, but all hesitation and irresolution when called upon to act; so that, resolving to do everything, he in fact does nothing. He is full of purpose, but void of that quality of mind which would lead him at the proper time to carry his purpose into effect.

Anything finer than this conception and working out of a character is merely impossible: Shakespeare wished to impress upon us the truth that action is the great end of existence—that no faculties of intellect, however brilliant, can be considered valuable, or otherwise than as misfortune, if they withdraw us from or render us repugnant to action, and lead us to think and think of doing, until the time had escaped when we ought to have acted. In enforcing this truth, Shakespeare has shown the fulness and force of his powers: all that is amiable and excellent in nature is combined in Hamlet, with the exception of this one quality: he is a man living in meditation, called upon to act by every motive, human and divine, but the great purpose of life [is] defeated by continually resolving to do, yet doing nothing but resolve.

Coleridge on Shakespeare: The Text of the Lectures of 1811-12, edited by R.A. Foakes. Routledge & Kegan Paul: London, 1971, 124–28.

From "Lectures on The English Poets: On Shakespeare and Milton" in *The Complete Works of William Hazlitt*

William Hazlitt

William Hazlitt (1778-1830) was a Romantic critic whose insights into the poetry of the plays influenced, among others, the poet John Keats in seeing the gusto and "negative capability" of Shakespeare.

I T HAS been said by some critic, that Shakspeare was distinguished from the other dramatic writers of his day only by his wit; that they had all his other qualities but that; that one writer had as much sense, another as much fancy, another as much knowledge of character, another the same depth of passion, and another as great a power of language. This statement is not true; nor is the inference from it well-founded, even if it were. This person does not seem to have been aware that, upon his own shewing, the great distinction of Shakspeare's genius was its virtually including the genius of all the great men of his age, and not his differing from them in one accidental particular. But to have done with such minute and literal trifling.

The striking peculiarity of Shakspeare's mind was its generic quality, its power of communication with all other minds—so that it contained a universe of thought and feeling within itself, and had no one peculiar bias, or exclusive excellence more than another. He was just like any other man, but that he was like all other men. He was the least of an egotist that it was possible to be. He was nothing in himself; but he was all that others were, or that they could become. He not only had in himself the germs of every faculty and feeling, but he could follow them by anticipation, intuitively, into all their conceivable ramifications, through every change of fortune or conflict of passion, or turn of thought. He had 'a mind reflecting ages past,' and present:— all the people that ever lived are there. There was no respect of persons with him. His genius shone equally on the evil and on the good, on the wise and the foolish, the monarch and the beggar: 'All corners of the earth, kings, queens, and states, maids, matrons, nay, the secrets of the grave,' are hardly hid from his searching glance. He was like the genius of humanity, changing places with all of us at pleasure, and playing with our purposes as with his own. He turned the globe round for his amusement, and surveyed the generations of men, and the individuals as they passed, with their different concerns, passions, follies, vices, virtues, actions, and motives—as well those that they knew, as those which they did not know, or acknowledge to themselves. The dreams of childhood, the ravings of despair, were the toys of his fancy. Airy beings waited at his call, and came at his bidding. Harmless fairies 'nodded to him, and did him curtesies': and the night-hag bestrode the blast at the command of 'his so potent art.' The world of spirits lay open to him, like the world of real men and women: and there is the same truth in his delineations of the one as of the other; for if the preternatural characters he describes could be supposed to exist, they would speak, and feel, and act, as he makes them. He had only to think of any thing in order to become that thing, with all the circumstances belonging to it. When he conceived of a character, whether real or imaginary, he not only entered into all its thoughts and feelings, but seemed instantly, and as if by touching a secret spring, to be surrounded with all the same objects, 'subject to the same skyey influences,' the same local, outward, and unforeseen accidents which would occur in reality. Thus the character of Caliban not only stands before us with a language and manners of its own, but the scenery and situation of the enchanted island he inhabits, the traditions of the place, its strange noises, its hidden recesses, 'his frequent haunts and ancient neighbourhood,' are given with a miraculous truth of nature, and with all the familiarity of an old recollection. The whole 'coheres semblably together' in time, place, and circumstance. In reading this author, you do not merely learn what his characters say,—you see their persons. By something expressed or understood, you are at no loss to decypher their peculiar physiognomy, the meaning of a look, the grouping, the bye-play, as we might see it on the stage. A word, an epithet paints a whole scene, or throws us back whole years in the history of the person represented. So (as it has been ingeniously remarked) when Prospero describes himself as left alone in the boat with his daughter, the epithet which he applies to her, 'Me and thy *crying* self,' flings the imagination instantly back from the grown woman to the helpless condition of infancy, and places the first and most trying scene of his misfortunes before us, with all that he must have suffered in the interval. How well the silent anguish of Macduff is conveyed to the reader, by the friendly expostulation of Malcolm—'What! man, ne'er pull your hat upon your brows!' Again, Hamlet, in the scene with Rosencrans and Guildenstern, somewhat abruptly concludes his fine soliloquy on life by saying, 'Man delights not me, nor woman neither, though by your smiling you seem to say so.' Which is explained by their answer—'My lord, we had no such stuff in our thoughts. But we smiled to think, if you delight not in man, what lenten entertainment the players shall receive from you, whom we met on the way':—as if while Hamlet was making this speech, his two old schoolfellows from Wittenberg had been really standing by, and he had seen them smiling by stealth, at the idea of the players crossing their minds. It is not 'a combination and a form' of words, a set speech or two, a preconcerted theory of a character, that will do this: but all the persons concerned must have been present in the poet's imagination, as at a kind of rehearsal; and whatever would have passed through their minds on the occasion, and have been observed by others, passed through his, and is made known to the reader.—I may add in passing, that Shakspeare always gives the best directions for the costume and carriage of his heroes. Thus to take one example, Ophelia gives the following account of Hamlet; and as Ophelia had seen Hamlet, I should think her word ought to be taken against that of any modern authority.

'OPHELIA My lord, as I was reading in my closet,
Prince Hamlet, with his doublet all unbrac'd,
No hat upon his head, his stockings loose,
Ungartred, and down-gyved to his ancle,
Pale as his shirt, his knees knocking each other,
And with a look so piteous,
As if he had been sent from hell
To speak of horrors, thus he comes before me.
    POLONIUS Mad for thy love !
    OPHELIA My lord, I do not know,
But truly I do fear it.
    POLONIUS What said he ?
    OPHELIA He took me by the wrist, and held me hard
Then goes he to the length of all his arm;
And with his other hand thus o'er his brow,
He falls to such perusal of my face,
As he would draw it: long staid he so;
At last, a little shaking of my arm,
And thrice his head thus waving up and down,
He rais'd a sigh so piteous and profound,
As it did seem to shatter all his bulk,
And end his being. That done, he lets me go,
And with his head over his shoulder turn'd,
He seem'd to find his way without his eyes;
For out of doors he went without their help,
And to the last bended their light on me.'

Act. 2. Scene 1.

How after this airy, fantastic idea of irregular grace and bewildered melancholy any one can play Hamlet, as we have seen it played, with strut, and stare, and antic right-angled sharp-pointed gestures, it is difficult to say, unless it be that Hamlet is not bound, by the prompter's cue, to study the part of Ophelia. The account of Ophelia's death begins thus:

'There is a willow hanging o'er a brook,
That shows its hoary leaves in the glassy stream.'—

Now this is an instance of the same unconscious power of mind which is as true to nature as itself. The leaves of the willow are, in fact, white underneath, and it is this part of them which would appear 'hoary' in the reflection in the brook. . . .

The Complete Works of William Hazlitt, edited by P.P. Howe after the edition of A.R. Waller and Arnold Glover, J.M. Dent and Sons, Ltd.: London and Toronto, 1930, Vol. 5, 47–50.

From "Lecture on *Hamlet*" in *Shakespearean Tragedy*

A.C. Bradley

A.C. Bradley (1851-1935), Professor of Poetry at Oxford, 1901-06, was the author of Shakespearean Tragedy *(1904), long the most influential study of* Hamlet, Othello, King Lear, *and* Macbeth.

4

'MELANCHOLY,' I said, not dejection, nor yet insanity. That Hamlet was not far from insanity is very probable. His adoption of the pretence of madness may well have been due in part to fear of the reality; to an instinct of self-preservation, a fore-feeling that the pretence would enable him to give some utterance to the load that pressed on his heart and brain, and a fear that he would be unable altogether to repress such utterance. And if the pathologist calls his state melancholia, and even proceeds to determine its species, I see nothing to object to in that; I am grateful to him for emphasising the fact that Hamlet's melancholy was no mere common depression of spirits; and I have no doubt that many readers of the play would understand it better if they read an account of melancholia in a work on mental diseases. If we like to use the word 'disease' loosely, Hamlet's condition may truly be called diseased. No exertion of will could have dispelled it. Even if he had been able at once to do the bidding of the Ghost he would doubtless have still remained for some time under the cloud. It would be absurdly unjust to call *Hamlet* a study of melancholy, but it contains such a study.

But this melancholy is something very different from insanity, in anything like the usual meaning of that word. No doubt it might develop into insanity. The longing for death might become an irresistible impulse to self-destruction; the disorder of feeling and will might extend to sense and intellect; delusions might arise; and the man might become, as we say, incapable and irresponsible. But Hamlet's melancholy is some way from this condition. It is a totally different thing from the madness which he feigns; and he never, when alone or in company with Horatio alone, exhibits the signs of that madness. Nor is the dramatic use of this melancholy, again, open to the objections which would justly be made to the portrayal of an insanity which brought the hero to a tragic end. The man who suffers as Hamlet suffers—and thousands go about their business suffering thus in greater or less degree—is considered irresponsible neither by other people nor by himself: he is only too keenly conscious of his responsibility. He is therefore, so far, quite capable of being a tragic agent, which an insane person, at any rate according to Shakespeare's practice, is not. And, finally, Hamlet's state is not one which a healthy mind is unable sufficiently to imagine. It is probably not further from average experience, nor more difficult to realise, than the great tragic passions of Othello, Antony or Macbeth.

Let me try to show now, briefly, how much this melancholy accounts for.

It accounts for the main fact, Hamlet's inaction. For the *immediate* cause of that is simply that his habitual feeling is one of disgust at life and everything in it, himself included,—a disgust which varies in intensity, rising at times into a longing for death, sinking often into weary apathy, but is never dispelled for more than brief intervals. Such a state of feeling is inevitably adverse to *any* kind of decided action; the body is inert, the mind indifferent or worse; its response is, 'it does not matter,' 'it is not worth while,' 'it is no good.' And the action required of Hamlet is very exceptional. It is violent, dangerous, difficult to accomplish perfectly, on one side repulsive to a man of honour and sensitive feeling, on another side involved in a certain mystery (here come in thus, in their subordinate place, various causes of inaction assigned by various theories). These obstacles would not suffice to prevent Hamlet from acting, if his state were normal; and against them there operate, even in his morbid state, healthy and positive feelings, love of his father, loathing of his uncle, desire of revenge, desire to do duty. But the retarding motives acquire an unnatural strength because they have an ally in something far stronger than themselves, the melancholic disgust and apathy; while the healthy motives, emerging with difficulty from the central mass of diseased feeling, rapidly sink back into it and 'lose the name of action.' We *see* them doing so; and sometimes the process is quite simple, no analytical reflection on the deed intervening between the outburst of passion and the relapse into melancholy.[1] But this melancholy is perfectly consistent also with

---

1. *E.g.* in the transition, referred to above, from desire for vengeance into the wish never to have been born; in the soliloquy, 'O what a rogue'; in the scene at Ophelia's grave. The Schlegel-Coleridge theory does not account for the psychological movement in those passages.

that incessant dissection of the task assigned, of which the Schlegel-Coleridge theory makes so much. For those endless questions (as we may imagine them), 'Was I deceived by the Ghost? How am I to do the deed? When? Where? What will be the consequence of attempting it—success, my death, utter misunderstanding, mere mischief to the State? Can it be right to do it, or noble to kill a defenceless man? What is the good of doing it in such a world as this?'—all this, and whatever else passed in a sickening round through Hamlet's mind, was not the healthy and right deliberation of a man with such a task, but otiose thinking hardly deserving the name of thought, an unconscious weaving of pretexts for inaction, aimless tossings on a sick bed, symptoms of melancholy which only increased it by deepening self-contempt.

Again, (*a*) this state accounts for Hamlet's energy as well as for his lassitude, those quick decided actions of his being the outcome of a nature normally far from passive, now suddenly stimulated, and producing healthy impulses which work themselves out before they have time to subside. (*b*) It accounts for the evidently keen satisfaction which some of these actions give to him. He arranges the play-scene with lively interest, and exults in its success, not really because it brings him nearer to his goal, but partly because it has hurt his enemy and partly because it has demonstrated his own skill (3. 2. 286-304). He looks forward almost with glee to countermining the King's designs in sending him away (3. 4. 209), and looks back with obvious satisfaction, even with pride, to the address and vigour he displayed on the voyage (5. 2. 1-55). These were not *the* action on which his morbid self-feeling had centred; he feels in them his old force, and escapes in them from his disgust. (c) It accounts for the pleasure with which he meets old acquaintances, like his 'school-fellows' or the actors. The former observed (and we can observe) in him a 'kind of joy' at first, though it is followed by 'much forcing of his disposition' as he attempts to keep this joy and his courtesy alive in spite of the misery which so soon returns upon him and the suspicion he is forced to feel. (*d*) It accounts no less for the painful features of his character as seen in the play, his almost savage irritability on the one hand, and on the other his self-absorption, his callousness, his insensibility to the fates of those whom he despises, and to the feelings even of those whom he loves. These are frequent symptoms of such melancholy, and (*e*) they sometimes alternate, as they do in Hamlet, with bursts of transitory, almost hysterical, and quite fruitless emotion. It is to these last (of which a part of the soliloquy, 'O what a rogue,' gives a good example) that Hamlet alludes when, to the Ghost, he speaks of himself as 'lapsed in *passion*,' and it is doubtless partly his conscious weakness in regard to them that inspires his praise of Horatio as a man who is not 'passion's slave.'[1]

Finally, Hamlet's melancholy accounts for two things which seem to be explained by nothing else. The first of these is his apathy or 'lethargy.' We are bound to consider the evidence which the text supplies of this, though it is usual to ignore it. When Hamlet mentions, as one possible cause of his inaction, his 'thinking too precisely on the event,' he mentions another, 'bestial oblivion'; and the thing against which he inveighs in the greater part of that soliloquy (Iv. iv.) is not the excess or the misuse of reason (which for him here and always is god-like), but this *bestial* oblivion or '*dullness*,' this 'letting all *sleep*,' this allowing of heaven-sent reason to 'fust unused':

> What is a man,
> If his chief good and market of his time
> Be but to *sleep* and feed? a *beast,* no more.[2]

So, in the soliloquy in 2.2. he accuses himself of being 'a *dull* and muddy-mettled rascal,' who 'peaks [mopes] like John-a-dreams, unpregnant of his cause,' dully indifferent to his cause.[3] So, when the Ghost appears to him the second time, he accuses himself of being tardy and lapsed in *time*; and the Ghost speaks of his purpose being almost *blunted*, and bids him not to *forget* (cf. 'oblivion'). And so, what is emphasised in those undramatic but significant speeches of the player king and of Claudius is the mere dying away of

> This is mere madness;
> And thus awhile the fit will work on him;
> Anon, as patient as the female dove,
> When that her golden couplets are disclosed,
> His silence will sit drooping,

may be true to life, though it is evidently prompted by anxiety to purpose or of love.[4] Surely what all this points to is not a condition of excessive but useless mental activity (indeed there is, in reality, curiously little about that in the text), but rather one of dull, apathetic,

---

1. Hamlet's violence at Ophelia's grave, though probably intentionally exaggerated, is another example of this want of self control. The Queen's description of him (5.1. 307) excuse his violence on the ground of his insanity.   **2.** Throughout, I italicise to show the connection of ideas.   **3.** Cf. *Measure for Measure*, 4. 4. 23, 'This deed . . . makes me unpregnant and dull to all proceedings.'
4. 3. 2. 196 ff., 4. 7. 111 ff.: *e.g.,*
> Purpose is but the slave to *memory,*
> Of violent birth but poor validity.

brooding gloom, in which Hamlet, so far from analysing his duty, is not thinking of it at all, but for the time literally *forgets* it. It seems to me we are driven to think of Hamlet *chiefly* thus during the long time which elapsed between the appearance of the Ghost and the events presented in the Second Act. The Ghost, in fact, had more reason than we suppose at first for leaving with Hamlet as his parting injunction the command 'Remember me,' and for greeting him, on re-appearing, with the command, 'Do not forget.'[1] These little things in Shakespeare are not accidents.

The second trait which is fully explained only by Hamlet's melancholy is his own inability to understand why he delays. This emerges in a marked degree when an occasion like the player's emotion or the sight of Fortinbras's army stings Hamlet into shame at his inaction. '*Why*,' he asks himself in genuine bewilderment, 'do I linger? Can the cause be cowardice? Can it be sloth? Can it be thinking too precisely of the event? And does *that* again mean cowardice? What is it that makes me sit idle when I feel it is shameful to do so, and when I have *cause, and will, and strength, and means,* to act?' A man irresolute merely because he was considering a proposed action too minutely would not feel this bewilderment. A man might feel it whose conscience secretly condemned the act which his explicit consciousness approved; but we have seen that there is no sufficient evidence to justify us in conceiving Hamlet thus. These are the questions of a man stimulated for the moment to shake off the weight of his melancholy, and, because for the moment he is free from it, unable to understand the paralysing pressure which it exerts at other times.

I have dwelt thus at length on Hamlet's melancholy because, from the psychological point of view, it is the centre of the tragedy, and to omit it from consideration or to underrate its intensity is to make Shakespeare's story unintelligible. But the psychological point of view is not equivalent to the tragic; and, having once given its due weight to the fact of Hamlet's melancholy, we may freely admit, or rather may be anxious to insist, that this pathological condition would excite but little, if any, tragic interest if it were not the condition of a nature distinguished by that speculative genius on which the Schlegel-Coleridge type of theory lays stress. Such theories misinterpret the connection between that genius and Hamlet's failure, but still it is this connection

1. So, before, he had said to him:
    And duller should'st thou be than the fat weed
    That roots itself in ease on Lethe wharf,
    Would'st thou not stir in this.

which gives to his story its peculiar fascination and makes it appear (if the phrase may be allowed) as the symbol of a tragic mystery inherent in human nature. Wherever this mystery touches us, wherever we are forced to feel the wonder and awe of man's godlike 'apprehension' and his 'thoughts that wander through eternity,' and at the same time are forced to see him powerless in his petty sphere of action, and powerless (it would appear) from the very divinity of his thought, we remember Hamlet. And this is the reason why, in the great ideal movement which began towards the close of the eighteenth century, this tragedy acquired a position unique among Shakespeare's dramas, and shared only by Goethe's *Faust*. It was not that *Hamlet* is Shakespeare's greatest tragedy or most perfect work of art ; it was that *Hamlet* most brings home to us at once the sense of the soul's infinity, and the sense of the doom which not only circumscribes that infinity but appears to be its offspring.

Shakespearean Tragedy: Lectures on Hamlet, Othello, King Lear, Macbeth by A.C. Bradley, Macmillan & Co. Ltd: New York, 1960, 120–28.

"HAMLET," From SELECTED ESSAYS

T. S. Eliot

T.S. Eliot (1888-1965), the pre-eminent poet-critic of his time, (1) doubted the artistic integrity of the play and (2) used Hamlet himself as the stereotypical figure of insecurity in his early poem, "The Love Song of J. Alfred Prufrock," itself an implicit interpretation of the play.

HAMLET

Few critics have ever admitted that *Hamlet* the play is the primary problem, and Hamlet the character only secondary. And Hamlet the character has had an especial temptation for that most dangerous type of critic: the critic with a mind which is naturally of the creative order, but which through some weakness in creative power exercises itself in criticism instead. These minds often find in Hamlet a vicarious existence for their own artistic realization. Such a mind had Goethe, who made of Hamlet a Werther; and such had Coleridge, who made of Hamlet a Coleridge; and probably neither of these men in writing about Hamlet remembered that his first business was to study a work of art. The kind of criticism that Goethe and Coleridge produced, in writing of Hamlet, is the most misleading kind possible. For they both possessed unquestionable critical insight, and both make their critical aberrations the more plausible by the substitution—of their own Hamlet for Shakespeare's—which their creative gift effects. We should be thankful that Walter Pater did not fix his attention on this play.

Two writers of our time, Mr. J. M. Robertson and Professor Stoll of the University of Minnesota, have issued small books which can be praised for moving in the other direction. Mr. Stoll performs a service in recalling to our attention the labours of the critics of the seventeenth and eighteenth centuries,[1] observing that

> 'they knew less about psychology than more recent Hamlet
> critics, but they were nearer in spirit to Shakespeare's art; and as
> they insisted on the importance of the effect of the whole rather

---

1. I have never, by the way, seen a cogent refutation of Thomas Rymer's objections to *Othello*.

than on the importance of the leading character, they were nearer, in their old-fashioned way, to the secret of dramatic art in general.'

Qua work of art, the work of art cannot be interpreted; there is nothing to interpret; we can only criticize it according to standards, in comparison to other works of art; and for 'interpretation' the chief task is the presentation of relevant historical facts which the reader is not assumed to know. Mr. Robertson points out, very pertinently, how critics have failed in their 'interpretation' of *Hamlet* by ignoring what ought to be very obvious: that *Hamlet* is a stratification, that it represents the efforts of a series of men, each making what he could out of the work of his predecessors. The *Hamlet* of Shakespeare will appear to us very differently if, instead of treating the whole action of the play as due to Shakespeare's design, we perceive his *Hamlet* to be superposed upon much cruder material which persists even in the final form.

We know that there was an older play by Thomas Kyd, that extraordinary dramatic (if not poetic) genius who was in all probability the author of two plays so dissimilar as the *Spanish Tragedy* and *Arden of Feversham;* and what this play was like we can guess from three clues: from the *Spanish Tragedy* itself, from the tale of Belleforest upon which Kyd's *Hamlet* must have been based, and from a version acted in Germany in Shakespeare's lifetime which bears strong evidence of having been adapted from the earlier, not from the later, play. From these three sources it is clear that in the earlier play the motive was a revenge motive simply; that the action or delay is caused, as in the *Spanish Tragedy,* solely by the difficulty of assassinating a monarch surrounded by guards; and that the 'madness' of Hamlet was feigned in order to escape suspicion, and successfully. In the final play of Shakespeare, on the other hand, there is a motive which is more important than that of revenge, and which explicitly 'blunts' the latter; the delay in revenge is unexplained on grounds of necessity or expediency; and the effect of the 'madness' is not to lull but to arouse the king's suspicion. The alteration is not complete enough, however, to be convincing. Furthermore, there are verbal parallels so close to the *Spanish Tragedy* as to leave no doubt that in places Shakespeare was merely *revising* the text of Kyd. And finally there are unexplained scenes—the Polonius-Laertes and the Polonius-Reynaldo scenes—for which there is little excuse; these scenes are not in the verse style of Kyd, and not beyond doubt in the style of Shakespeare. These Mr. Robertson believes to be scenes in the original play of Kyd reworked by a third hand, perhaps Chapman, before Shakespeare touched the play. And he concludes, with very strong show of reason, that the original play of Kyd was, like certain other revenge plays, in two parts of five acts each. The upshot of Mr. Robertson's examination is, we believe, irrefragable: that Shakespeare's *Hamlet,* so far as it is Shakespeare's, is a play dealing with the effect of a mother's guilt upon her son, and that Shakespeare was unable to impose this motive successfully upon the 'intractable' material of the old play.

Of the intractability there can be no doubt. So far from being Shakespeare's masterpiece, the play is most certainly an artistic failure. In several ways the play is puzzling, and disquieting as is none of the others. Of all the plays it is the longest and is possibly the one on which Shakespeare spent most pains; and yet he has left in it superfluous and inconsistent scenes which even hasty revision should have noticed. The versification is variable. Lines like

> *Look, the morn, in russet mantle clad,*
> *Walks o'er the dew of yon high eastern hill,*

are of the Shakespeare of *Romeo and Juliet.* The lines in Act 5. Sc. 2,

> *Sir, in my heart there was a kind of fighting*
> *That would not let me sleep ...*
> *Up from my cabin,*
> *My sea-gown scarf'd about me, in the dark*
> *Grop'd I to find out them: had my desire;*
> *Finger'd their packet;*

are of his quite mature. Both workmanship and thought are in an unstable position. We are surely justified in attributing the play, with that other profoundly interesting play of 'intractable' material and astonishing versification, *Measure for Measure,* to a period of crisis, after which follow the tragic successes which culminate in *Coriolanus. Coriolanus* may be not as 'interesting' as *Hamlet,* but it is, with *Antony and Cleopatra,* Shakespeare's most assured artistic success. And probably more people have thought *Hamlet* a work of art because they found it interesting, than have found it interesting because it is a work of art. It is the 'Mona Lisa' of literature.

The grounds of *Hamlet's* failure are not immediately obvious. Mr. Robertson is undoubtedly correct in concluding that the essential emotion of the play is the feeling of a son towards a guilty mother:

'[Hamlet's] tone is that of one who has suffered tortures on the score of his mother's degradation. . . . The guilt of a mother is an almost intolerable motive for drama, but it had to be maintained and emphasized to supply a psychological solution, or rather a hint of one.'

This, however, is by no means the whole story. It is not merely the 'guilt of a mother' that cannot be handled as Shakespeare handled the suspicion of Othello, the infatuation of Antony, or the pride of

Coriolanus. The subject might conceivably have expanded into a tragedy like these, intelligible, self-complete, in the sunlight. *Hamlet,* like the sonnets, is full of some stuff that the writer could not drag to light, contemplate, or manipulate into art. And when we search for this feeling, we find it, as in the sonnets, very difficult to localize. You cannot point to it in the speeches; indeed, if you examine the two famous soliloquies you see the versification of Shakespeare, but a content which might be claimed by another, perhaps by the author of the *Revenge of Bussy d' Ambois,* Act 5. Sc. 1. We find Shakespeare's *Hamlet* not in the action, not in any quotations that we might select, so much as in an unmistakable tone which is unmistakably not in the earlier play.

The only way of expressing emotion in the form of art is by finding an 'objective correlative'; in other words, a set of objects, a situation, a chain of events which shall be the formula of that *particular* emotion; such that when the external facts, which must terminate in sensory experience, are given, the emotion is immediately evoked. If you examine any of Shakespeare's more successful tragedies, you will find this exact equivalence; you will find that the state of mind of Lady Macbeth walking in her sleep has been communicated to you by a skilful accumulation of imagined sensory impressions; the words of Macbeth on hearing of his wife's death strike us as if, given the sequence of events, these words were automatically released by the last event in the series. The artistic 'inevitability' lies in this complete adequacy of the external to the emotion; and this is precisely what is deficient in *Hamlet.* Hamlet (the man) is dominated by an emotion which is inexpressible, because it is in *excess* of the facts as they appear. And the supposed identity of Hamlet with his author is genuine to this point: that Hamlet's bafflement at the absence of objective equivalent to his feelings is a prolongation of the bafflement of his creator in the face of his artistic problem. Hamlet is up against the difficulty that his disgust is occasioned by his mother, but that his mother is not an adequate equivalent for it; his disgust envelops and exceeds her. It is thus a feeling which he cannot understand; he cannot objectify it, and it therefore remains to poison life and obstruct action. None of the possible actions can satisfy it; and nothing that Shakespeare can do with the plot can express Hamlet for him. And it must be noticed that the very nature of the *données* of the problem precludes objective equivalence. To have heightened the criminality of Gertrude would have been to provide the formula for a totally different emotion in Hamlet; it is just *because* her character is so negative and insignificant that she arouses in Hamlet the feeling which she is incapable of representing.

The 'madness' of Hamlet lay to Shakespeare's hand; in the earlier play a simple ruse, and to the end, we may presume, understood as a ruse by the audience. For Shakespeare it is less than madness and more than feigned. The levity of Hamlet, his repetition of phrase, his puns, are not part of a deliberate plan of dissimulation, but a form of emotional relief. In the character Hamlet it is the buffoonery of an emotion which can find no outlet in action; in the dramatist it is the buffoonery of an emotion which he cannot express in art. The intense feeling, ecstatic or terrible, without an object or exceeding its object, is something which every person of sensibility has known; it is doubtless a subject of study for pathologists. It often occurs in adolescence: the ordinary person puts these feelings to sleep, or trims down his feelings to fit the business world; the artist keeps them alive by his ability to intensify the world to his emotions. The Hamlet of Laforgue is an adolescent; the Hamlet of Shakespeare is not, he has not that explanation and excuse. We must simply admit that here Shakespeare tackled a problem which proved too much for him. Why he attempted it at all is an insoluble puzzle; under compulsion of what experience he attempted to express the inexpressibly horrible, we cannot ever know. We need a great many facts in his biography; and we should like to know whether, and when, and after or at the same time as what personal experience, he read Montaigne, II. xii, *Apologie de Raimond Sebond*. We should have, finally, to know something which is by hypothesis unknowable, for we assume it to be an experience which, in the manner indicated, exceeded the facts. We should have to understand things which Shakespeare did not understand himself.

Selected Essays by T.S. Eliot, Faber and Faber: London, 1953, 141-46. Used by permission.

HAMLET'S NEGLECT OF REVENGE

R. A. Foakes

AMLET HAS commonly been regarded as a revenge tragedy, its early impact being marked by works that capitalized
on its success, like John Marston's *Antonio's Revenge* and the
anonymous *Revenger's Tragedy,* possibly written by Thomas Middleton.
In the twentieth century, critics from A. C. Bradley, writing in 1904,
to the editors of the three editions that appeared in the 1980s, all have
had much to say about Hamlet's "task" or "duty" to carry out his
revenge. Hamlet could be seen as having to deal with "the predica-
ment, quite simply, of a man in mourning for his father, whose murder
he is called on to avenge" (Jenkins 126). Hence a central concern
for many critics has been the question of why Hamlet delays or avoids
taking his revenge on Claudius. He might be seen as pathologically
disabled by his speculative intellect and sensitivity in a world of
action, handicapped by weakness of character (Dover Wilson), tainted
by a "fatal aestheticism" (Nevo 162), or inhibited by the inescapable
condition of man (Mack); in any case, and for whatever reason, he has
been regarded as a failure in his "evasion of the task imposed on him"
(Dodsworth 297). All such accounts of the play have taken for granted
that the play's central concern is the need for Hamlet to carry out the
Ghost's demand for revenge, and his inability to act has been related to
the condition of "Hamletism," a condition that seemed to define the
disillusion, cynicism, or despair that marked a century in which two
world wars were fought, and in which the new-media technologies of
the film and television made all too familiar the horrors of Nazi gas
chambers, of atomic bombs, and of the resurgence of genocide.

Yet, as John Kerrigan observes, "Hamlet never promises to revenge,
only to remember"(126)[1]—that is, to remember the Ghost, and to
memorize his "commandment" (1.5.102). On reflection, Hamlet rea-
sonably resists the demand for revenge by a questionable Ghost that
appears strangely in armor, and that may come from the hell symbol-
ized by his voice from the "cellarage" under the stage. Hamlet later
identifies revenge with the figure of Pyrrhus taking vengeance for
the death of Achilles by "mincing" the limbs of Priam—this is the
horrid image that appalls Hamlet (2.2.513–14). Indeed, revenge is not
the dominant concern in *Hamlet,* as comparison with *The Revenger's*

Tragedy shows. This play adapts to new uses one of the property skulls thrown about in the gravedigger scene in *Hamlet* first by displaying it as an emblem of murder and of revenge to come, and then as a means of poisoning the Duke in a kiss. From the opening moment, the action is thus determined by Vindice's cry:

Vengeance, thou murder's quit-rent, and whereby
Thou show'st thyself tenant to Tragedy,
O, keep thy day, hour, minute, I beseech,
For those thou hast determined! (1.1.39–42)

The play looks ahead to vengeance being "paid" as a requital for murder, not only for the rape and murder of Gloriana by the Duke, but for the rape and Lucretia-like suicide of Antonio's wife, a "religious lady" (1.1.111), by the Duchess's youngest son. Most of the male characters in the play are caught up in a desire for revenge of some kind, since the law, as administered by the Duke, is corrupt, and the first act ends with a group swearing on their swords to revenge the death of Antonio's wife if "Judgment speak all in gold" (1.4.61). Vindice claims a high moral ground in his missionary zeal to "blast this villainous dukedom vexed with sin" (5.2.6), but his long obsession with obtaining revenge contaminates him, so that he is shown taking increasing pleasure in torture and murder. He becomes morally indistinguishable from other revengers in the masque of four revengers followed by "the other masque of intended murderers" in act 5, where all look alike and could substitute for one another. The play closes on a Christian moral pattern in which all of the guilty, including Vindice and his brother Hippolito, meet with retribution finally, so that Antonio is left in charge at the end, and can cry "Just is the law above!" But the action throughout is also self-consciously theatrical, as Vindice contrives plots and stages his own scenarios and plays within the play.

In so doing, Vindice often includes the audience in his denunciations of luxury, wealth, ambition, and lust, so that the unnamed court in the play may reflect the licentiousness and corruption perceived by spectators as present at the court of James I and in Jacobean London. The opening scene looks ahead to the completion of revenges, and the action presses forward, stressing the present tense. "Now" is the most frequently occurring adverb in the play, giving a sense of urgency as well as a sense of immediate relevance to the world of the audience (McMillin 282–3):

Now 'tis full sea abed over the world;
There's juggling of all sides. Some that were maids
E'en at sunset are now perhaps i' th' toll-book.

This woman in immodest thin apparel
Lets in her friend by water; here's a dame,
Cunning, nails leather hinges to a door
To avoid proclamation; now cuckolds are
A-coining, apace, apace, apace ...   (2.2.136–43)

The play thus speaks home to a London audience through images such as that of the woman letting in her friend by water (the Thames?), and by various forms of direct address. The Italianate setting permits the audience to associate the depiction of intrigue, lust, and murder with a foreign country, but at the same time to enjoy the frisson of recognizing satirical relevances to their own city and court. As in *Hamlet*, the protagonist is something of a misogynist, for whom women may represent an ideal of virtue, as embodied in his sister, Castiza (signifying Chastity), but more commonly are seen as a source of corruption, of the wealth and sex that fascinated people then as now: "were't not for gold and women, there would be no damnation" (2.1.257).

The opening of this play, which has no ghost, is dominated by the displayed skull of a victim of murder, whereas in *Hamlet*, by contrast, the early scenes are dominated by the Ghost, and Yorick's skull, handled by Hamlet, is seen only in act 5, where it recalls the Ghost in serving as a reminder of the past, a remembrance of Hamlet's childhood. In *The Revenger's Tragedy,* most of the characters are engaged in a feverish pursuit of pleasure, sex and power,

Banquets abroad by torchlight, music, sports,
Bare-headed vassals that had ne'er the fortune
To keep their own hats on, but let horns wear 'em;
"Nine coaches waiting,—hurry, hurry, hurry!"   (2.1.203–6)

When Vindice broods on his world as he contemplates the skull of Gloriana again in act 3, he questions this pursuit of luxury and pleasure, seeing the court as absurdist and the people in it as mad:

Surely we are all mad people, and they
Whom we think are, are not ...   (3.5.80–81)

He is right to include himself, and yet he speaks as the one rational character who is capable of reflecting on the conduct of others, and who is therefore able to manipulate them and control events. In Shakespeare's play the situation is reversed, as Hamlet himself feels estranged to the point of madness in a court that is going about its orderly business as usual. These differences relate to a more fundamental dissimilarity between the plays, for Hamlet is not in control, but rather is being watched and monitored in a court run with some efficiency by Claudius. Hamlet thinks of himself as subject to the whims of unstable Fortune, or assaulted by her "slings and arrows," which tend to disable the "discourse of reason."[2] As noted earlier, his neglect of revenge has troubled many interpreters of the play, who tend to see Hamlet as "a man with a deed to do who for the most part conspicuously fails to do it" (Jenkins 139–40, Foakes 35–40). Hence the long tradition of regarding Hamlet as irresolute, paralyzed in will, unhealthy, morbid, neurotic, a dreamer who appears a very disturbing figure in the context of Western ideologies that value men of decision and action who are ready to do their duty. It should not surprise that many actresses have taken on the role, and that Hamlet has been appropriated critically as "sensitive, intellectual, and feminine" (French 158, Foakes 24–6, Thompson and Taylor 42–50).

The idea that Hamlet fails to carry out an appointed task or duty is based on his encounter with the Ghost of his father in act 1, and our understanding of this encounter relates to the presentation of the Ghost in the opening scene. There the Ghost appears as a "warlike form," in "the very armor he had on/When he the ambitious Norway combated," according to Horatio, who speaks as if he had witnessed the battle with his own eyes. Not until near the end of the play does it emerge that the old King fought old Fortinbras thirty years previously, on the very day Hamlet was born (5.1.147), so that Horatio, his fellow-student, and presumably about the same age as Hamlet, cannot have seen old Hamlet at that time. This inconsistency is not noticed in performance, nor often in reading, and seems designed to establish an image of old Hamlet as a warrior king. Shakespeare had recently worked on *Julius Caesar*, which could have influenced his use of classical names in *Hamlet*, such as Horatio, Marcellus, Claudius, and Laertes, and also his references to Caesar and the classical deities, but this classical contextualization goes deeper. In the Quarto, Horatio recalls in this scene the apparitions that preceded the fall of Julius Caesar in "the most high and palmy state of Rome," thereby associating old Hamlet directly with ancient Rome, but these lines were omitted from the Folio, possibly cut in performance because they do not advance the action, or alternatively because they mislead by suggesting the Ghost is merely a portent of disasters to come. However, the passage shows how Shakespeare's mind was working to create a complex idea of the Ghost. He is represented as not only a sort of epic figure, at once associated with ancient history, with old battles fought against Norway, and with heroic values, but also as someone known to Horatio, and connected to a present moment when it seems that history may repeat itself in an invasion of Denmark by young Fortinbras.

The Ghost probably startled the first audience to see *Hamlet* staged by its appearance in armor—the only ghost in early modern English drama to be so costumed (Prosser 120, 255). With his "martial stalk" he seems to emerge from an ancient time when fighting was the normal way to conduct affairs, and this "portentous figure," as he is called by Barnardo, is linked by Horatio with the portents and ghosts or "sheeted dead" that squeaked and gibbered in the streets of Rome before the assassination of Julius Caesar (1.1.113–25). Yet he is also old Hamlet to the life, so that Horatio reports to Hamlet, "I think I saw him yesternight" (1.2.189), his beard grizzled "as I have seen it in his life" (1.2.240). By this time, Hamlet has already, in his "O that this too too sullied flesh would melt" soliloquy, compared his father with Hyperion the sun-god and with Hercules (1.2.140,153), so enhancing his association with the classical world. The Ghost who interviews Hamlet late in act 1 in effect becomes the living man again, gesturing, passionate, bearded, armed, and carrying his marshal's truncheon, an actor visibly turning into Hamlet's father when he begins to speak. He carries the authority not only of a "supernatural being, King and father"(Hibbard 185), but also of the martial heroes of the classical world. But Hamlet has responded to the appearance of the Ghost with his cry,

> Angels and ministers of grace defend us!
> Be thou a spirit of health or goblin damned,
> Bring with thee airs from heaven or blasts from hell,
> Be thy intents wicked or charitable,
> Thou comest in such a questionable shape
> That I will speak to thee. (1.4.39–44)

All those forms of authority are thus put in question in relation to a Christian pattern of values, and the Ghost is "questionable" not only as inviting question, but also as doubtful, of uncertain origin.[3] Furthermore, the Ghost's first words suggest he has come from Hell ("sulphurous and tormenting flames") or Purgatory (where his "foul crimes" are to be "burnt and purged away"),[4] and his intents appear to be wicked rather than charitable. When he addresses Hamlet directly, he speaks in the voice of a Senecan revenger, invoking classical values again in calling on Hamlet to "Revenge his foul and most unnatural murder" (1.5.25).

HAMLET	Murder?
GHOST	Murder most foul, as in the best it is,
	But this most foul, strange and unnatural.
HAMLET	Haste me to know't, that I, with wings

> As swift as meditation or the thoughts of love
> May sweep to my revenge. (1.5.26–31)

Hamlet's immediate reaction to the Ghost's words is often taken as signifying an acceptance of a duty to revenge: "He now also has his directive, a commission that is also a mission. His reaction to the Ghost is like a religious conversion" (Edwards 39, 45). Hamlet's first response, however, is spoken in the context of the Ghost's Christian qualification of his Senecan call for revenge: in condemning murder as "most foul" at the best, he thus exhorts Hamlet to kill his murderer and at the same time denounces the idea of revenge killing (Alexander 45–46).

As the Ghost continues with his long account of Gertrude transferring her affections to Claudius, and of Claudius poisoning him, his emphasis is on the sinful nature of these events and on the horrible effects of the poison on his body. The Ghost is troubled with a moral disgust on the one hand, and a physical revulsion on the other, and the two meet in his sermonizing about Gertrude's behavior:

> So lust, though to a radiant angel linked,
> Will sate itself in a celestial bed
> And prey on garbage (1.5.55–57)

The moral and physical disgust associated with lust and garbage is seen also in the Ghost's horror both at the appearance of his body, covered by the poison with a "loathsome crust," and at being denied the sacraments at his death. This talking Ghost becomes flesh, a living actor, in his anxiety about what happened to his body, and in his outrage at the idea that the "royal bed of Denmark" should become "[a] couch for luxury and damned incest" (1.5.83). The Ghost's moral outrage, expressed in Christian terms, echoes that expressed by Hamlet in his first soliloquy in 1.2, who, like his father, thinks of the marriage of Claudius and Gertrude as incestuous (1.2.157); the Ghost adds adultery as a further charge (1.5.41). Both also have a kind of voyeuristic horror in imagining what goes on in the "incestuous sheets" of the "royal bed."

In the Ghost's long narrative the idea of revenge becomes diluted, and almost lost, especially as he ends by telling Hamlet to leave his mother to her conscience and to heaven. His final imperative is "Remember me," and this is what catches Hamlet's attention:

> Remember thee?
> Ay, thou poor ghost, whiles memory holds a seat
> In this distracted globe. Remember thee?
> Yea, from the table of my memory
> I'll wipe away all trivial fond records,

All saws of books, all forms, all pressures past
That youth and observation copied there,
And thy commandment all alone shall live
Within the book and volume of my brain,
Unmixed with baser matter   (1.5.95–104)

Hamlet indeed dwells above all on remembering the Ghost, and wip-
ing away all other records he has kept in the notebook of his memory.
But what does he mean by the "commandment" he wants to register there? The Ghost's imperatives have shifted from "Revenge" (25)
through "bear it not" (81) and "Taint not thy mind" (85) to "Remember me" (91). The word "commandment" incorporates "command,"
appropriate to a figure appearing as a great warrior and wielding
a marshal's truncheon, and this is how Hamlet recalls this moment
later in 3.4, when he expects the Ghost, appearing for the third time,
to chide him for neglecting to carry out his "dread command." In
1.5, however, "commandment" had a much more immediate sense for
Shakespeare and his audience, one derived from its use in the Bible,
specifically in relation to the ten commandments given by God to
Moses, which were by law inscribed or hung on the walls of par-
ish churches in England. Prominent among them is the injunction,
"Thou shalt not kill,"[5] so that the term in itself contains the contradictory impulses that characterize both the Ghost and Hamlet,
namely a quasi-Senecan desire for revenge, and a Christian inhibition
against taking life.

In his study *Pagan Virtue*, John Casey argues that "we inherit a confused system of values; that when we think most rigorously and realis-
tically we are 'pagans' in ethics, but that our Christian inheritance only
allows a fitful sincerity about this" (Casey 225–6). He observes that our
society admires qualities derived from the ancient Greeks and Romans, what he calls the "irascible" virtues, "pride and shame, a sense
of the noble, a certain valuing of courage and ambition," as against
compassion, meekness, pity, and love, qualities that we associate with
Christ. He thinks *King Lear* shows that Shakespeare was confused, that
the play "uncomfortably combines, without reconciling, 'pagan' and
Christian elements" (Casey 212, 225). I think what *Hamlet* demonstrates is that Shakespeare was fully aware of the differences between
these inherited sets of values and used them in establishing the character and dilemma of his protagonist. Hamlet sees his father in ideal
terms, associating him with classical deities and heroes, Hyperion, Ju-
piter, Mercury, and Hercules. Old Hamlet is established for us in the
opening scene by Horatio as a warrior who challenged old Fortinbras
to single combat and killed him, and Hamlet's remarks about his father

confirm this image of a hero from the past, possessing "An eye like Mars to threaten and command" (3.4.57). Old Hamlet represents martial honor, is associated with the irascible virtues, and is distanced into something of a mythical figure—doubly distanced in the past history of Denmark, and by association with the classical world.

Hamlet is represented as a student, whose training in the classics is reflected in his language, in his image of his father, and in other ways, as when he invites the players to rehearse a speech describing the death of Priam based on the *Aeneid*. For Hamlet, his father is measured against the heroes of the Trojan war. In challenging old Fortinbras, old Hamlet behaved like the heroes of the *Iliad*, making courage a prime virtue, and courting death in war: "[I]n heroic societies life is the standard of value. If someone kills you, my friend or brother, I owe you their death and when I have paid my debt to you their friend or brother owes them my death" (MacIntyre 117). In that simpler world of masculine values, revenge could be seen as a virtuous act, but this is not the world invoked in the Player's speech narrating the revenge taken for the death of his father Achilles by Pyrrhus, whose "roused vengeance" drives him to butcher the old king, "mincing" his limbs in full view of Queen Hecuba. The speech brings out the full horror of what Pyrrhus does, insuring that, in spite of the classical imagery, and the attribution of blame to Fortune, as though it is Priam's bad luck to suffer thus, the "hellish" (2.2.463) deed of the black and bloody murderer is condemned.

Hearing this speech prompts Hamlet to a tirade against himself, first for not having spoken out, like the player, and then for doing nothing but unpacking his heart with words. He does not threaten direct action against Claudius,[6] and slides from cursing into reflection; though "prompted" to revenge, as for the moment he claims, "by heaven and hell" (2.2.584), he goes on to question whether the Ghost may be "a devil" tempting him to damnation. So he shifts from a heroic stance applauding the idea of revenge to a Christian anxiety about the nature of the Ghost, and ends by deciding to try to "catch the conscience of the king," using the New Testament term that specifically signifies a consciousness of sin, and might suggest that Hamlet relates Claudius to those sinners who condemned the woman taken in adultery and were "convicted by their own conscience" (John, 8.9).

Hamlet's shift from Thyestean revenge to Christian conscience parallels the Ghost's turn away from his demand for revenge to his call to Hamlet to leave Gertrude to her conscience. The Ghost does not represent the simple heroic warrior Hamlet imagines, but a more complex figure who defines virtue not in terms of a heroic code but in relation to lust. In the *Iliad*, women are taken by the victors in battle as spoils of war, but the Christian morality that the Ghost preaches is focused on sexual relations, and he is especially outraged by thoughts of incest and adultery, as if he has in mind Christ's sermon on the mount, "whosoever looketh on a woman to lust after her hath committed adultery with her already in his heart" (Matthew 5.28). The Ghost's concern here in 1.5 in turn echoes Hamlet's thought in his first soliloquy, where he, too, is already tainted in his mind by his disgust with sullied flesh, and by his mother's marriage to Claudius. Indeed, he begins by rejecting suicide because "the Everlasting" has "fixed/His canon 'gainst self-slaughter" (1.2.131–2), apparently recalling the sixth of the ten commandments, "Thou shalt not kill." When Hamlet modulates in his "O, what a rogue and peasant slave am I" soliloquy from cursing and shouting for vengeance into worrying that the Ghost may be a devil, he again seems trapped in the conflict between the heroic ethos exemplified for him by the image he has of his father, and the Christian values the Ghost and he also share, and which are assumed as a common frame of reference by the other characters.

Hamlet takes the performance of *The Mousetrap* as causing Claudius, "frighted with false fire," to reveal his guilt when he suddenly calls for lights and leaves the stage, though it may well be, as Guildenstern reports, that Claudius is angered and frightened by something else: He has heard Hamlet identify the murderer in the play as "nephew to the king" (3.2.244),—pointing threateningly to himself as a potential murderer of his uncle. However that may be, Hamlet seems prepared to act in "the witching time of night" (3.2.358) as he goes to "speak daggers" (3.2.365) to his mother and encounters Claudius at prayer. Claudius has just admitted to the audience his offense in a reference to the first murderer, Cain:

> It hath the primal eldest curse upon 't,
> A brother's murder.   (3.3.37–38)

Inevitably, it seems, Hamlet is inhibited from carrying out a murder that would be analogous, the killing of a blood relative, now that he has the perfect opportunity. It is, of course, ironic that his chance comes when Claudius is kneeling, as if he were a silent embodiment of contrition, so that Hamlet is stymied by the thought that his uncle might go to heaven rather than to hell if he is killed while praying. Whenever Hamlet reflects upon revenge, he cannot carry it out because the very idea clashes with his awareness of biblical injunctions against taking life.

What happens when Hamlet comes into the presence of his mother in 3.4 is therefore crucial in the action of the play. He forces her to sit down, physically handling her in a way that makes her cry out, fearing he may murder her, and in response to her shout, "Help, ho!," a voice is heard from behind an arras or curtain, "What ho! Help!" Hamlet does not identify the voice, but draws his sword and stabs it through the curtain.

It is the first time he has not paused to reflect, and his act seems spontaneous. When Gertrude asks what he has done, he replies, "Nay, I know not. Is it the King?" Hamlet has worked himself up in preparation for the "bitter business" of his verbal attack on his mother, and, concentrating with all his force on the harsh things he has to say to her, he cannot bear to be interrupted. His reaction to the discovery that he has killed Polonius is callous, since all his attention is concentrated on forcing Gertrude to share his disgust with her marriage to Claudius, and persuading her to forego

> the rank sweat of an enseamed bed,
> Stewed in corruption, honeying and making love
> Over the nasty sty.   (3.4.92–94)

She has risen to see what Hamlet has done, as he presumably draws the arras and reveals the body, and, bidding a quick farewell to Polonius as a "wretched, rash, intruding fool," he turns back to her, once again making her sit down and listen to him. What has he done? It is not premeditated murder, or a *crime passionel*, since his passion is directed against his mother in the scene, and he does not know whom he has stabbed. It is not an accident, though there is an accidental aspect to the deed in that stabbing blindly through an arras might merely wound rather than kill. Hamlet hopes he may have killed the King, but really has no idea who is hiding. One might argue that he transfers his anger with his mother momentarily to the figure behind the arras, or that his frustration in passing up the chance to kill Claudius at prayer causes this sudden act of violence, but there is no adequate explanation for why Hamlet behaves as he does. His killing of Polonius is best thought of as a lashing out, a spontaneous act that may in some way release pent-up feelings and frustrations associated with his uncle, his mother, Ophelia, and the general state of affairs in Denmark, but it remains in the end inexplicable. It is a primal act of violence.[7]

Hamlet continues for about 150 lines to excoriate his mother in his anxiety to persuade her not to sleep with her present husband, Claudius, and ends by pleading,

> Forgive me this my virtue;
> For in the fatness of these pursy times
> Virtue itself of vice must pardon beg . . .   (3.4.152–54)

His words, with their generalizing stress on gross physicality in the overtones of "fatness" and "pursy" or flabby recall the Ghost's confidence in generalizing about his "virtue":

> But virtue, as it never will be moved,
> Though lewdness court it in a shape of heaven,
> So lust, though to a radiant angel linked,
> Will sate itself in a celestial bed,
> And prey on garbage.   (1.5.53–57)

Like his father's, Hamlet's "virtue" is focused in his horror at her sexual behavior, and, as if to pull him back from his obsession with sex, the Ghost returns, seen only by Hamlet, to whet his "blunted purpose," and remind him of more important matters. In the first Quarto the stage direction calls for the Ghost to enter "in his night gown," not in the armor he wore in act 1, as if the actor who played in this shortened version adapted his costume to a bedchamber, and there may have been deliberate irony in so clothing the Ghost when his words are more appropriate to a warlike figure, since they serve to remind Hamlet about revenge. Since the Queen does not see the Ghost, the audience may think it is a hallucination perceived only by Hamlet, confirming his eccentric behavior, which Gertrude regards as madness and so reports to Claudius in the next scene (4.1.7). The ironies are compounded in Hamlet's speeches, which are rational except for their obsessive concern with sex, which is morally disgusting to him in a way that the killing of Polonius is not. Polonius is dismissed and then forgotten for 120 lines, after which Hamlet rewrites what he has done by appointing himself as heaven's agent of punishment:

> For this same lord,
> I do repent. But heaven hath pleased it so
> To punish me with this and this with me,
> That I must be their scourge and minister.   (3.4.172–75)

Here Hamlet abandons all of his earlier wrestlings with conscience and with the biblical injunction against killing. He casually pushes responsibility away from himself with no remorse, treating the corpse with a mocking detachment as he makes his exit, lugging "the guts into the neighbor room." Has the body of Polonius, bloodied from the sword-thrust, been visible on stage throughout the scene? If so, it would serve as a reminder of the disparity between Hamlet's fixation on sex and his lack of concern about a man he has killed.

Hamlet has accused his mother of making "sweet religion" into a "rhapsody of words," or meaningless medley, which is, ironically, what he now does himself by claiming to be the instrument of providence.

Gertrude tells Claudius that Hamlet weeps for what he has done (4.1.27), but the Hamlet we see again in the following scenes seems unconcerned, as he puts on his antic disposition in mockingly talking to Rosencrantz and Guildenstern and then to the King about what he has done with the body of Polonius.

After his sudden act of violence his attitude to the idea of killing and death changes rapidly, the biblical commandments are forgotten, and he openly promises that Claudius will soon follow Polonius on his way to heaven or hell (4.3.35–37). At this point Hamlet is dispatched to England, and is offstage for about five hundred lines, while the action focuses on Ophelia and Laertes. When we see him again, in the graveyard scene, he is brooding over skulls on the leveling that death brings. He links the first skull thrown up by the Gravedigger to Cain: "How the knave jowls it to the ground, as if 'twere Cain's jawbone, that did the first murder" (5.1.76–77). Whereas Claudius sees himself as Cain committing a "brother's murder," Hamlet refers only to the primal act of murder, something he repeated in killing Polonius. The scene points up his casual attitude to death since he stabbed through the arras, while also marking his acceptance of the idea of his own death and its insignificance in relation to that of Caesar or Alexander the Great. But then comes the great shock of discovering that Ophelia is dead, and he realizes that the gravediggers have been preparing for the burial of her body. This is the only death that moves him, not to a recognition that he might be to blame for her suicide, but rather to anger at the ostentatious grieving of Laertes: "the bravery of his grief did put me/Into a towering passion" (5.2.79–80).

Hamlet has no compunction about sending Rosencrantz and Guildenstern to their deaths in England ("They are not near my conscience," 5.2.58, F only), and now accepts (also in lines found only in F) the idea of killing Claudius, "is't not perfect conscience,/To quit him with this arm?" (5.2.67–68). This passage from "To quit him . . ." (5.2.68–81) may have been omitted by accident or cut in performance because it makes Hamlet's intentions too explicit, but it is revealing, especially in the use of the word "conscience" in a sense that conflicts with biblical usage, as in 1 Timothy 1.5 (Geneva text): "the end of the commandment is love out of a pure heart, and of a good conscience, and of faith unfeigned"—in biblical terms, it is not possible to kill with a good conscience.[8] After he stabs Polonius, Hamlet increasingly displays a sardonic acceptance of the idea of death, and learns to distance himself from what he has done by claiming he is an agent of providence, and that his conscience is untroubled. By openly showing his hostility to Claudius, he has insured that sooner or later they will clash as "mighty opposites" (5.2.62), and he resigns himself to providence in the knowledge that death awaits him: "If it be now, 'tis not to come. If it be not to come, it will be now" (5.2.220–22). What he has done has made him ready to accept his own death ("The readiness is all."), but still not dedicated to revenge. It is only after he has his own death wound that he turns the poisoned weapon on Claudius, not in a plotted revenge, but in a spontaneous act of retaliation.

In neglecting his revenge, Hamlet is not "stifled by remembrance" (Kerrigan 186) so much as by his inheritance of conflicting classical and Christian values. The heroic code he associates with his father urges him to action, while the Christian code that is given lip-service in Claudius's Denmark condemns revenge and inhibits him from murder most foul. A ruler, however bad, may be God's "minister" in punishing the evil subjects do, according to St. Paul, as "a revenger to execute wrath upon him that doeth evil" (Romans 13.4), and the people must accept this, "for conscience sake."[9] Hamlet is not the king, but he claims the prerogative of a ruler in the role of "scourge and minister" after killing Polonius. From this point on, he likes to associate his actions with Providence, whereas earlier he had seen himself as subject to Fortune, contrasting himself with Horatio, the embodiment of Senecan stoicism. As long as he contemplates the idea of revenge, Hamlet cannot sustain resolution, finding "conscience does make cowards of us all" (3.1.82), and it is his exploration of this issue that makes the "To be or not to be" soliloquy so central in the play.

Only in his last soliloquy, omitted from the Folio text, does he find in Fortinbras an inspiring warrior image resembling that of his father, marching off to fight a war merely for honor, who might prevent Hamlet from "thinking too precisely on the event" (4.4.41) if it were not that this encounter occurs as he is on his way to England; furthermore, this soliloquy is present only in Q2, not in the Folio or Q1, and was probably omitted in performance not only because it duplicates Hamlet's self-denunciation in his earlier soliloquy, "O what a rogue and peasant slave am I," without advancing the action, but also because the momentum of that action has already shifted toward a final showdown with Claudius consequent upon the killing of Polonius and the open hostility to the King shown by Hamlet. Another self-questioning soliloquy is unnecessary (Foakes 92–94). Fortinbras resembles old Hamlet as a warrior prince, but now he is not, as Horatio supposed in the opening scene, aiming to attack Denmark to recover lands old Hamlet fought to win, but setting off for Poland to fight for a worthless patch of ground in the name of honor.

Thus, insofar as *Hamlet* is a revenge tragedy, Laertes is the revenger figure, who, in Senecan fashion, is willing, unlike Hamlet, to reject "conscience" and "dare damnation" (4.5.133–34) to get his revenge for the death of his father, and cut Hamlet's throat in the church (4.7.126). He returns from France equipped with a deadly poison he can apply to a rapier (4.7.141), and proceeds to plot with Claudius a scenario that will insure the death of Hamlet. Laertes, of course, only finds out in 4.5 that his father has been killed, so the subplot of revenge is worked out swiftly, but in most respects Laertes from this point becomes a revenger like Vindice or Pyrrhus, and in his difference from Hamlet reveals something about the limitations of the revenge play. Revenge is a frequent motif in drama, but there are, in truth, few major revenge plays, since the basic plot offers limited possibilities of diversity. Revenge is always reactive, secondary, a response to some previous deed, and the most powerful tragedies develop from some primal act of violence.

Hamlet remains central in European and American culture as a work that continually challenges interpretation. Although commonly characterized as a revenge tragedy, a concern with the idea of revenge rarely figures in the way Hamlet has been characterized:

> The Romantics freed Hamlet the character from the play into an independent existence as a figure embodying nobility, or at least good intentions, but disabled from action by a sense of inadequacy, or a diseased consciousness capable of seeing the world as possessed by things rank and gross in nature, and hence a failure. Hamletism gained currency as a term to describe not only individuals, but the failings of intellectuals, political parties, or nations, and so *Hamlet* was restored to the public arena to characterize the condition of Germany, or Europe, or the world, or the decline of aristocracy in the face of democracy. As the idea of Hamletism prospered, so it came to affect the way the play was seen, and the most widely accepted critical readings of it have for a long time presented us with a version of Shakespeare's play reinfected, so to speak, with the virus of Hamletism, and seen in its totality as a vision of failure in modern men or even in Man himself. (Foakes 44)

Hamlet has often been extrapolated from the play as someone who reflects, hesitates, is inhibited from acting, or as one who is oppressed by a corrupt world in which action is useless. Such versions of the Prince ignore much that is in the play, but in focusing on action or inaction they are responding in some sense to a central issue in the play, which is not the matter of revenge, but rather the control or release of instinctual drives to violence. If the "How all occasions" lines are omitted, Hamlet's last major soliloquy is "To be or not to be," a question that has immediately to do not with suicide, but with action:

Whether 'tis nobler in the mind to suffer
The slings and arrows of outrageous fortune,
Or to take arms against a sea of troubles,
And by opposing end them.   (3.1.56–59)

To "take arms," like his father, would mean to kill, which was accepted
as part of a heroic code, but is rejected by Christian commandments.
Hamlet is trapped in the contradictions between the two codes, which
make him a great exponent of the problem of violence. There is no
solution; having passed up a chance to revenge himself on Claudius
and worked himself into a passionate state on his way to confront his
mother, he spontaneously stabs through the arras to kill Polonius. This
act is a rite of passage, and makes it easy for him to send Rosencrantz
and Guildenstern to their deaths, and to resign himself to his own.
His initial act of violence changes his nature, so that he reconstructs
himself as the agent of providence in punishing others. He needs to
do so in order to live with what he has done. In exploring Hamlet's
dilemma, the play probes deeply into the basic problem of human
violence and the moral limits of action, and it is a misnomer to call it
simply a revenge play.

NOTES

1. Neill, 251–61, finely analyzes the emotional and moral ambivalence
   of remembrance in the play in his treatment of Hamlet as a conventional revenger whose "dream of re-membering the violated past and
   destroying a tainted order is fulfilled only at the cost of repeating the
   violation and spreading the taint."
2. Frye, 113–21, shows how Fortune was opposed to prudence and
   wisdom in Shakespeare's age.
3. The first use of the word in this latter sense recorded in the *Oxford
   English Dictionary* dates from 1607, but Shakespeare surely had both
   meanings in mind here.
4. The Ghost refers to purgatory and says he was denied the last rites
   (1.5.77), but these Catholic associations conflict with those of the
   Senecan revenger, and with the suggestions of hell when the Ghost
   is heard like a pioneer or miner beneath the stage. Hamlet is
   understandably confused, but his first reaction is arguably Protestant,
   as limited to earth, heaven, and hell: "O all you host of heaven! O
   earth! What else?/And shall I couple hell?" (1.5.92–93). Hamlet has
   returned from Wittenberg, the most famous Protestant university,
   so that once he shakes off the overwhelming sense of his father's
   presence, he suspects the apparition may be a devil (2.2.595). The

religious affiliations of the Ghost and of Hamlet have been much debated, as by Frye 14–24, by Jenkins 453–54, 457–59, by Prosser 118–42, and by McGee 13–54. I think Shakespeare chose to provide mixed signals about a Ghost that remains questionable still; the significant polarity in the play I believe is between Christian and classical, not between Catholic and Protestant attitudes and beliefs.

5. The Geneva Bible has a marginal gloss here: "But love and preserve thy brother's life."

6. The cry "Oh Vengeance!" (after 2.2.581) found only in the Folio text is thought by many to be an actor's addition, a rhetorical flourish that runs counter to the flow of the soliloquy; it is omitted from many editions, such as the Arden and the Riverside.

7. In his interesting study of the play Gurr also argued, 76–79, that the killing of Polonius is a turning point in the action.

8. The Geneva text has a marginal gloss here: "Paul sheweth that the end of God's Law is love, which cannot be without a good conscience. . . ."

9. In the Geneva text a marginal note adds: "For he is the minister of God to take vengeance on him that doth evil."

WORKS CITED

Alexander, R. N. *Poison, Play and Duel*. London: Routledge, 1971.

The Bible and Holy Scriptures, Geneva version (Geneva, 1560)

Bradley, A. C. *Shakespearean Tragedy*. London: Macmillan, 1904.

Casey, John. *Pagan Virtue: An Essay in Ethics*. Oxford: Clarendon Press, 1990.

Dodsworth, Martin. *Hamlet Closely Observed*. London: Athlone Press, 1985.

Edwards, Philip, ed. *Hamlet*. Cambridge: Cambridge University Press, 1985.

Foakes, R. A. *Hamlet versus Lear: Cultural Politics and Shakespeare's Art*. Cambridge: Cambridge University Press, 1993.

French, Marilyn. *Shakespeare's Division of Experience*. New York: Summit Books, 1981.

Frye, Roland Mushat. *The Renaissance Hamlet: Issues and Responses in 1600*. Princeton: Princeton University Press, 1984.

Gurr, Andrew. *Hamlet and the Distracted Globe*. Edinburgh: Sussex University Press, 1978.

Hibbard, G. R., ed. *Hamlet*. Oxford: Oxford University Press, 1985.

Jenkins, Harold, ed. *Hamlet*. New Arden Shakespeare. London: Methuen, 1982.

Kerrigan, John. *Revenge Tragedy*. Oxford: Oxford University Press, 1996.

McGee, Arthur. *The Elizabethan Hamlet.* New Haven: Yale University Press, 1987.

MacIntyre, Alasdair. *After Virtue: A Study in Moral Theory.* London: Duckworth; Notre Dame: Notre Dame University Press, 1981.

McMillin, Scott. "Acting and Violence in *The Revenger's Tragedy* and its Departures from *Hamlet.*" *Studies in English Literature* 24 (1984), 275–91.

Mack, Maynard. "The World of *Hamlet.*" *Yale Review,* New Series 47 (1951–52): 502–23.

Neill, Michael. *Issues of Death Mortality and Identity in English Renaissance Tragedy.* Oxford: Clarendon Press, 1999.

Nevo, Ruth. *Tragic Form in Shakespeare.* Princeton: Princeton University Press, 1972.

Oxford English Dictionary, 2nd. Edition (1989)

Prosser, Eleanor. *Hamlet and Revenge.* Stanford: Stanford University Press, 1967.

Thompson, Ann and Neil Taylor. *William Shakespeare: Hamlet.* Plymouth: Northcote House in Association with the British Council, 1996.

Wilson, John Dover. *What Happens in Hamlet.* Cambridge: Cambridge University Press, 1935.

Hamlet: New Critical Essays, edited by Arthur F. Kinney, Routledge: New York and London (2002), 85-99. Used by permission.

HAMLET THEN AND NOW:
AN OVERVIEW

Ralph Berry

O F HAMLET the properties to unfold would seem to affect speech and discourse. There is too much of him. But there's a case for a few time-developed photographs of Hamlet, as we track the course of this star across the firmament of social time. Hamlet has changed. The cloud that masks him may look like a camel or a weasel or very like a whale. He is certainly not the man he was when John Gielgud, as all agreed, had taken on the "definitive" shape of Hamlet.

My first Hamlet was Paul Scofield's, at Stratford-upon-Avon. As is often the melancholy case with playgoers, the first was the best. Scofield was and is an outstandingly handsome and magnetic actor. His Hamlet was a solitary, brooding, immensely attractive individual at odds with a corrupt and repressive Court. He absorbed effortlessly the sympathies of the audience. Claudius, in a setting of mid-Victorian Gothic, was marked as the villain and focus of all that was rotten in Denmark. Hamlet, in brief, was right and the Danish Establishment was wrong. The play's ending, however poignant, was the victory of right over wrong. That was the essential play. Scofield had taken further the Gielgud tradition, and Kenneth Tynan said simply, "This is the best Hamlet I have seen."[1]

Cut now to December 1991. I had been invited to Cambridge, Massachusetts to take part in a panel discussion organized by the American Repertory Theatre (ART). The occasion was the *Hamlet* then running at the ART, a production directed by Ron Daniels and starring Mark Rylance. The ART has strong links with Harvard, and its audience is discerning and sophisticated.

The ART *Hamlet*, an updated version of a Royal Shakespeare Company (RSC) production seen in England a year or so earlier, starred a leading figure who lacked personal appeal. This was a neurotic, disturbed Hamlet who spent much of the play in soiled pajamas, lolling around on his bed (which featured in the now standard wrestling bout with Gertrude). The setting suggested one of those sanatorium plays so popular in the 1930s, and Hamlet thus became a patient. He divided his time between being offensive and being impossible to all around.

Gertrude and Claudius, by contrast, emerged as highly sympathetic figures. There was certainly something shady about Claudius's past, one gleaned. The man had cut corners on his way to the top. There are precedents for that. But here he was, doing his best to run the country and trying to draw Hamlet into the new system. Gertrude was fully supportive of her husband in trying to make the arrangements work. And much help they got from Hamlet, a misfit and a gifted trouble-maker. One saw the play differently.

Not, however, till the panel discussion did I take the point fully. The panel, seated on stage, addressed themselves to an audience of 300, all of whom had seen the production. And then the truth emerged. *Hamlet* had become a family drama. For the audience, Gertrude and Claudius were simply a middle-aged couple *en secondes noces*, trying to make a go of their new marriage. The new family that they con-stituted was merely the latest, provisional regrouping of diverse indi-viduals. It was a postnuclear family, with the amoeba breaking off into separate parts and then reforming into a new amoeba. Everyone in America has encountered it, at the organizing or receiving end.

Into these dispositions the new Hamlet fitted all too well. As Alan Brien wrote, "Unlike Hamlet, Claudius is a role which needs to be presented from the character's point of view."[2] Society today is superbly placed to see Claudius's and Gertrude's point of view. All we have to do is think of two words never mentioned in the text, "stepfa-ther" and "stepson." It is as simple as that. In 1.2 Claudius does his best to bring his new stepson into the fold ("Our chiefest courtier, cousin, and our son"), only to meet veiled insolence and sulky defiance. And Hamlet, seeing that his bluff cannot be called, presses his advantage more and more. In the play scene Hamlet's behavior is outrageous. He knows perfectly well that his stepfather would love to throttle the wretch, but cannot. Not with his mother looking on, anyway.

At the core of *Hamlet* is a domestic triangle in which Claudius's stepson does his level best to break up his mother's remarriage. From such a steely egotist one can expect little else. Look at the closet scene (3.4): Hamlet has just killed a man, yet heaps reproaches on his mother's head for daring to remarry. No wonder that Claudius, in the course of the play, moves from "Our son" to "Your son." Hamlet, one feels, is always going to achieve his psychic goal. He will destroy his mother's second marriage.

All this became clear during the panel discussion, with contribu-tions from the audience. One of the panelists, Dr. Bennett Simon, a Harvard psychiatrist, illustrated the play's domestic concerns from his own practice in Cambridge. One thing he said lodged in my mind, never to leave it. A patient of his, referring to the problems of a son inherited from a previous marriage, said "Nobody knows what we've been through with him." Let that line be the epitaph on many of today's Hamlets, as registered by those unfortunate enough to be caught up in the Claudius-Gertrude situation.

•   •   •

The Cambridge *Hamlet* came on the fault line of contemporary history, devised before and falling after the great event of recent times. When the Berlin Wall collapsed, so did the old-style *Hamlet*. Of course, Hamlets in the West had been antiromantic, more obnoxious than alienated, for many years. Ulrich Wildgruber's Hamlet really had been "fat and scant of breadth."[3] Anton Lesser's Hamlet cheated Laertes in the fencing match. (Laertes was shocked. So was I.) Jonathan Pryce was a "gangling, twitching neurasthenic."[4] The vestigial memories of "student" and "rebel" were clearly inadequate to fuel the modern Hamlets.[5] But there was always Eastern Europe to remind us of what the old-style *Hamlet* ought to be.

And then they packed it in. The Eastern bloc *Hamlet* used to contain the spirit of the play very well. As Dennis Kennedy wrote, "But if to the liberal west *Hamlet* is an expression of the individual spirit, to a censor in a more repressive land it is a threat."[6] Stalin, famously, had banned *Hamlet* during the war. It remained heavily loaded after hostilities had ended, and this was true for much of the century. Kennedy picks out his quintessential moment in Siegfried Hochst's production in the DDR (1989) "which treated Denmark as a literal prison from which almost everybody was trying to escape, just as almost everybody was trying to escape at that moment from East Germany. The stage was enclosed with three rows of wire fencing, and when Laertes was given permission to return to France in the second scene, he was handed a green document that looked suspiciously like the passports issued by West Germany. The audience howled in delight."[7]

Hamlet was always, in the East, code for the struggle between the individual dissenter and the apparat of State power. Kozintsev kept Rosencrantz and Guildenstern in his film (1964), notwithstanding a heavily cut playing text. They were the agents of surveillance, the Renaissance KGB. Olivier had cut them completely. The national dimension was modified by the country: the Czechs preserved a fairly traditional model of *Hamlet*,[8] the Poles saw the play as a direct rendering of recent history. As Konrad Swinarski remarked ironically to me, "*Hamlet* is always successful with us. Hamlet is always a Pole, and Fortinbras is the Soviet Army." He was mocking a cliché of Polish productions, bringing on a Fortinbras listing to port with the weight of his medals, and looking much like Marshal Rokossovsky. The Eastern model of *Hamlet* served its time well, and ended with the Romanian National Theatre's *Hamlet* that came to London in 1990.[9]

Whatever may be said in favor of the fall of the Wall, it was a disaster for *Hamlet*. The game was up for Western as well as Eastern *Hamlets*. It cannot seriously be maintained that Western society is oppressive. As for "Denmark's a prison," untold numbers are clamoring to be let in. The entire social problem coded as "Denmark" has shrunk, even shriveled, and now remains as cypher for the difficulties Hamlet faces in reconciling himself to his society. The world of Hamlet has contracted to the domestic, the private even. "How all occasions do inform against me" can be cut, and if performed, poses the question: what kind of violence ("my thoughts be bloody, or be nothing worth") is permissible to Hamlet today?

The escape from today's Elsinore must therefore be toward the past or some other foreign country, or into the inner world. I doubt if the past is a serious answer, setting aside such designed gestures as bringing Uhlan helmets into the Danish court or showing home movies of the Tsar at play in the snow with the Tsarevich. Hamlet must be of our time, and the task is to reconcile him with the text. The recent instances I have seen suggest that the problem is widening.

The problem can be put concisely: what can we do about Fortinbras? Two recent productions I have seen, both at Kronborg Castle (John Caird's for the National Theatre, 2000, and Bill Alexander's for the Birmingham Repertory, 2001) solved the problem Gordianly. They cut him. In this they relocated the play within an old tradition. Victorian playgoers never saw Fortinbras. Shaw, in a classic passage, writes of Forbes-Robertson's Lyceum *Hamlet* of 1897, a production "really not at all unlike Shakespeare's play of the same name." "I am quite certain I saw Reynaldo in it for a moment; and possibly I may have seen Voltimand and Cornelius; but just as the time for their scene arrived, my eye fell on the word "Fortinbras" in the program, which so amazed me that I hardly know what I saw for the next ten minutes."[10]

For Shaw, Fortinbras was the symbol of his campaign for a full-text Shakespeare. And the absent Fortinbras was coupled with the emetically mawkish ending dear to the Victorians, when the play halted at "And flights of angels sing thee to thy rest." In the light of Shaw's superb polemic, and a historically won battle, it seemed likely that no one would ever see a "flights of angels" ending in a serious production today. But I did. And in Helsingor, too.

The "full-text" doctrine has gradually weakened over the years. The RSC in its early and most famous years was strongly in favor of substantially uncut texts. As recently as 1993, Adrian Noble directed Kenneth Branagh in a *Hamlet* for the RSC that conflated the Second Quarto and the Folio. Branagh, when the time came to film his own *Hamlet* (1996), stuck to a full text. This led to "How all occasions do inform against me" as a pre-intermission aria, with the camera pulling back from the hero, centrally placed against a snowy plain. A martial soundtrack (Patrick Doyle) signified Hamlet's resolution to adopt Fortinbras as role model. Since then a reaction against the full text and in particular against Fortinbras has been marked.

This movement started, to my observation, with Matthew Warchus's *Hamlet* for the RSC (1998). This was heavily cut, losing the battlement scene (1.1) right away. Alex Jennings's disturbed prince, genuinely on the brink of a nervous breakdown, was trying to cope—for the first time in his life—with real adversity. Warchus cut the 4.4 soliloquy and excluded Fortinbras from his playing text. What colored the final scenes was a distinctly Scandinavian tinge. The mourners at Ophelia's funeral could well have come out of a Bergman movie. For the fencing match, the contestants wore the proper garb, including fencing masks, as they might in a Swedish gymnasium. At the end, Hamlet killed Claudius with sword and poison—and then, at last, brought himself to fire his revolver into the body of Claudius. This was Hedda Gabler territory, and the symbolic instrument "the pistols of my father, the General."

This was not a military Hamlet. The dimension of war was absent. Rather, it was a father-dominated Hamlet. There was no final appearance of Fortinbras, that unwanted role model, and the English Ambassador. Instead, the play virtually ended on "And flights of angels sing thee to thy rest," a shameless return to the Victorian tradition. Warchus went a little further, with an indistinct voice-over of Horatio's speech ending, "All this can I truly deliver." But this was Stoppard territory.

There's a certain family likeness between the Warchus *Hamlet* and the two more recent productions that I've mentioned. Simon Russell Beale's *Hamlet*, directed by John Caird for the National Theatre (2000), was an intellectual and peacenik: fortunately for him, he did not have to think about Fortinbras, who had vanished into the Helsingor night. Hamlet's capacity to act in the Fortinbras mode was coincidentally in doubt. As the *Daily Telegraph* reviewer remarked with suave accuracy, "He speaks 'O that this too too solid flesh would melt' with rare authority." Russell Beale was indeed fat and scant of breath, and when he defeated the trim, athletic Laertes I wanted to call out "Fixed!" The production ended with Italian church music (cue for "Pity") and "flights of angels sing thee to thy rest." Was it for this that Shaw suffered?

In 2001 Bill Alexander (who retains his connection with the RSC) directed Richard McCabe's *Hamlet* for the Birmingham Repertory Theatre, a production that was put on in the Kronborg courtyard. Room was found for Reynaldo—usually an early victim in the cutting room—but not for Fortinbras. McCabe was magnetic, always watchable, using his charisma to project the "antic disposition" that Hamlet puts on. Clad in a surplice, first black, then white, barefooted on the Kronborg stones, he endured four acts of self-inflicted discomfort. (It is always, I think, "a nipping and an eager air" in the courtyard in mid-August.) "To be or not to be" was spoken as direct address to Ophelia, who listened in silence as Hamlet strove, unavailingly, to explain himself. This was not a Hamlet whose private anguish could be assuaged or resolved via the Fortinbras role model. So though McCabe looked like a man who could handle his rapier—not always true of Hamlets—it seemed logical to delete Fortinbras from his mental screen. Some of Fortinbras's lines were retained by Alexander for the final clear-up operation, placed in the mouth of Horatio. "L'intendance suivra," as the French military say. These lines extended marginally the essential close at "And flights of angels sing thee to thy rest." Nowadays one might as well wait for Godot as for Fortinbras.

I make Fortinbras the cardinal test of the current *Hamlet*. The play has always contained two large scenarios, one of them the political dimension, the other the family or domestic dimension. It was open to the director to lay emphasis on either. On my reading, history has collapsed the political dimension. It will always be present, but now survives in attenuated or coded form. Fukuyama's thesis, the "End of History," has taken hold in directorial minds. The RSC *Hamlet* of 2001, for example (directed by Steven Pimlott, with Sam West the lead), made Elsinore a company HQ, with Claudius the new CEO charged with turning round the company's fortunes. He was surrounded by executives in gray suits (male and female). This is not so very different from the perception that governed Peter Hall's production for the RSC in 1965, and the moment that John Russell caught in David Warner's Hamlet: "When pursued by Rosencrantz and Guildenstern and the officers, his 'Here *they* come' is illuminated with a contemporary inflection that marks 'they' as a composite image of restrictive and uncomprehending authority."[11] Restrictive and uncomprehending authority will no doubt always be with us, but The Firm seems a mild enough version of the State power that Shakespeare wrote into his play. On current showing, Rosencrantz and Guildenstern—the Company sneaks—together with a few Palace security guards, do not add up to the Securitate. Western society lays a light hand on dissenters. Repressive tolerance is bad for Hamlets.

Nor does Fortinbras appear to the director as a feasible resolution. At the heart of the play's later stages is a great myth, that of violence—linked with war—as the solution to the tensions and failures of life. The dark glamor of war is the romantic myth closing Tennyson's *Maud*, whose protagonist, musing on his shattered life, sees a way out in volunteering for the great conflict of his day, and to fight the Russians. "No more shall commerce be all in all," says Tennyson, in a close rendering of Hamlet's "What is a man/If his chief good and market of his time/Be but to sleep and feed?" (4.4.33–35) Tennyson's penultimate stanza is:

> For the peace, that I deem'd no peace, is over and done
> And now by the side of the Black and the Baltic deep,
> And deathful-grinning mouths of the fortress, flames
> The blood-red blossom of war with heart of fire.

And the unnamed speaker of *Maud* ends on "I embrace the purpose of God, and the doom assign'd." That is not so different from Hamlet's "The readiness is all." Violence that fully expresses the self, linked with a noble cause, is the antidote to tragedy.

It is not, clearly, a solution that commends itself to today's directors and audiences. There was indeed a flicker in 1982, when the Falklands campaign brought out a latent regard for Fortinbras. *The Times* (June 3, 1982) published a letter from Malcolm Muggeridge, consisting of "the following exchange between Hamlet and a Captain would seem to have some bearing on the Falklands affair," and then quoting the entire exchange between the Norwegian Captain and Hamlet (4.4.9–30). The "little patch of ground/That hath in it no profit but the name" turned out to be a compelling analogue for the bleak and windswept Falklands, whose possession meant nothing but honor to both parties. That was a fleeting moment of history, and nothing has occurred since to restore Fortinbras. Peter Brook's *Hamlet*, transferred from Paris to London in the summer of 2001, followed much of the Warchus precedent. "Most of the great opening scene has gone, and so has Fortinbras and the play's entire political dimension."[12] Benedict Nightingale was not prepared to go along with Brook's new vision of the play. Fortinbras's absence "in so intimate a production does even more to transform the play from a public to a private happening. That great concerto *Hamlet*—Denmark the orchestra, the prince the soloist— has become a chamber piece. Moreover, it seems to involve the royal family only . . ."[13] Brook's *Hamlet* was a further reduction of the "domestic" play that I described earlier. Politics has made a temporary departure from today's scene, and *Hamlet* will have to await its return.

Fortinbras has been airbrushed out of the current history of Hamlet, and textual scholarship now sanctions his departure. In the past, *Hamlet* was always taken to be a conflation of Q2 and F, and the director's task was to keep as much as he could carry away from the giant quarry. The director had an open field. Following the controversy over the two-text *King Lear*, *Hamlet* has also in more muted form taken on two-text status.

That is, it is now seriously held that the Folio *Hamlet* is Shakespeare's revision of his play, and must represent Shakespeare's second (or final) thoughts. The dropping of the 4.4 dialogue between Hamlet and the Norwegian Captain, and the loss of the final soliloquy, is on this view purposive. It is not a mere accident of transmission, a missing sheaf of some MS pages. Besides, the idea of a single, "authoritative" text has been much under fire of recent years. "Conflation" has lost a great deal of its old standing. Consequently, G. R. Hibbard made his Oxford edition (1987) into a Folio-based text. Passages found only in Q2 were banished to Appendix A, rather than printed alongside F in a full-text version. Hibbard argued strongly for this point of view, and his position came down to "The soliloquy ['How all occasions do inform against me'], for all its felicity of phrasing, is redundant. It tells us nothing we do not know already, except that the Prince has become unrealistic ... The cutting of Q2 is, then, the most important part of a logical and coherent process of revision designed to make a better acting version with a wide appeal."[14]

Whether one accepts Hibbard's reasoning (I don't, for one) is not the point. There is now decent scholarly authority for a director who wants to make away with Fortinbras. Peter Brook ran into great trouble in 1962 for cutting a dozen lines of servants' dialogue from the post-blinding passage in *King Lear*. "After such knowledge, what forgiveness?" asked Maynard Mack.[15] But then it turned out that the passage so blasphemously cut could be seen as a considered revision. If Shakespeare could do it, why not Brook? The same order of defense applies to Fortinbras. A director can now abandon him—or retain vestigial allusions only—without having boulders hurled at him by textual traditionalists among the critics. And all the latest evidence points toward directors taking advantage of this new licence. They are no longer compelled to mix socially with Fortinbras, and have quietly dropped him.[16]

So the Dane has to get by without his Norwegian role model. Someone of great power has fallen out of Hamlet's universe. It is possible that Hamlet may be missing him.

NOTES

1. Kenneth Tynan, *A View of the English Stage* (Frogmore, St. Albans: Paladin, 1976), p. 77.
2. *Sunday Telegraph*, October 27, 1963.
3. See Werner Habicht, "Shakespeare in West Germany," *Shakespeare Quarterly* 29 (1987): 298.
4. Francis King, *Sunday Telegraph*, April 6, 1980.

5. I have covered some of this ground in "Casting Hamlet: Two Traditions," in Berry, *Shakespeare in Performance: Castings and Metamorphoses* (Houndmills, Basingstoke: Macmillan, 1993), 57–65.

6. Dennis Kennedy, ed. *Foreign Shakespeare: Contemporary Performance* (Cambridge: Cambridge University Press, 1993), 4.

7. Ibid., 4–5.

8. See Jarka Burian's "*Hamlet* in Postwar Czech Theatre," in Kennedy, 195–210.

9. See Joan Montgomery Byles, "Political Threatre: *Hamlet* in Romania," An Account of A. Tocilescu's 1990 Production, *Shakespeare Bulletin* (Spring 1991), 25–26.

10. G. Bernard Shaw, *Our Theatres in the Nineties* (London: Constable, 1932): III.200.

11. John Russell Brown, "The Royal Shakespeare Company 1965," *Shakespeare Survey* 19 (1966): 113.

12. Charles Spencer, *The Daily Telegraph*, August 23, 2001. The review headline was "Brook Makes a Travesty of a Tragedy."

13. Benedict Nightingale, *The Times*, August 24, 2001.

14. G. R. Hibbard, ed. *Hamlet* (Oxford: Oxford University Press, 1987), 109.

15. Maynard Mack, "*King Lear*" *in Our Time* (Berkeley and Los Angeles: University of California Press, 1965), 40.

16. Michael Boyd did indeed retain Fortinbras in his production (2004), with Toby Stephens in the lead. But the final soliloquy cut the first 21 lines and began with "Rightly to be great," ending, after another cut, with "My thoughts be bloody or be nothing worth." The masculine and soldierly charge that Fortinbras provides was much weakened by the ghost. Chalk white and clad only in a loincloth, Hamlet's father was an anguished, purgatorial spirit, with no trace of the armor and "martial stalk" that the text demands. The "fair and warlike form" of Denmark's king had disappeared. One of Hamlet's ancestral voices had fallen silent.

Shakespearean Performance: New Studies, edited by Frank Ochiogrosso. Rosemont Publishing and Associated University Presses: Cranbury, NJ, 2008, 40–49. Used by permission.

'ENTER THE GHOST IN HIS NIGHT GOWNE':THE CORPUS OR CORPSE OF SHAKESPEARE NOW

Kathleen McLuskie

I. SHAKESPEARE NOW

Shakespeare Now, or the reproduction of Shakespeare, is currently moving in a number of rather contradictory directions.There has been in the last year a remarkable resurgence of interest in Shakespeare's biography,[1] led by Stephen Greenblatt and James Shapiro, together with equal and opposite anti-Stratfordian claims to unmask the real Shakespeare in the form of the Elizabethan courtier Sir Henry Neville[2] or a cryptic analysis of the 'real meaning' of the plays.[3] In the academic world, New Historicism is being replaced by Presentism but again there is an equal and opposite move to insist on the significance of 'Cultural Memory' which analyses the way that the early-modern world and its memories are being reinstated in the cultural memory of today.[4]

These intellectual oscillations ripple round the continuing central conflict over the ownership of Shakespeare that has taken place throughout the 20th century. On the one hand, Shakespeare is firmly embedded in the National Curriculum of state schools and, on the other, the publicly supported theatre is engaged in a huge educational offensive to insist on the centrality of performance to Shakespeare, training teachers to bring performance methods into classroom teaching and training children to become the next generation of audiences.[5] Most recently Lenny Henry, a popular Afro-Caribbean comedian has emerged as a new Shakespeare champion, rehearsing the now familiar conversion narrative of how he was bored by Shakespeare at school but found the truth of the bard in the theatre. Lenny Henry's conversion was the subject of a television programme and followed a season of new BBC Shakespeares in which the narratives of the best-known plays were turned variously into a chick flick (*Much Ado*) and a murder mystery set in a kitchen (*Macbeth*).[6]

The debate over whether Shakespeare is most fully represented on the stage or on the page has been going on since Shakespeare's own time. Linking that debate to the question of accessibility and innovation is, however, a more recent phenomenon. It reflects both the constant need for innovation that characterises the new cultural marketplace together with the recurring anxiety that the culture of the past might be ignored or rejected by those who are in thrall to the appeal of mass culture enhanced by new technologies of reproduction. These concerns are further complicated by the continual desire to dethrone the icons of cultural authority. In this debate the different sides assume that performance will always be more appealing and so the discussion centres on the extent to which performance can also be true to the ideals of the cultural heritage that performance reproduces. That debate rages particularly energetically with regard to performance on film. However, in this paper I want to pay attention to the evidence for and the debates over performance from Shakespeare's own time in order to explore the way in which that historical knowledge might help us to configure the relationship between text and performative reproduction at this point in the new millennium.

In order to explore that relationship between Shakespeare's text and performance we need to do more than simply accumulate examples of different ways in which the texts have been realised on stage. That study of the history of theatre has produced some fascinating accounts of particular performances but it pays scant attention to the different realms of knowledge produced by the text itself: the knowledge of a narrative that was enacted on stage at different historical moments as well as the experience of an audience who attended that enactment. Both of those two knowledges are necessary to gain a full understanding of the dynamic nature of a Shakespeare play.

Robert Weimann who writes of 'the unhelpful dichotomy between stage-centred and text centred approaches' has discussed the relationship between those two knowledges. Weimann's solution is not merely to replace one approach with the other. It is to focus on difference, on 'the duality of the concept itself':

> It is not enough to dispense with the text/performance dichotomy; performative action itself needs to be relocated at that crucial point where dramatic language and cultural representation can be seen to interact.

He distinguishes between performance as 'representation' (creating in physical terms the narrative and action of the play) and performance as *being*, embodying in real time:

> The inalienable strength and agility of the agent, with all the traces of his/her body, gender, age and other forms of existence that go with and counterpoint the histrionic representation of fictitious roles.[7]

Weimann's distinction between the performance of a role within a narrative and the real-time physical action of a performer seems to me critical. It helps to focus on the distinction between interpretation (of characters or narrative) and performativity. The interpretation will affect the mimetic reproduction of roles within the narrative but the performativity depends upon the particular skills of the performer (in recitation or dance or song or athletics) and exists only in the real-time relationship with a particular audience. Performance as representation and performance as being are both evident in the texts of Shakespeare's plays but the relationship between the two was changing and contested in Shakespeare's time and has continued to be so to our own.

2. 'ENTER THE GHOST IN HIS NIGHT GOWNE' (HAMLET QI: II. 57 SD)

This stage direction, from the so-called 'bad' quarto of *Hamlet* (QI) presents a particular case study for exploring the connection between performance as representation and performance as being. It does so because the existence of different texts of *Hamlet* has complicated the relationship between the play's narrative and the particular features of its performativity. The three distinct texts, QI, Q2 and the text from the Folio collection of Shakespeare's 'Works', have provided additional speeches, different stage directions and some changes in the order of scenes that have called into question the exact nature of the cultural object known as *Hamlet*. This textual dimension has been complicated by the critical attention that has made the play generate an expectation of meaning.

Every reader and audience comes to the play with a sense that it will provide more than the pleasure of seeing the actor's skill, the designer's imagination, the musicians' art. The play is expected to 'say' something about the modern condition or provide a universal truth. Even if, as in Peter Brook in *Qui est Là?* (1995) or Lepage in *Elsinore* (1995–96)[8] or Almereyda in his film set in a dystopic contemporary New York (2000), a director produces a work that precisely seeks to erase conventional readings of the play, there lingers behind their productions the ghost of an ideal *Hamlet,* one in which performance and meaning will be reconciled.

Theatre historians often try to effect this reconciliation between performance and meaning by addressing the provenance or significance of the stage directions or by tracking the multiple ways in which different moments of the play have been presented in multiple past productions.[9] By choosing a tiny stage direction that occurs only in one of these texts, and the least authoritative of them too, I was trying to find the smallest unit of a Shakespearean text in order to examine the process by which 'Shakespeare' has been assigned meaning, and how we might understand the passage from early performance instruction to the full blown locus of cultural value that we perceive in Shakespeare Now. In order to do this we must open out the critical space that exists between stage events and the surrounding words, trying as far as possible *not* to link them in interpretation; *not* to create a new narrative that performance only dimly represents.

The difficulties of resisting interpretation are particularly evident when we consider the editorial commentary on the texts of *Hamlet*. Faced with the possibility of irreverent giggles at the prospect of a ghost in his nightgown, one editor sternly reminds his reader that 'what it (the ghost's nightgown) signifies is a *dressing-gown* and, it can be assumed, a very splendid one at that'.[10] Those schoolmasterly editorial injunctions shoo us gently from experience to commentary and from event to meaning. These editorial comments play a critical role in turning an early text into a readable modern one but they do produce an extra layer that smoothes over the texts' inconsistencies and makes it suitable for meaning.

Scholarly attention to the 'bad quarto' of *Hamlet* has been divided between those who see it as a memorial reconstruction of the full play and those who see it as based on an early production prepared for touring outside London.[11] The scholarly consensus that favoured the 'memorial reconstruction' thesis, has, according to Thompson and Taylor, broken down completely:

> To begin with Q1, very few now see it as an early draft of a play by Shakespeare ... It clearly contains versions of many of the F passages not found in Q2 ... and lacks many of the Q2 passages not found in F. This suggests some kind of causal link between Q1 and F, but those scholars who see such a link are not agreed on the precise relationship ... [they] find it difficult to agree whether it is a memorial reconstruction or an adaptation—or a memorial reconstruction of an adaptation or an adaptation of a memorial reconstruction—and whether what is being reconstructed or adapted is the text behind F or a performance of the text behind F.[12]

Clearly post modern chaos reigns and so the desire to reject particular parts of the early quarto or to favour one stable reading of the text over another is severely compromised. The debates over the authenticity of the text have often been connected to attempts to recreate Shakespearean authenticity on the stage. In 1881, the scholar/director William Poel, presented a staging of Q1 in an attempt to recover an authentic Elizabethan original from under the overblown historicist productions of the mainstream theatre he knew. The iconoclastic gesture at that stage in history was to oppose textual truth to theatrical tradition and it could be equally achieved by playing the conflated text of Ql, Q2 and F as Frank Benson did in Stratford in 1888.[13]

In all these experiments, editors, critics and theatre directors were engaged in a search for the full realisation of the play's significance. That significance is inevitably bound up with meaning and meaning depends upon authority, whether that is the authority of author, or in the modern world of theatre and film, the control over meaning exercised by the director.[14]

At this stage in the history or Shakespeare criticism and performance it would be true to say that the controversy over Bad quartos is played out. Modern editors routinely reproduce the Q1 reading of the stage direction '*Enter the ghost in his night gowne*'. However the justification for using that reading in a conflated text is in itself interesting. By the late twentieth century, the Shakespeare Revolution (as J. L. Styan called it[15]) was complete. No one doubted that Shakespeare's plays were most fully realised in performance or that Shakespeare wrote for the stage. Nonetheless, meaning could not be abandoned. The gesture of arriving in his night-gown must mean something to both ghost and audience. The physical elements of the theatre exist to be *read,* to be turned into interpretative discourse. G. R. Hibbard's Oxford note is typically instructive. He claims that the ghost's 'night gowne' 'modifies our previous impression of him greatly by bringing out his humanity'.[16]

This humanising of the ghost emphasises his role as a character in a narrative rather than his role as a stage phenomenon. In Weimann's terms, discussed earlier, it focuses on his representational aspects at the expense of his histrionic ones.[17] The ghost becomes a character whose role in the play deflects attention from its immediate moment of performance and onto the play's narrative time, the characters' past existence that might provide clues about their motivation or the ethical significance of their actions.

3. 'MY FATHER, IN THE HABITE/AS HE LIVED' (Q1: II.79).[18]

This process of reading the play in terms of character, of assimilating all the physical stage action into meaning has become so naturalised in modern discussions of Shakespeare's plays that it is easy to forget that it has a history. That history is bound up with the textual and theatrical strategies of *Hamlet* itself. In all of the texts of *Hamlet,* the stage directions for the ghost's appearances are surrounded by explanatory commentary.

When the ghost appears 'in his night gowne', in Q1, Hamlet describes him to his mother as 'My father, in the habite/As he lived' (11.79). His description does nothing to corroborate or deny the stage direction. (It would be foolish to suggest that old Hamlet lived 'in his night gowne'.) Rather it draws the figure of the ghost away from the histrionic moment back into the representational narrative world where he has a past. He connects this, the narrative world, to the moment on stage with a further direction:

> [W]hy see the king my father, my father, in the habite
> As he liued, looke you how pale he lookes,
> See how he steales away out of the Portall,
> Looke, there he goes.   *exit ghost.*   (Q1: 11. 78–82)

These lines could be used in performance as instructions for the ghost's action: to look pale and steal away out of the portal. However they also, within the narrative are addressed to Gertrude, explaining to her what she cannot see and Hamlet can.

In Q2 the role of the lines as an instruction to the performer is even more explicit. Hamlet's reaction to the ghost, left to the actor in Q1, is elaborated by Gertrude:

> Foorth at your eyes your spirits wildly peep,
> And as the sleeping souldiers in th'alarme,
> Your bedded haire like life in excrements
> Stand up and stand an end.   (Q2: 3. 4. 119–22)[19]

It would be very hard for an actor to create this somatic effect of fear (Garrick had a mechanical wig that stood on end made for the purpose). The surrounding commentary ensures that a reader as well as an audience can be in no doubt that the effect of the ghost is powerful. Any possible failure of performance is held firmly under writerly control. Between Q1 and Q2 additional lines have appeared that not only instruct the *actor*—if we want to emphasise performance—they also help the *reader* to visualise the scene.

A similar process is evident in the ghost's earlier appearances. In Q1 soldier 2 (Barnardo in Q2) asks 'Lookes it not like the king?' And Horatio replies 'Most like, it horrors (Q2 harrowes) mee with feare and wonder'. The gradual revelation that the ghost is the King of Denmark is an important part of the narrative suspense in this opening scene but it once again indicates that the scene's theatricality, the excitement of the arrival of the ghost, is being firmly assimilated by the narrative verisimilitude of the on-stage world. The characters' reactions are given more attention than the immediate impact on the audience.

The importance of narrative representation is made even more clear in Horatio's further corroboration of the King's identity:

Such was the very armor he had on,
When he the ambitious *Norway* combated,
So frownd he once, when in an angry parle
He smot the sleaded pollax on the yce,
Tis strange.   (Q1: 1.49-53)

Horatio's lines not only describe the ghost's action and costume. They also connect them to the play's narrative past and give Horatio authority in describing it. The historionic effect of the ghost's arrival is assimilated into its narrative significance.

In their efforts to render the edited text a seamless reading experience that pays attention to staging effects, modern editors nearly always address the theatrical logistics implied by this speech. All three early texts have '*Enter Ghost*' as the stage direction and it is routinely changed to '*Enter the ghost, clad in complete armour, with its visor raised, and a truncheon in its hand*.[20] The narrative and commentary of the play are assumed to determine stage action rather than the other way around. The significance of the ghost's angry frown is more important than the frown itself; the reaction of the onstage audience is more significant than any spontaneous reaction that the audience in the theatre may have to the events on stage.

These efforts to control the stage action in the interests of narrative are still problematic for Shakespeare when writing *Hamlet* and indeed for early modern theatre at the same time. The anxieties felt by authors faced with clowns that speak more than is set down for them is palpable throughout the play.

Modern readers who have endorsed a notion of art that holds the mirror up to Nature readily accept Hamlet's strictures against the performances of such clowns. However it is interesting to look again at the theatrical dynamic that is discussed in these famous lines—especially as they occur in Q1:

And doe you heare? let not your Clowne speake
More then is set downe, there be of them I can tell you
That will laugh themselues, to set on some
Quantitie of barren spectators to laugh with them,
Albeit there is some necessary point in the Play
Then to be obserued: O t'is vile, and shewes
A pittifull ambition in the foole that vseth it.   (Q1: 9. 23-29)

In this speech Hamlet is clearly stating a preference for the narrative coherence of the play and is anxious to avoid the immediate collaboration between performer and audience that is essential to the pleasures of clowning. The clown on the other hand cares more about the spectators—albeit barren ones—than he does for the 'necessary point in the play'. He cares, in other words, more for the histrionic pleasure than he does for narrative representation.

In Q1 the speech continues with a further elaboration of Hamlet's contempt for the clown's role:

> And then you haue some agen, that keepes one sute
> Of ieasts, as a man is knowne by one sute of
> Apparell, and Gentlemen quotes his ieasts downe
> In their tables, before they come to the play, as thus:
> Cannot you stay till I eate my porrige? and, you owe me
> A quarters wages: and, my coate wants a cullison:
> And your beere is sowre: and, blabbering with his lips,
> And thus keeping in his cinkapase of ieasts,
> When, God knows, the warme Clowne cannot make a iest
> Vnlesse by chance, as the blinde man catcheth a hare: (Q1: 9. 29-38)

The contempt for immediate theatrical gratification is palpable and it provides a tiny glimpse of the theatre as a pastime that spoke to the immediate needs of gentlemen, lettered enough to note down the clown's jests but happy to take theatre as an entertainment that reinforces familiar pleasures rather than creating innovation.[21]

The jokes and catch phrases reproduced in this speech seem, to a modern reader, completely pointless. They may have had a similar comic impact to the catch phrases of modern television comedians, but that comic impact, by its nature cannot be reproduced. It remains locked in the histrionic moment and its point is that it is extra-narrative, it makes no contribution to the 'necessary point in the play'.

Hamlet's contempt for Clowns that 'laugh themselves, to set on some Quantitie of barren spectators to laugh with them' is only a little mitigated when he had considered the tragic player in 2. 2. who wept in reciting tragic events. In the Q1 soliloquy after the player's recitation on the fall of Troy, Hamlet marvels that 'these Players here draw water from eyes / For Hecuba' but he contrasts the emotion aroused by the player's fictional story and the emotion that ought to be wrought by his own experience of loss and betrayal. Q1 merely states the contrast but in Q2, its folly is elaborated on:

> Is it not monstrous that this player heere,
> But in a fixion, in a dreame of passion
> Could force his soule so to his owne conceit
> That from her working all the visage wand,

Teares in his eyes, distraction in his aspect,
A broken voyce, an his whole function suting
With formes to his conceit; and all for nothing.   (Q2: 2. 2. 577–83)

The player's performance of the Hecuba speech is remarkable. However it is less tainted than the clown's performances for it produces admiration in the spectators—including, grudgingly, Polonius—not empathy. The Hecuba speech is not a mimetic enactment of a narrative, it is a recitation that evokes both the story of the fall of Troy and the appropriate response to it. The player describes the scene, the revenge of the rugged Pyrrhus, and the arrival of Hecuba, 'the mobled queen' to see her husband's massacre. The player's empathy with Hecuba is both enacted by the player/reciter and attributed to the Gods themselves who would 'have made milch the burning eyes of heaven/And passion in the gods' (Q1: 7. 374–75). The thrust of Hamlet's aesthetic is towards plays that provide meaning and significance that can be controlled by an author, where audience's empathy can be directed by the feelings of the characters, described in the poetry of the play.

As a writer for the theatre, Shakespeare makes explicit the difficulties of securing meaning through performance. In the Q1 preamble to the play within the play Ofelia is insistent about understanding the meaning of the silent action of the dumb show:

OFELIA What doth this meane my lord?
HAMLET [Y]ou shall heare anone, this fellow will tell you all.
OFELIA Will he tell vs what this shew meanes?
HAMLET I, or any shew you'le shew him,
   Be not afeard to shew, hee'le not be afeard to tell. (Q1: 9.86–90)

This exchange is often glossed as bawdy but to do so diminishes the insistence on the problem of telling and showing in the theatre: the problem of creating art that will hold the mirror up to nature but also produce a powerful local and immediate effect. The presence of an audience in the theatre, of course, often undermines the effect. Hamlet asks his mother for her view of the performance and finds her unmoved—'The Lady protests too much' (Q1: 9. 130); Claudius, on the other hand is 'frighted with false fires'. His reaction, though it provides the evidence that Hamlet wants, comes from his own guilt, not from the effectiveness of performance.

This desire to control performance, to make it offer the intended effect, is especially evident in the additions to the dumb-show that occur between Q1 and Q2. Q1 offers the brief but perfectly adequate instructions that provide the basic actions, leaving the performance to the actors:

Enter in a Dumbe Shew, the King and the Queene, he sits downe in an Arbor, she leaues him: Then enters Lucianus with poyson in a Viall, and powres it in his eares, and goes away: Then the Queene commeth and findes him dead: and goes away with the other. (Q1: 9. 82)

In Q2, by contrast the dumb-show offers more elaborate suggestions for ways in which the actors might reproduce the feelings and emotional responses of the characters:

The Trumpets sounds. Dumbe show followes.
Enter a King and a Queene, the Queene embracing him, and he her, he takes her vp, and declines his head vpon her necke, he lyes him downe vppon a bancke of flowers, she seeing him asleepe, leaues him: anon come in an other man, takes off his crowne, kisses it, pours poyson in the sleepers eares, and leaues him: the Queene returnes, finds the King dead, makes passionate action, the poysner with some three or foure come in againe, seeme to condole with her, the dead body is carried away, the poysner wooes the Queene with gifts, shee seemes harsh awhile, but in the end accepts loue. (Q2, 3. 2. 145-50)

The Q2 directions were possibly added for a reading audience but if so, their relationship to performance is worth considering. They add a sense of emotion to the bare narrative of the Q1 dumb-show and even give direct suggestions for the physical action (*declines his head vpon her necke*) that will represent love. The additions in F take the control of the scene even further. In that text the queen 'makes show of protestation' and the '*seemes harsh*' of Q2 is replaced by '*loath and unwilling*'.

All of these added directions indicate the importance of the character's interiority and motivation and the difficulties of communicating them to an audience by non-verbal means.

What is even more difficult is the problem of communicating interiority with an additional moral gloss. The Q2 direction offers an implied commentary in the recurring use of 'seems', and 'seeming', an addition that allows the possibility of falsehood as well as performance. But as Hamlet indicates in response to his mother's request to put his nighted colour off, the signs of performance cannot always distinguish between seeming and reality: 'Seems, madam? Nay it is, I know not seems'.

The Q1 version of this exchange transfers the issue of how performance can deal with emotion to a consideration of the stark opposition between inner feelings and outer action:

My lord tis not the sable sute I weare:
No nor the teares that still stand in my eyes,
Nor the distracted haviour in the visage,
Nor all together mixt with outward semblance,

Is equal to the sorry of my heart,
Him have I lost I must of force forgoe
These but the ornaments and sutes of woe.   (Q1: 2. 33–39)

In Q1, Hamlet is responding to the King, not the Queen but the problematic of emotional integrity is linked to the effectiveness of performance: Hamlet's integrity is not communicated to his mother or step-father and he needs a soliloquy to communicate it to the audience.

In the final scene of the play, Hamlet is given further commentary to try to control his audience's reaction to the murderous events they have witnessed. They have seen an action that, he suggests, affects them and he begins to explain its meaning:

You that looke pale, and tremble at this chance,
That are but mutes, or audience to this act,
Had I but time, as this fell sergeant Death
Is strict in his arrest, ô I could tell you,
But let it be.   (Q2: 5. 2. 345-49)

None of this appears in Q1. There Hamlet simply returns Laertes's forgiveness with 'And I thee' and adds 'O, I am dead, Horatio, fare thee well' (Q1: 17. 101-02) before charging Horatio with telling his story. In Q2, Hamlet's extra lines paradoxically draw attention to his silence. In doing so they insist on the realism of his action on stage. He no longer has to unpack his heart with words and he can instruct the off-stage audience in the most appropriate reaction by commenting on the demeanour of the on-stage witnesses to his suffering and death.

The on-stage audience have a somatic reaction attributed to them—they look pale and tremble. However that very description of an appropriate somatic reaction uses the same phrases as are used to describe Horatio's reaction to the first appearance of the ghost: 'How now Horatio, you tremble and looke pale'. The audience are in effect instructed to respond in the same way as actors since both share the language of emotional and physical reaction. The clown sets on the audience to laugh by laughing himself; the tragic actor invokes tears by forcing his soul to his own conceit that he produces tears. The audience looks pale, because the ghost in Gertrude's closet also 'looks pale' (3. 4. 135) whether because of anger[22] or because he is dead.

Faced with the instructions on how to respond, an imaginative (and practised) reader or audience can fill in the gaps, can engage empathetically with the situation of the prince. In Shakespeare's own time, however, the collaboration of the imaginative audience seems not to have been able to be taken for granted. In both metatheatrical gestures and in prologues to the plays, writers insisted on the appropriate reactions to their effects. These reactions were vital to ensure the coherence of the plays' narrative world and there was a growing consensus that this desired affect in the audience could not be achieved with ghosts.

Thomas Lodge, in *Wit's Misery and the World's Madness* (1596) talks of a devil who looks 'As pale as the vizard of the ghost which cried so miserably at the Theatre, like an oyster-wife, "Hamlet revenge"'.[23] This reference is most often used to signal the existence of a Hamlet play before Shakespeare's. However it also mocks the theatre effect with bathetic comparison. Similarly, in *A Warning for Fair Women* performed by Shakespeare's own company, the figure of Comedy denounces the tragedies whose theatrical effects demand but cannot ensure audience affect. The narratives tell 'How some dam'd tyrant to obtaine a crowne/Stabs, hangs impoysons, smothers, cutteth throats' but the theatricalisation depends upon conventions that do not match the narrative: 'And then a Chorus too comes howling in/And tells us of the worrying of a cat'. Ghosts are reduced to conventions. They do not succeed in making the audience 'tremble and look pale' for in performance what this sceptical viewer sees is

> a filthie whining ghost
> Lapt in some fowle sheete, or a leather pelch
> Comes screaming like a pigge halfe stickt,
> And cries *Vindicta,* revenge, revenge (54–57)[24]

These comments are not, of course descriptions of actual theatre practice. They are part of a negotiation around changing theatre styles. They signalled a trend away from the theatre of spectacle and towards the theatre of empathy and affect. But it was also an attempt to close the gap between theatrical time in which the audience could mock the actual effect on stage and the narrative time in which events have consequences that build a narrative. For the writers, like Shakespeare, who also put their work into print, the debate about effective theatricality also reflected a trend away from spectacle (that could only dimly be represented in print) and towards the insistent commentary that turns action into meaning.

4. SHAKESPEARE NOW

I have been suggesting that the characteristic features of the Shakespeare that we expect were created in that historical negotiation at the turn of the seventeenth century. They favoured a theatre of narrative that resolved any tension between immediate production values, effective mimetic performance and 'some necessary question of the play'. In favouring narrative over histrionics and spectacle, they were able to create plays that could be reproduced both in print and in a variety of different theatrical conditions. They thus ensured their longevity that has allowed them to become part of the culture of the present.

In the academic and theatrical climate at this point in the millennium, we have constructed a Shakespeare and a theatre that values all of these features of the early modern stage. We expect our plays to offer production values that can compete with those of technologised entertainment, to present a credible mimetic narrative and to offer a sense of a significant 'question of the play' being addressed. The remaining tension between these different characteristics are the subject of our continuing debates over Shakespeare's authority, authenticity and accessibility. The technologies of production and the training of actors have narrowed the gap between narrative and performance but the same gap has been exploited to provide a space for inventiveness and innovation. There is no longer any need to consider the quandary of the ghost in his nightgown (or a foul sheet or leather pilch) for the expectation that the ghost will be of a piece with the narrative demands of the theatre is fulfilled by the roles of director and designer. If the ghost appears playing a white grand piano, or is played by the same actor as Hamlet, the familiarity of the story can assimilate the innovation. Moreover, the sense that the performance will bear significant meaning allows connections to other arenas of meaning in the life-world of the audience. An important part of this meaning comes from the ghosts of other productions but also from the ghostly figure of Shakespeare himself. The enormous modern commitment of resources from the arts and educational budget is directed towards continuing a modern Shakespeare who is available for adaptation and reinterpretation, who is part of global culture and who is the source. and the locus of theatrical energy that defines the high culture of our time.

In exploring both the changes made to the texts of *Hamlet* for their final presentation in the Folio and the packaging of those changes in the prefatory material to the Folio text itself, I have tried to show the connection between the texts of *Hamlet* and Shakespeare's position in the commercial theatre of his day. I have also been suggesting that the current debate over the relative importance of Shakespeare read and Shakespeare performed is a part of a recurring dialectic that contributes to the continuing value of Shakespeare and ensures that Shakespeare Now will have the latent energy to be transformed into new Shakespeares tomorrow.

(The Shakespeare Institute, University of Birmingham)

NOTES

The original version of this essay was delivered at the 45th Anniversary Conference of the Shakespeare Society of Japan at Tohoku Gakuin University on the 9th October 2006.

1. Stephen Greenblatt, *Will in the World,* London: Cape, 2004; James Shapiro, *1599 A Year in the Life of William Shakespeare,* London: Faber, 2005.
2. For example, Brenda James and William D. Rubenstein, *The Truth Will Out: Unmasking the Real Shakespeare,* London: Pearson, 2005.
3. Clare Asquith, *Shadowplay: The Hidden Beliefs and Coded Politics of William Shakespeare,* London: Perseus Books, 2005.
4. See Terence Hawkes, *Shakespeare in the Present,* London: Routledge, 2004; Garrett A Sullivan, *Memory and Forgetting in English Renaissance Drama,* Cambridge: Cambridge University Press, 2005.
5. See Neil Thew, *Teaching Shakespeare: a survey of the undergraduate level in higher education,* (The English Subject Centre, 2006) available at http://www.english. heacademy.ac.uk.
6. See www.bbc.co.uk/drama/shakespeare/.
7. Robert Weimann, 'Performance-Game and Representation in *Richard III*, in Edward Petcher, ed., *Textual and Theatrical Shakespeare,* Iowa City: University of Iowa Press, 1996, pp. 66–85.
8. See Andy Lavender, *Hamlet in Pieces,* London: Nick Hern Books, 2001.
9. See, for example, R. A. Foakes, '"Armed at point exactly": The Ghost in *Hamlet*', *Shakespeare Survey* 58, 2005, pp. 34–48.
10. G. R. Hibbard, ed, *Hamlet,* Oxford: Oxford University Press, 1987, p. 282.
11. See Kathleen O. Irace, *Reforming the 'Bad' Quartos,* Newark: University of Delaware Press, 1994 and Paul Werstine, 'Touring and the construction of Shakespeare Criticism' in *Textual Formations and Reformations,* ed. Laurie E. Maguire and Thomas L. Berger.
12. Ann Thompson and Neil Taylor, *Hamlet, The Texts of 1603 and 1623,* Arden Shakespeare, 2006, p. 9.
13. See the discussion of these issues in Dennis Kennedy, *Looking at Shakespeare,* Cambridge: Cambridge University Press, 1993, pp. 25–34.
14. Jeremy Erlich, 'The search for the *Hamlet* "Director's Cut"', *English Studies* 83. 5. 2002, pp. 399–406.
15. J. L. Styan, *The Shakespeare Revolution,* Cambridge: Cambridge University Press, 1977.
16. Hibbard, p. 282.
17. Weimann, 'Performance-Game and Representation in *Richard III*', p. 67.
18. In quoting from Q1, I have used the Shakespeare Quarto facsimile of the text prepared by W. W. Greg and Charlton Hinman, Oxford University Press, 1965, but have added in the line numbering from Ann Thompson and Neil Taylor's *Hamlet, The Texts of 1603 and 1623,* The Arden Shakespeare, 2006.

19. *Hamlet,* Second Quarto 1604–5, Shakespeare Quarto Facsimiles, Oxford: Clarendon Press, 1964.
20. See Hibbard, 1987; Wells and Taylor, See Ann Thompson's comment Q2 p. 90 on the use of 'heritage spelling' that Wells and Taylor use for the old spelling version of the text that includes this interpolated stage direction.
21. It was a dichotomy that was reinforced in para-textual discussion throughout the period. See Kathleen McLuskie, 'Figuring the Consumer for Early Modern Drama,' in Bryan Reynolds and William N. West, eds, *Rematerialising Shakespeare Authority and Representation on the Early Modern English Stage,* Basingstoke: Palgrave, 2005.
22. Compare, *MND,* 2. 1. 103–04: 'Therefore the moon, the governess of floods/Pale in her anger washes all the air'.
23. Cited in Geoffrey Bullough, *Narrative and Dramatic Sources of Shakespeare,* volume vii. (London and New York: Routledge and Kegan Paul, Columbia University Press, 1973), p. 24.
24. *A Warning for Fair Women,* ed. C. D. Cannon, The Hague: Mouton, 1975.

Shakespeare Studies, Vol. 46, The Shakespeare Society of Japan, 2008, 1–15. Used by permission of The Shakespeare Society of Japan.

FURTHER READING, VIEWING, AND LISTENING

READING

Adelman, Janet. *Suffocating Mothers: Fantasies of Maternal Origin in Shakespeare's Plays, "Hamlet" to "The Tempest."* New York: Routledge, 1992.

Bruster, Douglas. To Be or Not to Be (Shakespeare Now!). London: Continuum, 2007.

———. *Quoting Shakespeare: Form and Culture in Early Modern Drama.* Lincoln: University of Nebraska Press, 2000.

Charnes, Linda. *Hamlet's Heirs: Shakespeare and the Politics of a New Millennium.* New York and London: Routledge, 2006.

de Grazia, Margreta. Hamlet *without Hamlet.* Cambridge: Cambridge UP 2007.

———. "Hamlet the Intellectual," in Helen Small, ed., *The Public Intellectual.* Oxford and Malden, MA: Blackwell, 2002, 89–109.

———. "Shakespeare, Gutenberg, and Descartes," in Terence Hawkes, ed., *Alternative Shakespeares*, vol. II. London and New York: Routledge, 1996, 63–94.

Dutton, Richard. "*Hamlet, An Apology for Actors*, and the Sign of the Globe," *Shakespeare Survey* 41 (1989), 35–43.

Everett, Barbara. *Young Hamlet: Essays on Shakespeare's Tragedies.* Oxford: Clarendon Press, 1989.

Greenblatt, Stephen. *Hamlet in Purgatory.* Princeton: Princeton UP, 2001.

Guillory, John. "To Please the Wiser Sort: Violence and Philosophy in Hamlet," in Carla Mazzio and Douglas Trevor, eds., *Historicism, Psychoanalysis, and Early Modern Culture.* New York and London: Routledge, 2000: 82–109.

Holland, Peter. "Hamlet: Text in Performance," in Peter J. Smith and Nigel Wood, ed., *Hamlet.* Buckingham and Philadelphia: Open UP, 1996: 55–82.

Honigmann, E.A.J., "The Politics in *Hamlet* and 'The World of the Play,'" *Stratford-upon-Avon Studies* 5. New York (1964): 129–47.

——— "The Date of *Hamlet*," *Shakespeare Survey* 9 (1956): 24–34.

Isaacs, Jacob. "Coleridge's Critical Terminology," *Essays and Studies* 21 (1936): 94–5.

Kewes, Paulina. "The Elizabethan History Play: A True Genre?," in *A Companion to Shakespeare's Works: The Histories*, ed. Richard Dutton and Jean E. Howard, 3 vols. Malden, MA and Oxford: Blackwell, 2003: II: 170–93.

Lee, John. *Hamlet and the Controversies of the Self.* Oxford: Clarendon Press, 2000.

Nelson, Robert J. "The Ancients and the Moderns," in *A New History of French Literature*, ed. Denis Hollier. Cambridge, MA: Harvard UP, 1989: 364–9.

Parker, Patricia. "Black *Hamlet*: Battening on the Moor," *Shakespeare Studies* 31 (2003): 127–64.

Powers, William. *Hamlet's Blackberry: A Practical Philosophy for Building a Good Life in the Digital Age.* New York: Harper, 2010.

Rothwell, Kenneth S. *A History of Shakespeare on Screen: a Century of Film and Television.* Cambridge: Cambridge UP, 1999.

Shakespeare, William, Richard Appiganesi and Emma Viecell. *Manga Shakespeare: Hamlet.* New York: Abrams, 2007.

Stabler, A.P., "Elective Monarchy in the Sources of *Hamlet,*" *Studies in Philology* 62:5 (January 1965): 654–61.

Stallybrass, Peter, Roger Chartier, et al., "Hamlet's Tables and the Technologies of Writing in Renaissance England," *Shakespeare Quarterly* 55:4 (2004), 379–419.

Stoppard, Tom. *Rosencrantz and Guildenstern Are Dead.* New York: Grove Press, 1983.

Welsh, Alexander. *Hamlet in his Modern Guises.* Princeton, NJ: Princeton UP, 2001.

VIEWING

Branagh, Kenneth. *A Midwinter's Tale.* VHS. Richard Briers, Nicholas Farrell, Julia Sawalha. Dir. Kenneth Branagh. Turner Home Entertainment, 1995.

Brady, Pam and Andrew Fleming. *Hamlet 2.* DVD. Steve Coogan, Catherine Keener, Elisabeth Shue. Dir. Andrew Fleming. Bona Fide Productions, 2008.

Coyne, Susan and Bob Martin and Mark McKinney. *Slings and Arrows: The Complete Collection.* DVD (television series). Paul Gross, Martha Burns, Don McKellar, Rachel McAdams. Dir. Peter Wellington. Acorn Media, 2008.

Oguni, Hideo and Eijiro Hisaita. *The Bad Sleep Well.* DVD. Dir. Akira Kurosawa. Criterion, 1963.

Penn, Zak and Adam Leff. *Last Action Hero*. DVD. Arnold
Schwarzenegger, Austin O'Brien. Dir. John McTiernan. Columbia
Pictures, 1993.
Shakespeare, William. *Hamlet*. DVD. Laurence Olivier, Peter Cushing,
Eileen Herlie, Stanley Holloway, Esmond Knight. Dir. Laurence
Olivier. Two Cities Films (UK), 1948.
———. *Hamlet*. DVD. Derek Jacobi, Claire Bloom, Patrick Stewart. Dir.
Rodney Bennett. BBC TV, 1980.
———. *Hamlet*. DVD. Mel Gibson, Glenn Close. Alan Bates. Dir. Franco
Zeffirelli. Canal Films, 1990.
———. *Hamlet*. DVD. Kenneth Branagh, Julie Christie, Billy Crystal,
Gerard Depardieu. Dir. Kenneth Branagh. Warner Home Video, 1996.
———. *Hamlet*. DVD. Ethan Hawke, Bill Murray, Julia Stiles. Dir. Michael
Almereyda. Miramax, 2000.
——— and Adam Long, Reed Martin, Austin Tichenor, and Daniel
Singer. *The Reduced Shakespeare Company: The Complete Works of
William Shakespeare* (Abridged). DVD. Adam Long, Reed Martin. Dir.
Paul Kafno. Acorn Media, 2003.
Stoppard, Tom. *Rosencrantz and Guildenstern Are Dead*. DVD. Gary
Oldman, Tim Roth. Dir. Tom Stoppard. Image Entertainment, 1990.

LISTENING

Shakespeare, William. *Hamlet*. Audio CDs. Simon Russell Beale, Imogen
Stubbs, and Jane Lapotaire. BBC Audiobooks America, 2005.
———. *Hamlet*. Audio CD. Sir John Gielgud, Marian Spencer, and Celia
Johnson. Naxos Audio Books, 2006.

Select Online Resources

Shakespeare in Europe (SHINE). May 2003. English Department.,
U of Basel, Switz. http://www.unibas.ch/shine/linkstragmacbethwf.
html. A finding list of translations of a number of Shakespeare plays
in multiple languages.
Shakespeare Performance in Asia (SPIA): http://web.mit.edu/
shakespeare/asia/. A growing video archive with robust search
functions.
Opensourceshakespeare.org, http://www.opensourceshakespeare.
org/. An online resource with excellent concordance and selection
functions (allows printing by character lines/cues as well as by scene).
Should only be used in conjunction with a modern edition (such as
the Evans Edition) because its text is a nineteenth-century edition
that contains some errors.